Teaching Lives

Teaching Lives

Essays and Stories

Wendy Bishop

UTAH STATE UNIVERSITY PRESS
Logan, Utah
1997

Utah State University Press
Logan, Utah 84322–7800

Essays reprinted here were previously published as indicated on page 345, which constitutes an extension of this copyright page. Thanks to the publishers for their kind permission to reprint.

"Traveling through the Dark" © 1962 by William Stafford, is reprinted by permission of
Harcourt Brace. All rights reserved.

01   00   99   98   97   5   4   3   2   1

Library of Congress Cataloging-in-Publication Data

Bishop, Wendy.
    Teaching lives : essays and stories / Wendy Bishop.
        p.   cm.
    Includes bibliographical references and index.
    ISBN 0-87421-224-3
    1. English language—Rhetoric—Study and teaching. 2. English
language—Rhetoric—Study and teaching—Theory, etc. 3. Creative
writing—Study and teaching. 4. English teachers—Training of. I. Title.
PE1404.B575   1997
808'.042'07—dc21   97-21168
                                                            CIP

Contents

Preface
Why Write About Teaching Lives?

WHY INCLUDE AUTOBIOGRAPHY WITH RESEARCH, CLASSROOM STORIES with theories of genre and reading and writing, facts with fictionalized explorations? And why bundle this up now?

I'm not terribly old, though some days I feel old enough. This is not a self-generated *festschrift* or my swan-song before retiring. I've included some teaching failures and a story about teaching paranoia, and I'm far from ready to retire. I taught my first writing class in 1978 at the University of California, Davis. I've been learning from my teaching—fashioning a teaching life—ever since, in classrooms around the US—California, Arizona, Alaska, Florida—and in other countries—Guatemala, Morocco and Nigeria. I've held every position in the book, teaching introduction to literature, ESL, basic to advanced writing, teacher education courses, creative writing in every genre, and I've done this at each college staffing level, as adjunct, instructor, visiting assistant professor and on up the ladder; I've run a writing center, a writing program, and special services program, taught on an airbase and in an American Embassy, at two and four year colleges and at research institutions. My students have been Athabaskan and Nigerian and Anglo and Navajo and African-, Asian-, Mexican-Americans, though usually the proportions of students were more like me—white middle class American college students—than unlike me. I've explored many academic roles too—teacher, researcher, scholar, writer, administrator.

Through it all, I found that writing was the common denominator. This collection presents a portion of a self-education through writing about that education, this teaching life. For a while, I wrote about every class I taught. And, in fact, I still have portfolios collected from those classes I didn't write about, when the volume of projects and life itself caused me to fall behind; I still feel I let those classes and me, as teacher of those classes, down a bit. I completed these writings, at first, to discover more about the fascinating/frustrating classroom arenas that I thrived in, tired of, recuperated from, and came back to refreshed, term after term. My students taught me how to learn and how to write better. I did this secondly, because, as an introvert of sorts, I need to put myself in dialogue with others. By sharing published teaching stories I learned how to have a voice and a place in the composition community. I'm grateful to this community for enlarging my life and my thinking. In some ways, these essays work as love letters to the field, affirmations and also queries (as I got bolder, sometimes scoldings and "Why nots?" "Why can't wes?"—for I realize the field is far from uniform, perfect, or congenial to all). In some ways these writings represent excesses of zeal or enthusiasm—"This is neat. I tried it; why don't you?"—and rebellious "Why nots?"

And thirdly, of course, I gained professionally by publishing. Coming into publishing in composition was a real pleasure. The collegiality and general receptivity of editors in the field was impressive, particularly since I had already spent some time in the fiercely competitive and heart-breakingly difficult arenas of professional creative writing.

I argue that these three reasons hold for all teachers of writing. In writing about our own teaching lives, we figure out our classrooms, we speak to others, and we compose ourselves in beneficial ways. At the same time, teaching life journeys reflect a lot of hard work and a lot of figuring-it-out-through-words and putting those words into circulation and practice.

A graduate student came to my office recently and said, "I want to do what you do, combine two fields." I said, "Faith, it's not that easy and it's not exactly what you see." Meaning, my teaching life has been one of searching, bumping up against problems, and writing my way out of them into more celebratory stances. And the fields of composition and creative writing certainly don't yet comfortably align themselves. I had to tell her: "I see creative writing as a very competitive profession where each student is grooming him- or herself to be the *best* writer, thinking in terms of *service for* (oneself). I find the field of composition to be more collegial (although certainly there *is* competition), filled with colleagues who are trying to solve problems in writing classrooms; these are people who tend to think in terms of *service toward*. I find a better home in the latter," I told her, though I want to and try to do both—serve the writer in me and serve communities of writers.

I believe that constructing a teaching life through our writing about writing and about teaching writing may be one way to do this.

Why this book at this time and for whom? Certainly it's a retrospective learning experience, seeing how themes in my own teaching life surface, play out, recycle and are refined across the years (in this case, 1986 to 1997). For instance, the first section "Composing Ourselves in the Writing Classroom" offers a few of the teaching essays I often undertook as a teacher who was beginning to study composition theory and trying to return with it—usefully—to my classrooms. I wanted to better understand classroom issues and then decided to offer those developing understanding to others. While I wouldn't write the same essays the same way now, my early forays into product/process discussions, peer writing group dynamics, portfolio evaluation, issues in co-authoring, and grammar instruction debates are shared here chronologically, showing how one's practices do (must?) grow and change. For a few of these earlier essays, I have added endnotes pointing out current sources of thinking on the subject at hand.

I believe there's a lot to be said for the how-to article although it's little valued during academic reviews or acknowledged as a contributing part of a developing teaching career. I think the how-to teaches me how to talk as well as how to teach, how to develop a personal voice within the public matrix of professional communities. It is the foundational social action that encourages the expressivist-leaning teacher to move from the enclosed space of one classroom to discussions of classrooms in general.

At the same time, by including an opening how-to oriented section, I affirm that my initially expressivist position toward writing has not changed—any more than fingerprints change—but I try to show in subsequent sections how that position has been tempered, modified, and I hope improved: call me a committed social-expressivist (I'll use the term proposed by Sherrie Gradin in *Romancing Rhetorics* as the best approximation of a position no one has found a perfect word for). That is, expressivist-centered teachers are not *merely* or *just* expressivist, for they are highly social when they examine and incorporate theoretical discussions and findings and conduct classroom research.

A teaching life is a complicated creation. To understand writing, I had to teach myself about reading. To enter the profession of composition, I had to understand very different cultures and communities, those I electively joined and those that the academy prepared for me. I had to consider relations within English departments and across the university. I had to negotiate administrative positions. It helped to take a researcher's position at some of these times, given that no single individual can change administrative inequities or solve long-standing departmental and collegial disputes. I had to learn that I grew a space for teaching by becoming a good administrator, and I became a better administrator by studying what I did in that position. Learning the history of writing programs, researching administrative and teaching issues, returned me full-circle to the individual teacher and her or his writing classroom.

As I've explained, my expressivist self derived from my writing practice, my entry into the academy as a creative writer. In the fifth section, I show how that understanding of a writing self was broadened and strengthened by my entry into the writing communities of composition. Neither, I argue, has to be over- or under-valued, and creative writing and just writing are often the same thing. Teachers in those areas—teachers of writing—should be and could (productively) be more closely aligned. In the last section, "Composing Ourselves Through Teaching," I share essays that investigate the pleasures of maturity, of endurance, of commitment, adding up what I've learned from being in the classroom and the department meeting, the administrative session, the writers contest, the conference panel, and again, and always, the classroom. After twenty years of teaching and writing—and an intensive ten years of writing about both— I've come to see that teaching is a way of life that I can't and wouldn't do without. And one I feel lucky to participate in. It is a wonderful way of staying challenged and alive. It is one this collection seeks to offer to others—not in a starry-eyed or naive way, but in a hard-working, look-what-you-get-out-of-it-if way.

In the writing years covered here, I had to negotiate and explain my commitment to expressivism (for want of a better term) as new -ists and -isms came to challenge teachers (that's good) and intrigue theorists (that's good too). A chameleon, or just an adaptable life form, I've made my way by adding what works; I add genres, and I add theoretical understanding. I deepen my commitment to speaking and saying as a writer as I become more involved than ever in communities of writers.

I hope this collection speaks to teachers who are seeking to learn their own ways, who are busy (re)constructing their own teaching lives and who care to share stories together. I hope this book encourages teachers to keep writing about teaching and their lives in teaching long after they close the book. They may argue with my position, tire of my voice, or conversely—and hopefully—be energized by one observation or another and start to write. They should write into the gaps between essays, scribble end-notes and encouragements to themselves. If this collection acts as a teaching journal, encouraging others to keep their own, formally or informally, or to write teaching essays for professional journals in composition, then it will have accomplished my goals.

There are many people to thank.

Peter Stillman read a draft of the collection and shared generous responses and good poetry by return mail. Alys Culhane put up with lots of e-mails and then an overfull manuscript of essays, helping me cut and cull and then (re)shape what remained. She's been a long-time teaching friend, available, co-contributing, and enthusiastic during all the years these essays cover; and besides that, she provides great dog-raising advice. Michael Spooner has been the alpha and omega of editors, supporting my writing from a first, post-dissertation query letter to today's draft that he'll put into careful production—thank you, again. This book wouldn't be, of course, if Morgan and Tait weren't with me every revision of the way on our travels together.

The names of many other teaching friends are found in the works cited list and are looped and threaded through my writings.

I appreciate the support I've received from the editors whose journals I list on the back page—all the welcoming and challenging editors and all the difficult and encouraging anonymous and not so anonymous readers.

Thank you to my students—all of them—the hard and the easy, the challenging and the challenged, the unsatisfied and the satisfied, those past and present . . . and those just out of sight there, around the corner, in the teaching future.

Part I

Composing Ourselves in the Writing Classroom

The five essays in this first part of Teaching Lives *focus on classrooms as locations for growth. Composition—of word, person, or practice—is never simple or linear. Because of the complex nature of teaching writing, what worked one day doesn't always work the next. One classroom often seems more productive or more demanding than another classroom. Like all teachers, I experience doubt and elation, the confusion of circumstances ("Do I attribute this moment to genre, personality, age, accident, experience?") and the confidence that develops from improvement ("Oh, so this worked. Maybe, then, this will work!") But growth is usually incremental and contingent.*

I believe we can construct and compose ourselves across our teaching years through narrative, comparison, analysis, reflection, and action. The essays in this section can be read as partial maps of where one teacher went, useful to the degree that they share practical classroom knowledge and show how such knowledge is constructed. I try to illustrate the ways a teaching life improves when a teacher reflects on classroom communities only just disbanded in order to build new communities on another day, in another place.

In "Writing Teachers and Writing Process," readers will notice how reliant I am on the voices of others. With this essay, as a writing–teacher–turned–re-entry–graduate–student in composition and rhetoric, I begin to look to writing specialists for classroom help. New to essay writing, I scatter citations behind me as I build my own authority and apply the work of others to my classrooms. Such application takes time. Most of these activities—having students write literacy autobiographies, teaching students to respond to each other's drafts (and do it effectively), experimenting with classroom evaluation methods—took semesters of tinkering with after I was introduced to them. My bold plan—described in "Writing Teachers and Writing Process"—to institute a collaborative process classroom according to five theorized goals was formulated after two years of graduate study. The essay, though, began as an answer on my qualifying exams in the fall of 1986 before some reshaping resulted in publication in a state writing journal.

"Helping Peer Writing Groups Succeed" and "Designing a Portfolio Evaluation System" were both drafted while I taught at the University of Alaska Fairbanks during the academic year and studied in the rhetoric and linguistics doctoral program at Indiana University of Pennsylvania in the summers. "Helping" began in 1987 as a seminar paper based on my writing classroom experiences. In 1988, "Designing" grew out of my desire to share my teaching practices with other teachers. Having committed to collaborative and process-oriented classroom goals, I needed to make my writing groups work better than they were working. Having committed to writing portfolios as a method of classroom evaluation, I needed to develop a workable portfolio schedule. An adjunct teacher at the time, I was balancing the usual load of too many writing students that works against informed instruction.

In "Helping," the drive I felt to create authority as a student writing my essay for my rhetoric program professors is mediated by the developing authority I felt in my own improving classrooms. I chose to use vignettes of the situations I was grappling with in order to encourage teacher-readers to supply their own vignettes. By the time I composed "Designing," I had begun training other teachers to use portfolios. Because of this, I felt an urgency to make what I did that seemed to work accessible to those just starting out and to those who were suspicious of newfangled ideas. Though I am beginning to proselytize my positions in this essay, I cover this up somewhat with a distanced voice. This author-evacuated stance I take is not surprising since I was apprenticing in social science ethnographic methods which encouraged me to adopt the more distanced researcher's tone. In "Designs," there is not a first person pronoun in sight when I tell teachers—much more authoritatively than I ever felt—just what to do. Still, when I think back on it, this essay does represent a growing professional certainty, for I was thriving on the reading I was completing and the study I was undertaking in the graduate courses.

By this time, my classroom trials were also proving more successful. The final two essays in this section mark the point when I realized I had a flair for articulating the practical, a flair that developed as a spin-off of my investment in the field of composition and rhetoric. "Co-Authoring Changes the Writing Classroom" is author-saturated—written in the first person—in fact, it opens with the word I. My positions are offered on the basis of my (at that time) somewhat unusual background as a graduate of both creative writing and composition programs. Today, in 1997, many creative writers are educating themselves in composition, but this was not true as the decade began. In "Co-Authoring," composed in 1994, I urge my composition colleagues to join my creative writing colleagues; whereas, for the previous five years—in other published work—I had been urging creative writers to consider the knowledge of compositionists. Notably, this essay showcases "student" writing and my own attempts at the exercises I advocate.

Although Teaching Lives *is not arranged in strict chronological order, this section of the collection is—"Teaching 'Grammar for Writers'" was begun slightly after "Co-Authoring." It presents a very personal formulation of my always-in-progress answer to a writing teacher's age-old concerns with writing conventions and writing correctness. In this essay, I recall where I started and tell where I got to. Also, I predict where I see myself going as a writing process classroom advocate who does not see such classrooms as simple constructions of unexamined activities. By 1994, when I'm developing this position, I've graduated, have moved to Florida to teach at the Florida State University, and have completed my first years as an assistant professor and as a writing program administrator. I'm finally practicing what I preach (and preaching wholeheartedly what I practice).*

I composed portions of "Teaching 'Grammar for Writers'" in an alternate style because I'm advocating alternate style instruction in classrooms. Instead of broadly surveying the "field's" position on the issue, I aim at this point to affiliate with those theorist-practitioners I find most valuable. Instead of offering readers a literature review and then a smorgasbord of options, I define my position ("examined" process classrooms) and invite readers to join. I do this because, already in 1994, process instruction is undergoing (often useful but not often friendly) social-constructionist critiques that appear to me to simplify and then abandon much of what I have only recently found so powerful and convincing.

While "Teaching 'Grammar for Writers'" is the last essay in this section, it certainly is not the last how-to essay I have written or plan to write. The selections I share here showcase the many directions the how-to essay can take (and the many writing styles I undertook within the form). The brassy, assertive (but often, underneath, unsure) new teacher's voice of "students will" that I hear in "Writing Teachers and Writing Process" has evolved—or composed itself—into the more collegial, yet also more comfortable, voice found in "Teaching 'Grammar for Writers.'" I chose this voice to close this section in order to assert what I still believe: that we writing teachers are in the same how-to boat together and that we're always better off for thinking about our teaching and for sharing such thinking.

Writing Teachers and Writing Process
Combining Theory and Practice

WRITING TEACHERS AT EVERY TEACHING LEVEL USE THE TERM "PROCESS" when discussing writing but no single description of the writing process, developed from research into composing, adequately synthesizes current theory and research in the field. To develop an adequate and current model of the writing process in general, and the composing process, specifically, it is necessary to discuss work by many researchers and many theorists, some of whom do not agree with the theoretical basis of the other's work.

In his October 1986 *College English* article, "Competing Theories of Process," Lester Faigley discusses many of these theories and offers a useful framework from which to synthesize information about writing process. Faigley divides process theory into three broad categories: expressive, cognitive, and social. Of these categories, cognitive theories provide a research based starting point for building a model of the composing process. This essay will review research which develops models of basic and expert writers at work and then offer suggestions for using what is known about writing process to enhance writing students' growth in the classroom.[1]

Writing Process Theory

Research in the cognitive domain of writing has developed dramatically in the last twenty years. Not only have cognitive models become more sophisticated, but techniques for studying them have improved. A generally accepted starting place for cognitive research is Gordon Rohman and Albert Wlecke's 1964 model of writing which included three stages: prewriting, writing, and rewriting. These researchers were studying invention and not intending a complete description of the composing process yet their model prompted further research. The main drawbacks to the model were its linearity and the fact that it was derived from products, written texts, and not the observed process of writing, writers at work.

By 1971, Janet Emig had studied the composing process of twelfth grade student writers and expanded both the research model and research methodology. Emig used case studies and composing protocols, observing writers and interviewing them to verify her observations. She expanded Rohman and Wlecke's categories of prewriting, writing, and writing. For instance, in the writing stage she observed that writers exhibited silences and hesitations; areas studied by later researchers. She broke down the rewriting stage into correcting, revising and rewriting (which meant stopping and starting over). One of her most important discoveries involved the recursive nature of the composing activity. She found writers planning in the prewriting *and* the writing stages, and so on. An examination of recursiveness and the development of new research techniques were Emig's strongest contributions at that time.

By 1980, the composing process appeared much more complex than formerly thought. By observing writers as they wrote, a great deal could be inferred about their cognitive activities and more questions presented themselves for study. Specifically, what were the differences between basic and expert or professional writers, what were the steps in the revision process, and what kept certain writers from becoming more successful in their composing process?

In a landmark study published in 1977, Mina Shaughnessey defined and explored the problems of basic writers. Basic writers she found—contrary to the expectations of teachers—were working by a rule-governed system. Their mistakes were often the result of mis- or over-applying rules in their writing. With careful error analysis and attention to their writing process and classroom development, Shaughnessey found ways to enable basic writers to become more fluent, successful writers.

Interest in the problems of basic writers (who flooded schools in the 1970s due to open admissions policies) led researchers to study the differences between basic writers' composing strategies and the strategies of traditional college students or experienced professional writers. In 1979, Sondra Perl found that basic writers were doing exactly what Shaughnessey had said they were doing, applying ineffective rules throughout the composing process. These writers would often stop and scan and correct their papers at the sentence or word level. This self-imposed interruption would keep the students from achieving any type of global development in a piece of writing.

Perl found more efficient writers participating in projective structuring (worrying about audience) and retrospective structuring (checking the text so far in order to guide future development). She found successful writers listening to what she termed a "felt sense" which helped them negotiate the demands of their text in process.

Sharon Pianko also found basic writers to be overly rule-governed and concerned with correction. Basic writers in Pianko's study spent little time prewriting or writing and did not appear to value writing. However, the traditional students that she observed did have more successful writing strategies than did the basic students.

In 1980, Nancy Sommers and Lillian Bridwell both studied revision. Sommers found that basic writers relied on two main types of revision— addition and deletion—neglecting substitution and reordering. However, experienced writers used all four types of revision techniques. Experienced writers also had metacognitive awareness of their revision process while student writers, on the other hand, spoke of "cleaning up" their writing and showed underdeveloped revision strategies.

Bridwell's study supports this difference between successful and unsuccessful writers. In her study, the most effective writer revisions occurred between first and second drafts while writers were rereading their work. However, less successful writers, as in earlier studies, interrupted their work to make meaning destroying, sentence-level corrections.

In 1981, Linda Flower and John R. Hayes developed a full-scale cognitive model of the composing process. They divided composing into generating, translating and reviewing. Further, they discovered several important aspects of composing that connect to the results of the research I have reported so far. First, the composing process is also dependent on the text so far (as in Perl), and the rhetorical situation (audience demands, and so on) and is limited by the capacity of long-term memory. In this case, memory is linked to metacognitive and metalinguistic ability developed through previous writing experiences. Finally, and most important to their model, writers are influenced by self-developed goals. Flower and Hayes found successful writers relying on a hierarchy of sub-, mid-, and high-level goals which took them from sentence level to global concerns. Less successful writers seemed to lack mid-level goals and became stuck at the sentence level (as in the revision studies by Bridwell and Sommers) or on more global concerns.

Three other studies need mentioning to round out the composing picture. In 1980, Mike Rose published work on blocked and unblocked writers. He found blocked writers were often applying inappropriate, algorithmic rules to their writing, a characteristic of basic writers. On the other hand, unblocked writers had flexible planning and composing strategies which allowed them to write in a variety of situations for a variety of audiences (like Sommer's expert writers).

In 1979, Flower discussed writer-based prose. Writer-based prose is generally narrative and associational in structure, internal, expressive, and intended by the writer to explore a situation. Nonetheless, many writers have trouble moving from the useful medium of writer-based prose to the more public medium which Flower termed reader-based prose. Reader-based prose is expository in nature and organized with the reader in mind. Work by James Collins and Mike Williamson (1981) provide some insight into the problems experienced by composers of writer-based prose. Often these writers seem to be writing down speech, relying on unavailable references which are external to the text.

Cognitive research, then, develops a picture of the basic writer as someone who is rule-governed (generally inappropriately so), who has trouble imagining audiences other than himself, who doesn't value "school" writing, and who has inflexible revising and writing strategies and an underdeveloped sense of the composing process. Successful writers are much more closely aligned to the Flower and Hayes model, able to decide upon audience and able to tailor the developing text to audience demands and rhetorical demands. The successful writer not only has flexible composing and revising strategies, but also has a wealth of successful previous writing experience to draw upon, enabling her to make and adjust writing goals to suit a particular writing situation.

Unfortunately, as developed as this model is, it is not complete. For instance, those who believe in expressive theories of composing see the writer as an individual who is learning through writing. Theorists such as Ken Macrorie, James Moffet, Frank Smith, John Mayher, Nancy Lester and Gordon Pradl and others, view writing as a natural process, and many of their theories are derived from observing writers in the classroom. They are opposed to the cognitive model, arguing that those researchers, in order to study writing, had to break down writing activities into unnatural and unrealistic stages, procedures, and so on. Additionally, they point out the problems which arise when such studies take place in unrealistic testing contexts and settings.

Other theorists like Cy Knoblauch and Lil Brannon feel that breaking down the writing process into stages greatly misrepresents the composing process and encourages teachers to take a smorgasbord approach to writing instruction—picking and choosing those stages or those models they wish to emphasize—and that such an approach will lead to misinformed instruction (1984). They prefer to emphasize a holistic approach to the teaching of writing.

Expressive theorists have made valuable contributions to composition instruction. They suggest that we start where the student is, use student-centered classrooms and help students develop as individuals as they develop as writers. Unfortunately, these theorists do not offer enough in the way of classroom pedagogy that takes into account the very real constraints under which composition teachers work, such as large classes, department or district control of curriculum, diverse student literacy backgrounds, and so on. However, expressive theorists do offer an important corrective voice when considering cognitive theory which still, as yet, offers an incomplete model for the complex activity we call composing.

A different outlook for composing theory comes from the social theorists. Structural social theorists like Patricia Bizzell (1986), Marilyn Cooper (1986), and Kenneth Bruffee (1984) insist that neither the cognitive model nor the expressive models are complete, for composing does not occur only for an individual (expressive), or in the head (cognitive), but also in complex social settings which affect the ways in which both basic and professional writers write. To define a new, contextual base for composing, Bizzell explores the idea of discourse communities, Bruffee interpretive communities, and Cooper an ecological system that supports writing.

Equally as important as these social theorists is the work being done by ethnographers like Shirley Brice Heath (1983) and Jerome Harste, Virginia Woodward and Carolyn Burke (1984). These researchers point out that composing is negotiated by writers within households, schools, and communities, and that these social/biographical factors also affect the writing of any individual.

Rather than seeing these strands of theory and research as single items on a smorgasbord from which teachers and students pick and choose, I prefer to see current work in composition as confirming and extending previous work. A single writer certainly does need to express herself and to learn through writing. If she is offered demonstrations (a teacher or member of a work group writing), then she becomes engaged and sensitive to writing (Frank Smith 1983, 1994).

At that point, she is ready to participate in classroom activities that nurture her metacognitive awareness (writing process journals, peer group discussions of writing, invention heuristics). This awareness will result in more fluent texts; she will write more freely and for longer periods. Practice and *attention* to writing will result in improved writing correctness. Having real audiences, such as a supportive teacher and a writing work group, will allow her to move from writer-based to reader-based prose because she will want to and she will have every expectation of communicating successfully. Additionally, extended, ungraded practice will allow her to move from the conventions of spoken language to the conventions of written language as they are negotiated in her classroom community

Writing Process and the Writing Classroom

My understanding of current theory leads me to the development of a student-centered, process-oriented writer's workshop based on the collaborative models of Kenneth Bruffee and Thom Hawkins which are in turn based on earlier work by Carl Rogers in the US and M.L. Abercrombie in Great Britain. I believe the collaborative method allows students the greatest chance to achieve the following course objectives:

- Students will take responsibility for their own writing and view themselves as writers.
- Students will develop a more efficient and effective writing process.
- Students will learn to critique their own and other students' work, and participate supportively in peer writing groups.
- Student writing will improve and students will make fewer errors.
- Students will develop flexible writing strategies which allow them to write in a variety of writing situations.

These are certainly not the only course objectives I would work for, but they are the ones that develop naturally out of a study of current research in composing as outlined in the first section of this essay, for research suggests that basic writers have problems in most or all of the areas listed above. It should be noted that writing change occurs slowly and a course may only *begin* a process of writing change that may not be manifest until after the course has ended; therefore, a writing course should include both short and long-term objectives (Charles Cooper 1975).

It would be useful to sketch the organization of a collaborative classroom. First, when possible, topics for writing are student generated. Second, student texts are the students' own writing. Third, writing and revision take place in and out of class, and students are offered opportunities for non-graded writing. In my classes, students submit a writing portfolio in the middle and the end of the semester. When they do so, they write letters of self-evaluation and I respond in writing. In 1986, Peter Elbow and Pat Belanoff shared a departmental level portfolio system which can be used as a proficiency examination at the college level.

Next, the two major activities of the class are participation in writing peer groups (students talking to each other about their writing) and student/teacher conferences. Class lecture is kept to a minimum and limited to general information dissemination.

Students will take responsibility for their own writing and view themselves as writers.

Basic writers are often the victims of years of schooling which has depreciated their own sense of worth. These writers view successful writers as people who sit down and write a perfect draft every time. Basic writers are also often working against their own instincts and applying teacher-given rules of writing that do them little good (see Hartwell).

The collaborative classroom places these students in the center of the curriculum. Students are asked to develop their own topics and start to learn within the supportive social context of a writing work group that offers them a real audience (see Murray). By sharing drafts, and eventually writing portfolios, with other students, writers come to see themselves as individuals who are in control of their own writing: deciding when to revise, which pieces of writing to submit for final grades, and so on. Once they begin to view themselves as writers, basic and student writers will be much more receptive to information that the instructor is able to offer in the way of invention techniques, grammatical explanations, and so on.

Students will develop a more efficient and effective writing process.

Research in the composing process shows that professional writers have a great deal of metacognitive awareness of their own writing techniques. Student writers need to develop a similar awareness. This will be done by having students write literacy autobiographies (see Hartwell), share entries in process journals (see Mayher, Lester, and Pradl), and discuss a process model (see Reigstad and McAndrew) under the guidance of an instructor who is familiar with such models. After discussing their own composing process in small groups, class members together will use the blackboard to list the elements of the composing process familiar to them from their own writing and then compare it to a process model handout. In subsequent journal or log entries, students continue to analyze their own composing processes.

Students will learn to critique their own and other students' work and participate supportively in peer writing groups.

Peer group work is one of the foundations of the collaborative classroom (the other being conferences where many of the activities described in these sections can be modeled and reinforced). Learning to critique other students' work helps a writer to gain necessary self-editing skills. It helps a writer learn to step back from his own work and evaluate it. This type of distancing skill is often lacking in basic writers or writers who are overly reliant on writer-based prose. Thom Hawkins and Tom Reigstad and Donald McAndrew agree that students need to be trained to work in groups. They need to learn effective group roles (timekeeper, historian, general member) and they need to learn what to look for in a paper, what Reigstad and McAndrew call developing a priority of concerns. Students can be given preliminary critique sheets (see Beaven), or develop them through discussion with each other and the teacher. Several researchers have studied the ability of work groups to stay on task and a study by Anne Ruggles Gere and Robert Abbott found that groups were effective.

Student writing will improve and students will make fewer errors.

The collaborative classroom offers students a non-threatening environment in which to explore and take risks. Jerome Harste, Virginia Woodward and Carolyn Burke (1984) found that these were important classroom attributes for primary school writers. In the same sense, the basic writer needs to participate in successful adult literacy experiences (see Hartwell, Shaughnessey).

Students who are offered an environment which values revision will certainly improve their writing over the course of a semester, and this improvement can be traced in by reviewing student writing portfolios. As students write longer pieces, they will revise more often, achieve greater writing clarity, and eventually begin to make fewer errors even in earlier drafts. Additionally, through individual conferences, students will focus on the same priority of concerns (higher order—focus, organization, tone—before lower order—spelling, punctuation) as they focus upon with writers in their work groups. However, in conferences the teacher and student can review necessary grammatical or mechanical problems together in the context of an actual piece of student writing which will benefit from such a discussion.

Students will develop flexible writing strategies which allow them to write in a variety of writing situations.

The teacher in a student-centered classroom is seen as a coach or resource for students. He can offer a student a variety of invention techniques as the occasion demands. Working with individual students in conferences or with small groups of students, the teacher offers techniques such as nutshelling, twenty questions, tagmemic grids, or Kenneth Burke's pentad (see Reigstad and McAndrew). If the student doesn't like a draft or doesn't know where to begin, a short session with invention techniques may get her started. Students will also be encouraged to find real audiences beyond the teacher and beyond the classroom. They will be encouraged to work on papers that relate to other classes or real life concerns which they have. To reinforce the reality of such audiences, students will be encouraged to publish in the school newspaper or mail letters written about subjects of concern to them; that is, every opportunity for publishing student work formally or informally will be encouraged.

It seems clear that research into writing processes, particularly the composing activities of basic and expert writers, has broadened our understanding of the complexities of the writing experience. The difference between Gordon Rohman and Albert Wlecke's early, linear model of the composing process and Linda Flower and John R. Hayes's cognitive model of the same activity are monumental. To become more effective in the writing classroom, a writing teacher needs to understand these models and to apply theory to actual teaching situations, for a writing instructor is the single most important agent of change, turning writing theory into sound teaching practice in the writing classroom each time she begins a class.

Note

1.   While Lester Faigley's 1986 essay still offers a strong and useful initial set of categories for understanding how research into writing processes informs our field, much has been done in the eleven years since its publication to discuss, complicate and amplify Faigley's overview. My own bookshelf includes *Rhetoric and Reality* (Berlin);); *Academic Discourse and Critical Consciousness* (Bizzell); *The Construction of Negotiated Meaning* (Flower);

Making Thinking Visible (Flower et. al); *Romancing Rhetorics: Social Expressivist Perspectives on the Teaching of Writing* (Gradin); *The Making of Knowledge in Composition* (North); *Taking Stock: The Writing Process Movement in the 90s* (Tobin and Newkirk, ed.) to suggest a few starting places for further reading. In addition, many of the essays mentioned here can be found in *Landmark Essay on Writing Process* (Perl, ed).

2

Helping Peer Writing Groups Succeed

IMAGINE YOU ARE ENTERING A FRESHMAN LEVEL COMPOSITION CLASSROOM. It is the tenth week of a fifteen–week semester. The teacher sits to one side of the room, conferencing with a single student about the student's paper which rests on a table between them. The rest of the twenty–student class has been divided into peer writing groups of four to five students. The class is noisy, for each group is busy discussing a paper and students talk freely, offering revision suggestions. The writer and a group historian note these suggestions, and a group monitor moves the discussion on, seeing to it that the group reviews at least some of each member's writing before the one hour class is over.

After the teacher conferences with several students, she then moves for a time from group to group, offering additional suggestions and encouragement, and checking on work accomplished. A few minutes before the class ends, the groups briefly summarize their work and each discussion is transcribed into written notes by the group historian. Finally, the teacher checks to make sure that the class as a whole is clear about future class sessions and/or assignments.

I have just described an idealized but obtainable writing classroom, one in which students join together in collaborative work and develop their writing abilities in a non–threatening environment. The teacher is guide and assistant to the work at hand. This holistic approach to writing and the teaching of writing makes many new demands on both students and teachers who need to change their attitudes and expectations to participate in such a classroom. Because of these sometimes unexpected demands, teachers trying to introduce peer writing groups into their curriculum often feel let down by a method that has been presented in glowing terms yet can prove problematic in practice. Has group work been overrated? Have teachers been deceived? Or, have teachers become confused by the apparent simplicity of a rather complex teaching method?

I would like to explore these questions by reviewing research that discusses the use of peer writing groups, by profiling successful and unsuccessful peer writing groups and, finally, by offering a plan for preparing and training students for the method. Such a plan must also include guidelines for evaluating the effectiveness of peer writing groups in the composition classroom.

Research on Peer Writing Groups

The value of using peer writing groups as a teaching method if not overrated has sometimes been oversimplified. A brief review of current research and practice shows this. In general, collaborative peer writing groups do benefit the student. The claims for the efficacy of the method are many and various. Mary Beavan, discussing peer evaluation, claims that the collaborative method allows students to develop audience awareness, to check their perceptions of reality, to strengthen their interpersonal skills, and to take risks; the entire process results in improvement in writing and students' ability to revise. Thom Hawkins agrees that students strengthen their interpersonal skills and risktaking or creative abilities.

Kenneth Bruffee found that peer tutors and tutees at work in a collaborative environment deal with higher order concerns such as paper focus and development. Tutees feel comfortable enough with peers to bring up these concerns which go beyond the usage level, and the writing abilities of tutors also improves as a direct result of the collaborative writing act. Researchers like Francine Danis, who found that 75% of the students in her study correctly identified both major and minor writing problems, and Anne Gere, who felt that student responses (grades five to twelve) did deal with meaning, would seem to support Bruffee's contention that students in peer groups do more than simply act as proofreaders of each other's work. Other research by Anne Gere and Robert Abbott reaffirmed the power of peer writing groups to stay focused on discussions about writing. Their research also shows that group discussions where teachers are present are significantly different from those in which teachers are absent.

Drawbacks to the method must be noted. First, collaborative learning can be time consuming (see Beaven and Abercrombie), for those writing about this method agree that some training of group members is necessary.

Mary Beaven also notes that some instructors are unable to allow students the freedom required (student- rather than teacher-centered, discussion rather than lecture dominated classrooms) and therefore end up doing double work, designing *and controlling*, directing *and correcting* the groups. This problem seems to be one of teacher awareness and training rather than an inherent flaw in the method.

A final criticism develops from close research observation of groups and from student evaluations. Francine Danis found that students are not always sure of their group role, aren't able to stand back from their own writing, don't know what they want to know, and have a reluctance to offer critical comments. Elizabeth Flynn felt students lacked critical ability and attributed this to students' tendencies to supply missing information in a paper in order to make sense out of what they were reading. Again, these are problems that can be somewhat alleviated by student and teacher preparation for the method. The fact that students do need to develop a critical vocabulary from which to discuss their works is supported in Kenneth Bruffee's articles concerning the importance of language communities. Clearly, there is a need to introduce writing students to the vocabulary and terminology of the composition community.[1]

Profiles of Peer Writing Groups

Now let us enter another freshman composition classroom. Again, it is the tenth week of a fifteen-week semester. Again, the teacher is conferencing with one student and four or five peer writing groups are in session. We will observe three of the groups.

In Group A, students form a tightly knit circle. Members are discussing organizational changes that would benefit a group member's paper. The writer of the paper listens and makes notes as does the group secretary. Soon, the group monitor reminds the group that other papers remain to be discussed. The transition to the next paper is made smoothly. If the teacher were to come over to the group, she could slip into a nearby seat and participate; talk would continue, although it would be altered somewhat by the group's awareness of her presence.

If you asked members of Group A how the group method was working, members would most likely be enthusiastic, pointing out changes they have made in papers as a result of the discussion, showing how every member of the group helps by offering suggestions, explaining that they appreciate the teacher's comments but also enjoy developing their writing skills together. Group A is a successful, fully-developed peer writing group.

Here is an evaluation from a member of such a group:

> This is the first time I've had an English class where groups were formed. I found that I had an easier time talking in the groups then in class discussion. So I must say that it has value in letting me get my ideas across to other people in class, with much less apprehension.

Group B looks a lot like Group A. Most of the members are concentrating on a single paper. However, comments on this paper are tentative. The group gets stalled on a grammar point that no one is really interested in discussing nor competent to decide. When this happens, the writer of the paper starts to explain what she meant to do in the paper and other group members look bored. They've heard her talk like this before. Still, the members are polite and wait until the writer stops talking before moving on to another point: they find several misspellings in the paper. When the class ends, this group has only discussed two of four papers as the monitor forgot to move them on. The historian suggests that the group forego the end of session summary and no one cares. When the teacher moves toward the group, discussion wanes and dies awkwardly. When asked how the group is doing, members can't articulate their group's progress, but insist that everything is okay. Talk picks up slowly as the teacher moves away.

Group B is finding the group method only mildly successful, for members are never really sure if they are talking about writing "in the right way." They don't feel that other members give them truly honest evaluation of their work and don't trust the evaluations they do receive. They are confused when they get teacher-graded papers returned that have low grades. They wonder why group members didn't catch more of the problems the teacher marked. They feel comfortable with each other but are sometimes lazy and unsure of their own abilities to discuss or change their writing. They accept working in groups but are constantly waiting for something to happen. Group B is an under developed peer writing group.

Here is an evaluation from a member of such a group:

> I do like the idea of the groups. But could you please float around & insert "starter" statements for some groups if need be? Sometimes our group doesn't go very far under the analysis that we write in our journals.

Group C looks different than either Group A or Group B and looks different every time members try to start working together. Members of this group often don't come to class or come late and try to leave early. Some members are easily distracted; they look through their own bags or papers or watch other groups covertly. When this group does have more than one or two members, a single student may dominate the talk. No one has volunteered or been elected for the positions of historian and monitor. Often the group drifts, finishing work too quickly or not moving along at all. When the teacher comes to join this group, a single member enters into a private dialogue with her. Other group members may try to avoid contact with the teacher, both in and out of class.

Group C is sure the group method is useless. No one in the group knows what is going on and the class is boring. The dominant member is resentful, feeling he is doing too much work, and the other members feel they are in the grip of yet another un-elected teacher–dictator. Group members feel unsure of their own writing and do not see how they can teach each other. They have strong suspicions that the teacher is holding back something or is too lazy to really teach them. Group C is not simply underdeveloped; it is really not a peer writing group at all.

Here is an evaluation from a member of such a group:

> Individuals a little lax in group to have assignments read (including myself). We don't know what to write about, probably because we don't know what you want and don't know how to find it in the stories.
> What are we looking for?

The observer of this writing class and the teacher might agree: when peer groups are fully developed (Group A), the method is exciting and rewarding for students and teacher alike, but when peer group interactions are under developed (Group B) or break down (Group C) the method is discouraging and group work all too often feels like a matter of luck.

Obviously, these profiles are only useful in that they give a teacher a way to begin to sort out group interaction patterns. Each teacher will vary in the way she labels her groups. For instance, I evaluate group success on a continuum between fully developed and under developed groups as distinct from non-cohering groups. Diana George in her article "Writing with Peer Groups in Composition" distinguishes between task-oriented, leaderless, and dysfunctional. In both cases, in-class observations have taken place and serious consideration has been given to groups in order for a teacher to improve future group work. By profiling her own writing groups, a teacher can learn how writing peer groups can become useless and sometimes lifeless. If even one of several important problems is present in a group, such a problem can quickly move the group from success to failure. Therefore, teachers need to be aware of the attributes of successful groups and learn what can be done to move groups from failure to success and doing so will enable composition teachers to feel more comfortable using peer writing groups.

The following list shows ways groups can fail or succeed and notes the names of researchers or writers who touch on these concerns when discussing peer writing groups. I have developed my profiles of group weaknesses and strengths after reading these writers and observing composition and literature classes which I conducted by group method at the University of Alaska, Fairbanks campus, from fall 1985 to spring 1987.

Ways Peer Writing Groups Fail
1. Too much or too little leadership (Hawkins; Elbow 1977; George).
2. Poor attendance or participation or preparation of some students leading to resentment between members (Hawkins; Flynn 1982).
3. Unclear group goals; group doesn't value work or works too quickly (Johnson and Johnson; Hawkins; George).
4. Group doesn't feel confident of group members' expertise or members are afraid to offer criticism (Lagana; Danis; Flynn).
5. Group doesn't understand new role of instructor (Ziv).
6. Group never develops adequate vocabulary for discussing writing (Danis; Bruffee).
7. Group fails to record suggestions or to make changes based on members' suggestions; (George)

Ways Peer Writing Groups Succeed
1. Group successfully involves all members (Johnson and Johnson; Hawkins; Elbow).
2. Group works to clarify goals and assignments (Johnson and Johnson; Elbow 1977; Danis).
3. Group develops a common vocabulary for discussing writing (Beaven; Bruffee; Danis).
4. Group learns to identify major writing problems such as organization, tone, and focus, as well as minor writing problems such as spelling errors, and so on (Bruffee; Danis; Gere; Gere and Abbot).
5. Group learns to value group work and to see instructor as a resource which the group can call on freely (Rogers; Danis; Flynn).

Most writers are in agreement, students and teachers need preparation and training for successful peer group work. Those teachers who divide students into groups merely to provide momentary relief from the lecture classroom will develop failures similar to those listed above.

Preparing for Peer Writing Groups

Although the peer writing groups profiled in this paper show students critiquing each other's drafts, groups can serve a broader variety of purposes. Students can work together to discuss readings, to complete exercises, to explore writing invention strategies, and to help members with forming very early drafts. Additionally, the peer group method can be adapted to classes at the primary and secondary level, to advanced or creative writing classes, and to diverse academic disciplines.

Teachers who want to use peer writing groups in their classroom should plan ahead. They need to realize that the group method rests on a theory of collaborative learning and they will be more successful if they read widely in this area. While reading, a teacher should ask several questions:

1. Do I understand the theory behind peer writing groups?
2. Do I have a clear use for this method in my classroom?
3. What are my goals for students when using this method?

Additionally, because group work is based on a theory of learning that students may be unfamiliar with or resistant to, the well prepared teacher will acquaint students with concepts of collaborative learning through prepared handouts, class discussion, and continual monitoring of group work. After gaining a deeper understanding through reading, teachers need to visualize the place of peer writing groups in their entire curriculum. Students need to develop a group identity and participate in a new writing community. To function well, group members must be present, which requires a class attendance policy. A teacher might decide to use groups for a certain percentage of class time. I have found using groups 50 to 75% of my available class periods most effective. This percentage allows my students to develop a group identity yet regroup into a class on a regular basis in order to maintain a class identity also.

Classroom communities are formed by the school registrar, academic departments, and the enrolling student. How should peer group communities be formed? To start, teachers may divide a class into sets of four to five students or students may start working collaboratively in pairs and then pairs may be joined. Although many criteria could be presented for forming such groups, nothing in the peer group literature supports any one in particular. First week diagnostic writings may be used to organize groups with a balance of strong and weak writers. Students may rate themselves on matters such as ability to lead, to help, to take risks, and so on, and groups may be balanced with a member strong in each area. In addition, I try to balance groups by gender and by age.

Once groups are formed, there is no certain number of sessions needed to develop a strong sense of group community. Some groups develop rapport immediately and some take much longer. Groups can develop a radical (sometimes disruptive) streak and also a conservative (and equally disruptive) bent. Groups work best when they are balanced, focused, and comfortable. Depending on my course goals, I try to let groups work together for at least four sessions, and I rarely leave a group together for an entire semester.

The more groups are used, the more adept a teacher becomes in divining group personalities. Sometimes a teacher needs to intervene and change group membership (placing an overly dominant member in another, more challenging group, and so on), but often it is wiser to let the group itself solve group problems. Ideally, groups that stay together over a long period develop a strong group identity and sense of shared community. Equally, groups that change membership, partially or wholly, are often revitalized and ready to undertake new course challenges with greater enthusiasm.

Because groups develop as real writing communities, choosing a group name can help members identify with their new community. Ordering and clarifying group members' roles such as monitor and historian and general member also assures that group work will be carried on in an orderly manner. Groups are formed to work together, so group projects should be clearly articulated in handout form or as directions on the chalkboard, and group work should be real work, contributing to each member's writing development.

Time should be allowed for groups to share their work, conclusions, and progress with the whole class in order to support the class as a larger community and to keep groups from becoming too isolated. Reporting on what the group accomplished each session, in the form of historian's notes in a group folder, provides useful artifacts for group self-evaluation and teacher evaluation of the group session. To review, when forming groups for the first time, I ask the members to give themselves a name and to chose a monitor (timekeeper) and historian (secretary). Each group is given a folder for saving work and recording discussions.

Training Peer Writing Groups

To work well together, peer writing groups need training in two areas in particular: group roles and writing response. It is not enough to ask the groups to elect a monitor and a historian, but those individuals should have clear directions as to their roles. If a monitor does not act as the group caretaker, making sure each member gets time to respond to writing and time to have writing discussed and making sure the group performs the group tasks in time to share with the whole class, then the group will risk failure. If the historian does not record group discussions, there will be little continuity from session to session and no product to show the group and the teacher where the group has been and what it has done. When groups are first formed, handouts to elected members, as well as a handout detailing the responsibilities of a member in general—attendance, support, sharing, and so on—can speed the training in this area.

Even more important, group members will be teaching each other to talk about writing. This talk can be initiated by the teacher, reinforced by the class text, and nurtured by whole class discussion, but it will be brought to fruition in the group itself as members learn to improve their writing. In this effort, the teacher functions as the conduit linking the class to the academic community. She may begin by teaching the class necessary terminology (concerning writing process and writing analysis) and by training writers and readers to work together through role playing, reviewing sample essays, and so on. In their initial critique sessions, groups can work to answer set questions or can learn to develop their own critical concerns for papers. If composition terms such as prewriting, drafting, revising, focus, organization, and tone are introduced in class discussion, show up on group handouts, are reinforced in peer writing group discussions, and recorded in group minutes, such terms will soon become part of the peer group's working vocabulary.

Monitoring Peer Writing Groups

During group work, the teacher is extremely busy, although not necessarily appearing so, for she is the group and class facilitator, deciding when to intervene in groups and when to reconvene the groups into a class to share results, review strategies, or speed up information dissemination. Sometimes the best thing a teacher can do is to listen and watch her groups quietly and unobtrusively; sometimes she must participate in groups to insure that each group is working efficiently, but there is no single right way to help groups succeed.

A teacher needs to experiment, but she should do so carefully. She should keep records of her groups (a personal journal is a good place to start), for she learns from each one of them. She can monitor groups by sight (regularly noting what is happening in each by direct observation); by sound (listening to tape recordings of groups at a later date); by direct contact (visits to and participation in groups); and by reviewing group or individual artifacts (learning logs, group weekly reports, group self-evaluations questionnaires). It is important to remember that the teacher should be actively involved with the groups on a class by class basis.

Evaluating Peer Writing Groups

A teacher can evaluate the effectiveness of her peer writing groups, although few methods for doing so are quantifiable. Good evaluation results from good planning and from sensitive and careful review throughout and at the end of each course.

Teachers can determine if students are attaining the goals she set for group work. Group folders when examined tell a story of good attendance, completed work, and enlarged understanding. Self–evaluation on the part of students and teacher can chronicle success with the method and pinpoint areas for future work and improvement. And, most important, gains in individual student writing can be assessed.

In brief, a teacher can use any of the monitoring documents (group folders, tapes of group work, group self–evaluations, and so on) as well as her own journal of group work to develop a fairly clear profile of how successful each group was.

Measurements of student growth in collaborative learning techniques and writing in general can be accomplished with pre and post testing in the following areas:

1. pre and post written descriptions of what students feel can be accomplished in writing groups,
2. pre and post written descriptions of students' writing process,
3. pre and post writing apprehension tests,

4. pre and post essay samples.

Teachers would hope to find that post written descriptions of the group method show a greater understanding of and enjoyment of the method. Post descriptions of students' writing process should show a greater awareness of the writing process in general and as it relates to an individual student. Post writing apprehension tests should show a decline in writing apprehension. And post essay samples should show an improvement in writing when holistically evaluated (Bishop "Qualitative").

A teacher who hopes to use peer writing groups in her classroom should prepare for success. She needs to understand her writing groups will not always be completely effective but can be made more effective if she is willing to train herself and her students. In a sense, a teacher using peer writing groups must become a researcher in her own classroom. She plans for her class, trains group members, monitors and evaluates them, and, the next semester, begins the process again, refining and developing her talents as a group facilitator based on her own observations. This teacher will be willing to experiment, to redefine group failures as steps in a larger process that leads to success, and to have realistic expectations for this holistic teaching method. Before long, those expectations will be met and, hopefully, surpassed.

Note

1. This review of research into writing peer groups was completed in 1986, and significant amounts of work have been done on this subject since that time. I'd send readers to *Small Groups in Writing Workshops: Invitations to a Writer's Life* (Robert Brooke, Ruth Mirtz, and Rick Evans) for recent scholarship and bibliographic references.

3

Designing a Writing Portfolio
Evaluation System

WRITING PORTFOLIOS PROVIDE AN ORDERLY PRESENTATION OF A DISORDERLY process. When compiling a writing portfolio, student writers learn that revision is a long-term, recursive process. As they share drafts with peers, tutors, and their teacher, these writers become aware of a variety of audience needs. Through reflection on and response to such conversations, students revise their work into a portfolio representative of their best academic prose. In this classroom, the teacher works as both advocate *and* evaluator, helping writers select and present work for end of semester evaluation in the portfolio. And when student work is "published" in this manner, writers can take pride in their own maturity of expression. Surveying a completed portfolio, they realize that they *have* written a lot (portfolios often contain many layers of drafts) and that they *did* grow as writers from the first day to the last day of the class (last papers look more expert to writers than first papers); students, literally, become practicing writers. These are only a few of the ways students benefit from preparing portfolios.

Portfolio evaluation isn't necessarily easier for teachers; it is, however, a more adequate evaluation process for any classroom in which students learn to revise to improve their writing. In such a writing classroom, teachers want to guarantee that writing evaluation includes both "*measurement* (or grading or ranking) and *commentary* (or feedback)" as described by Peter Elbow ("Trustworthiness" 231). In such a writing classroom, teachers make an effort to assure that evaluation goals match class goals, thereby avoiding what Linda Brodkey calls practices that contradict curriculum ("Modernism" 414). Further, portfolio evaluation may be adapted to every type of writing class, including creative writing, technical writing, freshman composition, and writing with literature classes. [1]

Papers in portfolios must go through drafts

Since portfolios present students' best work, submitted after papers have been discussed and improved, generally, all portfolio pieces will have gone through drafts. Depending on the teacher's class organization, drafts may have been thoroughly critiqued (although often not graded) in peer response groups, in student/teacher conferences, and in tutoring sessions.

Over time, students bring three levels of drafts to class: *rough* (zero or discovery drafts), *professional* (draft #2 to #10+, depending on a students' own writing process), or *portfolio* (drafts submitted for mid-semester or end-of-semester teacher evaluation). Draft levels, audiences, and formats are summarized in Figure 1.

Although this overview distinguishes between three draft levels, papers may go through many more revisions than three (and in rarer cases fewer

Figure 1: Overview of Portfolio Draft Levels

Rough draft:
- written for student as she generates her ideas, and
- written for the student's peer group
- must be legible to writer for oral sharing with peers in order to receive verbal critiques

Professional draft:
- written for student as she reviews, revises, and refines her ideas, and
- written for the student's peer group, the teacher, friends, writing center tutors, etc.
- drafts must be legible to other readers (*preferably* typed)
- when shared with peer group, copies are provided for all group members who respond with oral critiques and/or written critiques
- when shared with teacher, teacher responds with written or oral (conference) critiques to discuss revision directions

Portfolio draft:
- written for the public—including student, teacher, and interested readers—after incorporating earlier revision suggestions
- typed and then presented with *rough* and *professional* draft versions in mid-semester and end-of-semester portfolios

---

revisions may occur). Equally, a mid-semester *portfolio* quality draft may receive further consideration and drafting for end-of-semester portfolio evaluation.

In any event, portfolio presentation requires some version of a planned drafting cycle. To review, students generate their own topics or write on assigned topics and share papers during a draft cycle—rough to professional to portfolio quality. Drafts can be requested on set due dates to help students meet their semester writing commitment. Teachers who feel they need to provide graded critiques to give students a formal sense of their academic progress could continue to grade papers, providing grades on the professional draft.

Two points about grading drafts should be remembered. The teacher must truly consider that grade as temporary (in-progress) for the later mid- or end-of-semester portfolio evaluation to be effective. And, grading a paper may send a negative message. The teacher who grades before collecting and evaluating mid-semester portfolios will surely be seen as less of a writer's advocate than the teacher who doesn't grade at this point. Finally, lack of grade should not be confused with lack of evaluation; with each paper, the student writer is receiving considerable, valuable, oral and written commentary from class peers, tutors, friends, and teacher.

How to evaluate a writing portfolio at mid-semester and the end of the semester

Having students collect all classroom writing at mid-semester to submit in a writing portfolio can lead to a productive student-teacher dialog. Mid-semester portfolio evaluation allows teachers to talk to students about where they have been and where they are going.

At mid-semester, teachers may ask students to place their writing in a two pocket portfolio folder. In one pocket are *rough* and *professional* drafts for each essay and possibly a writing process journal. In the other pocket are *portfolio* quality drafts of required papers and, possibly, a *letter of self-evaluation*. For each student, a teacher will read the portfolio drafts carefully, review other portfolio materials briefly, and respond a) to the portfolio as a whole and, b) if used, to the writer's letter of self-evaluation.

It is possible to write long and effective mid-semester responses to student portfolios, but such an activity will overtax most hard-working writing teachers. In doing so, there is also the possibility of allocating evaluation time unfairly as a teacher lingers over some portfolios and speeds through others. Evaluation sessions that fluctuate with stamina may become less than fair.

Designing a one-page response sheet for each class can regularize a teacher's response time, allowing him to check off class requirements, thereby making sure the portfolio is complete, and to respond briefly in writing to portfolio content across three categories:

1. an overall response to writing development (what is successful?);
2. suggestions for improving writing during the second half of the semester (suggestions at this time are particularly important as they may refer to the student's self-evaluation. If teacher and student estimations exhibit great variance, teachers will want to describe what changes will help the student progress more successfully); and
3. a mid-semester grade-in-progress with a sentence or two of explanation.

End-of-semester evaluation echoes mid-semester evaluation but it is summative in nature rather than formative. Because this is the last time a teacher can respond to students, the response sheet will include only numbers 1 and 3, above. Figure 2 below shows a sample evaluation sheet designed for a first semester, freshman composition course.

How to assure fairness in grading

Evaluating portfolios on their own, teachers may develop grading concerns that parallel the concerns they have had when grading individual student papers. For instance, what constitutes an A, B, or C level portfolio? How does a teacher assure that she is fair in her evaluations, not awarding a "fat" ineffective portfolio more credit than a "thin" focused portfolio, and so on? Such concerns are central for any teacher instituting a portfolio system. Several practices can help:

1. Begin a portfolio system by outlining goals for portfolios *as used in that class* and write a rubric that details what is expected from a portfolio in each grading category (A, B, C, etc.).
2. Share this rubric (or concepts from the rubric) with students during class discussion, in conferences, and in mid-semester evaluation commentary.
3. Use a formalized response sheet (like the one in Figure 2) for critiquing. By checking off materials received and recording responses *in categories*, teachers are forced to look up from the mass of writing collected and evaluate it as a whole effort. The checklist can include an "improvement" category or a "participation" credit as well as an evaluation of portfolio draft quality.

Figure 2: Sample Mid-Semester Evaluation Sheet for Writing Portfolios

English 111 Mid-Semester Evaluation Sheet

___ Paper 1 (Interview) _____

___ Paper 2 _____

___ Paper 3 _____

___ Paper 4 _____

___ Paper 5 _____

___ I-Search Paper _____

___ Portfolio Drafts for all papers _____

___ Letter of Self-Evaluation _____

___ Writing Process Class Journal _____

[Outside reader's evaluation of one paper:
P (C or above level)
NP (below C level)]

General response to the portfolio:

Suggestions for the second half of the semester:

_____

Evaluation summary:
Journal (10%) ___
Class Participation (20%) ___
(includes attendance, group work, readings, etc.)
Writing Portfolio (70%) ___

Mid-semester grade in progress: ___

_____

Portfolio evaluation does not take less time; it takes different time

Portfolios do not provide a grading panacea. Evaluating student writing does and probably always will take up a large portion of a writing teacher's available time. But writing portfolios change the quality of the time and the pacing of the time demands.

For instance, evaluating *professional* quality drafts does not require that a teacher carry papers home and make copious marginal and end comments. A teacher critiquing *drafts* might address content level concerns by writing a summary response paragraph and usage concerns in a student/teacher conference.

In a draft-oriented classroom, student drafts become familiar. By the time a teacher reads a mid- or end-of-semester portfolio, he is looking at well-known student work and making a holistic judgment about writing quality and writing improvement. Careful reading is required but not hand (and mind) numbing paper marking. Additionally, if grades truly are "in-process," they do not need to be recorded, whited-out, rerecorded. Students are expected to save their drafts and present them for consideration when portfolios are collected. Teachers may wish to record *professional* drafts as received or not received or to record grades, should they choose to grade, but they may feel a new freedom not to keep time-consuming class records.

A teacher's week-by-week grading time commitment may decrease with a portfolio system. However, a teacher's evaluation time commitment will increase temporarily when she collects mid- and end-of-semester portfolios. A teacher with a full teaching load of three to five writing classes will, reasonably, find the portfolio reading period daunting. When instituting the portfolio method and tailoring it to her classroom needs, this teacher will have to start with what works. Although it seems likely that a mid- and end-of-semester full reading of each student's work is the fairest possible evaluative review, teachers may not always be able to devote as much time as they would like to each writing portfolio and still submit grades on time. One of several possible modifications of the full-semester portfolio system may help.

1. Teachers can divide a portfolio evaluation period into two equal parts and evaluate the first half of the semester's work and then "retire" this work before going on to evaluate the second half of the semester's work. Teachers who do this may wish to weight the second half of the semester's grade

slightly (60%), expecting writing to improve more impressively the longer students work at developing their writing process. This choice, a two-part portfolio review, while less than optimum in that it reduces formative evaluation, still allows students involved in such a class to participate in two process-oriented, grade-in-progress drafting cycles, and the teacher benefits by not having to read seventy-five full-length, full-semester portfolios in a three-day grading period.

2. Teachers can have students submit a smaller number of "best" papers from the semester for portfolio evaluation. This can be a timesaving device for the teacher, assuring him that portfolios will never include more than, say, three already familiar essays and a student's self-evaluation. Additionally, students learn to weigh and evaluate their own writing ever more objectively, working with the teacher, class peers, or writing center staff to decide which of their essays are most effective from a reader's viewpoint.

   Additionally, choosing and focusing on selected "best" essays may support an end-of-semester transition from developing students' revision facility to developing their proofreading facility. Students have a greater incentive to proofread *portfolio* quality drafts than rough or professional drafts and may have greater success learning to proofread and edit when working with this limited number of papers.

3. Teachers may work out a class-by-class exchange with like-minded teachers and use their final portfolios as a class proficiency evaluation procedure. Early in the semester, these teachers enforce their advocate role by letting students know the teacher is helping the student to prepare work for an outside reader. Additionally, having an outside reader allows the student to visualize a new and important academic audience for her writing. Teachers may wish to exchange entire "short" portfolios or single "best" papers. The outside reader's evaluation can be figured in to the student's portfolio grade (try starting with a pass or no pass reading, set by reader agreement based upon an articulated rubric). Obtaining an outside reading can be useful for the new teacher who may be worried about grading subjectivity as well as for the continuing teacher who often has the same concern. Sharing reading and evaluation concerns also promotes teacher collegiality.

4. Teachers can collect portfolios up to two weeks before the end of the semester, offering the teacher more review time under less time pressure. During the final week or two of class, students can be refining their "best" essay for the outside reader, preparing and "publishing" a photocopied "class book" of peer chosen and edited writing from each student, and so on. Additionally, if the teacher's institution allows for such a substitution, conferencing time can be scheduled for the last week of class so that teachers can return the portfolio to each student and come to a satisfying sense of class closure. This slightly earlier due date can also help to assure that

students are not trying to make extensive and often unsuccessful revisions while cramming for botany or calculus exams.

Choosing Writing Portfolio Evaluation

Participants in portfolio evaluation generally find that it's one of the best ways to demonstrate a consistent classroom philosophy. Portfolios promote formative evaluation in the writing classroom and also provide a method for fair summative evaluation. Portfolios help students and teachers better respect a student writer's progress and effort while engaging in necessary evaluation of his final class products.

Teachers who want to move to portfolio evaluation need to review their class goals and design portfolio evaluation into their curriculum in a manner that enhances student learning without overtaxing their own energies so they don't abandon portfolio evaluation before it begins to work for them. To do this, they should develop a portfolio drafting and critiquing cycle, consider issues of fairness in evaluation, and, overall, understand the necessity for careful time management. Teachers who design and utilize an evaluation procedure such as this, one that is consistent with their course goals and teaching pedagogy, will learn the pleasures of using evaluation to *im*prove rather than to prove instruction.

Note

1. Since 1987 when the research review in this essay ends, there has been a dramatic development of interest in portfolio evaluation: many collections have appeared, conferences have been held, and universities and state legislatures have interested themselves in portfolio evaluation issues. A solid introduction to these developments can be found in *Portfolios: Process and Product* (Belanoff and Dickson, eds); *Portfolios in the Writing Classroom* (Yancey, ed.); and *Situating Portfolios* (Yancey and Weiser, eds).

Co-authoring Changes the Writing Classroom

Students Authorizing the Self, Authoring Together

I TRIED COLLABORATIVE WRITING AND RESEARCH PROJECTS OFF AND ON for several years in my composition classes with some success, but it wasn't until I experienced the benefits of co-uthoring poetry myself with a fellow poet that I took these active ties into my creative writing classrooms. Changing my creative writing classes to include co-authoring broadened my students' and my own understanding of what it means to compose creatively. In addition, these activities challenged us as readers in ways that I hadn't expected. Now, I'm again recirculating this knowledge back into first-year writing with literature courses, for I find asking students to imitate a poet, together, is one of the best methods I've found for teaching them close reading in the most beneficial sense: a reading that gets inside an author's rhetorical moves.

To begin, imagine you are hearing this small portion of the transcript of a five-minute collaborative poetry audio tape titled "I Grew Two Voices" by Pamela K. Gordon and Monifa Love. The poem is recited over a background of instrumental jazz. (Voices should follow the notations but only as general parameters. The voices should begin and end together. Call and response and meanderings of the spirit are integral parts of the piece.):

Voice #1	*Voice #2*
She sits straight-backed in the	jump back sally sally sally
rusty old red and white porch swing	jump back sally sally jump
her long zebra-stripped hair	jump back sally sally sally
brushed into a neat bun	jump back sally sally jump

a bowl of snapbeans in her lap
creaking back and forth   who is sally?
as the long green tubes pop in half
Her ancient bronze hands work   Great grandmother
rhythmically   stone-faced and gracious
She looks so good for her 81 years   snapbeans in her lap
"My life has been so fruitful" she tells   daughters at her feet
Her blue and white checked sack dress
has risen above her knees   Any y'all named sally
exposing the tattered garters
holding up her stockings
I wonder what will I be like when I
become her age?   little sally walker
                                                           sitting in a saucer
                                                           rise sally rise

I suggest that collaborative composing isn't taking place in all our college writing classes because, in the humanities, we produce such a small amount of co-authored writing that is judged meritorious. Unlike writing in the sciences, where collaborative research and authoring is common, in English studies, the single authored text foundational. When co-authoring takes place, it may be suspect, limited to devalued genres like textbook writing. Additionally, until recently, our theories of texts did not take into account the intertextual influences of other texts or the broader social contexts of all authoring.

What seems at stake for most of us in the humanities is evaluation, the need to measure and rank our members through their writing. We know how hard writing measurement is in the first place, but it becomes even more problematic if we try to award merit to two different authors—how, annual review and tenure committees want to know, can we be sure one author isn't carrying another weaker author—and, how, teachers ask, in a similar vein, can we award a grade to two (or more) class authors?

Since I'm a writing teacher within an institution, I too have accept the responsibility for evaluating student work, and if I move to collaborative work I must evaluate those class products, also. But I think it's possible to evaluate collaborative texts as it is possible to evaluate single-authored work (which means only subjectively possible) and perhaps even easier to respond to collaborative texts since the product of two writers is often superior, in my opinion, to the texts those writers may produce individually.

I believe in collaborative projects, then, because they allow students to pool their strengths, whereas individual projects so often highlight students' individual weaknesses. Think back to the audio-tape collaborative poem transcript you read above. Surely it is possible that one co-author did more of the work. Perhaps Pam (or Monifa) wrote it all, and Monifa (or Pam) just stopped by for a few minutes to help to record the product. Perhaps friends who were listening as they recorded suggested alternative readings, chantings, singings? While I don't think evaluation is the central issue for my teaching, if I want to keep track of student effort, I don't have to be suspicious of Pam and Monifa, for I can ask that each keep a process journal, or write a summary essay reporting on their learning. I think we're so suspicious of collaborative writing because it's strange to us, maybe even because it's often quite pleasurable.

I'd like to raise two other issues concerning classroom collaborative authoring before leaving problems behind and suggesting projects that you and your students might undertake. First, collaborative writing takes different time commitments. Second, since students have few naturally occurring literary models of collaborative work (though I should point out they have strong models of collaborative performance via rock videos), they need to be allowed a great deal of experimental space, and teacher and students need to be trained to read and respond to collaborative writing.

First, the time issue: Quite simply, it takes a different type of time to participate in successful out-of-class work groups. Collaborative projects should be designed so they don't ask more of a student than single-authoring might ask, but collaborative writing will demand better planning and less procrastinating. The smaller the work group—pairs or triads—the easier the work is to schedule and accomplish. The simpler the technology or media—audio tape rather than videotape—the more students can focus on composing, performing, and revising texts and the less they focus on arranging for and mastering the technology.

Finally, learning and work styles come strongly into play for collaborative work. Though I often mix in-class response groups heterogeneously, asking for students to form groups with members having different genders, ages, major areas of study, and so on, for out-of-class co-authored projects, I have learned to let students self-select partners who are more like them, particularly in terms of work habits. The procrastinator yoked to the detailed scheduler can create untold crises and recriminations.

Second, the models and reading problem: Those of us who read literature in graduate school know that Joyce's later work and Stein's work of any period are difficult to read no matter how rewarding. Experimental work taxes our reading schemes. Instead of quick reliable matches"Once upon a time" means relax and listen to the fairy tale unfoldthe "Once upon a time" of a Robert Coover short story throws us into a topsy-turvy world of challenging textual stress. When writing experimental collaborative texts, students are asked to—and readily and stylishly do—break conventional text expectations.

When I sat down with my first batch of Autobiographical Collages, described below, I wanted to cry. The first five were exciting and depressing. One seemed to "work" and the next to "fail miserably" in relation to the one that had just "worked." After I forced myself to read and then reread the collages, I started to see that, although each collage was stylistically unique, text strategies could be identified. Some students wrote snapshots, others produced textual video collages, texts torn and applied like magazine photos, others created new amalgams, fragments sewn together into prose crazy quilts. I had to have patience and tenacity as a reader—perhaps more than students had to have—because I had to set aside my English teacher's hyper-literacy and stop judging students against an implicit canon of genres in my head while I investigated the convention making and breaking they were engaged in.

I'd like now to share three types of co-authoring projects. I developed these in poetry workshops but they suggest ways to approach co-authoring in any writing course. In addition, there is no reason students can't follow these approaches with a literary author's text(s).

Autobiographical Collages

In my classes, the collage exercise is completed after sequenced introductory invention exercises, allowing students to weave invention exercises back into a productive whole. To explore each writer's personal archeology, I ask class members to produce a name acrostic poem (on what their name means to them or on how they were named); students bring in poems of poets whose themes or language are important to their lives and write imitations. In addition, we write self-portraits, compose poems about heirlooms or talismanic objects, write narrative poems that tell a family or neighborhood story, and so on. Each activity is valuable for the technique it explores and the product it may foreshadow, but after a week or two of rapid in- and out-of-class writing like this, we combine fragments from these texts into an autobiographical collage.

Before doing so, we discuss familiar and unfamiliar collage techniques: linear, spatial, and chronological order, listing, genre pastiche, dialog, interrupting narrators, and so on. And I emphasize that exercise is graded pass/fail (if at all) and that all collages will be published; in a class book to further introduce members of our writing works community to each other.

Since classroom writers are often not yet comfortable with their writing, collaborating with another writer early in the semester might be too intimidating; instead, through collage writing, class authors collaborate first with different aspects of their own identities and with their pasts, learning that they are not mono-vocal while exploring the boundaries of genres. Here is a section of Sean Carswell's collage:[1]

Depression:
    I once wrote a poem called "All I Have to Say About Depression":

> I close my eyes
> and see nothing
> I open them
> not much better

but that poem was written a long time ago and my record needle was broken.

Breeding:
    I have three Peter, Paul and Mary albums and I blame that on my breeding. "Where Have All the Flowers Gone" is one of my favorite songs in spite of myself. I know all four verses to "Home on the Range," and I almost ran away from home several times because of this.

Poetic Evolution:
    The first group of poems I handed in was during my senior year of high school and I titled it *Assorted Genius by Sean Carswell.* A poem I wrote last week describes me as:

> Etherized and I feel
> Like I should just join the rest of my poetic
> Generation and just write song
> Lyrics.

Influences:
    While reading *Walden,* I decided I should move to the woods and live deliberately, but I should wait until the end of the semester to do it. I felt the ghost of Henry David Thoreau slap me upside the head.

I'd never read any Gary Snyder before this class, but after reading "Four Poems for Robin," I wrote this poem about the time I hitchhiked two hundred miles to see a girl I thought I loved:

> Sometimes when   the air is cold enough
> and it tickles   my nose enough
> to smell like   melancholy the fruit
> I think of her   the frozen waterfall
> The time I thumbed   two hundred to turn around
> the mountains and   the beds of trucks
> the sheet rock hanger   the Cherokee reservation
> and her mother   telling my future
> I wonder why her   mother didn't warn me
> but the bed was warm   if the face wasn't
> and I guess I mistook   stick-to-itiveness for love.

Drive Words, Poetry Trading Cards, and Group Poems

The drive word exercise asks students to list single words that are important to them in a variety of categories—favorite colors, smells, sounds, months, types of weather, etc.—forty to fifty words total (example, flannel, shattered glass, potatoes, collard greens, Texas, October, panty hose, cats, belly or belly button, pool cue, calluses, saliva). The aim is to develop an evocative set of primary concrete nouns (although drive words don't have to be limited to nouns). Students review their lists and write their most interesting words on a set of fifteen three-by-five poetry trading cards. Then, in small groups, they read each others cards/words and negotiate a common list which must have some words from each member (example: pool cue, shattered glass, okra, sandpaper dry, camel hair, nails, thighs, panty hose, bus fumes, liquor store). After compiling this list of ten words, each group devises its own composing rules: members can change word tenses, from nouns to verbs or not; in the poems group members write, they must use eight out of ten words, all ten words, etc. Groups reconvene to examine four individually authored poems which utilize the agreed-upon drive words. A sample of mine, shared when I participated with a class group, follows:

READING DETECTIVE FICTION INTO THE NIGHT

> requires a street,
> straight as a **pool cue**,

lined with leaves
and heaps of **shattered glass**.
Here **okra**-shadowed curbs of Saturday night.
Here the pimp in a **camel-hair** double-breasted coat
flapped wide
bitter wings
in the proud heat of a not yet
switched on afternoon.

Soon,
night along the alleys—
hands and **nails** breasts and **thighs**:
lace **pantyhose**
exhibit irregular ladders of tension
on the city proper's
many legs.

At the right moment,
bus fumes rise to cover the proprietor's
name on that familiar **liquor store**
window as the wind-up action begins.

One day I asked each class group to share with the class as a whole their set of drive words and one of the poems authored by one of their group members. A group in the back corner refused to choose just one poem and decided to read all four poems aloud simultaneously. Suddenly we heard a plainsong of chant and repetition and answer, the drive words chiming through the chaotic but still inter-woven text.

I particularly like the way the drive word collaboration loosely introduces students to co-authoring. Group members are not constrained to write together by meeting out of class, but their work is "related" in linguistically powerful ways.

Co-Authoring Poetry

The co-authored poetry tapes I'm describing and sharing briefly in transcript were produced by writing students with little help from me because I didn't know how to give them help. The first time I suggested co-authoring, I asked for an end-of-semester co-authored video or audiotape. I let the groups self-select. The tape by Monifa and Pam was one of only two audio tapes from that class. Most students chose video as their medium, and their products were impressive. Many class members, though, admitted that the demands of video production nearly overwhelmed them. It's wise to remember that video production skills and technical support will vary by classes and by campus.

Pam was taking poetry writing for the first time; Monifa was an experienced and published poet. Pam first wrote a prose poem for class about her grandmother. The poem did not strike anyone—Pam included—as successful. She revised the prose poem and she and Monifa used it for a base, Pam refining the imagery as Monifa added African-American chants and songs. Together, they produced a piece that highlights their talents.

Here is a portion of a collaborative poem by Rex West and Devan Cook. They achieved entirely different—but, I think, equally effective—poetic effects. Rex and Devan used no background music and did not overlap their voices when they recorded this poem:

PATRIMONY: PATRIMONY

Reader #1   *Reader #2*
The road slinks, a sheep trail dropping
between two bare hills

                               covered by sage grass—
                               blades bend and rattle

The mine is hidden

                               and the town that went with it.
My father was an engineer.
I am a writer. I lie.

                               My great-grandfather was a coal miner.
                               I am a writer. I lie.
We're all concerned more with what works
than *why* it works

                               Don't let the facts get
                               in the way of the truth.
In his career my father invented new processes
for producing phosphate;
he mined mountains, aspen leaves yellowed young,
fell through still air to creeks fuming black
from smelter runoff: in snow melt spring floods
washed the bank with water that killed

everything. At the plant, two men died
in thirty seconds from a phosgene leak.

>Words explode, white-hot scraps of poems
>scatter.

My father's leg burned white to the bone;
bandages off, he went back to work
like the others wearing melted skin, welts,
scraps of hair, boots that glowed.
This all disappears when it snows.
Everything buries quietly
But mines are full of holes.

>My great-grandfather said the first steam engine
>pumped water out of a mine
>the first canal was cut to carry ore from Worsley
>to Manchester,
>the first railroad—at Newcastle—took coal from
>pit mouth to river.
>He had a human voice.
>*A collier,* he said, is a coal miner
>and gets used to being damp.

Devan and Rex's tape was produced during the second semester that I assigned collaborative poetry in my writing workshop. In this class, we listened to the tapes at mid-semester rather than as a final project. The benefit of moving the collaborative tapes up in the schedule were twofold: co-authors seemed to continue to work as careful editors for each other's work through the semester, and some authors re-recorded their tapes—essentially revised—after listening to their work juxtaposed against the work of classmates. Again, for each of these assignments, grading rested on good-faith efforts. If and when I want to grade the experiences of co-authoring more actively, I'll ask for an essay about the process of completing the work and grade that like any other reflective essay.

These collaborative activities have supported the traditional workshop in every way. Students pay more attention to the aural dimensions of their poetry while they explore issues of influence, authorship and intertextuality. They "listen" to peers with an eye to finding a congenial or challenging collaborative partner. Reading aloud in class takes on real importance. Due to collaboration and performance, students appear to me to read more ably and to listen to readers with better critical attention. And, as I mentioned earlier, I've taken these activities back to the first-year classroom, asking students to form collages from a literary author's work, to tape those collages, to imitate writing styles, to form their own works by identifying drive words in another author's text and freewrite from those drive word prompts, before shaping this material into their own text, and so on. In the last year, I've found that instead of asking why they are being asked to co-author in the writing classroom, students—as I hope you will—tend to ask why they haven't been doing this all along.

Note

1.   Sean's full collage and other samples of these activities can be found in the teacher's guide that accompanies *Working Words: The Process of Creative Writing* (Bishop). Both Pam and Monifa's and Rex and Devan's collaborative poems have been accepted for publication by literary magazines; the excerpts are used here with their permission.

5

Teaching "Grammar for Writers" in a Process Workshop Classroom

WE ALL KNOW THE PROBLEM WITH FALSE DICHOTOMIES—HOT AND COLD, good and bad, old and young cannot comingle—although they do as warm, complex, or midlife. So too, we think, process never includes product, or so it would seem, since products would short -circuit the recursive, non-linear, reiterative, exploratory and therefore open-ended flow of a pedagogy meant to encourage further and deeper thinking about and through writing.

But we don't live in a kinetic universe; it's not simply that we get the fly-wheel of process started and, like a perpetual motion machine, it keeps on moving, always. Process writing workshops, contrary to labeling, continuously result in products. Writers start again, explore, push, examine. Texts are produced, published, stopped, conflated, interwoven, reshaped. In the same way, writers' themes and topics are investigated and avoided, rewoven and never discarded, borrowed and begged and rebraided into new understandings. We assume far too easily, it seems to me, that process classrooms have abandoned instruction, activities, or writing opportunities that would result in well-edited, well-written products. When we teach writing as writers, it is inevitable that we include instruction in grammar for writers, for we must examine content, structure, linguistic, and cognitive choices that form the congeries of style(s), usage(s), and grammar(s) that are available to all authors and from which professional writers constantly draw. In addition, this choice-making and analysis takes place in an examined matrix of ongoing writing activity as writers use classrooms, and their out-of-classroom time to read and write their own and others' writing more fluently and accurately.

When "process" is viewed as a mindless perpetual motion machine, as if we kick-start student writers and let them generate words for a long fifteen weeks, then process instructors are ethically remiss: they are not teaching and they are not teaching writing as the process we know it to be. When we examine writers' processes in our classrooms, we teach better, for we look at the product payoffs that all invested writers strive for: texts that go out into the world and make meaning when read by ourselves and others.

Product Is Part of Process: Examined Process Classrooms

Let's look at some of the benefits of process theory writing classrooms. Why did compositionists jump on the process bandwagon in the 1970s and '80s, seemingly leaving issues of grammar and style and producing final products in the classroom dust? A writing process, workshop classroom, what I've termed a transactional workshop (*Released*) and what Robert Brooke describes as a response workshop, situates students as writers in writing communities, either drafting teacher-assigned essay sequences or, more often, generating their own topics, often through drafting. Idea and topic quickly became a focus of this type of classroom, resulting in a great number of exploratory invention heuristics like looping and cubing and asking reporter's questions. Invention was important since students were often enrolled in compulsory first-year writing courses and teachers noted a not-unreasonable lack of investment from students when they were so assigned. Students asked to write canned themes in strict forms could sometimes do so, but little learning beyond canning and forming seemed to be taking place, and teachers who were sometimes teaching five sections of twenty-five writing students were overwhelmed with, basically, bad writing. While it was easy to translate this scenario into a disdain for college students, it was more reasonable to see the problem as one of curriculum and context.

> Our texts are "safe" when we do what we know we've gotta do to get a good grade, rather than approaching a paper creatively. Regardless, you must make your point, but a safe paper is one you write, stylistically, for others, not yourself. I hate safe. Freshman English teachers try to "unteach" this style, yet freshmen must stick to it in history classes and humanities (sometimes).

Writing researchers in the 1980s started to understand the nature of professional writer's processes and the nature of basic writers' lack of progress when given traditional writing instruction. Traditional instruction relied on reading and examining model essays that were often culturally inaccessible to these students; class consisted of discussion of an essayist's exemplary text, and a command to emulate that text outside of class, and to submit student-written imitations for a close reading by the teacher who gave a one-time grade. During this period, we began to understand that expert writers undertake multiple drafts and have an ability to plan, generate, revise and refine at both the global and local level. Students did not become more fluent, however, from grading. They did not transfer corrections from an initial, graded paper to the next graded paper, and, when faced with a daunting writing task, many students simply did not write at all, or wrote in a mad rush, just hours or minutes before class.

> Just before the deadline, I would type those works out. I still do this style of pre-editing, making sure that when I type the words, they are the words that I want on the page. However, now [after a process workshop class] I allow at least a day or two to look at a hard copy for editing.

Even as we began to gain a more sophisticated view of professional writers' revision processes and basic writers' underdeveloped revision strategies, we found also that simply assigning "a revision" or multiple drafts did not clarify the process for students. In fact, assigned process sequences too often produced a "clunk" curriculum, with invention on Monday, drafting on Wednesday, and editing on Friday, inculcating still a linear and unitary sense of writing. Second drafts, then, were seen by students as nothing more than a call for implementing a teacher's red-inked corrections, again seemingly never transferring learning about writers' grammars and choices from one paper to the next.

In studies of revision processes, less expert writers usually drafted less and hesitated more. They instituted fewer global changes and often chose safe subjects and simple syntax rather than push their learning through exploration and questioning and language play. We have learned that years of assimilating competing and conflicting writing rules in school can block or stymie a writer: one teacher insisting first person voice is never appropriate and another plaintively asking for it. One teacher pushing for correctness and another for complexity.

> My past writing classes had not developed too much of me. I've either analyzed texts without really including personal views, or I've written stories that sounded pretty but had no depth.

Writing process classrooms attempt to foreground all these issues by setting up communication between the writer and her readers. Audience is broadened from the teacher only to, at a minimum, the teacher and class peers. Often previous writing issues and histories are examined as students write literacy autobiographies or voice analyses. Knowledge about writers' writing processes are shared as each writer examines her own processes through the use of cover sheets on essays or letters of writing self-analysis at the end of term.

When we moved to classrooms emphasizing the recursive nature of the drafting process, by asking students to draft and re-draft an essay, we also had to develop methods of response and evaluation that rewarded and complemented such a movement. If a text is viewed as revisable, then a student should not be encouraged to edit at the local, sentence level while pushing to develop ideas because those very sentences may disappear in a future draft. If a student spends too much time at this initial thinking-through stage on local issues, he's much less willing to discard an ineffective sentence or paragraph in the interest of improving the global effect of the paper. After all, like us, students are pressed for time in every facet of their lives, and writing classes represent just a small portion of their lives; they can't be expected to explore and take risks unless exploration and risk are valued, tangibly, through revision instruction and credit for such work in course grades.

Evaluating workshop products in a final course portfolio assures students that their processes and journey through the class were valuable. It also offers a chance to highlight products, since well-written, well-edited texts are always included, and to teach grammar for writers. By examining a term's work and then choosing to refine the best texts, a student puts her products firmly at the center of the writing workshop experience. The writer's past is explored, the drafting process valued, peers and teacher offer responses toworkshop drafts, and then the writer is allowed time to reflect on and improve work he has become invested in.

> I'm very proud of the material I've produced in here [portfolio]. Writing, revising, editing, workshopping, revising again—these all motivated me to rework my texts (or at least think about different ways to revise as I showered, walked to class, brushed my teeth, and ate lunch).

In this sense, grammar for writers has never been absent from the writing process workshop, but it has certainly been under-discussed and, I'd argue, under-taught. Most composition textbooks and teachers speed dizzily through revision discussions, assuming assigning drafts and allowing for peer response will do the work that needs to be done. It doesn't. We need to be teaching grammar(s) for writers. We need then to be paying much more attention to how we teach drafting, to examine what we mean by and how we teach revision, ditto for style and editing. We need to do this as frequently and as well as we've learned to teach topic generation through invention strategies. In the rest of this chapter, I'll address just how we might.

Grammar(s) for Writers

In her book *Grammar for Teachers*, written in 1979, Constance Weaver ends her considerations of the pro-grammar and anti-grammar instruction arguments this way:

> Indeed, formal instruction in grammar may have a harmful effect, partly because it tends to alienate students, and partly because it takes time that might more profitably be used in helping students read, write, listen, and speak more effectively. (89)

An underlying assumption of examined process classrooms has been similar to the point Weaver makes: writers need time to explore their ideas, to push and challenge received thinking, to experience the many frustrations *and* rewards that professional writers experience. they need to write, *often*, with support and feedback, in a variety of genres and styles. Given the artificial constraints of the writing classroom and the school calendar, it is not surprising that the many studies referenced in this book have shown that time spent on decontextualized grammar instruction provides little to no support for the developing writer. Weaver does argue that teachers may benefit from a good knowledge of language history and understanding of grammatical terms and vocabulary. And, certainly language use is the central discussion in all writing classrooms. Each teacher needs to find his best terms for discussing language use and rhetorical choices with writing students. However, many of us function very well with our personal amalgam of traditional terms, journalists' vocabulary, class-generated or invented terms. Our technical talk and discussion focus has to be relevant to our developing community of writers, even if that community is artificially convened.

In *Grammar and the Teaching of Writing*, written in 1991, Rei R. Noguchi comes to similar conclusions, though he pushes them one step farther:

> While formal grammar instruction seems to offer little in the area of essay organization, it does seem more potentially beneficial in the area of style. "Style" here is used broadly to encompass characteristic or recurrent linguistic features. Style includes not only syntactic and morphological forms but also salient features of punctuation and spelling. (11)

I intend to use a definition of "grammar as style" for the remainder of this chapter. In teaching grammar for writers I am advocating teaching characteristic or recurrent linguistic features of writing within "recognized" forms *and* "alternate" forms. Certainly, it's easy to "name" those broadly repeating features in conventional forms like the compare/contrast essay or the *bildungsroman*. However, it's less easy to tell what is recurring or characteristic when a conventional form is being challenged, say when we write a prose poem which partakes of fiction and poetry writing conventions, or when we choose to use fragments for effect in the manner of the new journalists or literary authors; still, even alternate forms recur, internally within the text, or externally, due to an author's repeated attempts to map her "new" territory by trying the form several times and creating "comparability."

I find it interesting that neither Weaver or Noguchi mention what for me has been an influential work, Winston Weathers's *An Alternate Style: Options in Composition* (first published in essay form in 1976 and expanded to a book-length study in 1980). Weathers argues for the expansion of the tools of a writer's trade. He argues that by neglecting to teach grammar(s) of style we are teaching students to play only bridge with a deck of fifty-two cards when many other games, options, alternatives, actually exist. He claims:

> Any number of such "grammars" or "stylistic families" may theoretically exist and be available to a writer at any one time. Yet on a practical level, in today's classroom we keep all our stylistic options within the confines of one grammar only—a grammar that has no particular name (we can call it the "traditional" grammar of style/or for my purposes Grammar A) but has the characteristics of continuity, order, reasonable progression and sequence, consistency, unity, etc. We are all familiar with these characteristics, for they are promoted in nearly every English textbook and taught by nearly every English teacher. (6)

Essentially, we do not make this diversity of grammars available because we are busy inculcating the dominant grammar, what Weathers terms Grammar A, and we do this because "what is socially prestigious, or 'correct,' in (formal) writing depends on which social variety of language, officially or unofficially, gains acceptance within public institutions" (Noguchi 115).

There are two problems here. We may severely limit grammars for writers in order that their formal writing approaches the official norm. We also tend to do this when we ignore the options and grammars of informal and exploratory writing which researchers like James Britton and his colleagues have argued are essential for thinking through writing. And, we decontextualize grammar instruction—foregrounding the dominant grammar and muting or silencing alternate grammars—so a writer has no sense of the "whys" or "hows" of textual choices.

Weathers's work helped me begin to reconceptualize how I taught grammar for writers, but he also borrows heavily from literary writers, though he argues these techniques should not ever be limited to literary texts; indeed, he advocates for Grammar B in composition classrooms. Grammar B Techniques include crots (prose bits or fragments that are strung together, though each terminates abruptly), labyrinthine sentences and fragments, lists, double voice, repetition and refrain, orthographic schemes, synchronous time and collage/montage.

Feminist theorists have done much to revolutionize academic writing in the last twenty years by using Grammar B techniques in their own writing and by attempting to define and advocate for non-patriarchal forms of discourse. Composition as a marginalized, many argue feminized, field in English studies now allows alternate styles in the professional journals, although it's unclear to what degree the students of these authors are encouraged to undertake similar explorations. For instance, the February 1992 issue of *College Composition and Communication* has Donald McQuade in his 4Cs Chair's address presenting an impassioned personal narrative and Nancy Sommers exploring the relationship between her writing and family life in a text full of alternate expression (including orthographic schemes!), and stories that have crot-like pungency. Terry Myers Zawacki presents a single-authored, multi-voiced text while Beverly Lyon Clark and Sonja Wiedenhaupt present their research in bold- and regular-type dialog.

In "Rendering the 'Text' of Composition" Sheryl Fontaine and Susan Hunter (1992) invited a reader's active participation in text-making when they assembled many prominent "voices of composition" to "render" instead of analyze the field in order to challenge and disrupt textual boundaries. The reader plays a game with this collaged text, identifying authors and documents and then listening to the way those voices amplify and echo and invoke meaning by juxtaposition and association, each text voice altering the text voice it is placed near. Their essay, which is as much the text of others as it is the text of authors, seems exciting but not surprising since the range of grammar(s) of style in composition publications continues to broaden rapidly.

In October of 1992, Lillian Bridwell-Bowles published an essay in *CCC* urging just such stylistic diversity; this essay can be read as a summation of the new directions we've taken since Weathers's work and may serve as a lens for understanding what was being practiced in the February *CCC* and Fall *JAC* issues I've just mentioned. She suggests that alternatives allow us to include other world views: "Our language and our written texts represent our visions of our culture, and we need new processes and forms if we are to express ways of thinking that have been outside the dominant culture" (349). Like many feminists, she challenges traditional models of argumentative writing (see also Frey), and advocates what she calls "diverse discourse"—we may posit this, perhaps, as Grammar C?

> Personal/Emotional Writing
>
> Breaking the Boundaries of Textual Space
>
> Language Play
>
> [Writing] Not [as] the Mythic White Woman
>
> Breaking Out of Linguistic Prejudice
>
> [Writing that Challenges] Class Barriers, Sexual Orientations
>
> [And Acknowledges or Encourages] Different Composing Processes

These stylistic suggestions are the subheadings of Bridwell-Bowles's essay. More or less.

How to Teach Grammar for Writers and/or What's In It for Me and My Students?

Warning: More serious attempts at Grammar B follow. Reading farther should challenge your textual expectations.

Questions: At what point in their writing are writers (usefully) (actively) revising? When do they need to obey conventions (Do they? Can they know them all first?) and when do they need to break with convention (Can they? Do they have ideas about how to?). When should grammar(s) of style be introduced? Which grammar(s)?

Ideas: **A planned drafting sequence that introduces and incorporates revision (Fulwiler "A Lesson" and "Provocative"). **A term plan that includes an intensive period of revision (*portfolio preparation can function this way in any class*) or a time when a single paper is revised (Bishop "Risk-Taking and Radical Revision"). **A term of intense drafting where ideas are explored and followed in informal and exploratory writing (Elbow suggests setting up "evaluation-free" zones) and near the end of term, ideas from this matrix are shaped into formal texts (*hey!*) use journals in the same way. **Students revising the same paper all term long (*sounds a bit rough for the many but possibly profoundly useful for certain writers*). **Analysis of the grammar (*style, rhetorical*) choices of student writers at any point in the term. **An examination of exemplary texts (*on overhead projectors, in published class books*) during the *revision* rather than the invention stage (*it strikes me that we might begin prompting writers with media other than the overwhelmingly awe inspiring professional text— use movies or ads or MTV or music to provoke spoken/written discussion, inner/outer voices—and then later when the writer is jogging along, but a bit out of energy and breath, offer the pick-me-up of written texts from writers who are exhibiting provocative moves so the writer [runner] can imitate, find the new spark that leads her on*).

A few more ideas: **Discuss writers' options, ask for suggestions about how texts can be made riskier and more conventional, how style can be altered. **Ask what it means to write into one's own strengths and weaknesses— what is learned when drafting or revising in this manner? (*that is, don't we learn different important things when we push on where we're already good **and** when we push into the difficult, sore, raw, hard-to-do part of our work?*)

Don't you think certain of these ideas need more flesh?

Let's go global.

In "Provocative Revision," Toby Fulwiler suggests four assigned provocations that will teach writers needed revision vision. They can be asked (when completing multiple drafts) to limit their writing (time, place, action, scope, focus); they can add to their text (dialogs, interviews); they can switch (point of view or voice) in their work; they can transform their writing (recast into a different genre entirely, essay to letters or diary, journals to research reports, and so on). (*If you want to see student samples and a three-draft version of "taught revision," look at his "A Lesson in Revision.")*

Q: He says students should be *assigned* revision—but we know every writer doesn't really need to go through multiple drafts while others need to go through countless drafts. Isn't this draconian?
PA (Possible Answer): But how do you know revision options, grammars other than the ones you've been introduced to, what you can do well (what you need to practice more) unless you try a canny and well-designed sequence to show you? Unless you try this or other sequences several times, in fact (who ever learns anything the first time)?

In my classes: I work with semester-long writing contracts—asking students to decide on a plan for drafting five papers a term. The fifth paper is automatically designated a "radical revision" of papers one, two or three. Four is not up for radical revision—initial writing of that paper takes place too close to the revision assignment for writers to have either the glow or weariness of initial drafting diminished. The radical revision must represent a risk for the writer—this leads us to class discussions of

a) conventions
b) how writers know and understand their strengths and weaknesses, and
c) what is radical? We brainstorm on the chalkboard all the ways we think a paper can be revised:

time changes, genre changes, style/voice changes, topic deviations, experiments with the physicality of texts, being conservative when you're normally flamboyant (vice versa), multi-media, multi-voice, borrowing, and so on (other "revision" grammars have been reviewed above)—resulting in

essays turned into crots with photographs woven through, into songs that are performed, into t-shirts that must be read, into collaged paintings, into applications to graduate school, into poems, into bumper stickers, into multi-voiced arguments of self and soul, into harangues, into papers that cannot be graded or they would not be written, so . . .

I ask for process narratives of what was learned about revision and grade on the exploration that was undertaken (in good faith) and how well it was narrated (in fact, writers may need to fail to produce learning through radical revision).

I launched on my radical revision, which attempts to bring the piece "out" from the constrictions of a straight essay. Instead of using italicized motifs to represent the letters, I decided to reconstruct the letters themselves. With assorted pieces of stationery I rewrote these letters with as much authenticity as I could (using an old typewriter, intentional misspellings, smudges, and my own handwriting). [Here indeed is a way to teach local concerns, traditional grammar, this student must know how to spell to misspell intentionally.] To further bring the piece out, I included the photographs of which I spoke and cut them up as to represent which segments of the essay were "mine" (the things I recall) or simply my parents'. What results is radical in that it accomplishes what I only spoke of accomplishing in past drafts, making the text more clear, more visual. More accessible.

One problem: we have to learn to read radical revisions, to honor the learning in the exploration, to value grammars of style, to understand the alternate ways they show us how much has been mastered and mistressed of the dominant grammar:

Lights off. Sitting down in
front of the glowing green
phosphor letters on the screen.
Fingers
wanting to move rapidly.
Twitching
to make the keys rattle.
Straining
through thoughts.
Sifting.
No. Yes. Maybe. What about the
lady on the subway today?
Too cliché.

The trick was to pick the
right hole. He had often
spent days working on an idea,
just to finally reel in and
face the fact that things
weren't biting on that hook.
Normally that would have been
fine, just change the tackle
and throw it out again, making
sure to keep the line taut.
But he had to face her each
time.

It's hard, isn't it, to stop fleshing out these ideas because revision is itself generative.

Time's running short, let's go local.

- Examining writers' productive and nonproductive writing rules may aid revision. If a writer believes his first paragraph has to be perfect before he moves to the next, revision has too high a price. So beliefs must be examined and contradictory rules must be defused.
- Writers change their writing habits and rituals lifelong—that is, they keep many, but abandon some due to external pressures. When I have this draft due, as it is, I'm writing late at night (*normally, I can't*) with a glass of white wine that should make me sleepy (*but it's not, because I'm not used to drafting at night, so I forget to sip from the glass as I find an idea and follow it to earn the end to my evening*). Students may more easily explore alternate grammars and attempt drafting if they change their physical writing conditions and experiment with altered processes—not forever, just to try new muscles, flex new wings.
- Introduce just a few new ideas (grammars, terms, encouragements, freedoms) concerning style. Although my students always critique Weathers's own writing style—a bit dry when advocating innovation—they take to his terms—crots is a particular favorite—and understand his concepts readily. Grammar B allows them to name what they have often, already, been attempting in their texts; it is a great relief for them to have terms for discussing alternate ways of writing and this fluency leads to more expert class discussions.
- Publish writing—there is nothing like performance to make us try to make ourselves and our writing presentable. Publish class anthologies for writing presentable. Publish class anthologies for writing workshops even if only five essays are to be discussed that cycle, everyone (*cleans house*) straightens his or her prose when they know it will be inspected. Emphasize final portfolios as a site of publication; insist that students spend time preparing final copies by offering:
- Editing sessions. These can occur at various points in the classroom and range from tapping group members' skills as copy editors, fine spellers, comma squad participants, and so on. My favorite editing device is what I call *wall editing*. The first time a "product" is due, I ask how many class members have read their papers aloud. In a class of twenty-five, usually only two to five have done so. I ask each writer (and I participate) to find a blank piece of classroom wall and read aloud to check for errors before publication. I offer myself as a resource for advice and I've already asked writers to come prepared with white-out and black pens to make corrections. Soft and loud, a manic murmuring of written texts takes place. Inevitably, I see nearly every class member return to his/her desk to make a grammar level improvement in the text being prepared to represent him/her to the world of readers.

Haven't you really already added to this list of items yourself, though? All your editing and grammar tricks and wisdoms and advice and tools don't have to be abandoned in the process classroom. We just need to find the right balance and the right places for this essential type of instruction. Teaching grammar for writers is nothing more (and usually less) than teaching writing itself.

Part II

Composing Ourselves as Readers

Dividing anything into sections or categories is necessary for those with a drive for organization and analysis, but the practice can be problematic, as we in the field of composition who pit ideas of expression and construction against each other know all too well. Of the three essays in this section, "The Literary Text and the Writing Classroom" could have been included in Part III, which deals with institutional issues, the politics of the profession. However, it functions here to provide an overview, an entry point to the discussions at hand: what do writing teachers know about reading? What assumptions about reading do we bring to writing classes, writing instruction and writing students? In our instruction, how do reading processes and writing processes work together and apart?

While this first essay considers the college-level first-year writing classroom— it moves from that classroom in two directions. I argue that the second-term first-year writing-with-literature classroom is the site where the stresses and strains of all our English studies' beliefs about writing and reading are situated. By studying this site, we study ourselves. I look backwards through institutional history to understand how the writing-with-literature classroom developed and look forward again to problems with such classrooms. I end by urging a difficult solution, that we teach writing and reading within the curriculum as tandem, better understood, equally valued and interdependent processes.

This essay was begun, as most of my essays were, from interest and from necessity. As I worked to revise the first-year curriculum at Florida State during 1991–1993 and began training graduate teaching assistants to teach the new courses, I met surprising resistance from these already fluent readers. The resulting essay made the rounds of journal reviewers who asked for more this and that—more institutional history and a more useful vision of where we might go next. The four-year drafting, critique, revision cycle of this essay led me to realize the issue of "what to do about reading" was not going to go away.

In 1995, Mariolina Salvatori offered me a chance to write about the teaching of teaching for a special issue of Reader that she was editing. Because I had been listening closely to reviewers of "The Literary Text" as well as to new teachers of writing, I began to struggle with the issue once again. This time I didn't feel as obliged to look at the "why" but instead at the "how". "Teaching Writing Teachers to Teach Reading for Writing" opens with three quotes as does "The Literary Text." My impulse to include opening epigraphs comes, I believe, from my experience as a poet who avidly collects prompts for poems to the point that I can now almost "feel" a poem originate as a result of reading. Choosing composition epigraphs allows me to undertake interior discussions when I go running. These often turn into exterior rehearsals, ideas talked-out to others interested in the same subject, often friends on the Internet. In this way citations are less a call to authority than they are a call to conversation. Meditating on others' thoughts on a subject has for me become a dependable invention habit; like a dog gnaws happily on a bone—or a writer-to-learn edges bravely into new territory, word by word—when faced with or when looking for a "subject," I first collect ideas and let my own developing ideas rattle up against them.

"Teaching Writing Teachers" exhibits other of my creative writing tendencies, relying as it does on repetition and circularity. In this essay my audience shifts from the field at large (which I address in "The Literary Text") to a subset of the field, writing teacher–educators. I use student and teacher voices and my own experiences to investigate the subject: arguing, essentially, that we need to be making the unseen reading processes we've internalized as expert readers more explicit for new teachers who are going to be working with what I call "disfluent" writers—writers who may have chosen not to read. The question is vexing: how far can a disengaged reader progress toward becoming a fluent writer?

The final essay in this section, "'Traveling Through the Dark': Teachers and Students Reading and Writing Together," began as an exercise in a graduate course in critical theory, that I enrolled in during the summer of 1987. For my class report, I chose reader-response theory to share with my peers and completed a reading of William Stafford's poem in order to illustrate and to learn the method. At this time I was first introduced to the work of Patricia Bizzell, David Bleich, Louise Rosenblatt, Frank Smith, and Jane Tompkins (and all the authors in her edited volume on reader-response theory). These individuals offered me important, stealable insights and techniques for understanding and teaching in my multi-cultural Alaska writing classrooms. This essay represents a first thinking-through of what it might mean to teach reading, and in it you see me, as I later saw the teachers I would train in Florida, trying to figure out how I did what I did that my students couldn't seem to do (or want to do): read a poem or short story with pleasure and involvement, read it in a way that sparked further thinking and writing. In this essay, I worked to make connections between composition theory and research and classroom practice and I found the connections were profitable. Stealing the idea of reading-aloud protocols from cognitive research did work. Stealing techniques of close analysis and poetic imitation did work.

Composing myself as a teacher of writing who reads meant, in one sense, de-composing myself—reaching back to remember how I learned to read, watching my students read or not read, seeing new teachers of writing ignore or profess ignorance of—or indifference to—reading processes. All these things made me study reading for writing. In fact, I continue to do so; one current project includes looking at how we use the same reading theorist/theories differently in the three main strands of English studies; for instance, trying to understand what it signifies that Mikhail Bakhtin's work is read differently by creative writers, compositionists, and literary critics.

Considering reading via history, theory, practice and process leads a teacher deeply into the politics of literacy instruction. Considering the relationship of reading to writing and writing to reading leads a teacher quickly into ongoing arguments over what should be read and written, how, where, by whom, and for what ends. In this section, however, I urge teachers first to consider their own composition as writers-who-read and readers-who-write and to examine how their literacy autobiographies affect their lives.

The Literary Text and the Writing Classroom

Required composition is the course that everybody wants all students to take but that nobody wants to teach.

CCCC Committee on Professional
Standards "Progress Report" (337)

Wrenched apart by skills teaching and patched together in curriculum plans and textbooks, reading and writing are not so much learned together as taught together.

Hepzibah Roskelly "A Marriage of Convenience" (139)

They were not deliberately ignoring the directives I had published for the course; they just could not resist the siren call of literature.

Edward P.J. Corbett "Literature and Composition" (181)

CONSIDER THIS IMAGINARY NEW WRITING TEACHER. SHE ENTERS OUR graduate program and is inducted into writing pedagogy by composition specialists. She then finds this knowledge undervalued by her literature professors. Another day she is told, in contradiction, to pay *some* attention to *some* of the compositionists' knowledge by critical theory professors, who, with the feminist studies professors, bemoan the backwardness of creative writing professors, who resist critical theories—which undercut the authority of authors—and who worry that their art is being diminished by the non-humanistic empirical research of the composition professors, who themselves feel the literary establishment is despairingly elitist and old-fashioned, while, at the same time, those composition professors also seem too easily to ignore the power of products, of texts, in their eternal questing after underlying activities, writers' processes.

I know these confusions exist and misdirections take place because I myself have moved across the strands—BA in literature, MA in creative writing, and Ph.D. in rhetoric—and because I train new writing teachers. A few years ago I began to study one group of eight teachers during their first year of teaching, choosing, on purpose, a mix of those who intended to produce, or to study the production of, texts and those who intended to consume texts: future writing and literature professors (see "Attitudes and Expectations"). As I observed these teachers during their first year, I also discussed with them the ways they were being educated and supported in their own graduate classes. I interviewed literature graduate teaching assistants (GTAs) who didn't feel like writers; only "creative writing graduate students" enrolled in graduate writing workshops could call themselves that. I interviewed creative writing, rhetoric and literature GTAs who found great disjunction between how they were being trained to teach writing and how their writing was treated in graduate seminars. Little or no drafting was required or encouraged as part of graduate level literature courses (see also Patricia Sullivan's study) and even creative writing workshops could prove surprisingly traditional, focused on the analysis of final drafts only.

I talked to perplexed GTAs who found themselves "playing school" to an unexpected degree—trying to produce the "right" reading for a literature professor and rarely to never receiving sufficient insight into the politics of the profession(s) that might explain why one professor still teaches New Critical approaches while another offers deconstructive readings and another swears by the new historicism.

In this essay—from the view of a writing teacher educator—I locate the tensions of disciplinary turf, professional allegiances, and unexamined teaching practices that intersect in the first-year, writing-with-literature class. Within these classrooms English studies starts to get earnest about its business of sorting students for the institution, and it is here also that we begin to distinguish the literature teacher from the writing teacher. I want to share my understandings of these courses, examine confusions that surround these courses for new teachers and for English departments in general, and address the problems inscribed in the very language we use for this work (which results from historical and political developments in the field). I hope in this process to begin to clarify a very muddy situation. Finally, knowing change in this area within English departments will be difficult and slow, I still suggest changes.

What Is Writing-with-Literature?

When I observe first-semester, first-year writing sections, called Freshman Rhetoric and Composition at my university, I am comfortable as a teacher educator. These are writing workshop classes. Students and teacher together work to understand and improve each writer's process of composing written texts. With a handbook and rhetoric as textbooks and students' primarily essayistic texts as reading materials, there is rarely a confusion of purpose.[1]

When I observe second-semester, first-year writing sections, called Freshman Writing About Literature at my university, I am often uncomfortable. These classes are meant to continue in the workshop model. However, with the addition of a literary reader—which traditionally consists of selections of poetry, stories and plays (and more recently essays)—students' writing often moves from primary reading material to subservient text, students using their essays to prove knowledge of canonical literature and literary techniques. Here students' essays inhabit the classroom sidelines, always "apprentice" work, attempting but never managing to attain the substance of the central works studied by the class (see Scholes *Textual Power* for an in-depth discussion of this hierarchy).

For those who devote themselves to the literature strand of English studies, this may seem a necessary and normal progression. After students study rhetoric and their own writing, they quickly move on, studying the best written texts available, literature. In this scenario, composition serves the university by delivering basic skills to a large entering freshman class, while, within the English department, first-year, writing-with-literature courses act as feeder classes, recruiting for literary studies.

At many universities, the second semester class can also migrate to the sophomore year and/or become the class taught most often by literature faculty members who need to meet their composition instruction commitment. At some universities, that leaves the first semester—or writing *without* literature—course staffed exclusively by teaching assistants and adjuncts, non-empowered academics in training (or worse, non-tenure-line academics in limbo).[2] Peter Elbow observes:

> In meetings to decide who teaches a writing course and who teaches a literature course, I often discover decisions being made on the premise that someone must be smarter to teach literature than to teach writing. Now that I'm sensitive to that premise, I see it often. Thus people often assume that only

advanced and experienced graduate students should teach literature but that raw, first-year [graduate] students are ready to teach writing. (*What* 127)

However, the new teacher or adjunct may not be "raw" in relation to writing pedagogies, having often been trained (no matter how swiftly) to meet the needs of preparatory or first-year *writers*. But older literature faculty members, hired in the 1970s or earlier, may remain untrained—and resistant to training—in composition research, theory and (new) practice(s). And these professors may view first-year students merely as naive *readers* with abominable writing skills that need to be fixed in order to allow them to better discuss the literary texts that remain, for such professors, at the core of the writing course. In fact, these faculty members often see their assignments in composition as "punishment":

> Every semester, some of these classes fail to garner the needed enrollment, and the faculty member is bumped down, down, down, into God forbid, Freshman English. Generally, professors in such situations are gracious; they put the best possible face on it and may even claim to hold no particular preference for teaching Seventeenth-Century Poetry over teaching composition. But given any choice at all, they will always seek an advanced composition course over one for freshmen, and a second semester freshman course over a first. (Martin 122–123)

Such teaching assignments are inevitable given current enrollment statistics in English departments since, at many universities, literature enrollments continue to decline and composition enrollments continue to rise.

At the same time, in the second-semester writing class, the study of reading—the complicated, interactive reception of texts—gives way to a more narrow definition of reading. In the traditional approach to consuming texts, students are asked to read the print before them while paying little to no attention to history, criticism, and the authors' actual, possible, or probable methods of composition: "Literary criticism is still imagined as the 'reading' an individual student produces rather than as a discourse he or she participates in" (Sullivan 296).

And a writing course that focuses on reading, the consumption of texts inevitably engulfs the teaching of writing, the production of texts; for instance, Maxine Hairston feels: ". . . when discussion in the class focuses on finished products rather than on how those products came into being, the writing component of the course suffers. What *should* be the focus of

any writing course—*the study of the writing process at all levels,* both amateur and professional—gets lost" (180). However, even those in composition do not uniformly agree on the purpose of this course as evidenced in
the Erika Lindemann and Gary Tate debate, started at a meeting of the
Conference on College Composition and Communication in 1992, that
resulted in a sequence of essays (and readers' responses) in the 1993 and
1995 issues of *College English.* In 1993, Lindemann argues for re-defining
the first-year course as one that "offers guided practice in reading and
writing the discourses of the academy and the professions" (312) and Tate
feels that literature in composition courses was often mis-taught and
would prefer a literary focus to Lindeman's academic discourse focus.

Clearly the issues involved are problematic, resulting in feelings that as a
profession we're rearguing an old (and, for some, a useless) issue and by
others that we need to revisit the history and purposes of these courses. In
1995, Erwin Steinberg argues along the lines of the Corbett quote that
opens this essay, more or less that there's enough work to do in the writing
classroom without adding the complications of imaginative literature.
Michael Garne argues for fictionalizing the curriculum. As he sees it,
"imaginative texts. . . .hold multiple points of view and are by nature mul-
tidisciplinary' (282). And he worries that "our graduate student teachers—
at least those in the humanities and even in the social sciences—usually
have just begun their own theoretical reading, and if anything are too eager
to impart these powerful ways of seeing to their students" (283). Finally, in
this 1995 issue, Lindemann and Tate recap their positions—Lindemann
arguing, again, for those in composition to define the goals of first-year
writing (she offers three models, product, process, and system). Tate revis-
its his own arguments and finds that the issue is less the disappearance of
literature from the classroom than the disappearance of *discussions* about
the place of literature in the first-year classroom: "In other words, although
we might still be using literature, we weren't talking about it" (304). He
argues that the current debate signals a need for such discussion. I feel the
need too even though I realize the topic can raise a groan of "haven't we
been here before" from teachers (as it did from a reviewer of this essay). As
a teacher-educator, I find myself returning to considerations of this course
again and again.

Even as I try to situate myself in the "should we, shouldn't we?" discussions, I find it more important to consider the degree to which—
whenever we teach literature and writing together—we've not been
integrating this instruction with teaching reading in the broadest and

most useful sense. I find it problematic, that, from first-year classes through graduate classes, reception theories and skills often are not taught as much as they are assumed. In the current-traditional writing about literature course, novice readers may be asked to undertake increasingly more complicated "readings" of literary texts without ever having theories of reading explained very clearly or explicitly. And at the graduate level, critical theories are applied to canonical texts but not to GTAs' texts; for instance, we may punish "gaps" in graduate student text, yet praise the free-play available to us in the "gaps" of texts by famous critical theorists. And in one sense, *assumptions* concerning reading ability always privilege those who read best (teachers) at the expense of those who would read better (students): "The primacy of reading in the reading/writing dichotomy is an act of locating authority away from the student and keeping it entirely in the teacher or institution or great figure" (Elbow "The War" 13).

While those in composition have made strong cases for there being writing processes and a need to illuminate those processes, the case for teaching reading processes has not been as uniformly made. And the graduate student teachers who are providing the bulk of composition instruction are themselves not guided through their own graduate level reading and writing tasks in a way that allows them, later, to model or illuminate text processes. Edward P.J. Corbett's testifies to large gaps in these teachers' pedagogical preparation: "Many English teachers come from the ranks of those who were omnivorous readers and, having learned to write mainly through this process of osmosis, quite naturally believe that others too can learn to write by being exposed to great literature" (170).

In addition, for graduate students in English, their own writing may go unattended. In her study of English graduate student writing at four universities, Patricia Sullivan found: "Graduate faculty tend to teach literature in the primary sense but assume that graduate students will master (or have mastered) the writing of scholarly and critical texts on their own" (296).[3] In fact, professors in her study seemed to be so unreceptive to current thinking concerning writing instruction, they felt writing "processes cannot or ought not be taught because discussion of the writing task would mean intervening in the writing process either in superfluous or counter-productive ways" (294).[4] The net result of such thinking moves the burden of instruction from professor to graduate students, with problems being "attributed to personal deficiency, not institutional *praxis*" (288).

Given a documentable lack of guidance received by graduate students when they undertake their own reading/writing assignments, it is not surprising that—despite their own preparation for teaching first-year writing—GTAs might neglect to provide guidance to students in the area of reception, since graduate students, as I pointed out before, are generally lifelong readers, who have consumed text after text. And for good readers: "the reading process is more hidden—and also quicker—it seems less fraught with struggle for someone who is good at it. Therefore literature teachers often fail to experience themselves in the same boat or engaged in the same process as their weak students" (Elbow *What* 131). Equally, these new graduate students might inherit some troublesome assumptions during their coursework, for instance, the habit of attributing first-year writing students' writing and reading problems to personal deficiency rather than to teaching practices. That is, the way they have been treated as graduate writers will conflict with the way they are being *taught* to teach first-year writing.

And there is a sadder assumption that is all too often made—that those in literature and certainly those in first-year writing only "serve" or "study" creative texts although many came to literature via the excitement of trying to make literature, just as many of their writing students might benefit from "making literature." Despite this, creative writing is often banned from first year writing classes and graduate students have forsworn their earlier pleasures in text production:

> I've noticed a striking feature that is common in literature students that I don't much see in graduate students from other disciplines: a wry and sometimes witty but always condescending tone they take toward their younger selves who were usually excited with writing and eager to be great writers. Behind this urbanity I often see a good deal of disappointment and even pain at not being able to keep on writing those stories and poems that were so exciting to write. But instead of acknowledging this disappointment, these students tend to betray a frightening lack of kindness or charity—most of all a lack of understanding—toward that younger self who wanted to grow up to be Yeats or Emily Dickinson. Instead, I see either amused condescension or downright ridicule at their former idealism and visionary zeal. (Elbow "The War" 8–9).

Whether GTAs began primarily as readers (Corbett) or as writers (Elbow), when they abandon their pasts, their teaching may suffer. I think this lack of literacy self-understanding compounds in negative ways in the writing-with-literature class where text appreciation is foregrounded; where literary text-making is often, at the same time, forbidden; where newly cynical GTAs "discover" their own writing students are not "motivated" to write on restricted topics and in limited forms; just as these GTAs are folding away their own dreams of "being writers" as they write single-draft "academic" essays for their own professors who, long ago, folded away similar dreams. This is not to argue that every writing class should focus on creative genres, that every GTA is a bitter former-poet, or that all English professors are urbane and unapproachable, but I do argue that when such suppression occurs, we might locate its beginning in the second semester writing course. For it is here, that teachers' individual histories play out against a broad sweep of field and institutional history.

For the second half of this essay, then, I explore the problems that develop when the literary text slips into the writing classroom, and I aim this exploration in two directions. First, I look at the confusion that arises for new teachers of writing when they enter the contradictory culture of English studies. Second, I explain the confusion by looking at the dichotomous language we use to separate production from consumption—teaching writing from teaching literature—and the way that our language reflects our institutional history and our everyday lives. Both explorations should illuminate my basic thesis. Writing-about-literature classes present new teachers with too many tacit and conflicting demands. These demands exemplify, in microcosm, the long-term and continuing conflicts that trouble English studies.

Teachers' Confusions

Currently, I teach two main categories of new teachers of writing: those hoping to become creative writers or rhetoricians, both focusing on the production of texts, and those hoping to become literary scholars, those focusing on the consumption of texts: to simplify, I'll refer to these groups as writing GTAs and literature GTAs.[5]

When preparing to teach the first semester of our writing sequence, literature GTAs are worried, sometimes unhappy, although often successful; they all look forward to the second semester class which uses readings texts—predominately literary readings—although our common curriculum downplays literary value and plays up understanding of textual strategies, in part, by now requiring a reader that includes advertisements, films, imaginative nonfiction, and culture-in-general as "texts".

Teaching during the second semester, the writing GTAs are the ones who are often less happy; some claim they don't know how to deal with the literature readings since they can't supply what they assume is necessary historical or critical background. Some describe being more comfortable in the previous semester with the rhetorical discussions and the focus on student texts shared in a workshop.

Certainly there are new teachers who break through these stereotypes; literature GTAs who fall in love with writing process and find out that they too are "writers," and writing GTAs who have always read literature and are able to make a brilliant segue to our second semester writing course, often because they have no trouble including "student-writing-as-literature" and "Literature" in the same universe. Our programmatic assumption—which broadens the category of literary (valuable) texts to include student work—does, however, give some literature GTAs great pause.

Teachers' basic field preferences aside, the second semester course is problematic for many. New GTAs often teach it in a traditional manner—as an introduction to literature to resistant non-majors—or they may teach it quite loosely, as a writing course with no center, one, perhaps, that just looks lightly and in an atheoretical manner at a variety of texts. There is of course a problem with the literature readings textbooks themselves. The textbooks are high on canonized content and low on innovative teaching apparatus; in most large programs, textbooks are pre-ordered for teachers and function to teach the teachers.[6] Therefore, if textbooks provide current-traditional introductions, teachers receive current-traditional reinforcement. Also, the new teacher may be involved in a teacher education course that looks seriously at current theory and research in composition, advocates a process pedagogy, and provides a well-defined introductory curriculum, but time is always short in these courses and the new material—production theory—dominates while reception theory is rarely (re)visited. Generally, it is assumed that graduate students need to be trained to teach writing. And, as I have shown, it is equally easy to assume that they already know how to teach reading, having been "trained" to do so through their own participation in English studies as undergraduate English majors: the osmosis theory.

To further complicate the education of new teachers of college writing—and easily the majority of our new faculty members start out their academic life as graduate teaching assistants—new teachers will find that some in English studies are willing to define writing as a subject while others are very reluctant to assign content to the field. When writing is not viewed as a subject, it is also not viewed as a subject about which to talk: there is often an unwillingness (or inability) of those in English studies to discuss the historical, political and economic factors that have led to this development.

Departmental Confusions

Within my own program and despite the department's good intentions and efforts, I found at least some confirmation that English professors offer little direct instruction within the overall curriculum regarding academic publishing, tenure systems, the relationship of writing programs to literature programs, and so on. Most English departments like mine still adhere to the field coverage model of English studies (Graff *Professing* 4–10). Field coverage tends to reduce the questions we ask about time periods, genre categories, theoretical choices and our own ideologies by marking a professor as a specialists (within a limited area) who has no need to consult or interact with professors in other areas: Chaucer doesn't speak to the modern British novel or American literature since 1875, and both of those areas in turn don't speak to English literature 1500–1560, and so on. The field coverage model encourages isolation rather than conversation. As a result, programmatic meta-knowledge has been placed perhaps too conveniently into the Introduction to English Studies courses that were designed to teach bibliographic methods and now have been enlarged, slightly, to provide a whirlwind tour of competing critical theories, and, lately, some of a growing body of institutional history. Gerald Graff in his history reminds us that our willingness to segregate such information within a single course (rather than conduct meta-discussions within all courses) often has the (desired?) net effect of de-fusing on-going self-inspection and self-critique. He points out:

> The boundaries that mark literary study off from creative writing, composition, rhetoric, communications, linguistics, and film . . . each bespeak a history of conflict that was critical to creating and defining these disciplines yet has never become a central part of their context of study. (*Professing* 258)

However, Graff's study itself participates in such segregation in the very way he sets up his history to focus centrally on the study of literature and not at all on the study of composition. Composition scholars like Richard Miller and Susan Miller point out the ways critiques like Graff's keep composition at the margins; Richard Miller suggests we need to readdress the work of composition by seeing it "as the institutional site reserved for investigating acts of reading and writing as evidenced in and by student texts" (Richard Miller 169). To consider classrooms (students and teachers) as core sites for performing our academic work is to refocus Graff's understanding of disciplinary conflicts in important ways.

While Richard Miller makes an admirable case for refocusing on the student writer, I'd also like to argue for a focus on the new teacher of student writers who hopes to become a new member of an English department somewhere. For instance, at my university, the only other regular venues for institutional instruction beyond the introductory class are informal preparations for the English job market: colloquia and individual conferences and advice offered for MLA bound job-seekers. These meetings, of course, occur after graduate students have survived many years in the confusing English studies culture; survival, in fact, may be premised on the candidates' ability to intuit the necessary tacit knowledge that will enabled them to move through our complicated profession.

The lack of meta-knowledge on the part of many of our GTAs, then, predicts that they will find the second semester writing class an unsuspected scene of struggle where old and new-found allegiances are suddenly strained. After moving from first-semester teaching, the only course in the required undergraduate curriculum dedicated primarily to discussions of text production, GTAs enter a site where writing and reading vie for time and attention.[7] And literature GTAs in particular, answer the siren call of literature. Heeding the training they are receiving within the culture of English studies, they will turn their classes from writing to reading (and a very particular and limited brand of "reading") despite the best efforts of their rhetoric-trained composition director who tries to subvert the siren by tying teaching assistants to the masthead of a firmly outlined curriculum.

Our Language *Is* Our Institutional History

The language of English studies helps to compose our departmental lives, lives which in turn reflect our complicated histories. Consider the following list:

Literature	Composition
Consumption	Production
Theory	Practice

Reading	Writing
Easy	Hard
High	Low
Old	New
Few	Many
University	High School
Meritocratic	Democratic
Conserves	Serves
Perpetuates	Accumulates
Product	Process
Leisure	Work
Heads	Hands
Professional	Novice
Masculine	Feminine

When this list is shown to the new graduate student, I have no doubt that the most familiar and powerful language will reside in the left-hand column: Literature, Theory, Reading, University, Professional. As a new teaching assistant, however, the student's entrance to the profession takes place via the right-hand column: Composition, Practice, Writing, Hard, Work, Hands, Novice. Overnight, what looked like the easy life of the literature professor, reading and talking about famous literary texts to classrooms of eager listeners, becomes the more frantic life of the writing teacher. And no one can quite tell the novice how to complete this understandably difficult indenture:

> The task, most people would agree, is not to teach students in writing courses grammatical theory, but to make each student pass somehow from a condition in which he or she cannot write well to a condition in which he or she can write well. First the student cannot write well and later he or she can. To make this happen is perhaps more difficult than to make that camel pass through a needle's eye . . . . (J. Hillis Miller 48)

As soon as there were composition courses to teach, there was the need for this almost mystical pedagogical transformation. And the responsibility for transforming first-year students into productive university students was not taken in hand by university English professors but, rather, was placed into the hands of their graduate students and other more marginal department members.

Not until the renaissance of interest in writing instruction that took place in the 1960s would the process of moving from the condition of not writing well to the condition of writing well receive adequate attention. Until that time (and even now for most writing instructors) teaching writing has been some of the most difficult work undertaken in American universities, akin to the effort needed to make *many* camels pass through the eyes of *many* needles.

In "A Personal Essay on Freshman English" Sharon Crowley argues for the abolition of the universal requirement, claiming that these courses "originated as punishment for failure to master a highly idealized version of the written dialect of the dominant class" (159) and therefore represent an institutional and political problem of gigantic proportions:

> But the problems that plague Freshman English are not merely curricular. Its repetitive and repressive curriculum is directly linked to its institutional status as a required, introductory-level English course. Since it is universally required, the Freshman English course is attached to a huge administrative enterprise on almost every college campus in the country. Its very size subjects its administrators, teachers, and students to unprofessional and unethical working practices on a scale that is replicated nowhere else in the academy . . . ." (157)

Required first-year writing has always required the difficult, hands-on work of despairing but aspiring young professors who now work in tandem with part-time and adjunct staffs. Required writing courses came into being at the end of the last century to solve certain institutional and professional problems which, in turn, were responsive to historical, political, and economic developments in the country as a whole; problems that continue, as Crowley (and all those who worked on the Wyoming Resolution to improve working conditions for postsecondary teachers of writing) points out.

The Dominance of the Literary Text

The study of literature has dominated English departments from the late 1890s on, and it has done so for several reasons. Before the ascent of literature, the study of classical rhetoric contributed enormously to the four years of a gentleman's education at the undergraduate American university. But around 1880, the university—an exclusive training ground for ministers, doctors and lawyers—transformed itself into the modern comprehensive university with graduate level programs designed along the model of German universities with their "scientific" graduate research programs. Rhetoric did not survive this transformation, in large part because ". . . there were not German Ph.D.s in rhetoric. There was, simply, no important German intellectual tradition of rhetoric active at all after around 1810, and thus there was no German field to export in the form of a Ph.D." (Connors 61).

The movement within English departments to a focus on literary texts constitutes "a revolutionary development in language studies in the U.S. In the nineteenth-century high school and college, by contrast, the literature studied was more likely to be Roman or Greek while the focus in the study of the vernacular was rhetoric, both oral and written" (Berlin *Writing* 183). The study of literature would offer a chance to affirm a national culture: "The very decision to divide the new language and literature departments along national lines was an implicit assertion of pride in 'the English speaking race'" (Graff *Professing* 71). Also, literature offered an engaging content for study and such texts were accessible to the philology-based German model.

Equally, the development at the new university of graduate programs continued to stratify that institution along class lines. Its proliferating programs and levels of study, increased the pressures on high schools to prepare graduates for further educational advancement. The development of the new university was accelerated by "the passing of the Morrill Federal Land Grant of 1862, establishing state institutions designed to apply the findings of science to the managing of economic affairs" (Berlin *Writing* 185) and resulted from other complicated social conditions: "Western expansion, post-Civil War dislocations and unease, industrialization, 'the impact of science'" (Susan Miller 48). Land-grant institutions offered more educational opportunities and broadened the enrollment base of universities to include women and minorities. Between 1890 and 1920, high school college enrollments grew rapidly.

Such stratification—graduate programs for the professional literary scholar and undergraduate programs for the mass of new college students—was supported by the implementation in 1874 of "a test of the student's ability to write English as a part of the Harvard entrance requirement" (Berlin "Rhetoric" 23). The test was a written essay on a literary text. Rapidly, Harvard's reading lists began to drive high school preparation. However, since the lists changed, it was difficult for high school teachers to decide what literary works to teach, resulting in the creation in 1894 of uniform reading list, compiled by the National Conference on

Uniform Entrance Requirements. As English departments developed, literature became the core subject for elective undergraduate and graduate study and composition became the common basic literacy requirement for entering undergraduates. Over time, composition courses formed the financial base of the modern English Department pyramid, funding graduate students and large proportions of full-time faculty positions.

The Relationship of High and Low Work and the Results of Dominance

The English department represents a hierarchy of workers and products. James Slevin suggests that those in literature derive power by separating texts from the taint of production, turning literary works into:

> . . . "timeless" objects that demand sophisticated powers of analysis and synthesis. The importance of these texts, and the value of reading them, derive precisely from their separation from history and utility, from other discursive and nondiscursive practices and cultural formations. From that ethereal perspective, they consider the work of those in the composition camp as impoverished in both its subject and the intellectual powers upon which it draws. As a result, those who do the work we generally include within the category of "composition" are seen as marginal to the real (as in "really important") work of English departments, at both the graduate and undergraduate levels. Those in composition are stained by their immersion in history, by a preoccupation with social practice, and by a concern with the uses of language that refuses to privilege canonical texts and forms. (Slevin 6)

Literature to a great degree still derives its power through its focus on "the text itself"—what feminist critics have often objected to as ahistorical, apolitical, "timeless" masculinist object lessons in human life. The high literary text was intentionally divorced from low popular texts, for low texts included "18th- and 19th-century popular women's magazines and novels—genres scorned by the literary male elite whose views influenced canon-formation . . ." (Kaplan 18). In this vision, politics and literature do not go together and the life of the mind is unlike the mind preoccupied with the social practices of the home or workplace.

On the other hand, composition teachers have always known that they are in the world, a world where students from various literacies attempt to enter the democratic discussions promised, but not always delivered, by a university education. The timeless view of literature works to uphold a traditional canon and a traditional world-view. Composition is dangerous to the degree to which those in composition use literature in a new and threatening way (just as those in critical theory do), asserting that: "Literature is in the world in the same way that students are in the world" (Clifford 102). And teachers of college writing are "preoccupied by social practice" because they (and their many students) form the base of all that takes place in English studies.

Because of their own ranked and tiered system of part-timers, GTAs, instructors, assistant, associate, and full professorial classes, English departments readily fall into the higher-up, lower-down way of looking at education: often assuming that those in composition are less meritorious than those in literature just as high school teachers are less able than university teachers (or why wouldn't they have chosen the more prestigious course, the left-hand column of terms that I offered earlier?). In the higher-up, lower-down scenario, gender comes strongly into play:

> . . . higher-ups sustain their ability to project apparently more mundane work onto lower-downs by also projecting onto lower-downs personality characteristics which make them seem suited to this work. Lower-downs are seen as more emotional, less critical; more dependent, less capable of self-assertion; more caught up in the everyday, less theoretical; more content with their work, less capable of the more "pure" work which takes place at advanced levels; more concerned with people and nurturance, less concerned with ideas and with criticism . . . . The obverse of this tendency to project mundane work downward is the belief that knowledge should be created at advanced levels of the educational system. It is then applied or carried out at lower levels by persons whose personalities are suited to this mundane work. (Schultz, Laine and Savage 148)

Women, traditionally, are assigned mundane pedagogical work. In the elementary and secondary classroom, they are valued for their ability to nurture young minds and their willingness to be guided by curricular controls. Once a work force starts to be valued for such attributes, it also becomes viewed as having those attributes. Certainly women are viewed as being very good at lower-down work.

In a profession like composition, which is seen as lower-down work in the English department, even men who move from higher-up to lower-down suffer the taint of their descent. In moving from literary work as a Chaucer scholar to work as a composition scholar, Peter Elbow claims: "I've felt my former 'profession' treat me as less serious, intellectual, and scholarly—indeed, less a member of the profession than before" (*What* 127) and in discussions "between literary theory and composition theory, I've often encountered the assumption that of course all the learning will proceed in one direction" (*What* 127). It is no surprise that many compositionists are rebelling against the higher-up and lower-down assumptions and exploring what it means to see the field of writing instruction—positively—as a feminist enterprise that may change English studies.

In a higher-up, lower-down world, scholarship which focuses on "pedagogy"—the traditional work of lower-downs—will be dismissed. At the same time, the work of lower-downs is essential to the smooth functioning of the meritocratic society of the university:

> We have helped inculcate the discipline—punctuality, good verbal manners, submission to authority, attention to problem-solving assignments set by someone else, long hours spent in one place—necessary to perform the alienated labor that will be the lot of most. And more important still, by helping to sort out those who will succeed in school from those who will not, we have generally confirmed the class origins of our students, while making it possible for a few to rise (and others to sink). The effect—unintended of course—is to sustain the *illusion* of equal opportunity and convince the majority that their failure to play a significant and rewarding role in society is a personal failure rather than a systemic one. (Ohmann "The Function of English" 8–9)

In Richard Ohmann's arguments, I hear support for my suggestion that the ways we educate our graduate students encourages them to assume that their failures in reading and writing are failures of people (they're not good critics, close readers, students of literature and might just as well consider a career doing lower-down work in ESL or community college teaching or poetry in the schools or. . .) rather than systemic failures. In essence, by withholding English studies' meta-knowledge, we confirm the class origins of our own graduate students and encourage them to do the same with their writing students. In an apolitical, non-dialogic learning system, only those who are personally mentored by teachers and professors *most like themselves* will rise to the heights now held by those teachers and professors.

English departments insist that composition programs sort students for the universities—by agreeing to screen those who should progress to higher levels of education from those who are not meeting institutional or state-wide proficiency requirements—and then those departments sort students for themselves:

No department I know of would think of instituting a common syllabus and uniform final examination for all the sections of Shakespeare, The Comedies. Yet such arrangements are routine in freshman writing programs, and they are commonly explained as quality control measures . . . freshman writing is in general viewed by departments as a fundamentally different enterprise from the rest of the department's work: an assembly-line endeavor, essentially remedial, not especially demanding on the intellect, taught by interchangeable workers, managed by composition specialists, the segment of the regular faculty whose status is most dubious. (Martin 132)

Always, inculcating literacy skills and assuring future literate behavior is the work of department lower-downs, graduate students and part-time faculty members. Only when the mass of first-year students have been, essentially, civilized, do the senior faculty expect to meet them in upper division courses (this is particularly the case at research institutions). When students have not been judged as sufficiently groomed by literature faculty, complaints about writing and reading skills are sent down to the first-year writing program.

In this vision, the literary enterprise is one that is itself steeped in self-preserving motives—an attempt to create a beneficial work environment for its members rather than to offer students, as is often espoused, free access to life-transforming literary texts. Literature avoids socioeconomic responsibilities through the tacit agreement to observe and enhance the conventions of a highly structured university social system. Literature has long prided itself on being ahistorical, apolitical and set apart (as mentioned above, in a "timeless" manner) from the socioeconomic concerns of the nation at large. In fact, English departments promote a very particular view of liberal culture.

To see the left-hand column of terms that I provided earlier as dominant, then, is to see English studies as the truly conservative edifice that it is, not as the liberal, transformative, humanistic discipline of its literature classroom, liberal culture, self-advertisements. Basically, after first-term, first-year writing fulfills its institutional function, second-term writing begins to inculcate the status quo. These classes exist as currently configured because they work—for those who are higher up.

Responding to Institutionalized Inequity

Literature in the writing classroom tends to overwhelm the study of writing just as the study of literature has traditionally overwhelmed creative writing and composition—the study of the production of texts—in

English departments. Literature faculty are not ogres of bad intention. However, they are dominant in a social system based on inequality—both of funds and of prestige—and extreme social stratification. However, such efficient self-blinding is becoming more difficult as the numbers of writing professionals and the department funds generated by writing programs increase and as cross-disciplinary study becomes more sanctioned.

When I point to writing-with-literature courses as sites of struggle, I am far from believing that literary texts should be abandoned entirely, particularly since I am life-long reader of canonical *and* non-canonical texts. Instead, I believe these courses are a place to start as we move in two directions. First, and most problematic, we need to be teaching writing (and advancing literacy) in all English department courses, particularly by attempting to re-envision upper-level and graduate literature courses. Pedagogy needs to be part of our thinking not a threat to our thinking.

Second, we need to offer students who are new to the university, those in their first and second years, a far more sophisticated introduction to the world of texts and text-making than is usually provided in current-traditional writing about literature courses (see Graff *Beyond*). Peter Elbow suggests that we teach reading processes more actively and offers solid suggestions for doing so ("The War"). Patricia Sullivan's study of graduate-students-as-writers indicates we need to do a better job guiding and inviting these students into our subdisciplines, making our own ways of reading, learning and knowing more tacit and offering graduate students opportunities to develop their own disciplinary reading and writing *processes* as they work to produce degree- worthy final products.

Simply, it is not enough for compositionists to try to become the dominant member of some new hierarchy, with a new subdiscipline on top, in the middle, or on the bottom. Instead, in days of shrinking state educational budgets, of disciplinary self-examination, of fluctuating university enrollments, it will be far more productive for all members of English studies to look not at dichotomies but at continuums, not at stratification but at forms of collaboration, not at fields as competitive but as complementary, not at the university community as apolitical but as highly political, representative of our country at large and responsive to our lives in particular. Some institutions have gone much farther. At the University of Vermont there are now discussion-based introductory courses focusing on reading, writing, and the study of literature within the English major core curriculum (see Fulwiler). At SUNY Albany, the graduate programs in composition and creative writing have been combined to grant Ph.D and MA degrees in Writing, Teaching, and Criticism (see North).

I have had some success in the teacher education course by embarking on a journey of self-education. Teaching second-term first-year writing for the last year, I've asked students to tell me about themselves as readers through reading literacy autobiographies and writing-to-understand-reading exercises (for many ideas in this area, see W*hen Writing Teachers Teach Literature*, edited by Art Young and Toby Fulwiler). I've taught the second-term course as reading-for-writers and returned to our summer teacher-education classes sure that I need to include more instruction in reading processes (see "Teaching Writing Teachers to Teach Reading for Writing"). At the same time, I continue to raise the larger issue—discussing GTAs' own reading and writing education within the English department. I am making explicit my goal of encouraging these teachers to translate their learning to the introductory literature and creative writing courses they will eventually be teaching; together, we look for ways this can (and should) be done.

In a sense, I am asking for these teachers to help me institute writing-and-reading-*within*- the-discipline, for, in the field of English studies, we need to acknowledge what connects those who are marginalized with those who are dominant, to understand that there are multiple modalities for learning and knowing (reading and writing and speaking and listening), and to encourage our programs to accept the many career paths we inevitably travel—some starting in composition and moving to literature, some the reverse, some moving from literature to creative writing—and so on. Even more, it is time to consider how these "paths" constitute the same path, one that too often has been divided primarily for institutional convenience.

I am suggesting difficult undertakings and to some of us such changes will be almost impossible to imagine. Still, we must be more active. We need to know our history, understand our political and economic situation, and work in concert with any colleagues who indicate a willingness to talk and consider departmental conditions. Whether it means changing the curriculum or abolishing the requirement , we *can* examine ways to keep first-year writing from remaining the national course in silence that Susan Miller claims it has become (55). We *can* refuse to keep writing and reading in "an unnatural partnership [that] obscures the fact that both processes are directed and produced by the force of the imagination" (Roskelley 139).

This will only happen, of course, if we include writing and reading instruction in *all* our English classes. Literature professors *as well as* writing professors need to become writers involved in writing (just as writing professors can't exist without reading). English departments need to include self-study and historical/political study in all their courses—from the survey of world literature to beginning drama writing to advanced rhetorical theory. Of course, all these suggestions are premised on a changed and changing English department. For those who were in the low position and are intent on moving to a higher one, for those whose work life is shifting from the language of the right hand column of terms to the language of the left-hand column of terms—it is time to challenge dichotomous thinking, to resist the complacency of "having just arrived," and to argue that "this" is no place to be. I'd suggest we start by changing the writing with literature course and then move outward, bravely. Our graduate students are feeling the ground swell of change already, and we have an opportunity—to continue to fight until someone (probably everyone) loses—or to change with—and for—them.

Notes

1.   This is certainly a broad sketch and I don't mean to imply that these classes are free of problems; confusions of purpose sometimes certainly occur since no one has yet designed a first-semester workshop class that all composition programs accept as definitive.

2.   If a two-term sequence is to be reduced to a single term, as has happened at many institutions, the class that is retained will likely be the writing about literature class.

3.   It may be useful for the narrative arguments I am developing here, to point out that Sullivan's research survey was administered to four English departments, including my own. See the note on page 298 of her article; her results are congruent with my interviews but I did not know of her work or see her results until my own conversations with graduate students had been completed.

4.   Discussions of writing processes may result in challenges to the traditional manner of producing academic texts, a manner that Olivia Frey suggests is particularly masculinist:

     In any event, I would not describe the conventions of mainstream literary critical writing as feminist. These conventions include the use of argument as the preferred mode for discussion, the importance of the objective and impersonal, the importance of a finished product without direct reference to the process by which it was accomplished, and the necessity of being thorough in order to establish proof and reach a definitive (read "objective") conclusion. A common denominator of each convention seems to be "to get it right," that is, establish cognitive authority. (509).

In the traditional literature classroom, these conventions are certainly valorized and usually there is only one "real" authority.

5.   In non-essayist actual life, creative writing and rhetoric GTAs are not so easily conflated. Both are greatly interested in understanding text production but some seek to "read like a writer and produce publishable work" (creative writers) while others wish to "understand more of the writing process in order to improve instruction" (composition and rhetoric students). Many rhetoric GTAs do not view themselves as writers and are not willing to make strong claims of writing proficiency. I have met creative writing GTAs who may be ambivalent about their skills in a particular genre, but never any who doubt their essential writing talents.

6.   Recently, after a year-long textbook review conducted by our first-year writing committee composed of volunteer, experienced GTA writing teachers who worked with me, we easily narrowed the field of "innovative" readers to three: *Textbook* (Scholes et al.), *Making Meaning* (Gould) and *Reading(s)* (Summerfield and Summerfield). Our program is undergoing a curricular transformation, turning from a writing *about* literature course into a *writing with literature and other texts* course. Previously, we used *The Lexington Introduction to Literature* (Waller et al.) which helped start that transformation with its strong reader-response and feminist theory apparatus. Even these four texts, we believe, don't begin to outline the possibilities for an innovative writing about literature textbook (or more reasonably, a writing with "texts including literary texts" reader). And this essay points out that more thoroughgoing changes need to take place to improve this course and our GTAs' course of study and teaching within our English departments.

7.   Some departments might like to claim that first-semester, first-year writing isn't the only course dedicated to discussions of text production by pointing to their advanced courses. But business and technical writing, advanced expository writing, and imaginative nonfiction courses are often extremely product-oriented and under-theorized and/or taught by professors untrained in writing pedagogy who are seeking to meet their writing instruction assignment in the company of "advanced" students (see Bishop "Revising").

7

Teaching Writing Teachers to Teach
Reading for Writing

. . . normal writing is really both-writing-and-reading.
Peter Elbow, "The War Between Reading and Writing" (10)

Teachers' own theories of how texts mean influence their daily practice.
Richard Beach, *A Teacher's Introduction to Reader-Response Theories* (3)

*Research in reading, no matter what else it has demonstrated, has found
the teacher to be a most important—perhaps the most important—
factor in the theoretical process. Theoretical movements come and go, but
change comes slowly. In the classroom, teachers often fall back on the
ways of their own teachers, because of lack of practical implementation
of new theories or because of fear of failure in trying new methods.*
Louise Rosenblatt *Literature as Exploration* (xi)

To begin, I read through Donald Murray's book *Shoptalk* to find a
section on reading as part of a writer's process. I don't find it and worry
that my basic premises are undercut: that what writers do when they aren't
writing is reading; that we need better ways to teach teachers writing/read-
ing and reading/writing together; that what we're doing in writing classrooms is creating a chance for students to develop writer-and-readers'
habits of mind. Not finding the section I expected, I start to worry.
Maybe all writers don't need to read?

I worry because so little time in writing teacher education courses seems
available for this issue although I'm aware that there is a history of argument that writing teachers *do* need such training. For me, this history
begins with Louise Rosenblatt's now well known, but originally all but
ignored, analysis in *Literature as Exploration*, a prescient blue-print for reor-
ganizing literary instruction. The history continues with the introduction
of a variety of reader-response critics in Jane Tompkins's 1980 collection,
continues with Mariolina Salvatori's research in 1983 on the teaching of

reading with writing, continues with Peter Elbow's discussions of the inter-connections of reading and writing for writers, continues with Richard Beach's 1994 overview of practical applications of reader-response theories. Strong voices, faintly received, I would argue, profession wide.

To begin, I reread my abstract, finding what I want, the kernel of this essay, only in the paragraph at the end:

As a teacher educator, I find that my clear need to share contemporary writing research, theory and practice with new teachers has over-whelmed and hidden an equal need to discuss reading processes as more than a set of study skills, requiring pinching oneself awake to highlight opaque texts or offering critical lenses that can be applied by already expert readers. Teachers need to examine their own reading processes, making the invisible visible. They need to be encouraged to teach second term writing classes as classes in reading for writing. Student writers read to understand text strategies, read to understand their own stances toward and uses of texts, read to understand how they construct texts and how other readers construct *their* composi-tions. For my own classrooms and for the teachers I'm helping enter classrooms, I'm interested in better balancing the talk about writing with equally useful talk about reading. Toward this end, I've collected teachers and students' reading literacy autobiographies and their own understandings of their reading strategies and connect these to the work of reading and discourse theorists. My goal in this essay is to refine my position from a place of real need: this summer I will be teach-ing new teachers once again, and I'm determined to allow reading the place it needs to have in our discussions and writings. This essay will offer the rationale for a major refocusing of my previous curriculum.

To begin, I go to my office and gather up more things to read—students' literacy autobiographies, a book—*Writers on Writing*—that has one essay where the author Harry Brent lists all the readings (many) on his bedside table as part of his writing process. But I'm frustrated, I can only find vol-ume two, not volume one. I start to think about all the books I've lent out to my students—*Women of Academe* to Dawn, forced it on her, really, to help her solve her writing block. The latest P.D. James mystery to Devan, another forcing, to help her relax a bit. I start to see that my reading-as-a-writer leads me to share, to distribute information to those writers to whom I think it will matter. Tom has *Romancing Rhetorics. The Peaceable Classroom,* missing, but I can't remember who I loaned it to or loaned it on.

Last, I go upstairs and borrow a book myself, from Ruth, Frank Smith's *Understanding Reading,* because I feel I need his support. I've always found him a calm and clearheaded author. His observations about children's learning are applicable to adult readers in my classrooms since he focuses on similarities between reading theories in particular and learning theories in general. I read the third edition years ago and am not surprised to find the fifth edition in hand.

To write about teaching teachers about reading, I sit down and read.

To begin, I re-skim Peter Elbow's essay "The War Between Writing and Reading and How To End It." I worry again—I love this essay but suddenly it's backward to what I want to say—yes we've overprivileged reading, but the answer is not found solely in teaching more writing. I highlight his ideas about making reading processes explicit—that's where I hook in, showing students drafts of reading, yes, and how we read drafts. I think about the struggle I've had understanding reading-for-writing, myself, and where it fits into the writing curriculum.

At a recent inservice workshop, I invited teachers to describe their own reading processes. On the whole, they were surprised by and hesitant about fulfilling my request, assuming I was asking them to state the obvious. As they began to write, they found the "obvious" was difficult to articulate. As readers, we found we used comparable strategies (taking notes, breaking reading sessions into do-able chunks) and idiosyncratic ones (standing while reading, falling asleep while reading and continuing when the reader woke). We had different attitudes, tastes, levels of ability. We had developed sophisticated and complicated methods for efficient "schoolreading" (even though most of us came to English Departments because we were aesthetic readers, loving certain texts, authors, periods of writing history). Somehow, we had also learned to mediate between the sometimes very different requirements of schoolreading and pleasure reading. Still, this group had never considered the need to teach reading to writers. Such a charge was easy to overlook in the assumption that such processes were not accessible to study nor were they part of the writing process as it is often (too) simply described.

Teachers' reports:

My own reading process? Well, hell, that's a dumb question (only because I haven't thought about it!). There is no single process that I employ. It's as varied as the texts, contexts and purpose are. I mean, take a short story. If I'm reading it for the first time, for a class that I'm taking, I'll approach it slowly, lovingly and relaxed but alert. On the other hand, if I'm rereading it for the same purpose, I will then underline, highlight, asterisk, etc. Various areas that I find crucial to my understanding. Thirdly, if I'm reading it after a class discussion or lecture, my approach will be to read quickly the parts not discussed in class while slowing down for areas that had drawn critical discussion. Fourth, if I'm reading the same story for a class I'm teaching, my approach will be entirely different. I will read with an eye toward understanding fully the sections that I think may present trouble to the class or readers that I'm teaching. In the same vein, I may also read it quickly with the thought of creating a few quiz questions that, while not requiring extended answers, will have required a reasonably close reading of the text at least once. —Greg

For Greg, that's five reading processes and at least two, if not more, reading personas.

When I was assigned readings, I would treat them as pleasure reading. Now I read books that a few years ago I would have abhorred—it finds its way into my writing: history, philosophy, theology, mythology—it doesn't matter. I usually read several books, both fiction and non-fiction, at a time so I'm always in the mood for something I have on the reading table—it keeps me from getting bored with one subject . . .I keep a dictionary beside me now when I read and write down definitions of words I don't know. I'm primarily a libracubucularian (a person who reads in bed). —Ron

Ron is clearly a fluent reader, but, as Frank Smith would point out:

For beginners and experienced readers alike, there is always the possibility of fluent reading and the possibility of difficult reading. There is no sudden transition from beginning reading, when nothing can be read without difficulty, to fluent reading, when all reading is easy. The more we read, the more we are able to read. (177)

Understanding this, I began to get interested in understanding what I'll call "disfluency". Not used in a negative sense, it indicates those who aren't fluent readers, who chose to read less, who move fairly comfortably through the world reading little, until faced with a schoolreading assignment in first-year college writing.

For instance, students' responses (anonymous, from a second-term, first-year writing class, fall 1994, describing their reading processes), are not inferior to teachers' responses, simply less involved:

For me, factual material is like putting a stew together, if you read or skip over something, everything is messed up or will fall apart. For me, reading imaginative material is like a bird gliding over the oceans. It's fun. And free. For me, reading my own writing is like clearing my room. I have to make sure nothing is wrong and everything is in the right place. Reading

student writing is like going to hear an unknown band. Sometimes it is a
pleasant surprise and sometimes you want your money back.

For me, the process of reading factual texts is like listening to the news.
For me, the process of reading imaginative texts is like letting your mind
run free and thinking about what the text means to me. It is probably different for everyone. It is similar to watching a play. One person might
see something that another person may not. For me, the process of
reading student texts is like learning a new word.

To begin, I read and answer e-mail because I don't want to begin. I read
and sort through the junk mail on the counter. I read and reply to the
papers in my home office. I wander into the front room, rereading the
interior, deciding it's time to move a painting, hang another, and maybe
vacuum.

To begin, I run and read the day, lovely May Florida early summer. The
nesting mockingbirds are keeping a guard on my cat Cypress who sits,
belly-flat and snarling on the patio pavement as the parents dive bomb her,
to head her away from the nest in the palm tree. I can hear Cypress move
down the street, mockingbirds at each house forewarning the others. I pass
the new houses being constructed—I think about a contractor named
Price Vincent (who would name a child this, to be listed as Vincent, Price
on school rosters?) and how his houses are identifiably similar, one on the
lower road, one up here on the high road. I read a stand of trees—yellow
tags mark the pines and live oaks that will be saved. The first signs of clearing before construction. I read myself. Started weight-lifting this week and
today, the fourth day of my May resolutions, I'm folding a bit, not running
well, going to use writing about reading as an excuse to stop running just
as running was an excuse not to begin. I think about the options and ramifications of this essay—each possibility takes me down a road, then I come
back, circle, run, yes, no, this is part, this isn't. I read the draft in my mind,
presenting it in several different versions, eliminating this one and that
one, until I'm ready to return, I think, and write.

Most of what we know about language and the world is not formally taught.
Instead, children develop their theory of the world and competence in language by testing *hypotheses*, experimenting in meaningful and purposeful ways
with tentative modifications and elaborations of what they know already. Thus
the basis of learning is *comprehension*. Children learn continuously, through
engagement, whenever they have *sensitivity*, from whatever is demonstrated to
them. (Smith 199)

I know that running provides me with a writer's habit of mind, medita-tive space to help me map out the alternatives, explore and modify, should I use this rhetorical devices or that? Should my essay sound this way or that way? In the same way, I've been running through the stacks of infor-mal research on my desk—abstract, journals, student writings, cut and paste, cut and paste, eliminating alternatives. While I'm reading to write, I'm deeply engaged in the demonstrations—words, thoughts, rhetoric— of others as I try to shape my own learning.

> The basis of comprehension is *prediction*, or the prior elimination of unlikely alternatives. By minimizing uncertainty in advance, prediction relieves the visual system and memory of overload in reading. Predictions are questions that we ask the world, and comprehension is receiving answers. If we cannot predict, we are confused. If our predictions fail, we are surprised. And if we have noth-ing to predict because we have no uncertainty, we are bored. (Smith 23)

In my writing-with-literature class last spring, I asked students to read three short short pieces of fiction and then to chose one they felt strongly about, liking or disliking it. They paired with a student taking the oppo-site position and discussed why each had such reactions. Then, I asked them to write a letter defending their taste and swap with their partner who they knew took the other side. They were to read each other's letter and write a response letter. The stories were "Girl" by Jamaica Kincaid. "The School" by Donald Barthelme. "The Man to Bring Rainclouds" by Leslie Marmon Silko (all found in Hansen and Shepard).

> Dear Christine,
> When I read "Girl" by Jamaica Kincaid, my first impressions were one of dislike. I still feel this way. Even though it was easy to read and short, I did not like the content. Basically, the whole story was about a mother telling her girl how to act. I know I don't like to be told how to do some-thing much less everything I do. The mother seems hard-headed and doesn't listen to anything the girl has to say. She scolds the girl for stuff that the girl doesn't even do. I wouldn't want someone to do this to me much less read about it. Sincerely, Kate

> Dear Kate,
> Gee, you really took the story personally. I didn't internalize it as much as you did and I enjoyed it. You didn't think it was funny? You know, the way they talked, the references they made to things that we don't have in the USA. I thought it was so typical of an uptight mother and her daughter. Wasn't the story universal? —Christine

Kate is refusing the invitation of the story. She does not want to be the reader of this text, therefore she is a disfluent reader. Christine is able to see such a stance toward the story is interfering with Kate's comprehension—she gives Kate her own interpretation (explains how she became engaged) and offers Kate some reading tips, if Kate wants to see them as such: don't take the story personally, don't internalize it, look at the funny parts, think of how it's similar or different to your own experiences. The issue is not that Kate can't read—she won't. She has no questions about this text; she is bored.

> Dear Ann,
> This essay says "mom" all over it, can't you relate? I know she's telling her "Girl" what to do, but that's what is so funny. Just like your mom tells you to be home by dinner, take out the trash. . .this mom told her to cook pumpkin fritters and not to pick flowers. Even though some of the terms are unfamiliar to both you and me, the language is every-day: simple and honest. It isn't often that you can read something so easily, as if it were being said to you, rather than forcefully written. So reread "Girl" and try to look at the essay in a lighthearted way. —Kim

> Dear Kim
> I don't feel that it was easily read. The lack of complete sentences gets me confused. I like sentences that carry a complete thought. Yes the story is honest, and I can see the humor in it, but it just doesn't do anything for me. I don't care for the repetitive orders, and I probably wouldn't waste my time to read it again. —Ann

This is the second half of a two letter exchange. At this point, Kim is try-ing to offer Ann reading tips, also. She points out what she likes—the plain language, and more or less tells Ann to loosen up, to accept this as a text she will, can, and should read. Ann on the other hand, asserts her independence from the story. She sees that the sentences are fragmentary and declares them hard to read (as probably her own fragmentary sentences have been labeled in her schooling past). She thinks the story is honest and humorous, but seems, like Kate above, to identify too closely with the text—seeing the mother's speech as a set of "repetitive orders." She sees rereading as a waste of her time, and in her own world view she's right. Since she's declared that "Girl" is written in a way that confuses and distances her—a style where sentences don't carry a complete thought—there really is no point to her reading the story again. She cannot predict purposes for this piece (other than, perhaps like her own mother, to give her orders) so she is confused. In one sense, Ann and Kim agree—this is how mothers talk—and it may be their differing relationships to mothers as well as schoolwriting that affect their involvement here. Again, both can read, and both are fluent with this text to different degrees, and for different reasons.

Dear Andree,

I'm sorry you couldn't appreciate "The School" as much as I did. Beyond the morbid nature of the stories that Edgar tells, I find a lot of truth and humor. We've all been in a class where things haven't worked out according to the lesson plan. Nothing has ever happened as extreme as in the story but I think it makes a point.

I like the fact that once you start to see the pattern forming where you can predict the inevitable death of the new class project, he broke into the questions about the meaning of life or death. You picture young kids wondering for what reasons things happen. You see them asking questions that on the surface seem very innocent and almost juvenile. But through the eyes of an adult, these are profound questions that there are no definite answers for. And then, when you expect the normal response to these questions the children ask the teacher for, this "bizarre assertions" with a demonstration of love.

Anyway, if you don't like the morbid nature of the story, see if you can read it again looking for the humorous nature of the story and the writers voice. It was obviously an effective voice if you had such strong feelings. —Dawn

Dawn,

"The School" at first seemed to be leading up to a good point. But as the story progressed, the author just seemed to go beyond what was needed. The orphan girl, the parents, the suicides and the poor two children all dying made me forget about the point of teaching children about death and made me appreciate that I wasn't in this class. Also, like you said, at the beginning I picture first graders planting trees and playing with a puppy. But I have a brother in first grade and towards the end, when they ask if death is considered as a fundamental datum, the means . . .etc. would never come out of my little brother's mouth. That just seemed way too unrealistic. The whole story did. —Andree

Dear Andree,

In response to your letter on "The School." I can't tell you how to think when you read, but maybe next time you shouldn't expect anything from a story and just see where the author takes you. Realize that the kids weren't necessarily using that vocabulary to ask the teacher but the teacher saw these questions in this deep philosophical light. Happy Readings, Dawn

In this exchange, Dawn offers Andree some sophisticated reading insights. Andree counters with an important problem. She is reading the text as "realistic." Because she expects texts to be realistic and because she has a brother the exact age of the kids in the story, she assumes kids would never act as portrayed by Barthelme. Andree is not refusing to read. She doesn't have enough reading experience with experimental texts to pick up the textual clues that Dawn does as Barthelme's story intentionally becomes increasingly more surreal. While Dawn doesn't know exactly how to analyze Barthelme's techniques, she can spot the problem Andree is having and asks Andree to approach the text without genre expectations, to "just see where the author takes you."

This advice looks like but probably isn't the generalized, "go with the flow" or "I like papers that flow" talk that can easily arise in classrooms. Instead, Dawn is offering Andree part of her reading repertoire, saying, in effect: "increase your ability to sustain disbelief and judgment; make predictions, yes, but be willing to wait a while to see if they are fulfilled." Andree, like many students, did not have this engaged theory of reading. Studying the responses of her own students, Mariolina Salvatori characterized the problem this way. Her student "could not effectively 'relate,' that is, 'synthesize' the various segments of the text. She could not in Iser's words, set the work in motion, and herself in motion too" (663). And this seems to be true for Andree; she and the work are not set in motion.

These student letters show that accepting fluency in reading (which I argue leads to fluency in reading a writer's own text and intentions) is a complicated issue:

> Reading is not just a visual activity. Both *visual information and nonvisual information* are essential for reading, and there can be a trade-off between the two. Because there are limits to how much visual information the brain can cope with in making sense of texts, readers must make use of all forms of redundancy in written language—*orthographic, syntactic,* and *semantic.* Information may be regarded as the reduction of uncertainty concerning the alternatives among which a reader must decide. How much visual information a reader will require is affected by the reader's willingness to risk an erroneous decision. Readers who set to high a *criterion level* for information before making a decision will find *comprehension* more difficult." (Smith 63).

My students' reading letters exhibit all the complicated reading trade-offs that Smith outlines. They experienced—using Iser's terms again—the blocks and gaps and indeterminacies that Salvatori's students did. We can indeed illustrate these problems, but Salvatori raises the more pressing issue:

[M]y research suggests that the improvement in writers' ability to manipulate syntactic structures—their maturity as writers—is the result, rather than the cause, of their increased ability to engage in, and to be reflexive about, the reading of highly complex texts. However, if the two language activities are indeed related, the important question need not be "what causes what," but rather how to teach composition so as to benefit from the interrelationship of the two activities. (659)

Not *should* we, but *how* should we teach composition so as to benefit from the interrelationship of writing and reading. And how should we do this beginning with new teachers of college writing? Especially if a teacher educator believes, as I do, as argued here by Smith, that "teachers must show that reading is worthwhile" and that "teachers must themselves be conspicuous practicing users of written language" (210).

Back from my run, I tell myself I'm tired, so I finish reading a book about the malpractice death of a former professor of mine, Eliot Gilbert, written by his wife, the critic and poet Sandra Gilbert. The book *Wrongful Death* kept me up long last night. This morning, knowing I need/want/don't want to write about reading, I skim-read the book's last chapters. Last night I read for empathy and memory, this morning, I read with some guilt but also to finish the plot. I think about writing this author/professor a letter. I remember I need to begin an essay.

To begin, I think about ways to begin. And I realize, all these ways I've reread and read to begin, are—for me and many writers like me—the reading process of all writing, the reduction of alternatives, the long cultivation of a habit of mind that finds connections between what I've read in the past and want to explore-through-saying in the future. I want to stop now, take a shower, then re-read my students' reading literacy autobiographies from last term. I want to use student voices and teacher voices in this essay. I've been investigating literature in writing classrooms for several years now, resulting in an essay about the problems of bringing these texts into the second term writing classroom (see "The Literary Text"). During that time, and now again, I feel a little foolish. For God's sakes—I'm a former English literature major, a practicing writer and writing teacher. I read all the time. The teachers I train read all the time. What can I tell them about reading?

Last night, my family and I, for the first time, were all reading together in the Florida room; that is to say, for the first time the youngest joined us, still vocalizing, telling how many pages he read of one his sister's R.L. Stine

Goosebumps books while my daughter had just borrowed her first adult nonfiction book from me—*Autobiography of My Face* by Lucy Grealy. Just as he was proud of reading her book, she was proud of borrowing my library book and she was wrapped up in it as she curled herself in the green leather chair. Her father was reading the *Wall Street Journal* but he had also borrowed my borrowed copy of Frank Smith, thinking it might be relevant to his dissertation. Then, when I showed him the pictures of my former professor in *Wrongful Death*, he started reading the next page of the book until I asked him impatiently to give it back. This potlatch of reading was not schoolreading, and, in addition, I was reading us all, storing it up for later, perhaps, for writing. Why then did I think I didn't know enough about reading to teach writing teachers how to teach reading for writing?

> A survey accompanying the 1994 test [of reading reported in the National Assessment of Educational Progress scores] found that, compared with seniors who took the 1992 test, students were less likely to: read for fun on their own time, read more than 11 pages per day, or be asked at least once at school to discuss something they have read.
> Carol Lynch-Brown, a Florida State University professor of reading and language arts, echoed that finding: "The reading children do is done mostly in schools, so that doesn't give them the kind of practice time they used to have. (Democrat Staff and News Services)

Sometimes, about mid-term (each term), I think that perhaps the best way to teach the writing class would be to read aloud together (any text) half the period and then to write together (anything) the other half, or to write together and then read together—interactive, eclectic, equal weight for these interrelated processes, concentrated time, inculcating not critical thinking, reading, and writing *skills* but writers' habits of mind. I ask students to write writing process cover sheets for each essay and there learn about composing on the drug ecstasy; while watching TV; around a fight with a roommate who might erase the disks if they are left in the computer; after the fourth false early morning fire alarm; during the first twenty minutes of class and now just arriving, late, in class. Could the classroom, perhaps, be the only best oasis of concentration available?

One of my second-term, first-year writers, mentioned that reading *Waiting to Exhale* in a reading group in my writing classroom this spring (each group read and researched a different text—*Waiting to Exhale, Easy in the Islands, Self-Help, She Had Some Horses*—and then wrote essays growing out of those discussions) was the first time she had ever read a three hundred-page book. One athlete said she now found herself reading

Steven King on the road trips and that it helped pass the time and seemed good to her. One student, after reading *Easy in the Islands* in his reading group, wrote a story, setting his father and his family to sail in the Caribbean, learning in the process, a lot about how they'd all act under stress. But this isn't a brag session. I learned, mainly, that students know or believe there's no time for reading (they are focusing on law school and a boyfriend, they'll say, and don't read for pleasure any more, and so on). The multi-textured, paper-strewn, book-strewn environment I live in, I know, is rare. But it hit me how little time my writing students had for cultivating a reader-who-writes's habits: watching, detailing, categorizing the world, comparing new information to old memories, constructing meaning, having arguments with appearance.

To continue, then, I had to learn to see reading differently. Like every writing teacher educator, desperate to convince literature majors that there is merit to writing process theories and composition research, I often underpresented reading. My students are in college. Of course they can read. They need to learn how to write. My new teachers need only to learn to teach them to do so. I need mostly to guide literature majors away from canonizing the writing curriculum. Among a group of new teachers, I found those like Dennis, who chose to return from composition to his love of the literary (Bishop "Attitudes"):

8/1/90
Dennis: Finally, after nearly six weeks of abstractions, of rhetoric and composition duckspeak, I finally was able to get to my first love: literature. Now I understand that the ENC1102 class is structured as Writing *Through* Literature. But nevertheless, I was quite pleased to hear the names Faulkner and Kafka rather than Elbow and Murray.

Like Dennis, many teachers I teach have internalized good student habits that helped them survive in graduate school:

7/30/90
Dennis: He didn't want anyone else's opinion . . . Out of class, I argued with him and I didn't agree. . . . basically, I learned after the first exam, after *The Scarlet Letter*, the type of symbolism that he wanted. . . . and the same with another professor. I wrote basically the same essay on an exam roughly four times, almost word for word, I think. Or at least, types of sentences were the same. "Man's a creature in possession of language . . ." All I had to say for this one professor is that "Keats celebrates language as an event through this

particular device." Then the next time: "Virginia Woolf celebrates language in this way . . . I have yet to find a professor that doesn't want in some shape or pattern his own opinions. No matter how much [they] say, I want to see original thinking . . . that's a lie.

Like my students (graduate students particularly), like the students in Patricia Sullivan's study, Dennis had internalized appropriate reading processes for surviving in school. For him, "The reading of elaborate texts remains the province of knowledgeable critics whose expertise inexperienced students can only vaguely imitate through the memorization of an empty literary nomenclature, achieving at best knowledge *about* rather than *through* literature" (Salvatori, 658). Teaching Dennis reading and writing processes for any other purposes proved to be an uphill battle, as it proved to be last fall in my second-term writing class.

To continue, I re-examine a bad teaching moment—the student last fall, thumping on the front table as the room cleared out and saying "I don't have a reading process." I said, "Of course you do." "I don't," he said. It had been a several week struggle. This wasn't a course about reading literature no matter how named in the catalog; it was a course about how he (we) read for his (our) writing. "Well, your parents are going to be pretty disappointed," I snapped. This was the first class in years that I dreaded attending. And the students in this class did too. Each for his or her own reason:

> Children do not learn to read who do not want to, or who see no point in doing so, or who are hostile to the teacher, or to the school, or to the social or cultural group to which they perceive the teacher and the school as belonging. Children do not learn to read who expect to fail, or who believe that learning to read will be too costly, or whose preferred image of themselves, for whatever reason, is that of a nonreader. Children do not learn to read if they have the wrong idea of the nature of reading, if they have learned—or been taught— that reading does not make sense. (Smith 214)

This student did not have a reading process because he did not choose to. He had an image of himself as non-reader-in-general or non-reader-as-writer, as the type of reader I was trying to define. He was good at schoolreading and wanted to go back to the read the literature anthology for the symbol-searching he had been expecting. He was *disfluent* out of choice and distrust over what I was doing and suggesting, over the new roles I was offering him. Richard Beach, in the quote which heads this essay, suggests teachers' past experiences strongly influence the direction of the course; equally, Louise Rosenblatt suggests we need to account for the personality of the student:

> The teacher realistically concerned with helping his students to develop a vital sense of literature cannot, then, keep his eyes focused only on the literary materials he is seeking to make available. He must also understand the personalities who are to experience this literature. He must be ready to face the fact that the student's reactions will inevitably be in terms of his own temperament and background. Undoubtedly these may often lead him to do injustice to the text. (51)

Or, I might add, to the process.

The next term, to investigate whether it was possible *not* to have a reading process, I asked the class to construct reading literacy autobiographies. At first, they resisted drafting such an essay because they saw no way to access the hidden history of their reading. Several inventions at least got us to the discussion stage: I asked students to freewrite in response to this poem by Hans Ostrom that mentions how each member of his family reads:

OF READING

1
We receive letters of an alphabet
as if they wash ashore, lost ancient drums.
We pick them up, touch
them, stretched hide
thrumming like a bird's throat.
We turn and journey into deep
rhythms of a language.

2
I think of all the headlines
my mother has read with her sharp blue eyes.
She looks through a newspaper at History
the way a fierce bird looks at the forest.

3
My young son bounds
through my notebook till a blank page
opens like a meadow. He draws a giant spider
that has monumental legs.

4
When my father first looks
at a book, he looks it over
as if it were an occurrence
or an animal in the woods—
a deer walking through
manzanita in October.

5
Words and letters fall through the murky sky
of a computer monitor like wet snowflakes on a windless day.

6
There is a moistness to adventurous reading,
something that connects us to an astonished mud
of lore women and men of old tribes
used when they painted clothing and stone,
when they explained Night,
talked back to rain,
named the holiness of infants.

I asked them to draw a childhood home's floor plan and to write about any reading memories they could revive in each of those rooms. I asked them to try to remember favorite childhood books—calling parents if necessary—and to go look at those books in a library or bookstore. I asked them to broaden their definition from reading texts to reading their world—how did they learn about their family, how to dress, how to survive in school, how to cook, and so on? Our goal was to see in what ways we were or were not readers. I was surprised with my own discoveries as I wrote along with the class; for instance, I realized I couldn't remember ever seeing my mother read but did remember strange interludes like making church bazaar Christmas trees out of *Readers' Digest* magazines and positing from that memory that she must have read the magazine. Here are some of my students' discoveries, highly abbreviated:

This passion for reading that consumed my father skipped my generation. Looking back, I found I took a lighthearted approach to reading. . . . To be honest, the bathroom is where I did all of my coming of age reading. It was in the bathrooms of my house that I found *Playboy Magazines*. I remembered how they provoked many uncomfortable questions for my parents. The pictures I saw had women, in familiar places, stretched out naked. . . . Going to the dentist was traumatic enough. As naive as I was, I thought the dental assistants were to be naked while flossing my pearly whites. I figured if naked women were repairing cars, then that explains why my brother had so much difficulty with his '78 Chevy. It was in the bathroom that I also learned a lot about the female body by reading the little pamphlets that fell out of every Tampon box. —Dawn

Dawn had characterized herself as a dancer, and non-reader, but discovered that she was an incessant reader of labels in the kitchen, magazines and notices in the bathroom; she concludes: Reading materials other than schoolbooks have taught me more than any one encyclopedia ever could.

Kirk tells the story of avoiding reading life-long, making a game out of avoidance, trying to fool his mother who in frustration gave him tests on the Grimm's fairy tales. His essay begins:

Along with every other child in the world I knew that I could read, so what was the point of constantly reading books when you could just watch television. The stories on there were just as interesting and took about a fourth as much time . . . . Now when I look back at all of my attempts to get out of reading, I realize I learned a whole lot more than if I'd actually just sat down and read the book . . . . It also amazes me that this type of behavior didn't end with this one incident. I continued this type of juvenile behavior all the way up through high school, imagine that. I'd continue to attempt anything that appeared to be less work than the actual assignment. Of course, that would fail miserably and I'd be forced to go and do the original torturous assignment.

[two pages later in the essay] One of the examples that really sticks out in my mind was my unsubstantiated confidence in Cliff Notes. For some strange reason I thought that [high school] teachers had no idea that they existed and I was getting away with something. Once those myths were dispelled by my failure of the first quiz, I was again stuck reading the book, just with a little more guidance from my parents.

[concluding the essay] Now that I've reached the college level, I've discovered that skimming the pages and hoping that the lectures cover everything that will be on the tests doesn't quite cut it. . . . I discovered that common sense does nothing to help me figure out what Skinner's main focus in his psychological experiments were. That was probably my awakening to the world beyond high school. —Kirk

Corey, another student who assured me that no one in his family read, found a trigger from Hans's poem about family readers and wrote his an essay about the same topic—his mother read Danielle Steele and the Bible, his father books on sports officiating, his younger brother comics and himself, the Bible, the sports page, magazines, schoolbooks and so on. Then he completed a radical revision of this essay (see Bishop "Risktaking"), making collages of his family members out of the texts they read:

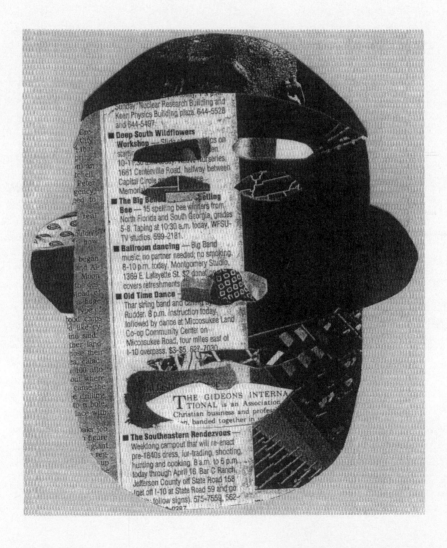

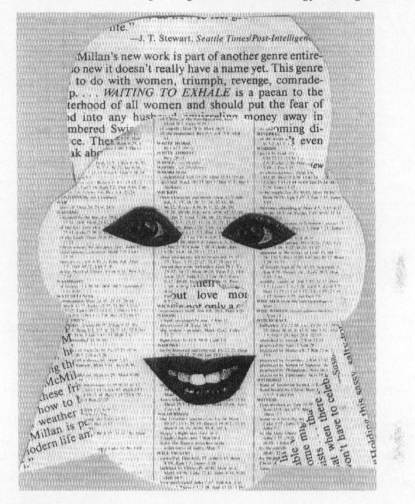

Through the essay and revision process, Corey realized he was a much more fluent reader than he had thought. He learned that his family did read and that he was the most fluent reader in his family because he addressed a variety of texts.

After much revision, I have had some success making reading, writing, and learning processes the center of my writing courses. I ask students to write letters to authors of their textbook. I ask students to compile their own set of reading tips for students in a future class:

Waiting to Exhale reading group:

- Read in a comfortable setting (eat, drink, lounge).
- Fall asleep reading, sleep, wake up and read again—it's okay.
- If highlighting is distracting, outline and read more than once.
- Read about things that you're interested in (when you need to find a paper topic, choose materials that interest you). There are a lot of choices out there; don't feel limited. Research!
- Take notes—you can review your notes to refresh your memory on what you read.
- Research the author—it helps to better understand the author's purpose behind writing the materials that you are reading.
- Ask others for their input about the book you are reading. The more inf. you have about the book, the better able you are to plunge into the work and better understand it.
- Read aloud. To hear your own voice can sometimes help to commit the words to memory.
- Stand while you read. It's a change from the usual way of lounging and reading.
- Try new things to break the monotony.
- Set a reading schedule (pages per day) for longer works; planning helps in accomplishing a goal.

These suggestions were compiled after a discussion of two handouts—several pages of teachers' reading self-reports and first-year writing students' reading self-reports.

I've had success using interactive reading techniques:

1. Cut a poem in three, sharing one third of the text at a time, asking the class for readers' responses, renegotiating meaning as each set of new lines is added.
2. After reading a story, ask different groups to prepare different responses: write a letter to the author; write another five pages that take place one hour, one day, or one year later; find a resonant quote and explore what the quote means to your group; pretend you're casting this story—what actors and actresses would you use, and so on.
3. Share reading protocols (see Elbow's suggestions in "The War" and "Being a Writer").
4. Ask students to self-assign readings from a class anthology and develop journal questions.
5. Ask students to facilitate class discussions.
6. Assign reading groups like classroom writing groups—have group and individual journal responses that engage the text:

- You're the editor of a publisher that has received this manuscript. What revision advice would you give the author to make this text more popular/accessible/a best seller for (a) your contemporaries and (b) your parents?
- Think of five very different people that you know. How would each respond to this text? If they're resistant to it, how would you argue to convince them to try it?
- Speculate on why you think I chose this text for this class? Would you suggest I use it again? Why or why not?
- Speculate on what this author might write next (or what you'd like to see them write about)—consider genre, topic, style, and so on.
- If this author came to campus to read his/her work—would you attend? Why or why not? Would you invite anyone to go with you? What do you think the author would look and sound like? What part of your text do you think he/she would choose to read and why? What part—story, poem, section—would you like to hear read aloud and why?
- What, from this author's writing style—techniques, voice, subjects, way with words, sentences, paragraphs, could you steal to spice up your own writing? Be detailed, quote some of the writing and explain why it's particularly stealable.

I'm not alone in developing interactive response and writing activities; in fact, some of these are adaptations, borrowed from colleagues who figured this out sooner than I did (see Qualley), and other similar activities appear in *When Writing Teachers Teach Literature*, edited by Art Young and Toby Fulwiler. But, in fact, I don't think it's enough to simply create engaging demonstrations alone. I learned that my whole course needed to be refocused on literacy, on experiencing, cultivating, developing a reader/writer's habits of mind. To that end, I'm announcing that agenda in my first-year writing classes and exploring ways to teach teachers to design curriculums that make the invisible visible, that invite fluency instead of engendering *disfluency*. Richard Beach suggests:

> In order to recognize how their own theories shape practice, teachers may find it useful to make explicit the response theories underlying how they themselves respond to texts. In such a process, knowledge or theory construction takes center stage in the classroom" (4).

To finish, I argue that it's imperative that writing teacher educators address this issue of writing-and-reading in more varied, theoretically informed, and engaging ways than we have before. Writing teachers are often former or current literature majors who are struggling not with reading fluency but with critical theories and theory wars. This background will lead them—as it's leading many of us today—to focus on something we call critical thinking when I believe we need to start cultivating habits of mind of fluent readers who are writers—predicting, questioning, engaging—and who are doing all this because they are constantly reading the world, because their world is valued, because reading and writing are meaning making moments. We have to care before our students will care, and we have to care in informed ways:

> The teacher's personal love of literature, however, has not always been proof against the influence of routine, pedantic notions concerning teaching methods. He is dismayed at the results indicated by the low level of taste about him; he undergoes constant frustration, or he consoles himself by focusing on the rare student who seems to possess the divine spark. To develop many such students the teacher must liberate himself as well as his pupils form self-defeating practices. (Rosenblatt 66).

To finish, I realize I can't finish. I could read more and write more about reading-to-write. There are half-followed arguments here, explorations, predictions that could be narrowed and tested. I am changing the way I teach teachers this summer, but doing it by writing about reading, because writing is how we will learn together. I'm asking teachers to write a reading literacy autobiography, to draft and share it in groups. I'm asking new teachers in this six-week teacher-education course to "read" themselves as tutors and to read the teachers they mentor with (sitting in on actual classrooms for two weeks), writing case studies of themselves in these locations (see Tobin). I'm asking them to learn about assessment by "reading" a student portfolio each from my last class as they would read an archeological artifact. To "read themselves" as teachers (see Rankin) who will teach for the first time in the fall, they will read the student portfolio, read the class they think I taught as they can glean it from this many-paged writing portfolio, and read the teacher-self they are constructing through these activities. I'm asking them to actively read literary texts and student texts together (realizing that they bring old information to new, like all readers—and that old information may include limiting assumptions about writers, about the gender of authors, and so on [see Haswell and Haswell for an interesting new look at this problem]).

To finish. To continue. To begin. I have to throw off my English depart-ment ingrained suspicion that these are basics, prerequisites, things that should have happened before, that to agree to teach reading for writing is tantamount to an agreement that I'm doing developmental work. I'm not. Disfluency is a social and a political problem when writing courses are required and too often taught by individuals who assume lack of reading equals lack of intelligence.

To teach teachers to teach reading for writers, I've had to understand that writing students (and teachers who write/teach) are adult learners who have already mastered the difficult code of language itself, long ago, and very well, and that now we need to begin working together, reading, writing, talking, listening. "It is possible to specify the conditions under which children [and first-year writers] will learn to read [and write], and these are again the general conditions that are required for learning any-thing—the opportunity to generate and test hypotheses in a meaningful, collaborative context" (Smith 202, my additions). Teaching our writing teachers to teach reading for writing will help assure that these basic and essential conditions and contexts are met.

8

"Traveling Through the Dark"
Teachers and Students Reading and Writing Together

[T]here is no way to escape all discourse communities, stand outside them and pronounce judgment. Furthermore, I assent to most of the conventions of academic discourse community and believe that students from other communities can benefit from learning about them, and learning them. But perhaps we can break up the failure/deracination dilemma for students from communities at a distance from academe. Through discourse analysis we might offer them an understanding of their school difficulties as the problems of a traveler to an unfamiliar country—yet a country in which it is possible to learn the language and the manners and even "go native" while still remembering the land from which one has come.

Patricia Bizzell "Cognition" (238)

IN WRITING CLASSROOMS, STUDENTS OFTEN STUDY WRITING BY READING literature and responding to it. That is, literature offers many students the content for their writing class experiences. However, teachers of writing and teachers of literature alike have found it more and more difficult to make relevant the canonized classics taught by English departments to classrooms of students with varied reading and writing histories. *King Lear* for the Korean/American immigrant or "The Lovesong of J. Alfred Prufrock" for the Athabascan-speaking Native American writing student clearly present a cultural and interpretive chasm. In addition, the gap between dominant culture students and their "academic" teachers is equally great. These teachers know and propound the virtues of expository prose and prose explicating "literature" to a generation which is more engaged with rock videos and computer games. The challenge is as great for such teachers as it was for Mina Shaughnessey when she began working with open admissions, multi-cultural, basic writers in the 1970s.

Two strands of thought in composition studies and contemporary criticism may help writing teachers create a more successful writing-with-literature classroom in spite of these widespread cultural differences between students and teachers. First, composition theorists and practitioners suggest that writing teachers must become writers within their own classrooms. Second, reader-response criticism shows teachers a new viewpoint from which to survey texts, whether student texts or literary texts. Thinking in these areas suggests that students and teachers must build an interpretive community within the classroom as a first bridge between disparate cultures. Doing so affirms writing and reading as interconnected, meaning making, social activities.

I will explore these two areas of thinking—teachers should write with and for students and texts are socially constructed artifacts—and then suggest a way in which teachers can explore their own reading and writing by offering a reader's response to William Stafford's poem, "Traveling Through the Dark," which illuminates the gap between teacher and student knowledge and points to those areas teachers must explore as they re-envision their participation in a multi-cultural reading and writing process classroom.

Writing Teachers Writing

In her article, "When Writing Teachers Don't Write: Speculations about Probable Causes and Possible Cures," Maxine Hairston summarizes one view about teacher-as-writer:

> . . . teachers who do not engage in the writing process themselves cannot adequately understand the complex dynamics of the process, cannot empathize with their students' problems, and are in no position either to challenge or to endorse the recommendations and admonitions of the textbooks they are using. (62)

And Donald Murray supports this stand, that teachers *should* be writers. He describes the writing process classroom simply: "The students write and the teacher writes (14)." This assurance that writing is a valuable learning experience for teacher and student can be traced back to Janet Emig's essay "Writing as a Mode of Learning." Emig pointed out that writing leads us to understanding because it is relevant: "Successful learning is also engaged, committed, personal learning." And some years later, in the article cited above, Hairston advances that claim by observing that:

> . . . your students are more likely to become interested in their own writing if they know that you write, that you understand the process firsthand, and that you share their problems and frustrations, but also their excitement. (70)

The question remains, are writing teachers experiencing the writing process with their students? Most indications lead me to say no. This was certainly true for participants in a research project where I studied participants in a training class for teachers of composition and focused on the learning of five composition teachers with an average of ten years teaching experience each. These teachers took coursework in a doctoral program in rhetoric and linguistics and returned to their home institutions to teach composition. Teachers in the study felt they were "average" writers and several expressed strong fears about writing for their own professors. Similarly, in their study of a doctoral program writer/teacher, Carol Berkenkotter, Thomas Huckin and John Ackerman had related findings; teachers as doctoral students can have as much to learn about writing academic prose in their discipline and be as frustrated writing for their doctoral program instructors as composition students who are writing for composition teachers.

In an ethnographic study of primary and secondary teachers, Sondra Perl and Nancy Wilson found that one of their elementary case study teachers was extremely hesitant to write and share her writing even with her first grade students. Finally, most of the writing workshops modeled on the Bay Area Writing Project and National Writing Project acknowledge the need to get writing teachers writing and premise many of their workshop activities on this perceived need: Workshops are designed to generate teachers' writing, training them to critique peers and enabling them to enter into the writing experiences of their own students more thoroughly (Daniels and Zemelman).

In addition, we can no longer assume that the writing teacher who follows a textbook and assigns students to write an expository essay comparing and contrasting characters in two Shakespeare plays has a real understanding of the challenges involved in that assignment. For some teachers this type of writing is not necessarily the kind of writing the teacher has done recently, if at all. And the stereotypical English literature professor who rages at the atrocious sophomore student writers in his

Introduction to American Literature course may be no more comfortable with his own academic writing pressures than his writing students; he has simply learned how to hide his own apprehension or chooses to write only those pieces he can succeed at writing. Hairston suggests "that at least two-thirds of college professors publish nothing after the dissertation (62)." Further, many writing and literature teachers, like myself, may never even have taken the courses they most often teach—freshman composition—after scoring high enough on their college placement tests to be excused from such classes. These teachers, and I include myself again, may have an understanding of graduate level academic prose conventions but no useful memory of the problems which thwart a student attempting to enter the academic community through the perplexing medium of writing-with-literature classrooms.

This description of teacher preparedness (or underpreparedness) for teaching writing, leads to important questions. Can we really consider ourselves process teachers creating a student-centered curriculum until we know the problems our writing students experience as they are socialized into the academic community? Can we really continue to demand that our students write, under pressure, in modes and on subjects we have little experience writing ourselves and which, frankly, would probably bore us if we did? Can we be sure that there is a developmental progression—freshman composition, to upper division literature classes, to graduate school in education or literature or rhetoric—that is productive for our students when we ourselves often short-circuited such a stage-model (not to mention the greater number of our writing students who go into other professional areas)? These are questions focused on writing. Looking at reading in writing-with-literature courses raises an equal number of concerns.

Writing Teachers Reading

Current interest in designing "best" reading lists—The Great Books or Cultural Literacy lists—brings up the omnipresent issue of writing-with-literature classroom texts. Just as writing teachers have varied writing backgrounds and proclivities and abilities, they have varied interests in and abilities to read "literature." Theorists in the area of reader-response criticism—Stanley Fish, Louise Rosenblatt, David Bleich, to name a few of the most well-known—vary greatly in their approaches to reading texts but one premise that they hold in common is that texts, to a certain extent, are socially constructed. That is, readers cannot help but bring themselves (and their emotional and social histories) to their interpretation of texts. Reader-response theory gains further support from readings specialists like Frank Smith who argue that the very act of reading is transactional; readers' ease in connecting to new knowledge increases in proportion to the amount of old, relevant, knowledge they have in the subject area being considered. Therefore, an Athabascan speaker who has lived his entire life above the arctic circle, can reasonably expect to have some difficulty reading Jay McInerny's New York novel *Bright Lights, Big City.*

This reader may begin to understand such a novel with reading support. He may have read other books about urban dwellers. He may go to Anchorage and get his first taste of urban congestion and begin to understand New York somewhat more. He may watch a number of movies set in large cities. He may talk to friends who traveled to New York and who slowly help him draw a picture of the place and its culture. But, reading cold, this reader may not be able to transact very thoroughly with the novel, however much we as writing teachers might hope he would. The impatient writing-with-literature teacher who teaches this student may have forgotten the transactional nature of reading and her own long reading history and cultural influences. With the help of her own New Critical education, she may tend to see books as artifacts, thinking, after all, that the text is just words on the page. Modern theorists and modern students teach us that such a view is simply not complete.

Instead, writing teachers find that every writing-with-literature classroom is made up of twenty or more interpreters who must negotiate meaning within the academic discourse community. Teachers who realize this may help their students bridge cultural gaps. As I have argued before:

> Our students need to interact with literature in the fullest possible sense, and to do so, they need to become fluent readers and writers. Additionally, they must be allowed to respond to literature, to write literature, to relate themselves to literature and literature to their lives, and to have an historical understanding of texts. In this way, they learn to participate in the world of readers *and* writers because the *are* readers and writers. (Bishop "Texts and Contexts" 194)

Such an approach is going to call for biographical criticism (students understanding the time and place out of which a text was written) and creative writing (students writing poetry parodies or short stories to discover the conventions that must be followed and the resources of the genre) and new study skills and gambits (students writing journal responses to readings and pooling those responses to acquire a wider knowledge-base from which to approach a text). To do this, they need an interactive classroom, one in which the teacher approaches texts in the same sharing way, pooling her resources (a more extensive successful reading history and technical or "insider's" knowledge) and experiencing some of her students' frustrations and anxieties in order to better help them. Such a teacher is in the unique position of growing and sharing along with her student. She will be less tempted to stand back and critically detail insurmountable cultural problems or to rail at declining standards. She will respect her students as individuals able to grow in knowledge.

This teacher, as Janet Emig points out, will find that writing is *the* mode of learning in the literature based classroom. She will also, like many social critics concerned with the teaching of writing, understand that she is participating in a new and somewhat revolutionary educational model:

> Reorganized under a rhetorical paradigm, [Terry] Eagleton argues, English studies would analyze how all kinds of verbal discourse, spoken and written, make meaning in their particular contexts. Eagleton hopes that the new English studies would produce students better able to critique the hegemonic culture in its entirety and so to conceive of liberatory social change. Interestingly enough, many composition theorists—such as James Kinneavy—have been calling for a very similar sort of change in English studies. (Bizzell "On the Possibility" 178)

To begin learning how to "critique" one's own culture, an ethnographic viewpoint is called for. Teachers must "make the familiar strange to come to an understanding of it" (Mehan 61). This defamiliarization can occur fairly simply by the teacher taking up pen or pencil and writing with students. First, teachers writing on their own class topics and in set formats will experience some surprising difficulties. I certainly did. In a writing-with-literature course I wrote a "sample" essay on "A Rose for Emily" to offer a model for some struggling writers in class. I *loathed* my own essay. It exhibited all the "school" writing devices I had been moving away from for years—a lumbering first thesis sentence, a boring comparison and contrast organizational pattern, and a leaden conclusion. There was none of Donald Murray's or Janet Emig's sense of writing for surprise and discovery in this sample. Needless to say, it was virtually unusable—I missed my deadline. I couldn't write that piece and

I had to think seriously about what deadly labor I was requesting from my own students.

This experience was a turning point for me. From that time on, I studied my writing-with-literature class. I made the too familiar composition classroom scene "strange." I started to read more widely in composition and criticism, leading to some of my observations here. I realized any writing samples I brought in to class had to be real in the sense that I needed to learn from them. And I realized that I hadn't much considered, in recent years, how it was I had developed and maintained my own identity as a reader and writer.

By sharing one such writing exercise here, and the discoveries I made writing, I would like to show how a few attempts to write *with* students, *for* students, and *like* students can illuminate a teacher's understanding of her class and of the works of literature she may love to read herself but have difficulty "teaching" to underprepared writing students.

Reader's Response to "Traveling Through the Dark"

I will be reading one of William Stafford's most widely anthologized poems, "Traveling Through the Dark." Having read it before, I know that I like the poem, yet my explanation of why this is so would be vague, something like: "The poem is emotional, power-packed, but controlled." When my sophomore-level writing-with-literature students read it last year, they only seemed to sense the control and not the emotion. For them, the poem was just okay, shoulder-shrugging stuff. A few young men with hunting backgrounds valued it as a poem with a recognizable subject (or an object which they could recognize—a deer), as opposed to other class poems, most of which they did not seem to value.

I wanted to attempt what would be for me a new reading of this poem, to try to "evoke" it in Rosenblatt's sense by recording *how* I read it. I aimed for an aesthetic rather than an efferent reading. In Rosenblatt's method, a work may be read efferently, for what the reader can take away, or aesthetically, for what happens to the reader during reading. Since the text that is evoked will be different with each reading, readers in the classroom would need to share aesthetic responses. Absolute subjectivity is avoided by distinguishing criteria such as unity, coherence, and so on, by which a text may be evaluated. "Clarification of the criteria that are being applied—not necessarily consensus—is the basis for critical communication" (Rosenblatt 49).

Instead of assigning my students the poem, offering them reading guides with which I might lead them to a preordained understanding of the text, I felt it was time for me to risk my own learning. By reading and writing about what I read, I would follow Emig, Hairston, and Murray's advice and have a document or ideas that could be shared with the students in my classroom community. (I use the present tense in my reading to try to describe my immediate reactions.) Here is the poem by William Stafford.

TRAVELING THROUGH THE DARK

Traveling through the dark I found a deer
dead on the edge of the Wilson River road.
It is usually best to roll them into the canyon:
that road is narrow; to swerve might make more dead.

By glow of the tail-light I stumbled back of the car
and stood by the heap, a doe, a recent killing;
she had stiffened already, almost cold.
I dragged her off; she was large in the belly.

My fingers touching her side brought me the reason—
her side was warm; her fawn lay there waiting,
alive, still, never to be born.
Beside that mountain road I hesitated.

The car aimed ahead its lowered parking lights;
under the hood purred the steady engine.
I stood in the glare of the warm exhaust turning red;
around our group I could hear the wilderness listen.

I thought hard for us all—my only swerving—
then pushed her over the edge into the river.

To start my reading, I slip past the title and begin with the first line:

Traveling through the dark I found a deer

Reading this line, I move quickly.

dead on the edge . . .

The first word of this line, "dead," stops me abruptly. I move back to read part of the first line again: "I found a deer/dead." I am impressed with the fast turn the poem takes after the precipice of the first line break, underscored by the alliteration of *d, d,* (and made more interestingly ambiguous as I write this draft in a confusion of dear/deer which I will go back and change).

I feel a need to begin reading the poem again. "Traveling through the dark" is an evocative phrase which I rushed over at first because I am familiar with it. It is stored in long-term memory as an efferent fact: William Stafford wrote "Traveling Through the Dark," rather than as a content-bearing phrase. I try to look at it aesthetically and find that it unfolds in a mysterious manner. It gives me no sense of time or place and yet draws me in; the poem does not pause to explain itself. *I* am traveling through the dark, reading myself into the "I" voice until I am brought up short by the word "dead." My easy acquiescence to the forward-moving first line ended when I encountered this word.

I continue to read, more warily now, and I gather more information:

> *dead on the edge of the Wilson River road.*

I find a first-person narrator who can pass over the shock of the dead deer in the prosaic effort to locate in a real-sounding place, Wilson River road. Distanced, I listen to the narrator tell a story which has a landscape which is beginning to form. But the next line confounds my narrative expectations.

> *It is usually best to roll them into the river.*

Again, I'm disturbed. The phrase, "It is usually best," implies a past (when is it not always best?) in which the narrator rolls "them" (an abundance of deer and many such movements) into the canyon (which gives more particularization of the landscape—now there is a road, a river, a canyon, a scene). As a reader, I realize that this scene is not in *my* past and I'm disturbed by the image of someone blindly rolling "them" into an unplumbed canyon.

> *that road is narrow; to swerve might make more dead.*

The narrator's choice of "that" insures my removal. I no longer feel "in" the poem. Perhaps it is being directed to a narratee. Insider's information is offered "*that* road is narrow" which seems like "already known" information being shared between narrator and narratee and functioning as a reminder of a mutually remembered landscape. I have moved from a very "felt" first two lines of the poem to a greater distance. "To swerve might make more dead," moves me to an intellectual distance due to its generality and ambiguity, emphasized by the narrator's avoidance of concrete words: *make* for *kills*, *more dead* for *more deer dead* or *more dead (humans)*. Is this generality directed to an outsider, this reader? It certainly stands outside of the narrative line which recommences in the first line of the next stanza.

By glow of the tail-light I stumbled back of the car

With this line, immediacy has been reinvoked and perhaps increased. As reader, I am again identifying closely with the narrator, supplying my memories of car-lights on dark nights, perhaps the numbness of unexpected accidents. I listen for water-roar from rivers in remembered canyons and supply a certain closeness of tree-darkened evening air. The line is loose and tumbling, not especially poetic until I notice the ambiguity in "stumbled back of." Is this stumbling to get to the back of *or* stumbling once at the back of the car. There is also a mannered heaviness to the dependent clause's prepositional phrase which drives the sentence inexorably toward the subject, "I."

and stood by the heap, a doe, a recent killing;

Now the narrator "stumbling" collides with "standing" and ends by the "heap." Before I am told, through the use of appositives, "the doe, a recent killing," I have already understood that this stumbled into heap is the center of contemplation: now inanimate, formerly animate, life. The secondary details are like blows after the knockout, ironic details that hurt less than they add to the numbness, "a doe, a recent killing," (which could have been prevented?) The next line works the same way, amplifying the already overpowering paralysis of *heap*:

she had stiffened already, almost cold.

When the next line begins with the phrase:

I dragged her off;

I am placed in the action again, as if *I* am dragging back the wounded deer. When I learn:

she was large in belly.

An alarm is triggered by the word belly, a very particular, redolent word. I read across white space to the third stanza.

My fingers touching her side brought me the reason—

This long, loping sentence leads me to expect an explanation yet I already feel I won't need it. The explanation has already been intimated by the words "a doe" and "belly."

her side was warm; her fawn lay there waiting,
alive, still, never to be born.

These lines overwhelm me with sensory and emotional detail. I, who have been dragging a stiff, dead deer, find, with a shock, that she is warm. As I register this information, I continue reading and learn that which I had already half-guessed: "her fawn lay there." Then, a second shock occurs, equal to the first, in the alliterative emphasis given to the words "warm" and "waiting." The fawn is personified and vivified and its essential tragedy is summed up abruptly in a horrible, oxymoronic sequence: "alive, still." Each of these words is set off singly and must be lived through: alive—hope; still—no hope (but the reading is ambiguous: still as in no movement *or* still as in continuing to be alive); and resolved uneasily in the final phrase "never to be born."

Here the narrator has stepped back again to the generalizing stance and I'm wrenched into a form of disengagement although half of me is still thinking: "Can't he cut the fawn out? Surely I've seen something like that in a movie." The next line wrenches me into greater identification with the narrator who, as if guessing my thoughts, says:

Beside that mountain road I hesitated.

As a reader, I'm poised also, stopped physically by the intersection of sentence and stanza end, and stopped emotionally by the narrator's contemplation, and by my desire to "do something."

The next stanza plays against this stasis by shifting my focus in a way that creates immediate distance.

The car aimed ahead its lowered parking lights;
under the hood purred the steady engine.

I'm back out in the darkness looking at a peculiarly personified car that aims its own lights. The machine is purring (as a dead deer can't.)

I stood in the glare of the warm exhaust turning red;

The imagery of car as beast is continued in the warm, breath-like exhaust. After all, another car, another beast, killed the deer and the confusing metaphor "glare of the exhaust" helps to evoke a scene that is simultaneously surreal and primeval. The first and only instance of color is the connotative mention of (blood) "red."

> *around our group I could hear the wilderness listen.*

Should I read myself into that group? There is certainly an insistence on shared experience. Jung's theory of collective unconscious and recurring archetypes comes to my mind. Instead of machine against beast, I sense beast against beast and man immersed in nature. The subtle personification continues. Everything in this poem is sentient and involved, whether willing or not—the group—this reader.

> *I thought hard for us all—my only swerving—,*

Here the narrator is interpreting for me, for "us all," yet describing the very impasse which I, as evoker of this poem, have been brought to. I too wanted to rewrite the poem. I wanted to swerve.

> *then pushed her over into the river.*

The action has a heavy abruptness and an almost too human identification, for narrator and reader, of "she" with a human rather than with a deer. At the least, "heap" has been specified and made over, movingly, into "she."

As I read, I think to myself, "hasn't this already happened?" I knew the swerve would only be a swerve. To verify this sense, I must re-read the third line of the poem, the formerly ambiguous "It is *usually* best . . ." The movement and development of the poem has allowed me to live through the narrator's moment of decision. With this particular evocation of the poem, I have grown into a fuller understanding of the implications of that singularly placed word: "usually."

I have finished one reading. I'm fairly tired. Exhilarated and exhausted. Some things I've surely missed. Some explorations are far fetched. But I've never quite looked at "how" a poem does in quite this way. I think, to my own satisfaction, I've understood Stafford's use of the word "usually." I learned a great deal about timing. To read, I moved backwards and forwards through the lines in a manner I've never charted before. I also detected the in and out movement of reader identification with the narrator and reader distance from the narrator, distances triggered by line turns and contextual juxtapositions as well as by meaning.

After such a reading, I understand more clearly how my students and I come to such different readings of the same text. For it took work and concentration to evoke the poem, just as it would take work and concentration to evoke it a second time. And what is evoked the second time will be different from what was evoked here. Certainly, I haven't done justice to the many technical facets of the poem: the enjambments, the stanzas, the understated diction. Yet clues to those things came out. I noticed the crescendo of emotion in the third stanza by living through it and now I can look at it more pragmatically. The poem has structure and shape combined with powerful content.

Working to evoke this poem has reminded me of the writing aloud protocols that are being used by researchers in composition theory (Linda Flower and John Hayes, among others). There are drawbacks to the method. It *is* artificial and there are moments of double-vision (when the shifting between efferent and aesthetic is not fully within my control or fibrillates disturbingly), yet I did feel successfully engaged with the text and able to record aspects of "reading the poem" that led me to new understanding.

Even as I made this type of reading, I was aware that I was being helped by past experience, by all the years I have spent as a careful reader of literature, which made me feel confident enough to take risks. I even had previous readings of the same poem as a buffer. In this reading I alluded to many literary terms and techniques, including alliteration, ambiguity, first person narrator, narratee, concrete detail, stanzas, poetic line, personification, oxymoron, connotation and denotation, collective unconscious. This list of technical terms won't be available to every reader, certainly not to my students. And the poem is not yet fully evoked: I haven't talked nearly enough about meaning. So, I have to conclude that this is not *the* way to read the poem but it is *a* very interesting way to begin reading the poem and an excellent way to realize that I must help students make the transition from their own reading pasts to our classroom reading present, enlarging and supporting their understanding with well-designed classroom interactions. These activities might include but not be limited to:

- Students and teachers writing reading protocols (typed or tape recorded) and sharing readers' responses.
- Students working in research groups to analyze group members' protocols.

- Generating craft discussions from class protocols; that is, teaching connotation, denotation, oxymoron, alliteration, ambiguity *as they come up as issues in* students' and teacher's readings.
- Allowing students to prepare biographical reports (what was the writer's situation, who did she know, what/who were her influences, and so on) and craft talks/ presentations (what is blank verse and what writers in our class anthology use it?), and reviews of reviews (historical survey of the author's place in the canon over time as reflected by book reviewers or literary critics) as alternate types of paper in addition to analysis or reader response papers [papers in these expanded areas can lead to guided library research projects using handbooks and reference books in literary studies].
- Exploring the writer's world through imitation and parody (such explorations are most successful, and easier to evaluate, if accompanied with a process journal entry or process cover sheet describing the writer's process in writing the imitation/parody and if the *process of imitation/parody* is evaluated rather than the *product,* the imitation/parody itself).

Any of these activities, will help me, as in the Bizzell epigraph to this article, allow my students to "'go native' while still remembering the land from which one has come" (" Cognition" 238), as they enter into *and contribute to* the discourse community of literary studies through a variety of shared approaches.

Part III

Composing Ourselves as Department Members and Administrators

Becoming a tenure-line English department member and a writing program administrator led me into some bad clothes days. Bad clothes years. I remember escaping my office at school and ending up at a mall department store looking at racks of sale suits. This was some sort of half-way house or Dantean limbo where I could escape identity, feel neither fish nor fowl, WPA nor my own person, partner nor parent. I paused before I returned home to my family and briefcase full of unfinished day's business. I knew there was something to this identity thing from the moment I left Alaska; even then, along the way, kids in strollers, I shopped, struggling to compose a new, hot climate, professional identity.

Becoming a department member is much like trying to dress right, to define oneself in and against one's community. For instance, I came to feminist theory and thinking late. By 1990, however, I would better understand women from my writing classrooms who would come in my office, close the door, and say "I didn't say anything in class because I don't want to be labeled 'feminist' "but . . . ." Time in the academy had sensitized me to the uses and abuses of gendered language, to the ways the men in my classes seemed to claim and be comfortable with my attention while the women—if I didn't work hard not to let it happen—could fall silent. And I was sensitized anew in my position as WPA to the "woman's work" I was asked to do as supervisor/mentor to a program of sixty teaching assistants, as wife to the English department. These positions, these identities, these practices didn't always suit me or feel comfortable and my insights into academic hierarchies was sometimes hard won, though it developed apace after networking at WPA conferences and studying the growing literature on institutional politics.

In "Learning Our Own Ways to Situate Feminist and Composition Studies in the English Department"—written in late 1989—I use the voices of others to find my own voice. Like the student who closed the door, I had been silent until that point on these issues. The many citations in this essay are part of my intentional collage and call to (self) action. I wanted to say, "hey, all these folks are saying something important." This essay resulted from mindless shopping and mindful reading, from going out of my way to find thinkers and theorists who felt right, who welcomed me, who helped me look under the surface of things, beyond appearance.

I smile as I see the asterisks between sections in this essay. When the piece was published, the asterisks were removed and descriptive subheadings were inserted by journal editors to make it conform to style, to add a linearity and inevitability I didn't feel. This essay marks the first time I got testy—calling to complain about these changes (I later called to apologize for complaining, like the good girl I am and probably will mostly remain). It was at this point in drafting essays I decided style was an important part of my self-presentation. And of course, after this, I pursued written style with a vengeance.

Two years as a WPA, life was getting harder not easier. "Writing Is/And Therapy? Raising Questions About Writing Classrooms and Writing Program Administration" is an attempt to pass on to the public my private dilemmas, but they were private only in that they weren't often enough, it seemed to me, talked about. Although I had prepared intentionally in graduate school to be employed as a WPA, by the 1992 composition date of this essay, I felt somewhat like I had made a precipitous moon landing. At the same time, having given up my creative writing identity for that of a teacher-educator and administrator, I started to find that past self calling to me again. As my theoretical and pedagogical positions were challenged by new teachers of writing (and this challenging is normal and necessary), I had to re-examine my own writing life history, my own values, my own investment in and beliefs about teaching writing—that is to say, about writing itself. It seemed clear to me that to say what our business wasn't about—not about therapy, for instance—wasn't helping me to say clearly to myself and others what the business of teaching writing and administrating a writing program inevitably was about.

This essay explores the unexpected confluence I continued to encounter between my identities as poet, compositionist, researcher, feminist, plain person: I started to realize I wasn't choosing one outfit or another but wearing them all in layers, different sides out for different occasions/situations. Structurally, this essay moves from the person I was as writer out to the teachers I worked with and the program I directed by asking the same question over and over again: what therapeutic forces and processes are at work? To do this, I suggest we explore the merit of certain analogies. As in other essays in this section, identity is investigated by paying attention to patterns, themes and metaphors.

In "You Can Take the Girl Out of the Center But You Can't Take the Center Out of the Girl," (a speech prepared for a conference jointly sponsored in 1995 by South Carolina Writing Center and Southeastern Writing Center Association became this essay), I explain why holding multiple identities can be productive. I don't ever want to lose the knowledge or experience I gained while directing a writing center and a writing program. I don't want to lose the empathy and admiration I feel for the relatively unrewarded work of adjunct and teaching assistant and tutoring staffs around the country who tithe to the university system. Nor do I want to lose the anger I felt and continue to feel for inequities that riddle this system. And finally, I don't want to lose the pleasure that I take (that I know fellow teacher/tutors take) in work well done in the sites of literacy we have managed to create, sometimes against great odds—fiscal, intellectual, emotional, and historical.

Because "You Can Take the Girl" is an essay written for an occasion, it is intentionally as celebratory as I felt on that occasion—a gathering of hardworking, like-minded individuals; my argument rests on personal testimony and I end with an invocation and call to further work and sharing of work. Obviously, a piece like this is a pleasure to write but it also creates a certain space for reasoned reflection and examination—it allowed me to reground my thinking about writing centers and the way physical spaces affect intellectual spaces.

The short story that ends this section was written earlier than any other piece included in Teaching Lives. *The factual portions of this fictional reimagination "Let Me Tell You About the Rocks" were lived out during my first period of intense adjuncting, at Northern Arizona University where I taught a 4/4 composition teaching load in 1981. The teacher who comes to observe the narrator's class was/is Sharon Crowley, my supervisor in the days before I knew the field of composition existed. Just returned from a year teaching in Nigeria, I was working for a living as I decided where to return to school for a Ph.D. in creative writing—a development that never took place. This story, published in a literary journal in 1986, captures the paranoid adjunct, the scared institutional member persona that I struggled with then (and some days still feel resurfacing in me from my deep identity pool). To update this essay I had to substitute computers for typewriters but, unfortunately, the daily strains and confusions of adjunct teaching cannot be so easily corrected and remain strikingly similar and problematic for many teachers I know. I moved on in my teaching. But some days, I certainly still feel like I'm waiting for that mysterious messenger to return—to (re)solve all our problems.*

9

Learning Our Own Ways to Situate Composition and Feminist Studies in the English Department

WE ALL KNOW THAT IT IS POSSIBLE TO HOLD CONFLICTING INTELLECTUAL and emotional positions simultaneously; many personalities inhabit us when it comes to our lives as teachers, mothers, scholars, fathers, community members, speed offenders, friends, lovers. It is primarily when we move into that rarefied air of our professional lives—say when we open the door to an English department meeting—that we give ourselves over wholeheartedly to what Mary Savage describes as "academentia." At that moment, our carefully negotiated and necessary composite personality shivers, cracks, faults and folds under, and we resay ourselves, become decontexualized as a "Shakespearean," a "Melville specialist," or, in the lesser ranks, a "feminist," "compositionist," "fiction writer" or "poet." When we label ourselves this way, we agree to the dominant method of distinguishing areas in English studies, what Gerald Graff calls the field-coverage model, which isolates and elevates the literature scholar and critic and isolates but devalues the generalist.

And too often, in entering these singular terrains, women travel nervously, alone, with few maps or guidebooks, while the current-traditional "body" of English studies is very able to absorb our nervousness and our discontent. By creating separate women's studies programs or field designations of composition and feminist studies, or by allowing only minimal authority for writing program administrators (see Olsen and Moxley), the establishment is free to conduct department business as usual. Meanwhile, the marginalized cultures within or beside the department's dominant culture, alienated, co-opted or about to be co-opted, sit silently around that meritocratic table, feeling concerned.

***

When I was a good girl in high school, I completed my classwork scrupulously and also found a part-time job in order to save money for my future college expenses. The first morning at Woolworth's, I didn't forge right out to the mixed joys of working the candy counter, but was kept in the drafty upper regions of the store to read the rules and regulations manual, after which I would sign a sheet of paper saying I understood and agreed. Most jobs I held after that, generally part time and poorly paid, sure to encourage me to continue pursuing the examined life, included a quick run-through of parameters. There was always a rules and regulations manual. Always, that was, until I entered the more discreet and more elite work force of the English department. During my years as a TA, part-time lecturer, full-time renewable instructor, and finally tenure line professor, there were rules, but they were not written; there were communities but they were usually not friendly nor open.

In my earliest days in academia, I wanted and needed more guidance in many ways. I was a woman. I was naive. And I was traumatized by much of what I experienced. I had "converted" suddenly and enthusiastically from studio art to creative writing and literature. Professors welcomed me to their undergraduate classes, but in the transition to graduate level work, something happened. My place as a class member in good standing was usurped. As Adrienne Rich describes it, I entered a world where the prevailing hierarchy was visible if not explicit:

> Look at a classroom. . . . Listen to the voices of the women and the voices of the men; observe the space men allow themselves, physically and verbally, the male assumption that people will listen, even when the majority of the group is female. Look at the faces of the silent, and of those who speak. Listen to a woman groping for language in which to express what is on her mind, sensing that the terms of academic discourse are not her language, trying to cut down her thoughts to the dimensions of a discourse not intended for her . . . or reading her paper aloud at breakneck speed, throwing her words away. . . . ("Taking" 244–245)

As female initiate into graduate English studies I was no longer expected to have a voice (see also Bolker and Sperling and Freedman).

Equally, reading the traditional canon with paternal guidance was going to change me. Patrocinio Schweickart illuminates the problem: "For a woman, then, books do not necessarily spell salvation. In fact, a literary education may very well cause her grave psychic damage: schizophrenia 'is the bizarre but logical conclusion of our education'" (41). For instance, although I thought I loved reading and writing and thus became an English graduate student, those texts I loved to read were no longer sites of enjoyment. They were, rather, sites of struggle where my, generally, male professors were enmeshed in a critical game of vast proportions. These professors were Titans struggling in the bleak academic "publish or perish" universe, while, uninitiated, I was naively still expecting to savor great works with their guidance. The critical wars were not seen as suitable for seminar discussion, the primacy of particular great works was not questioned, the woman literature student of my time progressed through literature studies as usual, reading against herself. Schweickart also reminds us of the disturbing end result of such reading. We create a personality untrue to itself, for this is ". . . the consequence of the invocation to identify as male while being reminded that to be male—to be universal—. . . is to be *not female*" (42).

***

After completing master's level work in creative writing, I continued on, through a quick unhappy stint in literature, to teaching composition and English as a second language (ESL). I should say I was guided into community college teaching by a literature advisor when I failed to pass one day of three days of qualifying exams for a Ph.D. in English (literature) program and, no longer a good girl, refused to take the exams again. Teaching composition and ESL was viewed at that time as a respectable "trade."

Years later, finally, excitedly, happily, *I chose* deeper work in rhetoric and composition. Yet I've never given up my allegiances to those first areas of study (I came to value and critique literature *more* as I read rhetoric and as I continued to write and publish poetry and fiction, and I learned more than I can say about cultural variety from students in second language classes), and I constantly work to reintegrate these areas back into my life. Not to do so, would be to lose my culture, which in this case is my pedagogical and writing life experiences. For me, today, to be only a poet, or a feminist, or a compositionist is not enough. Nevertheless, traditional scholars, those dominant in English studies, warn me not to try to cross field boundaries. Says Martin Mueller in an article published in the *ADE Bulletin:* "A great deal of interdisciplinary work in English departments is deficient precisely in the virtue it claims for itself because scholars approach interdisciplinary work too casually. Stick to your knitting is sometimes good advice. We would all benefit from a healthy respect for our own expertise and an equally healthy apprehension of the difficulties involved in venturing on other territory" (9).

Muller tries to find a middle ground in the critical theory/literature studies wars, never once mentioning feminist or composition issues. Sticking to my knitting in a traditional English department would include, I expect, not allowing learning from my low status pasts to inform my present professional status. That is, I should not dilute boundaries by admitting to having taught ESL or liking to write poems if I am intending to "do" criticism or direct graduate students' theses. Cross disciplinary work, it must be remembered, challenges the existing field coverage model.

As a participant in English studies today, I do not want to stick to my knitting, for, like many others, I did not want to endure the deracination that Patricia Bizzell predicts may occur to minority culture students who have to forget where they have come from to survive their journey through the academy. Bizzell sees students as trying to resolve a dialect problem as they accede to the preferred school dialect. They need to learn the ways in which school discourse is structured in order to successfully master the discourse conventions of their chosen field or of the academic community at large. Or they may need to learn a new way of thinking entirely, mandating a change in their world-view. Bizzell holds that the student who is asked to change his or her world view risks deracination. She argues for closer study of how academically enforced acculturation affects students (Bizzell "What Happens"). And, I would add, how academically enforced acculturation affects women, and those who are viewed as women, often all composition teachers.

***

Women risk deracination as they attempt to enter the tacit culture of the dominant strands of English studies, literature and critical theory. Often good girls are adrift without mentors and are offered few choices and denied voice: they may learn to read and act like a man, or they may be stopped short by the gatekeepers. "For gatekeepers," Dale Spender reminds us, "are in a position to perpetuate their own schemata by exercising sponsorship and patronage towards those who classify the world in ways similar to their own. Women are by no means the only 'outsiders' but they are a significant group and there is considerable evidence which suggests that women's schemata does not at times 'match' with men's" ("Gatekeepers" 191). When these gatekeepers hold the rules and regulations *in their heads* and don't share them, marginalized individuals won't succeed very well or very quickly.

Sometimes gatekeepers respond to critiques of the patronage system with counter-arguments: the relative oppression argument and the quality work argument. In the relative oppression argument, gatekeepers may compare ". . . (white) women's status with that of black and poor men (not black or poor women), as a means to label women's concerns trivial" (Aiken et al. 267). In the quality work argument, individuals, who are often men and always insiders, claim that access for women or marginalized constituencies like part-time teachers or graduate students *is* open. If they aren't succeeding it's probably because they didn't complete the requisite degree or do "quality work," not because they didn't know the rules or because they were denied necessary access. Here is a version of the argument:

> You will only be outsiders as long as you define yourselves that way. Any time you want to get on the bus, you can. All you have to do to get on the bus is some quality work. Yes, it is a meritocracy. But that's all it is. Nothing else— not race, professional status, gender, religion, clothes style, sexual orientation, or brand of underwear—decides whether or not you succeed in getting recognized. Graduate students can do it if they choose to, although usually it takes longer than graduate school lasts. You can certainly begin in grad school. I'm a reader for six different journals, and I can tell you from my experience that *good work gets published.* ("CCCC Voices" 213)

This quality-work view is held in literature studies but also in composition studies, as in this example, despite composition being a field for which members like to claim better things: that its professional meetings (CCCC, NCTE) and community are friendlier, more open, more accessible than say those of the Modern Language Association or Associated Writing Programs. That belief does not keep novices, women and men, in composition from sometimes feeling they've entered new and discouraging terrain without maps or guidebooks.

Here is part of an anonymous, graduate student written critique of CCCC which prompted the "quality-work" response above: ". . . if I am ever an Insider, standing at podiums reading my papers, extolling the virtues of teaching writing, what will I have really gained? A more comfortable room, a more self-assured voice, and a sense of uneasiness as I remember what I left behind" ("CCCC Voices" 199). Clearly, this *is* a voice worried about the effects of gatekeeping and deracination.

Both the relative oppression and quality work arguments ignore issues of marginality and feminism in composition studies where, as Elizabeth

Flynn reminds us, gatekeepers still flourish in fine health. She refers to her recent, and eventually successful, attempt to publish composition theory informed by feminism: "'Composing as a Woman'" is thoroughly feminist in perspective and method. . . . The reviewers of the piece seemed to be offended by my criticisms of the field, though, so I decided to shift the emphasis of my discussion, focussing on the positive rather than the negative" ("Composing 'Composing as a Woman'" 88). Flynn's view is at variance with the quality-work argument ("I can tell you from my experiences that *good work gets published*") offered by the male composition scholar above.[1] These voices of dissent should be enough to remind us that the rules and regulations manual is not always fairly available for everyone and that some of us *feel* they get a kick in the teeth in spite of quality work or *understand* that their quality work has to include a shifted emphasis so as not to offend the editors.

In the same vein, Maxine Hairston, in her 1985 CCCC address, reminds us: "But our experience [in composition studies] is much like that of the women's movement. One can look at how far we have come and rejoice at our progress, or one can look at the barriers that still exist and become discouraged. I believe, however—and once more the situation is analogous to that of many women—the major reason we get discouraged is that our worst problems originate close to home: in our own departments and within the discipline of English studies itself" (273).

As compositionists, we engage daily with what Hairston calls the "intimate enemy," members of the traditional English department. Her argument, at the time, was, possibly, the need for succession, that writing find a new home. Terry Eagleton has argued even more persuasively that this new home might be a new unified department called rhetoric. Also, succession has been the solution for some feminists who have built separate women's studies programs within existing university structures.

Separation has resulted in some cases in strength, in that separation allows marginalized cultures like composition or women's studies to circumvent the tendency of the field-coverage English department to absorb their interests in isolated intra-departmental pigeonholes. In other cases, succession resulted in further alienation and erasure of any campus profile, problems which seem similar, at times, to those experienced by some writing across the curriculum programs.

***

I want to argue that we in composition studies, involved with feminist issues, who intend to exist within English departments and to encourage such existences might do so by learning from Adrienne Rich when she reminds us that:

> Today women are talking to each other, recovering an oral culture, telling our life-stories, reading aloud to one another the books that have moved and healed us, analyzing the language that has lied about us, reading our own words aloud to each other. . . . To do this kind of work takes a capacity for constant active presence, a naturalists's attention to minute phenomena, for reading between the lines, watching closely for symbolic arrangements, decoding difficult and complex messages left for us by women of the past. It is work, in short, that is opposed by, and stands in opposition to, the entire twentieth-century white male capitalist culture. (*On Lies* 13–14)

We need to become active *for ourselves* while observing these issues with "a naturalist's attention to minute phenomena, for reading between the lines, watching closely for symbolic arrangements, decoding difficult and complex messages." We need to remain active while realizing we are a formidable challenge to the status quo.

Susan Aiken and her colleagues found that: "Curriculum integration is, however, an exceedingly complex undertaking. . . . Those who direct it should anticipate resistances that will shift—in both kind and intensity—according to the changing chemistry of the groups involved. Because resistance assumes such protean forms, there is no single right way to proceed . . ." (273). Nevertheless, we may accomplish much by learning from ourselves. To start, we can recognize that what we have learned from our study of multicultural students in our writing classrooms can illuminate our own positions. There is a connection between what we do to enable those students to negotiate academic lives and what me may do to resolve our own lives within our complex English department culture.

Certainly we need to explore new attitudes and practices for learning and knowing, including: neighborliness, praxis, feminist mentoring, and the encouragement of believing behaviors. Arguments for these positions come from composition and feminist theory and pedagogy. In the remainder of this essay, I examine our world—we *are* the multicultural populations within English studies—to see where we may go in light of such explorations, questioning whether through active intervention we may not be able to do for ourselves what Pat Bizzell suggests we do for our students: ". . . offer them an understanding of their school difficulties as the problems of a traveler to an unfamiliar country—yet a country in which it is possible to learn the language and the manners and even 'go native' while still remembering the land from which one has come" ("Cognition" 238). For we and our graduate students are much like the students Bizzell is considering, and we are traveling inward, into forbidden territory.

***

Discussing multicultural writing students, Terry Dean suggests that "teachers need to structure learning experiences that both help students write their way into the university and help teachers learn their way into student cultures" (23). A parallel understanding is voiced by Kevin Davis who finds "Basic writers are neither deficient and in need of remediation nor developmentally unadvanced; they are, instead, quite adept users of different languages, capable of explaining who they are, where they are headed, and why they want to get there" (35). Joy Ritchie adds to and extends these ideas when she explains: "Learning to write and teaching writing involve us and our students in a process of socialization *and* of individual becoming . . ." (153). All three writers pinpoint the transactional nature of such learning.

Additionally, Davis claims a need for "translation" so that "their language can be understood by members of other cultures" (35). Both Dean and Davis point out too that those from the dominant culture need to interact and enter into the minority cultures' concerns. But can we, as feminists and compositionists, engage the dominant culture of literature faculty members in our lives even as we engage in theirs?

More theorists working at the interface of marginalized cultures offer concerns which are equally insistent. Lucille Schultz, Chester Laine, and Mary Savage suggest that college writing teachers need to resolve their own class biases before trying to resolve intra-departmental biases. This would be accomplished by college writing teachers realigning themselves with elementary and secondary writing teachers through collaboration to break down the hierarchical and elite system of thinking which insists that "knowledge should be created at advanced levels of the educational system and applied or carried out at lower levels; and . . . that the language and discursive practices of each educational level should be separate and distinct" (147).

It is easy for us to see that such hierarchical thinking works against composition and feminist studies *within* the English studies department but less easy to see our own faults, that we also work against precollege writing teachers, who are often female, simply by ignoring any connection between our practices. In this sense, the enemy is even more intimate than was suggested by Hairston. We may be the oppressors of writing teachers in the precollege writing world even as we complain about our own impoverished positions.

***

What suggestions, then, do we receive from those working with individuals who are marginalized by culture? Terry Dean tells us he has found success in building bridges and translating across cultures by including cultural and language topics in class, by using peer response groups, by publishing class newsletters, by bringing campus events into classroom discussions, and by encouraging the use of anecdotes (28–36).

Patrick Hartwell suggests that in the freshman writing classroom we need to access "underlying postures toward language" and that we might accomplish this by "banishing teacher talk" and "investigating literacy events" and by looking at our metaphors and narratives. Reminiscent of Adrienne Rich's call for a naturalist's attention to detail, Hartwell suggests that we use classroom ethnographic observation, that we watch and explicate ourselves, teachers and students (12–16).

This anthropological model of teachers who learn *as* they teach is supported by the research of Mary Belenky and her colleagues in *Women's Ways of Knowing*. They argue for what they term "connected teaching" where the teacher views herself as a participant-observer in the classroom: "A connected teacher is not just another student; the role carries special responsiblities . . . an authority based not on subordination but on cooperation," and they claim: "Connected teachers are believers. They trust their students' thinking and encourage them to expand it" (227).

For compositionists at the English department level, Maxine Hairston offers several suggestions. She claims we should: 1) realize literature professors not listening to us, 2) stop being angry and wasting energy, and 3) pay attention to the inner voice, stop trying to be "good." To accomplish this, she offers general strategies: 1) be productive and publish, 2) network with fields outside our field, and 3) network with the professional (non-academic) world (278–282).

And finally, Mary Savage in "Writing as a Neighborly Act: An Antidote for Academentia" offers instant relief, claiming "Neighborliness is an antidote; it is not a new direction, paradigm, consensus. Rather it is an instant, homeopathic remedy that allows the body to come back to its senses" (16). For Savage, neighborliness is "praxis, practical activity, like teaching people to read, or helping women provide better nutrition for infants, or accompanying a grieving family at a wake" (16), and this type of praxis is founded on Freirean pedagogy and Christian ecumenical work where neighborliness "establishes both closeness and distance in the critical interrogation of life" (17). A critical interrogation of life is the one being undertaken by: "Pastoral workers in Latin America [who] are curing their own clericism by asking a central question: whose cry do I hear, toward whom do I move, whose interests do I serve?" (17)

And Savage's suggestion is strongly rooted in a feminist perspective. She suggests that "writing teachers capitalize on their womanliness, their 'limnality' (their living at the limits, on the margins of the system), and that they approach one another as neighbors . . ." (18).

***

Whose cry do I hear? At times I hear many, but I want to attend here to the cry of the novitiate, the official new member of the English department community. We need to pay close attention to our "young," those temporarily (and sometimes permanently) marginalized male and female TAs, the next generation in the changing Department of English, with whom we may come into contact in exciting and valuable ways. These are the individuals toward whom I move, for it just may be that the entrenched literature studies professional is too obdurate to change. Remember Hairston's intimate enemy and look at Hairston and others' "war" imagery.[2] Remember, Dean and Davis and Ritchie—they told us that those who develop critical consciousness, who enter into dialog with minorities, who cross cultural boundaries, are both change agents *and changed*.

Simply put, those individuals with strongly developed classification systems may find it impossible to change; they have more at stake, more to lose (Bishop *Something Old, Something New*). Additionally, intentional change for those in power can be seen as giving in, becoming the enemy, and in the case of men, becoming female. Susan Aiken and her colleagues found this occurring in an institutionally sanctioned project, a curriculum integration seminar, designed to aid university faculty in incorporating feminist concerns into courses: "Unfortunately, participants who transcended masculinist preoccupations and attempted to voice feminist positions frequently found their contributions ignored or discounted by others in the groups or found themselves subtly classed as 'female' by their [male] colleagues" (269).

Rather than go to war, to insist on change in those for whom change entails great risks, who may even react with punitive or repressive measures against department subcultures, I look toward the new graduate student in English who is not yet such a fixed product because she or he is still in the process of becoming.[3] No adult comes to a graduate program as a blank slate, but new English department graduate students are voluntarily enrolling in a process which can have profound effects on who they are and who they become. Carol Berkenkotter, Thomas Huckin and John Ackerman trace the writing development of a new student in rhetoric and linguistics who learns to write like a rhetorician, and John Schilb later critiques this case study in which these researchers, he felt, did not illuminate the ideological biases of the culture this student was asking and being asked to enter, nor, Schilb felt, did the researchers come to terms with the political and ethical issues of graduate student academic acculturation.

***

Since graduate students clearly represent great potential for English departments, we should explore public and private channels for teaching these soon-to-be-peers critical consciousness. As the next wave of composition and feminist workers, and particularly as newly aware literature faculty, these students have the potential to make the changes within the house of English studies we have sometimes despaired of making.

Public forums can, and I think should, include an introductory course in "English Studies" that goes far beyond the required bibliography, research, and criticism courses currently offered at most universities.[4] Such a course would be concerned with knowledge-making. To understand this, we need to refer to philosopher Gilbert Ryles's often quoted distinction of "knowing that" and "knowing how": "'Knowing that' and 'knowing how' are two different kinds of knowledge, not antecedent and consequence. 'Learning *that*' is 'acquiring information,' becoming 'apprised of a truth'; 'learning *how*' is 'improving in ability,' or 'getting trained in a procedure' (59). These two capacities are both exercises of intelligence, but are not associated in a simple cause-and effect fashion" (Foster 117).

In most graduate programs, bibliography, research, and criticism courses are focussed on knowing *how*, while knowing *that* about the professions is incidental information, program lore, the rules and regulations of the academy, transmitted by word of mouth from mentor to mentee or puzzled over by graduate students in midnight lounges. To exercise both knowing capacities, the introductory graduate seminar would also focus on knowing *that*.

In such a course, we may question the history of ourselves through examination of texts like: James Berlin's *Rhetoric and Reality: Writing*

Instruction in American Colleges, 1900–1985 for composition history; Gerald Graff's *Professing Literature: An Institutional History* for a discussion of the growth of English studies; Toril Moi's *Sexual/Textual Politics: Feminist Literary Theory* which provides an introduction to feminist theory; and Joseph Moxley's *Creative Writing in America: Theory and Pedagogy* which engages seldom discussed issues concerning academic creative writing[5] These authors are chosen from *my* eclectic and personal list—books that help me begin to *know that.* Still, these authors share a determination to examine the historical and ideological conditions that influence our lives within the modern English department.

By including works related to *all* areas of English, the redesigned, historically aware, multicultural English studies seminar begins to offer graduate students important context(s) and a forum for question-making. Questions must be asked in such a seminar about how each of our intertwined but varied subdisciplines have come into being and, often, have come into serious conflict. And such a seminar works against the traditional assumption that ". . . students should be exposed only to the *results* of the controversies of their teachers and educators and should be protected from the controversies themselves" (Graff 261).

Within this participatory seminar, we can use activities similar to those we rely on in multicultural classrooms, including anecdote and story-telling, for telling stories is a neighborly act that can illuminate the ways of the academy for those just entering. Our narratives can also be considered change-active. Linda Brodkey argues for *critical* ethnographies where the writer's voice "is made most audible by interrupting the flow of the story and calling attention to the fact of the narration" in order to be "theoretically sound and honest to draw attention to one's ideological position as a narrator" (73). Critically conscious historical discussion will bring up issues of politics and ethics in academic acculturation.

And, questions will be raised. What does it mean to study literature, writing, critical theory, and/or rhetoric in today's English department? Whose cry do we hear? Toward whom do we move? Whose interests do we serve? Questions promulgate dialog. As we do with our multicultural students, we may dialog in diaries, journals, and peer groups, telling anecdotes and stories, examining processes, developing critical consciousness on a range of department and profession specific concerns. Using Elizabeth Daumer and Sandra Runzo's suggestions, we could ". . . focus on experiences of being unable, or denied the right, to speak for oneself and on incidents of racial, sexual, and linguistic oppression and assertion" or describe "a time when someone changed or distorted their language," or consider "telling a story of personal significance to another who then retells it to the class," or encourage a student to "write about herself in a context that she thinks social conventions have generally denied her . . ." (55–56). As I did when I began this essay.

We can discuss whether quality work does count and how it counts and who says so and how this work should be done. We can discuss the gatekeepers and the conventions. Through such discussion we illuminate the ideological bases of *all* the groups involved, gatekeepers and gatecrashers, dominant culture and minority cultures, males and females.

***

Neighborliness can extend beyond the graduate seminar and function in those departments too small or too conservative to transform the curriculum. Women in composition (and men who value such alternatives) can provide new and positive mentoring models to female and male students new to the profession(s). Mentors can develop for and articulate to graduate students their sense of the operative rules and regulations governing that department and that field, and such articulation may well serve the mentor to better understand her position, too.

Kathleen Schatzberg-Smith reminds us that "Mentoring is not only an intellectual relationship but also an emotional one" and that "productivity is enhanced by affiliation with a mentor. This in turn stimulates the novice's career advancement. The protege also gains access to a professional network that would not be so readily available without the assistance of the mentor . . . the mentoring relationship provides in a sense a safe haven in which the protege can take risks and develop personal and professional values and style" (48). For those new to the field, mentoring provides a wonderful opportunity. Yet mentoring opportunities are often restricted for women (see Hall and Sandler).

We need new ways to view mentoring. Mary Belenky and her colleagues offer one, what they called the "midwife-teacher," an individual who utilizes connected teaching and believes in and cooperates with students: "Mid-wife-teachers focus not on their own knowledge (as the lecturer does) but on the students' knowledge. They contribute when needed, but it is always clear that the baby is not theirs but the students'" (218).

Dixie Goswami describes an analogous mentoring model. Goswami and Maureen Butler, who had studied under Janet Emig, develop their view in the course of an interview with Emig. When Emig explains that: "Teaching writing is more like what is classically the maternal role than the paternal role and that is to make certain that something grows. And you do that any way you can . . .," Goswami immediately points out that Emig, herself, practices this valuable form of feminist mentoring. Goswami claims that Emig works: "First, as collaborator with a student, next as reformulator for a student, and finally as audience, as a very particular kind of audience and that is a progressive role" (Emig "Non-Magical" 132). A non-hierarchical mentoring model makes sense, for by becoming a first collaborator, first reformulator, and first audience for a wealth of young academics, we might just reduce our collective "academentia."

The benefits of such mentoring is explained by Daniel Lindley in an essay titled "The Source of Good Teaching." From a background of Jungian psychology, Lindley claims that the successful teacher taps the "student" in herself and the "teacher" in her student to transfer authority from teacher to student by the end of a semester: "But at some point, or rather at various points during the school year, if things have gone well, a final stage occurs: the student finds that her inner teacher is all she needs. She can do the work on her own" (164). In essence, the successful teacher enables students to become successful self-learners, just as the successful feminist mentor would enable the graduate student, male or female, in literature, composition, or creative writing, to become a successful academic: one who has critical consciousness and expects to perform in a neighborly fashion; one who has achieved a measure of holism, being able to utilize both male and female behaviors; one who explores ideologies and can explicate and critique her or his beliefs. Being a positive mentor to as many students as possible is not an impossible task *if* we redefine our concept of mentoring as does Nell Noddings: "I do not need to establish a lasting, time consuming personal relationship with every student. What I must do is to be totally and nonselectively present to the student—to each student—as he addresses me. The time interval may be brief but the encounter is total" (qtd. in Belenky et al. 225).

***

Encouraging believing behaviors in and out of the seminar room can promote neighborliness within our departments, helping us to make sure something grows. Peter Elbow encourages us to develop both doubting and believing capabilities. Elbow views methodological doubting and believing as essential learning activities. He claims that we more often doubt than believe, needing only one disconfirmation to abandon an assertion. Proof of the nonexistence of a disconfirming instance, however, is very difficult (if not impossible to provide). He claims that doubt too often caters to "our natural impulse to protect and retain the views we already hold" (263). Elbow calls for balance and integration, doubting and believing both being necessary to broaden our intellectual repertoire.

By valuing believing behaviors and also by realizing their connection to praxis, we may attempt such integration. Schultz, Laine, and Savage discuss praxis, based on the work of Richard Berenstein: "*Praxis*, or critical practice, therefore, is neither the highly theoretical knowledge of the advanced scholar nor the technician-like knowledge of those asked only to carry out ideas, but practical activity which continuously involves judgement and reflection" (150).

We practice judgement and reflection in our classrooms and seminar rooms as we develop what Stephen North has called (not always flatteringly), teachers' lore. We can share lore, based on judgement and reflection, using anecdote and narrative if we gather our understandings carefully in diaries and teachers' journals and when we begin to see ourselves as teacher/researcher/ ethnographer naturalists. We reap the productive results of metacognition and are aligned with feminists who advocate praxis as well. Schweikert claims that: "Feminist criticism, we should remember, is a mode of praxis. The point is not merely to interpret literature in various ways; the point is to *change the world*" (39).

***

In this essay, whose interests do I hope to serve?

Again, Adrienne Rich in her writing offers insight: "What interests me in teaching is less the emergence of the occasional genius than the overall finding of language by those who did not have it and by those who have been used and abused to the extent that they lacked it" ("Teaching" 67–68). What interests me in teaching graduate students in English is not finding the original genius but helping to give voice to those who want and need voices. For silencing still occurs. Two simple examples passed into my critical consciousness lately. Reading *The Chronicle of Higher Education*, I learned, with little real surprise, that some academics intend never to change. Regarding the new MLA-sanctioned guidelines to avoid gendered language:

> Edward A. Cowan, an assistant professor of German at the University of Texas at Arlington, tells *The Chronicle* that using "he" is grammatically and stylistically correct because the masculine pronoun is by definition without gender when used as a generic pronoun. He writes that he plans to continue using "normal English," adding, "if that is 'sexist,' then so be it." ("In Box" A13)

And, while reading the *AWP Chronicle*, a newsletter which represents creative writing programs around the country, I listened to poet, Maxine Kumin, and learned:

> Every six months or so another critic of the contemporary culture parachutes among us with the bad news that poetry is dead. Joseph Epstein's Who Killed Cock Robin? essay [titled "Who Killed Poetry?"] employs so much ammunition in the service of cramping us poets even deeper "into the dark corner poetry now inhabits" that I can only throw up my hands and agree with him. Things are indeed bleak, but we women poets can hardly be held accountable. In this didactic and learned essay peppered with the names of the dead great poets. . . . we don't amount to much. Although, to quote Carolyn Kizer (not cited by Epstein), "we are the custodians of the world's best-kept secret:/ Merely the private lives of one-half of humanity," only the sacred deceased triumvirate of Dickinson, Bishop and Moore are mentioned. . . . It would seem that we have blundered into an all-male profession by mistake and may therefore ask to be excused. (Kumin 15)

Whose interests do I serve?

Well, of course, my own, but, also, I try to listen to graduate students. I listened recently to these MFA students, who also teach freshman composition, enrolled in a graduate level, creative writing pedagogy seminar in which I tried to practice what I preach here—critical consciousness, feminist mentoring, neighborliness, and the encouragement of believing behaviors. Certainly, I did not practice all these behaviors successfully, but in response to end-of-semester questions designed to gauge their learning in the seminar, they said:

> I hadn't considered the issue of sexism in the field of teaching creative writing. I had thought about it in terms of literature and the male-dominated canon but not in terms of the workshop.
>
> And I think when I sensed sexist behavior, such as male teachers flirting with female students, I told myself I was misreading the situation. Now I think I am more sensitive to it in the academic community—and more resentful when I see it going on. Across the board, male teachers are still setting the norms without being sensitive to female students.
>
> I guess I have changed in that with what I have learned, I'm a little more critical of how workshops are conducted and how teachers treat students. (Sandy)

> I was continually reminded to think as a young college student, rather than a jaded grad student. I learned to be patient, something, quite frankly, I'm tired

of learning. . . . Other issues [that I learned from] included a heightened sensitivity to gender differences because of some of the readings and the constant
vigilance, benign as it is, of the instructor. (Eric)

To get results from undergraduates the teacher must present a variety of exercises beyond workshopping. Before [this class] I wouldn't really have thought
so. I thought that sitting at the end of the table . . . was the way to go.
(Ripley)

Maybe what it all boils down to for me, is that students get the respect they
deserve in classrooms. I don't think it matters what we're teaching—literature,
composition or creative writing—what we're helping students to achieve is the
ability to empower themselves through language. When we understand this,
the tools—literature, essays or poems or stories or criticism—take on an equal
weight, one is no more primal than the other. What is most important is that
students experience language, discover it and clarify their relationship to it.
(Anne)

The older I get, the more I hate being told what to do (it's especially hard
being a student again since I sometimes feel that my teachers . . . treat me like
a dumb student instead of someone who's been out there for 16 years working
as hard on my professions as they have—and probably learning as much). . . .
I feel like every class I take changes me—hopefully a little for the better. This
one made me feel more like a writer and more like I'm part of a writing community. (Margaret)

Engaging in such "change-oriented" teaching means that we must proceed with care. Both for our students and for our own sakes. If we provide
new models, our students *will* consider them.

***

Maintaining a questioning stance in a seminar means, too, that we question ourselves. Listen to writer and teacher Katherine Haake as she doubts
and believes herself:

For me it is much easier to say what I do wrong: I talk too much, I am not
nurturing enough, I don't make effective enough use of collaboration. As for
what I think I may do right, what I want is not to be the focus of the classroom, and what I do to allow for this shift is not to read my own work, not to
teach drunk, and also to provide a theoretical context by addressing such
issues as how discourse operates to constitute ourselves and the world, and
what happens to writing in the absence of an author. I also make explicit my
own ideological assumptions, including my various stances as a feminist that

extend to embrace those who are marginalized in other ways as well, by race, by class, by belief, by status: blacks, for instance, or students themselves. I work to establish a common critical practice that can empower students by giving them control over their own work. And there is one other thing: I listen very, very closely, for we are all working this language together, clumsily, eagerly. . . . (Haake, Alcosser, and Bishop 2).

And listen to writer and teacher Kevin Davis as he considers his own writing classrooms:

And what I'm suggesting [about good teaching] is asking questions you don't know the answer to, letting students establish meaning, accepting whatever answer they produce as their answer, perhaps seeking a little clarification. . . . You don't have to know any answers to teach; you only have to know the right questions. And you'll know the right questions when you see them. (Davis, letter).

The questions we need to ask may be simple: whose cry do I hear, toward whom do I move, whose interests do I serve? Asking these questions helps us to cure our own clericism. And the mentoring model may be simple: first collaborator, first reformulator, first audience. Yet the results of our activities will be productive and dangerous. Neighborliness is not passive, it is active praxis. Feminist mentoring is not ideologically free; it is self-analytical and self-critical, based on belief, and premised on engaging ourselves to ask the right questions. The rules and regulations manual does and should change. Our constant endeavor is to help translate it into the language of these graduate students and then to be, in turn, translated by them into the best academics we can be.

Notes

1.   I contrast Flynn's assertions that gatekeeping does exist—she felt she had to modify her essay to pass the scrutiny of gatekeepers who did not value feminist claims—to Robert Connor's assertions that composition publishing is not based on "race, professional status, gender, religion, clothes style, sexual orientation, or brand of underwear" ("CCCC Voices" 213)—not to beatify or vilify either writer, simply to show that gender *has* influenced the perceptions of these two, equally prominent members of the composition community. In fact, as did other readers, I appreciate Connors's openness in insisting on identifying himself to the graduate students who wrote the "CCCC Voices" article.

Nevertheless, when James Raymond, *College English* editor, reviewed submission and publication patterns during 1985–1986 and compared them with earlier years' figures, his data shows that gender and professional status *do* influence editorial reality, at least in that prominent composition forum (556).

2. The metaphors we use in these "mandarin wars" (Hairston) are of great interest. Hugh Munby, in research on teachers' metaphors, found that they did use metaphors consistently and that "it is reasonable to believe that the metaphors used reflect something of how the speaker sees or constructs professional reality. If the metaphors are used persistently, then the case for their representing a construction of reality becomes more compelling . . ." (380).

    Women tend to resist war imagery. Maxine Kumin offers "my weapon is the manure fork, not the gun" (15) [Kumin lives on a farm]. War imagery is used by those fighting for primacy for creative writing studies (Bishop "Teaching Undergraduate Creative Writing"). Janet Emig uses householders' images: "By my own metaphor, in the house of English studies, literary study is in the parlor; writing, in the kitchen ("Literacy" 174) [and feminism. . . .?]. Casting issues in new metaphors may help us resist a war we don't want to fight and may help us to imagine new attitudes by accessing "underlying postures" toward English studies and by assuring that our "teacher talk" reflects and predicts a tenable reality.

3. See Donald Stewart for a story of curriculum change and resistance in which a department chair dismantles a threateningly successful rhetoric program within his English department.

4. See Donald Stewart for a suggestion that the same type of rethinking is needed in the undergraduate English major.

5. A fuller list of useful texts would include: *Tradition and Reform in the Teaching of English* (Applebee); *Women's Ways of Knowing* (Belenky and others); *Writing Instruction in Nineteenth-Century American Colleges* and *Rhetoric and Reality* (Berlin); *The Rhetorical Tradition* (Bizzell and Herzberg); *Teaching Writing* (Caywood and Overing); *Language, Gender, and Professional Writing* (Frank and Treichler); *Literary Theory* (Eagleton); *Singular Texts/Plural Authors* (Ede and Lunsford); *In a Different Voice* (Gilligan); *Writing Groups* ;(Gere); *Ideology, Culture and the Process of Schooling* (Giroux); *Professing Literature* (Graff); *Rhetorical Traditions and the Teaching of Writing* (Knoblauch and Brannon); *Invention as a Social Act* (LeFevre); *The Future of Doctoral Studies in English* (Lunsford, Moglen, and Slevin); *New French Feminisms* (Marks and Courtivron); *Sexual/Textual Politics* (Moi); *Creative Writing in America* (Moxley); *The Making of Knowledge in Composition* (North); *English in America* and *Politics of Letters* (Ohmann); *The New Feminist Criticism* (Showalter); *Textual Power*

(Scholes); *Man Made Language* (Spender); and *The Iowa Writers' Workshop* (Wilbers).

6.   Although these are not their actual names, I appreciate the way these graduate students always offered useful insights into their learning.

My thanks to Kevin Davis and Katharine Haake, peers whose thinking always helps me to think, and more recently to Bonnie Braendlin for careful and supportive reading. For Don McAndrew—a mentor in all the best ways.

10

Writing Is/And Therapy?
Raising Questions about Writing Classrooms and Writing Program Administration

IN MY YEARS AS A STUDENT AND TEACHER OF WRITING, I'VE OFTEN WISHED that I had been given more encouragement for investigating the personal, therapeutic, and affective aspects of our field. Daily, I find I need to know more about the least talked about and least researched areas of writing—how writing includes and celebrates the personal and how authoring, writing instruction, and program administration are thoroughly connected to our personalities. Possibly, we have not investigated these areas because we are unfamiliar with psychological theory and practice and remain uncertain about the legitimacy of translating those theories and practices to our own classrooms. However, I believe the unfamiliar only becomes familiar and more comfortable through discussions like the one I will share in this essay.

Comparisons of writing instruction to therapy often focus on the teacher and student interaction, but the analogy is necessarily more extended and complicated. In composition studies, we should be paying attention to issues of affect and providing teachers and program administrators with a course of study that includes introductions to personality theory, gender studies, psychoanalytic concepts, and basic counseling, even if such study mainly confirms that there are large differences between a teacher/administrator's and therapist's roles. "Perhaps it might be helpful to remind ourselves," says Ann Murphy, "that the analogy between the two professions is not symmetrical: analysis, as Shoshana Felman discusses, may be a 'pedagogical experience' [27], but teaching is not a purely psychoanalytic one" (179). Still, I would add that it may be crucial for teachers and writing program administrators to understand the degree to which both activities *are* pedagogical.

To help me define terms for this essay, friends knowledgeable about counseling offered this clarification:

> Therapy . . . is a change-process that takes place with another person (in our culture, a person who has undergone rigorous training, controlled and prescribed for the specific fields within the profession). Processes can be therapeutic; they can make you feel healthy and facilitate change, but the processes themselves are not "therapy." Thus, "therapeutic process" seems to be the more appropriate term for what happens in writing or in a writing class. (Reid and Lord)

My intention then is to hold a discussion based on this suggestion: we need to understand the degree to which writing may be a therapeutic process and the degree to which teachers and administrators can or should undertake counseling roles. By doing this, I hope to indicate where future research and discussions might take us.

Authors: What If Writing Is a Therapeutic Process?

Creative writers have long offered tantalizing hints concerning the therapeutic aspects of writing. For instance, Willa Cather acknowledges the power of early life experiences: "Most of the basic material a writer works with is acquired before the age of fifteen" and Milan Kundera sees the self as subject: "But isn't it true that an author can write only about himself?" (Murray *Shoptalk* 16–19).

And I can attest to the connections from personal experience. As a writer in the literary marketplace from the 1970s through the 1990s, I've learned that I write because I want to *and* need to; I try to publish because I've found pleasure and reward in sharing my private explorations publicly. In talking to a writing student recently, I found myself explaining that I didn't keep a journal even though I advocated journal-keeping. Instead, I write and publish poems and essays. The poems, in particular, I said, have two faces for me—the public face, a text I am willing to send out into the interpretive arena—and the inner diary. When I reread my own poems I remember the reason I wrote, the way I felt writing, the personal story behind the public story, and only then do I stop to (re)examine my craft. And of course the memory of the impulse of writing may be embedded for any author in any text, no matter the genre. Equally, composition students often tell us of the many ways they "use" writing for personal knowledge, savoring their texts and sharing them with friends, lovers, and families.

Why then, are many writing teachers (some are published authors, of course, and some are not) quick to deny the personal, therapeutic aspects of such work? For instance, I have heard teachers begin writing workshops by demanding that participants focus exclusively on the text, never on the author; workshop participants are reminded that their "constructed" texts allow them to share a (seemingly) safely distanced and artfully transformed personal experience; that is, writers may be encouraged to "draw from life" but are discouraged from discussing what it means to be living that life. Of necessity, tensions arise when writers create texts which closely explore aspects of their individual lives, and teachers (for reasons that will be examined below) choose to distance class discussions from those same lives-in-the-texts.

To resolve these tensions in some workshops, writing teachers are more likely to emphasize craft than to encourage discovery through writing: "The conference isn't a psychiatric session. Think of the writer as an apprentice at the workbench with the master workman (Murray *Writer* 154 qtd. in Tobin 341). And teachers do this despite their familiarity with authors' claims that writing is intensively a matter of self-exploration. As an example, Donald Murray who offers the apprentice, craft, master workman analogy above, has also gathered a contradictory bouquet of quotes from writers regarding self-expression. These quotes include the observations by Willa Cather and Milan Kundera, that I have shared, as well as the even more fervent attestations to the interrelatedness of writer and writing that follow:

> It seems to me that writing is a marvelous way of making sense of one's life, both for the writer and for the reader. —John Cheever

> Writing is a form of therapy; sometimes I wonder how all those who do not write, compose or paint can manage to escape the madness, the melancholia, the panic fear which is inherent in the human situation. —Graham Greene

> I wrote because it relieved me. —Jean Rhys

> (Murray *Shoptalk* 5,9)

Overall, I sense a profession-wide uneasiness regarding the connection of self to writing and from this uneasiness springs a substitution of attention: even our process workshops are under the sway of craft-based pedagogy and generally insist on the author-is-always-distinct-from-the-text ground rules from the first class onward. It is striking then to see a writer like Murray who inhabits both worlds—professional author and writing teacher—evolve in his thinking concerning the degree of connection between writing and writer. What he wasn't able to sanction earlier in his career, he emphasizes in a recently published essay "All Writing Is Autobiography." If all writing is autobiography, a life in writing must of necessity consider writing as a process of self-discovery and the writing classroom as a site of such exploration.

Professional authors, it seems, have strong intuitions about the degree to which their writing represents a therapeutic process of self-discovery, a curative journey with sometimes dazzling outcomes that can be shared with an interested readership. Writing teachers, though, have encountered the less curative aspects of this discovery process in student writings that are not controlled, in life stories that are not sublimated to purposes of "artful" re-envisioning, in classroom essays which seem indecorous or uncontrolled, in student conferences filled with emotional reactions, rebellion, personal admissions, tears. This set of experiences—students more powerful than expected and, perhaps, removing defenses before they have developed new, equally necessary defenses (for instance, the agreement that what they say on paper is not synonymous with fact, feeling, and life)—has perhaps led writing teachers to embrace a craft-based approach to writing instruction as a way to downplay the affective states students as writers negotiate when they begin to explore and express selves.

Also, in my experience professional authors who are teachers may become quite taken with their role of writer/artist, able to transform life experiences for others. Obviously, such a role is more valuable if few are able to undertake it. Think of the "apprenticeship" metaphor—it takes endless years to become a great poet or novelist—and the literary writing life necessitates initiation penalties, embodied in author myths: writers are wild, drunk, liable to depression and suicide; after much trauma, writers experience transfiguring and transformative emotional states; writers "feel" more and are "at risk" and therefore their life-style is not for everyone.

Long inculcated romantic beliefs about author/artists may lead teachers of writing astray. To solidify their own professional standing, creative writing teachers often fuel the art writing image. In doing this, they may fail to acknowledge writing more generally as a personally empowering, often curative, and necessary way to develop a literate self-in-society. Such a failure may disempower the majority of our students, those who don't plan to apprentice and don't view themselves as inspired and/or talented and because of such deficit views also don't view their writing (sometimes even themselves) as valuable. However, when writing is demystified—understood as a useful, personal, and productive activity, perhaps even as part of a therapeutic process of coming of age—then the activity of writing and teaching writing becomes radically more democratic. We all have life histories that are in need of and available for exploration.

To see writing as a democratic practice is to challenge traditional beliefs about the value of genres of writing and challenges writing teachers to change pedagogy. As in any "relationship," change threatens a working status quo and induces resistance. Therefore, strong curricular and aesthetic borders have been set up between creative writing and composition in most English departments, although borders are breaking down to the degree that certain teachers have come to know themselves as teachers of writing in general before they develop their abilities as teachers of "types" of writing in particular. At the same time, first-year writing teachers, who may or may not consider themselves professional authors or "creative" writers, are also hesitant to explore the strong personal relationships and undercurrents that develop in the workshop, due to the very power of writing to become for some students, at some junctures, a therapeutic process. As I pointed out earlier, first-year writing teachers have not been trained or encouraged to view writing in this manner. Instead, more simply, more safely, but equally problematic, many first-year writing programs have internalized a university perception that our job is primarily one of socialization, thereby constructing composition as a service course without content. If we believe this, we may too easily look to the student in the university before we look to the person that is the student.

Currently, some theorists and researchers are calling for an examination of the connections between the often separated areas of creative writing and composition instruction (Bishop; Moxley) as well as exploration of the interrelatedness of feelings and writing (McLeod; Brand *Therapy;* Pennebaker). Alice Brand has suggested that we need "hot cognition," that is research agendas that include attention to emotions. She outlines some of the work that is being undertaken:

We know that affective traits and personality overlap conceptually and empirically (Plutchik and Kellerman). We are just now recognizing that personality may govern discursive style (Jensen and DiTiberio; Selzer), just as discursive style has an impact on personality (Brand, *Therapy;* Denman). In fact, how personality influences the way writers function is the direction I think composition research is ultimately headed. (Brand "The Why" 441)

Robert Brooke through his research asserts that the study of writing is really the study of writers and of their developing writing identities: "The entire 'process, not product' revolution can be seen as a change of focus from results to behaviors, from texts to people—in its best forms, the goal is to teach people to be writers, not to produce good texts in the course of a semester" ("Modeling" 38). And this assumption—that we are teaching people to be writers, not simply to produce texts—has great import for the role of the writing teacher who is herself always in the process of developing her teaching identity. This is particularly true if she is new to the field and being trained to investigate her own writing. The basic tenet of the National Writing Projects—that writing teachers should be writers—is notably similar to that of Freud who required would-be analysts to undergo analysis (McGee 667). Process instruction and response pedagogies necessitate change, so the move to process requires that we give greater attention to the people undergoing, and resisting, those changes: writers and writing teachers.

Are Teachers Writing Therapists?

In a number of recent articles in the major composition journals, teachers have begun to explore writing teachers' relationships to their students, using personal experience and relying, often, on both clinical and therapeutic analogies. Diane Morrow, a doctor turned writing tutor and instructor, suggests that as a field we reject even metaphorical connections between writing and the health professions because they present a negative view of the teaching relationship, as that of an authoritative physician attending to a "sick" writer. However, Morrow claims the physician/patient relationship in medicine is changing, and that the metaphor may now be more relevant than before (218–219).

Gregory Ulmer uses the analogy quite comfortably, perhaps because he sees the "patient's" submission to therapy as elective:

> The patient agrees to put herself in the care of the analyst, but then she may resist all attempts of the analyst to cure her.
>
> Similarly, our students sign up for our classes with the intention of being educated, but then not infrequently they refuse to cooperate with the process . . .

because people tend to accept only that which corresponds to the opinions they already hold. (762–763).

In noting that resistance is one of the natural responses to submission, even when undertaken by the learner for the learner's own good, Ulmer suggests that the student's job is to become more open to change.

Lad Tobin supports Diane Morrow's claims that it may be time to explore the connections between health professions and the profession of writing instruction when he notes that a number of writing theorists bring up the connection between writing and therapy and then repudiate that connection as being no more than metaphorical. This is not surprising, for considering the teaching relationship in a therapeutic light raises questions about transference (students becoming deeply interested in the teacher's self) and counter-transference (teachers becoming deeply interested in the student's self) in the Freudian sense. Transference may involve teachers and students in emotional relationships with ethical dimensions (Torgersen), and transference and counter-transference may both have to be dealt with for a therapy or a pedagogy to succeed. If we don't label what happens as transference—a term some counselors prefer be reserved exclusively for professionally mediated interactions—teachers will certainly still note strong role identification among students, identifications that may be complicated by teachers' and students' gender, race and class.

Metaphors may signify real conditions or alert us to important new ways of conceptualizing a subject. Certainly when looking at writing and therapy more than just metaphor-making is at stake. For instance, as concerned writing teachers, we acknowledge our relationship to students through liberatory pedagogies, student-centered classrooms, personal discovery essay assignments and so on. At the same time, we sometimes finesse responsibility for students' actual responses and feelings. Or, if we acknowledge responsibility, we're still unsure of the degrees and limits of such responsibility. How do we respond to journal or essay discussions of suicide, incest, anorexia, and depression, the underside of the often-elicited writing about high school triumphs, personal bests, or greatest moments?

At this time, it is not clear if expressivist pedagogies (author-centered curriculums first popularized by scholar/teachers like Peter Elbow and Ken Macrorie) necessarily result in more personal issues being raised in the classroom. Expressivist pedagogies are often contrasted with social-constructivist pedagogies (often academic discourse oriented curriculums attributed to a widely varied set of composition scholars like David

Bartholomae and Patricia Bizzell) (see Faigley). For instance, in an expressivist classroom, students might certainly be encouraged to construct personal, often autobiographical essays, potentially leading to revelations that might prove curative and/or disturbing. At the same time, social-constructivist classrooms may ask students to consider political, social, or ethical topics (date rape, discrimination, gender bias in the workplace) which may in turn elicit curative and/or disturbing narratives, discussions, or memories for students who have been raped, discriminated against or experienced gender bias.

Overall, it is not surprising that students open up in writing classes since workshops usually enroll twenty to thirty students and aim to develop community feelings. This is a welcome contrast to the many impersonal, large-enrollment classes a student may experience in the modern university. In fact, university officials may understand that writing classrooms offer writing instruction but fail to understand the degree to which these classrooms often act as "home rooms" for a freshman class in transition. However, when community engenders connectedness and feelings, interpersonal relationships are at the center: "we cannot create intensity and deny tension, celebrate the personal and deny the significance of the personalities involved" (Tobin "Reading" 342).

Lad Tobin raises some of the issues I've been grappling with for several years, openly acknowledging teaching beliefs which I know have not generally been sanctioned:

> In my writing courses, I *want* to meddle with my students' emotional lives, and I want their writing to meddle with *mine*. Transference and counter-transference emotions are threatening because they are so powerful, but they are most destructive and inhibiting in the writing class when we fail to acknowledge and deal with them (342).

Unlike Tobin, I'm not sure that I've intended to meddle, but I have no doubt that I have. Whether they understand transference or counter-transference, experience identification or alienation, students see any sort of teacher intervention as authoritative, and they always expect to learn from their teachers. Robert Brooke by way of the writings of Jacques Lacan describes the teacher as the Subject Supposed to Know. "The mentor, the priest, the therapist, the lover, the guru, the martial arts master . . . helps us 'find ourselves,' helps us 'unlock our true feelings,' helps us know ourselves as we can't on our own" (682). We may be uncomfortable acknowledging that we are about to take such a momentous role in our students' lives because "unlocking" involves us in both transference and worries about counter-transference. However, the Lacanian version of transference is posited on the notion of the student forging an under-standing of separated parts of herself; the "other" is not necessarily the teacher but a part of herself that she needs to and can come to know.[1] It is worth noting that studies of the academy indicate that women may have particular problems forging identities in the postsecondary academic set-ting (Aisenberg and Herrington).

Teachers do affect students in a variety of complicated ways. Lad Tobin suggests that unknowingly we may "read" students and our instruction in ways that help us see our classrooms in the best possible light.[2] Additionally, he found himself "reading" classroom situations according to his personal scripts, for instance, not getting along with students who were unintentionally re-creating problematic scenarios from Tobin's own high school learning past. Tobin believes that being aware of the similari-ties between writing and therapy keeps him from preferring the student who makes him feel secure or avoiding the student who threatens him. He says: "And that is what I need to monitor: as soon as I find myself giving up on a student or, on the other hand, feeling tremendous personal pride in a student's work, I need to question my own motives. I need to discover in what ways my biases and assumptions—both conscious and uncon-scious—are shaping my teaching" (347).

The type of powerful "misreadings" that can take place between stu-dents and teachers is highlighted in Richard Murphy's article "Anorexia: The Cheating Disorder." Murphy describes how he misunderstood, mis-read, and intimidated a student who didn't want to claim the portrayal she had written for him concerning her experiences as an anorectic. For this student, writing involved her in a classroom transaction that elicited emo-tional reactions to her teacher and his instruction *even if he didn't know it.*. The anorectic student was in the position described by Ann Murphy:

> In encouraging our students to unlock and express their ideas, feelings, and beliefs more effectively, we are, like psychoanalysts, insisting that they confront lost or denied elements of themselves—itself a project filled with social, familial, and per-sonal dangers—and then that they express those elements in written, often alien discourse, the very use of which arouses a whole new host of terrors. (175)

However unwittingly, Richard Murphy's pedagogy elicited a confronta-tion between the student and her past which the teacher then did not believe.

Response pedagogies inevitably elicit powerful responses from our students. Ann Murphy suggests that we should be wary of creating this classroom; Lad Tobin claims he has come to seek this classroom; Richard Murphy illustrates how he could not avoid this classroom; and Robert Brooke suggests that our field's movement to process pedagogy has made this classroom inevitable. And for all we know at this time, social-constructivist classrooms may appear not to but may equally often do the same. Clearly, things are getting complicated these days in the profession of writing instruction.

Personally, I agree with Robert Brooke's suggestion that such classrooms are inevitable, particularly given a response pedagogy. Ann Murphy has noticed this is especially true for basic writers; she feels that:

> [J]ust as an analysand returns to and repeats ancient family traumas with her analyst, so too, I suggest, the writing student returns to and re-enacts an ancient drama of initial wonder at the brave new world of language and ideas and then subsequent, painful humiliation and defeat by teachers, institutions, and cultural/political forces. . . . (184)

I would enlarge her assertions by suggesting that such a movement may occur for any writer who enters the always dramatic acculturation process of writing within institutional settings. Writing classrooms are complex arenas: "students and their writing contribute to the linguistic, psychological, and social richness of the classroom, creating what Charles Schuster, describing Bakhtin's view of language, calls 'a rich stew of implications, saturated with other accents, tones, idioms, meanings, voices, influences, intentions' (597)" (Ritchie 159).

Part of this "rich stew" is the teacher. Writing teachers may co-author their students' essays as they assign and shape a text (through conference and draft review)—and then subsequently "create" a student over the course of the semester. For instance, Lad Tobin found himself reading a student's text: "in such a way that it reached a self-confident and successful resolution, by making *her* into a text with a happy ending" (335). The problem, he feels, is not that we do this rather that we deny that we do this. We need to examine teaching as a constitutive process, consider more deeply the idea of the teacher as the Subject Supposed to Know, and continue to explore the many complicated issues of gender, transference, and counter-transference in the writing classroom; if we don't, we will fail to act on available developments in reading and writing theory and research in our own field.

To start, we need to acknowledge these issues and investigate what we might learn from analogous psychoanalytic discussions; this is not necessarily a comfortable suggestion. Like "hot" cognitions, emotions are "hot" topics for us all and ones we tend to avoid. I believe, however, that issues of emotions and teachers' actions are becoming more important since they deal with the "why" of the workshop. Why did this class work? Why did this student stop trying? Why is teaching writing so difficult and so rewarding? And, finally, if emotions, therapeutic relationships, and hot cognition are important for teachers, they must also signify for writing program administrators.

WPAs As ?

Trudelle Thomas suggests that graduate students as apprentice Writing Program Administrators should be given training in five areas; they should apprentice through a practicum, should acquire a broad picture of the world of a WPA by serving on department and university committees, should teach a variety of composition courses, should be involved in teacher training, and should learn about testing and assessment.

This will be useful, but will it be enough? How, I wonder, will the WPA learn to counsel a teacher who comes to her to discuss a student who is experiencing ongoing sexual abuse from a father who is "putting her through school"? How will the WPA deal with the teacher who is concerned over a student's response to an autobiographical collage assignment that opens with a quote from the student's two-year-old journal entry—"Dear Diary, Die, die die! Death looks good compared to my life"—and is followed by a new freewrite titled "My Unorthodox Funeral." "My Unorthodox Funeral" is an account of the writer's imagined burial at sea: "Though she felt desperately depressed, my mother took control of her reactions and seated herself Indian-style with the urn between her legs. Feeling comforted, my mother began to recite my favorite poem."

What should a teacher and the WPA think, feel, and do when the student, as this one did, does not return again to class? Equally, how should the WPA react when a TA calls on the weekend to read a student essay in which two students describe how they plan to kill a third student that weekend. The story ends: "Tonight, Janet and I will fix everything with him, permanently."

Inevitably, a Writing Program Administrator will need to counsel teachers about highly charged problems, problems that can not be labeled exclusively "academic." Students *and teachers* resist their instruction, the program, and the institution, and the WPA is someone who is in a position of power and authority within the English department and the university; no matter how well-intentioned or how sensitive and right-minded, she helps to maintain those structures (Chase; Daniell and Young; Strickland).

Ann Murphy reminds us that Freud linked three powers—that of teaching, psychoanalysis and government. Students trust writing teachers with their thinking and their feelings because our classes are "friendly, intimate, and safe" (183). Teachers are asked during training to trust their WPA who helps them institute the response pedagogies which create intimate classrooms. Yet I've heard myself and other teacher educators say more than once: "You're not a trained counselor. The best you can do is get students to the counseling center quickly." And while that is a fact I believe in and a strategy I support, I know that strategy is longer adequate.

Such a response didn't help me early in my teaching career to deal with my guilt over a "problem" student who committed suicide the semester after he was in my class. It didn't help me to counsel an able new teacher who experienced "teaching anxiety" to the point that she resigned her TAship. It didn't help me endure the long weekend when I was "pretty sure" the student paper about killing another student was a satire, although the student's experienced TA was alarmed because the paper was so different from the assigned topic as to seem believable; that teacher and I both worried until a student's Monday conference confirmed that the paper had been a "joke."

When my current administrative office was turned over to me with its student-journal suicide file and the out-going director's listing of hot-lines and crisis support numbers, I felt then—as I feel today—that saying what we're *not* (*not* therapists, *not* counselors, *not* specialists in affect or dysfunction) is not helping us to understand and prepare to be what we are. I believe the WPA explores and participates in forms of "the talking cure" on multiple levels and from multiple perspectives. Perhaps it is time to enlarge WPA training by providing new teachers and administrators with an introduction to psychoanalytic theory and the basics of counseling to support them in their necessary work.

My own effort to become more educated in this area developed into a two-year process that has no clear end in sight. In the course of drafting this essay, I have contacted and talked at length with student health services counselors on my campus. They have provided me with a copy of their booklet (see Student), designed to help teachers detect, respond to, and support students who are undergoing stress. On our campus, teachers are encouraged to refer students to free campus counseling services but also to stay in contact with students, checking in on their progress, remaining available for informal talks. I shared copies of the booklet with my teaching staff and use the booklet as a teaching aid in my teacher education class.

In addition, I have regularized my department files, beyond simply asking GTAs to provide me with writing samples from students who are undergoing stress. Currently, I also ask the teacher to provide me with as much classroom context as possible. I plan to draw from some of these files to create anonymous "cases" of classroom/student problems to share with new teachers of writing (see also, Anson et al.). Next, I am exploring the legal implications of this active way of looking at student and teacher classroom relationships. There are many moments when my natural desire to counsel and help students puts me (or the teachers I direct) into situations where I may be violating students' rights, however well-intentioned my motive. I have sought counsel when I felt the need to contact a student's resident advisor and alert her to a student's emotional state. This student was talking in her journal (which her teacher shared with me) about having no friends and feeling suicidal. I could not leave my office that day, feeling that no one had been alerted to the student's situation, knowing that no one in her dormitory was actively seeking her out and offering her support. Yet I knew that my desire to support this student was potentially in conflict with her right to privacy, since my knowledge of her situation came from a private journal entry. In this instance, I sought the advice of a counseling center doctor who said to me: "You'd rather be sued for having intervened than for having not intervened, wouldn't you?" I called the resident advisor and wasn't sued—that semester. The counselor's advice was sobering though. Clearly, writing program administrators are themselves in need of legal counsel.

On my agenda, then, is an appointment with the university's lawyer to investigate the laws regarding students' rights to privacy, programs' legal responsibilities to students and parents, and so on. When we meet, I'm certain I will find a second use for the student "cases" I have been collecting, since I can share several with a lawyer and receive information that will help me make the most responsible decision when similar cases arise in the future. No doubt, legal advice will vary from institution to institution, and all writing program administrators will want to understand their own situation in order to better counsel their own teaching staff.

I have taken two other self-education steps. I continue to review data-bases to find other discussions of these issues, in order to find work like Mary Vroman Battle's essay in *Teaching English in the Two Year College*, "Suicide: Students at Risk," which offers a useful discussion, set of recom-mendations, and bibliography of books for further reading. And I have started a further course of self-education by way of reading introductory counseling books; I may continue this education by contacting colleagues in other departments and perhaps even enrolling in some of their classes.

When I read books like Kennedy and Charles's *On Becoming A Counselor*, or Moursund's *The Process of Counseling and Therapy* taken from my university library shelves, I don't feel like rushing out and prac-ticing without a license. I know that I need someone with more experi-ence to help me pick the best books and to curb what might be an overly facile application of what I am learning. But I do believe that I need to make a start. The analogies between writing instruction and therapy have something to offer me and something I need to offer to the teachers I train. Particularly, program administrators may begin by reading, but we all need also to investigate other avenues of support, contacting the cam-pus counseling center and the psychology department. Even more, though, we need to find colleagues who are open to these discussions and willing to share what they have observed, suspected, and learned in similar situations. We need to talk, share conference papers, and write journal articles. We need to include these topics and this training in graduate cur-riculums because we need to listen to and respect the affective needs of our writing students and our selves.

Notes

1. McGee and Brooke are discussing a theory of transference derived from the writings of Jacques Lacan rather than those of Sigmund Freud; the special issues (October and November 1987) of *College English* in which their arti-cles and Gregory Ulmer's article appear provide a good introduction to Lacan in relation to pedagogy.

2. Glynda Hull and Mike Rose on the other hand warn us that if we don't "read" students well, we miss the clues to student understanding which are embedded in students' personal histories.

11

You Can Take the Girl Out of the Writing Center, But You Can't Take the Writing Center Out of the Girl
Reflections on the Sites We Call Centers

site • the place where something is, was, or is to be.
Webster's New World Dictionary

Each night I am reluctant to close up because there may be some one who needs the cafe.
Ernest Hemingway, "A Clean, Well-Lighted Place"

IN THIS ESSAY, I CONSIDER WRITING CENTERS AS LOCATIONS WE CONSTRUCT in our minds and hearts as well as within our institutions—that is, as emotional/intellectual sites and as physical sites. In October 1995, I spoke at the National Peer Tutoring Conference at Ball State University in Muncie, Indiana. In a conversation there with Mickey Harris, my co-keynoter (and first publisher of some of my writings about centers in *The Writing Lab Newsletter*), she asked me if it didn't feel odd to be at a tutoring conference since I was no longer the director of a writing center. I was a little taken aback by her question and its implications until I realized she had put her finger on a slight uneasiness I had experienced myself when invited to attend. Who was I to talk about centers and tutoring when I wasn't any longer, day by day, entering one, facing the challenges and frustrations that center life can offer?

Was I like the writing teacher who didn't write? The administrator who taught teachers to teach first-year writing but herself rarely entered the first-year writing classroom? I worried about this in a flash but my face-saving verbal response was instantaneous: "I like writing centers" I explained, "They're some of my favorite places," as if that were reason enough to be there, as fan, as advocate, as appreciator. I think there are many satisfactions connected with centers. And I think those pleasures are not solely derived from the pleasure of being the renegade, outsider, dweller-in-borderland-spaces (though many of us are drawn to the radical potential of centers). Centers, in my experience, are often sites of exhilarating educational experience. So my response to Mickey was more than disingenuous; it was heartfelt. And I am a thoroughgoing fan, for I started, ran, and reluctantly left a writing center at the University of Alaska, Fairbanks, in the 1980s. I've been writing and reviewing for center journals and newsletters and following professional debates and issues since 1986. And for the last several summers, I've taught a course designed to prepare new teachers to tutor in our center. I've left a directorship, but I've never really left the milieu of centers or concerns about cooperative and collaborative learning, tutoring and co-authoring.

Reconsidering this involvement reminds me that centers have come of age. Our journals have urged and supported and detailed our growth. But lately I've been thinking about the emphasis on *how* and the absence of *what* in such writings, on a lack of thick descriptions of writing center life, of how seldom we publish stories similar to those we tell when we meet together at conferences. For example, consider the complete absence of poems and fictions about writing centers that might illuminate what we do. These omissions lead me to look at metaphors instead of history and professionalism and to challenge myself to write a writing center poem soon (though I'd be even more interested in reading students' poems about centers, hearing the stories they tell about their tutorials, the metaphors they use to describe their experiences).

To return to my narrative thread: I spent most of the two days of the Peer Tutoring Conference at Ball State hanging out in the center coordinated by Cindy Johanek, enjoying the tutors' engaged talking about their presentations and tutoring concerns, watching the occasional writer come in and receive tutoring even though the center was officially closed for the conference, tutoring a tutor who shared several poems with me, asking for response. I saw that center—as I see all centers—as a haven from the artificially controlled classrooms or class-break stairway thunder of students and teachers all trying to get somewhere fast. I see centers as stopping places, as clean, well-lighted spaces.

You may remember the Hemingway story that I quoted from as I opened: a young waiter, eager to get home to his wife hurries an older hard-drinking customer out into the night while the older waiter chides him for being in such a hurry to close, arguing that some of us in the world need cafes. "I am of those who like to stay late at the cafe," Hemingway has the older waiter say, "With all those who do not want to go to bed. With all those who need a light for the night." Hemingway's story is certainly about the ways we approach death, but for me, this phrase has long provided a metaphor for the writing center experience. I'm drawn to the metaphor of the clean well-lighted place and, in fact, we've probably all known or been tutors of the impatient young waiter *and* the patient old waiter variety. Anyway, experiences at the Ball State writing center, talking and drinking over-cooked coffee, were similar to my experiences earlier in the day talking to Joe Trimmer at the local coffee bar in downtown Muncie, discussing writing, watching individuals make notes in their journals as they sipped cappuccino in the corner. In both the cafe and the center, I was relaxed, at ease, with writers as a writer; I was happy. Of course, the more I elaborate, the more clearly you see *my* center metaphors and where holding such metaphors might lead me. Equally, those metaphors may not take me everywhere I need to go, so I think this through further.

Since that October visit, I have been considering the implications of carrying an internal architectural metaphor of writing centers around with me, asking: What does it mean that the center is in me even when I am not in the center?

The center in Alaska was no less crowded, dowdy, or second-hand than many centers around the country but it seemed well-lighted, warm and welcoming, when I entered from those dark Arctic days and heard the steady hum of involved discussion. A positive image like this, it seems to me, enlarges my teaching life the way we claim literature enlarges the life of readers of literature. Simply, if I image the center as a well-lighted cafe or my idea of a Burkean parlor—where conversation takes place and a newcomer enters, listens, joins when ready, as a variety of people come and go, swelling and enlarging the discussion, swirling off into side discussions, joining, parting, rejoining—I'm more liable to support my students who go to the center, to support center initiatives, and maybe most importantly, to spend time there myself. If I find the center lodges within me as a laboratory, a workroom, a (cell)block, clinic, annex or basement, I may be as liable as the next person to pass up spending time there or valuing the work that goes on there. But it's more complicated than "simply imagining"—for what you see isn't necessarily what you get and what you get isn't always what you see. What are the implications of a positive convergence of inner metaphor and actual site?

Cynthia Haynes-Burton says: "Writing centers often seem embroiled in rhetorics of advocacy which fight everything from misperceptions of the center to misappropriations of its function. As such, many writing centers face a common identity problem: that is, students, tutors, teachers, and administrators perceive the writing center in radically different ways" (113). If we're all—as I suspect—attached to slightly different metaphors that represent our center experience, we can't help but perceive the center in radically different ways as we play those metaphors out. It might be useful, then, to do some metaphorical work together, looking at the images we hold, wondering what would happen if those images should converge, examining the results we reap when they do—as they so often do—collide, and offering each other a wealth of metaphors with which to augment our closely held one. That is to say, we need to think in terms of metaphors plural, not metaphors either/or. What occurs, for instance, when a lab metaphor co-occurs with a center vision, as when a student-centered site is used to host institutional placement testing? As when the center is used most often after hours by tutors to do their own schoolwork and administrators to train their staff instead of by writers as a workspace and hangout?

I'm far from the first to consider the metaphors of our discourse—in fact, they arise and swirl around almost every discussion at every conference and appear in most essays in journals in recent years, from James McDonald asking why we don't consider centers "islands" or "gardens," to William McCall suggesting we think of tutors as "consultants" (implying a site that is more a think tank or clinic than Burkean parlor or writing studio), to Linda Shamoon and Deborah Burns suggesting we rethink tutoring on the model of master classes in music which allow for a more directive approach. These metaphors range from landscape to roles to social configurations—all worth exploring—but I want to consider in the most detail metaphors surrounding our actual sites and how those sites become originating schemas upon which we build our future relationships with centers and one-to-one instruction. For I think the work of the center goes out into the world with each (hopefully satisfied) writer and tutor and director, whether they participated for years at that site or only for a short while. And as the dictionary handily tells me, a site is a place of past, present, and future potential, more than the sum of its parts, more than its physical reality, its practices, its theoretical scaffoldings; it is the idea that I carry around with me, imposing my old ideas onto my new situations. As a "reader" of centers, I build future readings from past experiences, present expectations and future desires.

Once I see the degree to which I impose my center's memories, spaces, feelings, attitudes, on every center I visit, including the center at my current institution, Florida State University, I start to wonder what is actually there and what is coming along with me. For instance, I automatically feel good when I enter the FSU Reading/Writing Center though it looks not much like the one I developed at the University of Alaska ten years ago. Intrigued with this whole line of thought, I asked members of my poetry writing group, all GTAs who have tutored in the center, what image/architectural space they evoked in their mind's eye when they thought of "The Writing Center." Their diverging answers surprised me and took me farther down the road of this essay: Devan Cook imagined a coffeehouse but also a forum—as in Roman forum—and, yes, she studied Latin. Asked about the "actual" center, she characterized it as a comfortable friendly room, if a bit bedraggled, a room much improved from the room she entered three years earlier when "The ceiling leaked and there was no privacy for tutorials." Bill Snyder and Jennifer Wheelock, on the other hand said the physical center was unappealing, that they chose not to tutor, that they didn't like the run-down room, the noise of people coming and going, the way people hang around at the front desk, both eager and reluctant to receive help. And, as I returned to this room in my memory, I reimagined it as each of the locations they were describing and realized that Bill and Jennifer did see literally what is there—a large drab room, old chairs, front desk covered with papers, water-stained acoustic tile. What I (and maybe Devan) "saw" were teacher/tutors we've worked with smiling hello or busy in conversation with a writer.

But, unlike Devan, Bill and Jennifer had not had good experiences or long-term contact with the room, had not seen the center develop and grow. I had to admit, this actual site could be an off-putting place. The front desk isn't welcoming; it is more like a ticket-agent's desk at the airport where we process student travelers in and out. Realizing this, I wanted to rush back to campus from the bakery where we were meeting and tell Carrie Leverenz, our director, that she should tear out the front counter, because I wanted the center to work, to evoke the feelings I was so able—perhaps too able—to overlay upon it.

Personally, I look beyond the front desk, block it out really, because I'm a champion of alternative educational spaces. I hate the confines of traditional classrooms that jam too many students into too small a space, making desk moving and writing on chalkboards difficult and funneling all attention to a broken down podium, creating climates that are disrupted by late entering students or those who have to step out a moment to visit a drinking fountain; I'm enamored with learning spaces, like writing centers, that allow for movement. Regularly, I breeze through ours, usually using it as a short-cut to get to the director's office just outside the back door. But I saw, through Bill and Jennifer's eyes, that the center wasn't the friendly, if tacky, "coffeehouse" or "cafe" that Devan saw, or the "clean, well-lighted place" offering freedom and movement and a site for writing that I had brought with me from Alaska. For them, it was a waiting room, a way station, replete with all the anxiety of travel, insecurity about "equipment," as the airlines call their planes, and so on. Perhaps it will remain a place of transience and departure until it is redecorated *and* until their architectural image is reconstructed through their participation in center life. Perhaps they will not feel encouraged to participate until they are motivated to enter by the lure of a truly inviting location. Perhaps, then, it is worth asking: how does site shape sight? And, conversely, how does sight shape site?

If a writing center is a physical location embodying our ideas (theoretical/practical) but also an idealized space—an internalized location that we carry with us and modify—of what use is re-imagining, re-imaging our spaces internally as we often do physically? For example, I've inherited a lot of shabby institutional rooms in my career and my impulse is to tape up posters and batiks, to scrub the desks, dust the chairs, put a good face on the institutional drabness that unwanted locations on overcrowded campuses are always graced with. I believe the impulse is right, just as the impulse to optimize my internal metaphors for writing centers must be useful as long as it doesn't lead to denial.

We know that changing names from writing laboratories to writing centers changed teacher/tutor/client/administrator language of and about centers. The move from laboratory—an experiment in education, a place where processes would be applied over and over again, replicated with slight variation—helped encode our move to process pedagogy. In a center, there was possibility for centering, for composing, for collaborating, for being co-equal tutor and person tutored, writers together, rather than abandoning writers to a deficiency or "subject" role, under the power of the white-coated lab director. But it seems to me that while increasing our discussions about roles—tutor, client, consultant, master teacher—we've slowed the discussions about sites—perhaps because our sites are so often given to us second-hand, maintained less well than we'd wish, always less adequate than they might be to our visions of what centers might be or become. As centers serve large numbers of international students, how should our center be reconceptualized? As centers adopt a social-constructionist or social-expressivist theoretical scaffolding, do we need to remodel our actual site? An expressivist one-to-one tutorial center of cubicles and quiet conference places may give way to a constructionist site of small group tutoring, mini-classrooms without walls.

As I listen to the metaphors of others, I have to ask how does a "clean, well-lighted" writing center suit and augment my writing center pedagogy? And how would my seeing our center through the eyes and metaphors of others help me to change a particular center and to enlarge my ways of thinking about centers in general? For the moment, though, let me ask you to mine your own memory for center images within an architectural dimension: what is your center to you and how does it contribute to your sense of identity and work? Is your center a laboratory, a writing studio, an educational basement or a secret annex? If your center is two or more sites, do they co-occur comfortably or conflict? How does that affect the work of the center?

For me, often, metaphors arise in clusters. And I think of them like lenses of power on a microscope, that we can flip through to try to focus in on an image of what it is we experience in thought or practice. For instance, there are the social, generously populated, and conversational metaphors of a Burkean parlor, or family room, or local cafe. Each has its draw—the elegant conversation of the parlor, the warmth of the family, the urbanity of the cafe. The same cluster has drawbacks—the stiffness of the parlor, the dysfunction of the family, the isolation amid the din of the lone writer scribbling away in a cafe. So too with the industrious and product-oriented image of an educational business (so dear to the heart of legislators today). The laboratory or workroom in the wrong hands can lead to performance-solely-for-profit, assembly lines, can become impersonal places of testing or production. Of course, I color these metaphors from my humanistic biases and some might find them less oppressive by background, inclination, and training, or due to local circumstances (for instance, a center that serves a specialized writing population in a business, medical or engineering school might find different metaphors quite functional).

I try out the set of that lenses can be found in the spatial metaphors I have for a center—basement, ground floor, third floor, or attic in a real and/or an imaginary building of English studies. Location in the center of campus or on the periphery of the university property impacts a center's sense of worth. And yet another set of lenses are those of duration and stability: does the center reside at a busy crossroads? Is it set in the junction of differing paths? Perhaps it is a halfway house, a stop on a developmental underground railway? Or, do I propose the center as a sanctuary, refuge, salon, or settlement—not a place where the lost may be found, but a place where the interested may return and even stay a while.

Let me suggest several ways we can put site-based metaphors to work for us. First, of course, as I've been doing here. *We can continue to try on various metaphors* (for instance, see North "Idea" and "Revisiting"). We may identify a congenial cluster—say, in my case, the cafe—and we can focus the lens, evaluating what happens to our center with each click of increasing or decreasing power. A center as coffeehouse or cafe may be more useful for a multi-cultural, international writing centers while a writing center as family room may quickly become problematic, reflecting dominant values despite my desire to create a renegade space. Equally, as I move from an expressivist pedagogy to a social-expressivist pedagogy, I may find my valorization of the cafe, the writing space, doesn't allow for a more interactive pedagogy where many needs are met in small groups, in tutorials, in skill-specific workshops.

Second, *we can examine metaphors in combinations.* The metaphor of a clean, well-lighted cafe for writing includes several roles for those who come there (just as cafes include diverse clientele). I want my cafe to be a reading room, a warm way station for a deranged street storyteller, and at the same time to allow for energetic discussion between several invested writing "theorists." And of course it should be a place where writers are at work and work is in progress and a place where my poetry workgroup can unobtrusively read drafts in the corner. Maybe then my cafe can co-exist with a writing room and/or studio space metaphor. Conversely, perhaps as a center director with a vision, I'm trying to meet too many constituencies, offering corners of a center to technology and computers, turning over the center to holistic readings of placement exams, canceling tutorials for college achievement test preparation, making workbooks available for grammar review and preparing students for department exit exams, all the while squeezing in tutoring. We need to think about how doing this may produce competing images, roles, internal and external realities, resulting in a net loss: no site, no center, no life.

Third, I might *push my dominant metaphor until it breaks down*— somewhat as I've done in this essay. I have to admit that people have to buy something or pay to sit in the cafe, that my determinedly unworldly well-lighted room does not prepare me to step into the cold and dark out-doors. Perhaps my comforts are more hoped for than extant. Equally, I cannot forget or ignore the political dimensions of my work: theorists within composition do not agree on goals and procedures (as the long-term persistence of discussions pitting personal writing against academic discourse show us) any more than those who run centers agree with those who run universities. Therefore, I will serve myself well in negotiations with others, particularly with administrators, if I can help them see where their metaphors break down. I can explain that the center is not a "busi-ness" or that if it is, the business cannot declare tangible assets at year's end since we know writers' growth usually manifests itself outside our gaze. If my dean is a scientist and wants to know why this lab doesn't work like labs he has known, I'm better off if I know my own history, that writing centers once were language labs but that they grew beyond that model. As early as 1934, for instance: "Adah Grandy relates that the Minnesota lab was housed in the College of Science, Literature, and the Arts and con-sisted of a large well-lit room with writing tables and reference books, as well as a smaller anteroom where student and tutor could conduct individ-ual consultations (Carino 372–3)." In this description of a "lab," I hear the ideal of a language-library substituted for hissing gas jets and high lab tables and the future direction of tutoring spaces seem predicted in that smaller anteroom for consultations. The scientist's and the composition-ist's "lab," I'll need to explain to my Dean, have different requirements, functions, and physical dimensions. In fact, I'll need to explain why exper-iments with chemicals are not the same as experiments with words.

Fourth, I'd like to *capture the metaphors used by writers who come to the center.* What do they say about the "scene" of tutoring? Do they see the shabby walls that Bill and Jennifer saw or the friendly interactions that Devan and I hoped for? Is going to the center like pulling teeth (as some of my writing students readily describe revising) or is it more like practic-ing the piano or perfecting one's dance? Is the center more like a library to them or more like a classroom or like neither of those and like something else entirely? Is the noise of multiple activities in a center comfortably similar to the sounds of composing in a crowded but friendly dorm or is the center too sterile in the way many of their experiences of educational spaces are predicated on sterility. Perhaps, by evoking the sense of the cen-ter they carry, we'll understand and fine-tune our own that much better.

Fifth, I would suggest mining metaphors in several directions, asking *What metaphors does an educational theory suggest?* and *What metaphors do particular practices require or produce?* The banking theory of education as theoretical scaffold will produce far different center architectures than a collaborative theory of learning. And actual practices, as I've pointed out, require adjustments to actual sites—the writing center one-to-one tutorial cannot take place (well) in an overloud, distracting, echoing cafe and a conversation among peers does not fare well in the cramped cubicle of the tutorial or in the (sometimes) less free space of the master-teacher's studio.

I argue that you can't take the center out of the writer/tutor/director even if you take the writer/tutor/director out of the center. Proof positive—this essay was developed for and shared with conference participants who had traveled (through unusual southern winter weather conditions) away from their actual architectures but carrying along their equally important internal spaces. We spent two days together seeing where, how, and why our center metaphors converged and collided, conflicted and cohered. Asking who had the young waiter's world-view and who the older waiter's. Remembering that in the story they worked perfectly well together. Asking what do those views mean for the old man quietly and deafly sipping his drink?

The joys of such an occasion are that we gain strength through such examinations because a conference is itself a site—a temporary but crucial joining of like-minded individuals who can set aside advocacy for the time being and investigate understanding. We did so at Myrtle Beach, and we left, I believe, looking forward to continuing this process in the future.

Note

Those who attended the joint 1996 South Carolina Writing Center and the Southeastern Writing Center Association conference will see how this essay developed out of the keynote talk. They'll also remember how this conference depended on Phillip Gardner of Francis Marion University and Susan Meyers of Coastal Carolina University, hard-working co-directors of that invigorating gathering.

12

Let Me Tell You About the Rocks

MY SUBJECT MIGHT SEEM NOT WORTH REMARKING ON, BUT I FIND THAT IT sticks in my mind. For some time now, someone has been placing a large rock on the roof of my car while I am inside the General Classroom Building teaching a class. I come out of the class to the parking lot, carrying all my folders and notes and books and a thermos empty of coffee, and there I find a large, jagged rock placed directly above the driver's door on the car roof. I remove it carefully so as not to scratch the paint while thinking, momentarily, of how I might approach the class saying: "Tell me now, which one of you is putting a rock on my roof?" but I give up the idea. Twenty-three students would stare back at me, pretending to know nothing about what I'm saying.

I place the rock back in the nearby divider bed and forget about it until the next time it appears. I almost suspect that whoever does this uses the same rock each time, but that would be impossible. No one would wait, hidden from view until I throw away the rock, and then come out from hiding to retrieve it from the divider bed, all in order to use the same rock the next time.

The rock appears randomly. Sometimes on first seeing it, I am irritated and feel attacked or intruded upon, and I think of the trouble that might be caused if one day I didn't notice it and drove off without removing it from the roof. The rock would bounce down my back windshield and shatter in the road behind me. I would be tempted to go to my class the next Wednesday and say firmly: "Which one of you is going to replace my damaged windshield?"

But mine are useless fantasies, for now I'm convinced that I'll always notice the rock. I seem to look for it each day without thinking about doing so consciously and, eventually, I might go so far as to feel relieved to find it there.

Today I parked in another lot, the one on the other side of campus which is nearer to my office. When I came outside to go home, the day seemed especially beautiful. The early, cool fall weather had broken, and the days were momentarily warm again and clear. Light was reflecting off all the cars in the lot, even the poorly painted ones. When I got closer to my own car, I noticed two tiny stones resting on the roof, just at eye-level, above the driver's door. They looked almost as if placed there by accident, and at any other time in my life I might have assumed so.

Scanning the parking lot, I realized it would be impossible to find a large rock in that immense expanse of blacktop; only a few pebbles were scattered around the area. Resting on my car roof, the stones looked oddly innocent, as if someone had half spelled out a message and then run away. Reflecting, I decided a message *had* been created, for those two stones made me start thinking more deeply about the whole matter. The leaving of stones was coming to seem less like a prankish act and more like a very vulnerable act. What if I had come out too soon and caught him. (I am beginning to assume the person who leaves the rocks is a man simply because I am a woman.) Would he have been embarrassed? Relieved? Did he really have more stones to place and did I disturb him unwittingly? In that glaring morning light, with my poor eyesight, I could have actually seen no one until I fell over him. I decided I must eliminate hatred as a motive for placing rocks: the rocks and stones could have been used to deface, to scratch, to harm my car. Instead, each was lowered gently into place, admired perhaps, and left. I had to think about it. Really, it was almost nothing, but it intrigued me.

This is the moment, in late September, when I stop ignoring the rocks and start, instead, to concentrate on them. I decide to watch, speculate, record, and wait. A small amount of detective work can be illuminating. For instance, three weeks after the first small stone incident, I find, again, small stones on the roof when I park near my office. The four stones are arranged in a circle (or in a square, depending on how you visualize them). I've developed a theory: two people are working together to decorate my car. Subject A works the lot near my classroom and prefers one large stone. Subject B works the lot near my office and prefers small stones. The small stone preference may be due to ecological factors, supply and demand, availability, and so on, but I do not rule out personal preference for each size rock does make a different statement. It is true, I could also be dealing with a mild case of schizophrenia. Subject AB, if he is one person, may feel like A on one lot and like B on another lot, or he may view me as a different person according to location and, therefore, he chooses his rocks accordingly.

This idea led me farther: if I should encounter AB, or rather if AB should encounter what he must by now recognize as my car by license plate number in, say, a parking lot outside a local and well-known bar, might he not resort to different forms for his message, such as a handful of gravel? And if the location should be the city hall, why not a chip of onyx or marble or some other cold, durable material. This idea took hold of me and, contrary to my custom, I happened several days last week to park conspicuously in more public areas of the city. Nothing happened. But that was only a random sampling; I don't yet feel daunted.

It is October. This month there have been no messages left in the lot outside my classroom but several small stone rings, triangles, and even one octagon (again, this depends on how you interpret the configurations—which is a pleasant exercise in itself, much like figuring out how the ancients turned a set of eight or ten loosely grouped stars into a complex drawing of Orion or the Hydra) appeared when I occupied a place in the lot near my office. This led me to form conflicting hypotheses.

In the first, I directly relate the lack of rocks in the classroom parking lot to the idea that the messagee must be one of my students. I need to subdivide this idea: (1a) the student, because he has recently been traumatized by a death or major illness in his family is unable to devote his time to the large rocks. Conversely, (1b) the messagee is staying away from class because he is unprepared to take the mid-term examination. I don't know how many times I've tried to address this problem when talking to my classes.

"Please," I say, "Don't miss class simply because you are afraid you are unprepared for it; much of the good that comes to you from being here depends on your being in the classroom *unreservedly*."

Short of making a direct and obvious plea to the messagee, such as "Please don't miss class and, incidentally, I have noticed no large rock variety messages lately," I must leave events to the messagee's conscience. But, as I've been honest with the class, I have to prefer explanation (1a): the student is having family difficulties that preclude his direct involvement with his studies and with my car.

My other hypothesis (2a) works from another premise. For instance, there is a direct correlation between the disappearance of the large rock and the emergence of the small stone as the dominant motif. In other words, for some reason the messagee is located more topically in the area of my office parking lot this month. This brings me to a disturbing supposition: one of my new colleagues may be dallying with my car. I will, in the interest of honesty and fairness, examine this idea more deeply, but I refuse, on the face of it, to accept such a conclusion for as a conclusion it eliminates the vulnerable messagee I have come to admire and, I must admit, to almost enjoy.

If another faculty member should be the messagee, what would that mean? It might, among other things, indicate that I am undergoing an arcane departmental initiation rite. Perhaps I am being tested for sensitivity and endurance. It will all come out in one of those small committee meeting jokes where one member says something I don't understand, another enlarges and adds to it, wittily it seems, and a third, red-faced with pleasure, bursts into laughter while the kindliest member, seeing me as if for the first time and noticing my weak smile, explains the private meaning, saying, "Those rocks, you know, they're our doing. We wanted to see how you would take it. You dealt with them wonderfully. Why the time we kept removing Herman's diskettes from his office computer, now there was a case of panic."

As things stood though, the rocks kept appearing and I felt hypothesis (2a) was not a strong possibility. Was it, then, some single aberrant department member, I wondered a bit hopelessly, forming hypothesis (2b) almost against my will. Was someone slipping out of department meetings to place rocks on my roof, before disappearing for the day down one more dim, angled hallway? I gave up on (1a), (1b), (2a), and (2b) entirely. My messagee had more imagination than I had.

Later, two other questions occurred to me. I was at that time undergoing a reappearance of large rocks and a remission of small stones. Was the messagee right or left handed? It seemed essential that I know. I wanted to be able to visualize the person in the act of placing the stones, but I was receiving a fuzzy image. I couldn't decide which hand would hold the rock or stones.

Were these messages from an unexpected person altogether? I wasn't, God forbid, parking in the areas designated especially for handicapped persons; though at 8:05 on a freezing fall morning when late for class and driving through a crowded parking lot, those parking places looked tempting. But perhaps I had unknowingly parked in the path a certain independent looking blind student that I now recalled used for getting to the General Classroom Building. Did he get irritated when he encountered my compact car blocking his favorite pathway and might he not leave rocks there for a reminder, a warning, a legitimate complaint? Who besides him, sensitive to touch, could lower those stones so carefully to my roof? This would necessitate, of course, the geographical theory of rock distribution. The student I was remembering would use whatever came to hand: large stones in the classroom parking lot and pebbles in the office lot.

It is late November. To examine the roof I must first scrape off the frost. Rubbing the area dry, I look to see if I can tell anything more about the messagee from marks he may have left there in spite of his care. But I cannot make out, from the tiny scratches some of the latest rocks have left, whether he is right or left handed. I must attribute the scratches themselves not to the righteous irritability of the serious blind student, but rather to the cold weather. The scratches are slight and superficial and the weather, these days, would cause anyone's fingers to be clumsy. No, it is numbness and cold weather causing him to drop the rocks and not a change of attitude on my messagee's part.

It is early December. I have considered it prudent to reevaluate my earlier prediction of the messagee's sex, or what I assumed to be the messagee's sex. Is it not superficial to label the messagee male merely because I myself am a female? Certainly it is chauvinistic and underestimates my adversary. At first I adopted the male messagee theory, nay, I was forced to adopt it after a certain class period where my teaching was observed by my superior who had noted, and I quote from memory directly from her observation sheet which she showed me after the class: "Do you know that fellow in the back row is madly in love with you?" I rushed over her statement by laughingly saying, "Oh, that Eric!" We both laughed rather chummily and began to seriously discuss my intonation patterns, voice level, and, in general, the dynamics of the day's class, shelving the subject of inamorata entirely.

As I arrived at my car later that afternoon, I found an unusual offering: a circle of small stones with a jet black extremely flat stone placed perfectly in the center. I couldn't help but wonder and feel that perhaps I did have an admirer. I couldn't go into class and say: "All right fellows, I understand. It is only natural that one of you has a crush on me. This happens between teachers and students. But truly, rocks are not the way to my heart." As I prepared my speech I realized I could not deliver it. It would have been a bluff, for I was beginning to realize that rocks *were* the way to my heart. I was spending more time considering the situation than I had ever spent thinking of a lover, past or present. I wanted at that moment to return to my supervisor and to tell her: "Forget Eric, let me tell you about the rocks."

Wisely, I refrained, but now I have to see this through alone.

An infatuated young beau of a student is an explanation far too easy for the problem that confronts me on another gray December morning. I must take into consideration other sexual configurations. After all, we are a sexually liberated society, as my students never fail to mention in their writings. If that is the case, maybe I am appreciated by a gay. My psuedo-liberal remarks, made mainly to goad or to fill certain painful gaps in class discussions, might have caught the fancy and excited the sympathy of one of our local depressed homosexuals. Depressed, for they know like I know that ours is not a sexually liberated society.

I go out of the classroom to my car, retrieve a rock from the roof, and later in the day, when I retreat from my office and walk outside to the nearby parking lot, I must remove a hex of small stones from my roof. Two offerings in one day. Then I am convinced my shy messagee is gay. Surely he not out, hides his preferences, pretends to date, wears the eternal jogging suit that marks off the hale and healthy or the aspiringly hale and healthy from the rest of the campus population, but, at the same time, leaves these explanations, these manifestos on my car roof top. These messages symbolize the two conflicting halves of his psyche, the yin and the yang, petite feminine stones competing with large male stones. How he wishes he could unite them on an imaginary car roof top in a perfect parking lot that exists, in his imagination, equidistant from the north and south ends of the campus.

Do I really care to know who the messagee is? Christmas break is approaching and I am not unthankful for the promised succor from these rock patterns. The messagee is taking up too much of my time. In desperation, I made a chart of stone occurrences and plotted on it how many stones had appeared, what time they appeared, where they appeared, and what size they were when they appeared. I cancelled classes for a week, ostensibly for personal student conferences, but, more plainly, to entice my class, student by student, into my office where I made sure the chart was exposed on one corner of my desk. I watched each student's reactions carefully, which produced slight symptoms of nervousness among many of them, but no one, I repeat, no one, reacted in any perceptible way to the chart itself. I decided not to interrogate them individually.

One morning, after eyeing a particularly large specimen of rock that was nestled in the snow on my car roof, I decided to take action. The next Wednesday, before entering the building, I wrote: *Who are you?* in the ice crystals on the roof. I had to use the frozen nib of a pen to scratch through the ice and found out later that I had scratched too deeply, leaving an impression of the question there for all time.

When I returned, I found nothing. I was, at that time, in the large rock lot. Later in the day, when returning to my car, which was now parked in the office lot, I found the answer to my question framed in beautifully colored precious stones; it looked as if the messagee had been saving the stones for a very special occasion.

Why? the message said.

Christmas break arrived just in time. I parked nowhere but in my own driveway and found no rocks there. When the new term commenced, I was, it seemed, freshly charged and ready to face not only a new set of students who would of course be eager to learn, but, also, to face my messagee, whoever he might be. As you might have guessed, or no, not knowing the subtlety of this messagee at first hand, you might not have guessed the upshot: *I found no new messages.* The last message then was the one I received just before Christmas break. As I had expected, my messagee left me a Christmas testimonial.

I walked out to the lot, after I had returned final papers to a class anxious to be off to the ski slopes, and I found a Christmas star on my car roof. It was formed from small, polished stones. Set in the middle of the star, with the messagee's usual delicacy, was a beautiful turquoise bead. Not only were the small stones out of place, occurring as they did in the large rock parking lot, but the turquoise bead had been added. I gathered up the offering carefully. (The stones I keep in a small, hand-embroidered coin purse, imported from Rumania. The bead I have strung on a silver chain and I often wear it, hoping that one of the many people I notice admiring it might someday recognize it and give me a clue to my messagee's identity.)

As the new term progressed and it became clear that no matter where I parked no new rocks were forthcoming, I began to mourn my messagee and to make some final investigations. I took the stones and the turquoise to a geologist on campus who seemed nervous when I told him my story, but he finally complied with my request for an analysis of each stone. Where, I insisted on knowing, had they come from. Each he found, to his surprise and my pleasure, came from a distinct geographical area of the Southwest: Rainbow Bridge, Havasupai, Canyon de Chelly. To me these were names of mystery. He was an explorer, going out eagerly, returning reluctantly, hoarding the stones that he finally turned over, for safety, to me. My messagee was still haunting me with his subtlety.

And so it is today. Although I will never know his name, I do know he existed. I could tell by the shy way my colleagues looked at me. And my students, in their inimitable manner, sensed that something was going on and too often behaved too restlessly to be entirely innocent. But I know most surely from the reassuring hardness of the ten rare stones and the turquoise bead that I will keep waiting with me for the messenger to return from his last, his longest journey.

Part IV

Composing Ourselves as Researchers

I never expected to claim the title researcher. I do so now with pleasure but always with explanation. As an undergraduate art major and finally as a fifth-year-in-college convert to English, I was not a counter of texts or a comfortable user of numbers. I shied away from the specter of statistical research in my required anthropology classes, preferring cultural to physical. Hand me a primate bone and I'd muse over it, ask me to review population data and I'd excuse myself. Had the I-Search paper been in wide use when I went to college, I might have had an easier time and not done miserably in a literary bibliographic methods course during my first incarnation in graduate school. I could not get my mind around "researching" difficult to locate journal publications of a writer not of my choosing (of my professor's life-work choosing). Like my later writing students, I had to learn the value of research done in service of something. For me, this meant research done in service of classrooms, students, my writing, my genuine developing interests.

It took some time to develop a disciplined investigative approach to the world, to understand that research was a mode of thinking, of being more mindfully aware of life's patterns. I learned to range through library indexes and computer searches, to compile annotated bibliographies on subjects I wanted to learn more about, to enter a research discourse community by first reading citations at the end of articles, to recognize differing research models and traditions. As I did this, I became more schooled in what I'll call logical guessing, and found that the same ability to pay attention to patterns that helped me build a poem also helped me read across the translated transcripts of qualitative data. Auspiciously, I arrived on the composition scene just as that field was entertaining qualitative research methods and I found this way of thinking about culture and community congenial to my English studies trained mind.

In 1988, I dove in and undertook ethnographic writing research. When I resurfaced, several years later, having completed my dissertation and several more naturalistic classroom-based studies, I found myself immersed in issues of post-modern ethnography—ethics, representation, writing style, presentation of self and of others. "Students' Stories and the Variable Gaze of Composition Research" reflects this engagement. It was composed in 1992 after I began sharing primary research results with students in undergraduate and graduate classes both, only to have these students point out their own under-representation in researchers' agendas. After several such "what's wrong with this picture" moments, I realized I could more energetically be involving research "subjects" in research "projects." In a way, I was refiguring the I-Search into a We-Search and this approach seemed more responsive to the beliefs of our profession.

"Attitudes and Expectations: How Theory in the Graduate Student (Teacher) Complicates the English Curriculum" was written in 1994 but based on data collected three years earlier. In this essay, I've moved from the distanced, author-evacuated voice of my dissertation—where as "researcher" I interviewed "teachers"—to the more personally voiced account found in this study where the researcher persona/character "Wendy" interviews the student persona/character "Dennis." This essay highlights what is enticing to me about ethnography. It draws on all my writerly skills. As a reader of transcripts, I am author of a report/a representation. I am a close reader and a textual critic. I draw on metaphor to analyze culture. I use my developing understandings of institutional history and identity theory (borrowed from psychological theory) to meditate on and meta-analyse this student's partially shared experiences.

"Having Been There: The Second Ethnography and On" resulted from learning garnered teaching graduate seminars in ethnographic research methods (1990–1996), from the struggles inherent in drafting a methods book for ethnographic writing researchers (struggles that are still continuing), and from the invitation of the editors of a volume, Voices and Visions: Refiguring Ethnography in a Postmodern Era, *in 1996 to write about ethnography. This essay allows me to reflect on how ethnography changes the ethnographer, how research has become part of my writer's life, and how ethnographic processes represent a powerful way of thinking about our worlds.*

13

Students' Stories and the Variable Gaze of Composition Research

STUDENTS' STORIES OFTEN CONFOUND, CORRECT, EXPLODE, OR REFINE writing theorists' constructs, researchers' findings and teachers' assumptions. I intend to explore some of the conditions of composition research that have led to an under-representation of the student self-report in our research agendas, a result, perhaps, of the professionalization of our field. And I suggest there are dangers in using student-vacant research projects to inform instruction. In doing all this, I'll argue that composition researchers, from the fully-funded literacy expert to the beginning teacher-researcher, need to include students' voices in all discussions of student writing.

Finding Value in Students' Reports

For several years, I read and responded to composition research in graduate school. During the course of my studies, I memorized the results of cognitive research projects and found myself sketching the Flower and Hayes flow-chart on cocktail napkins or on exams. I knew what the state-of-the-art research in the field *said could be said* about students' processes, that is, what was scientific and therefore defensible, drawn from dependable, controlled, and well-analyzed "data," for I was intent on becoming a professional rhetorician after years spent as a writing teacher and writer. When reading empirical reports in graduate school, I had many questions, of course, about unsanctioned topics—what about school pressures, home pressures, love pressures, life pressures? What about writers-as-people, I had often wanted to ask? As a good student, though, I mostly kept those questions to myself and proceeded with my certification.

Not long after receiving my degree, I taught a class for junior and senior English majors at my university titled "Theories of Composition."

The course offered my students information about writers and writing, and they were interested, although often asking why research reports had to be written in such a dry and inaccessible manner. After training them as I had been trained, by taking them on a tour of sections of famous research articles, I gave them Kate Ronald and John Volkmer's research essay, "Another Competing Theory of Process: The Student's." Their response mirrored my own; when I first read Ronald and Volkmer I felt as if those authors had gone ahead and asked the questions I had pragmatically suppressed during graduate school.

Ronald and Volkmer claim our writing process models seldom reflect our writing students' realities; students compose in order to receive good grades and to please the teacher; they procrastinate and draft under less than ideal conditions (at three in the morning and so on); they suffer great anxiety; and they evaluate their own work primarily on the basis of the grade they hope or expect to receive.

My students valued this essay because it rang true to experience and to the discussions they had in groups on the first day of class, concerning their own writing processes, discussions that sounded like this:

> The members of our group are surprisingly similar with respect to the way we write. Almost all of us do some form of formal categorizing. Some of us outline, some brainstorm, some write lists, and some of us just write. One thing remains constant among all six of us—we all procrastinate. I used to think I was a horrible individual for waiting until the last minute, but now I realize that everyone procrastinates—maybe we do it to actually "psych" ourselves up. We all preferred to write straight through with breaks only for their nutritional value. Most of us need quiet in order to keep up our train of thought but one of us (surprisingly) preferred lots of loud music. With regard to writer's block we agreed that the only way to beat it is to keep working. We all seemed to have a lot in common—at least where writing is concerned.

These students compared their self-reports with Ronald and Volkmer's suggested, corrected view of the student composing process and found the previous research models and studies we had read strangely lacking. They resonated to Ronald and Volkmer's claim that more than texts are at stake in writing research. Students' habits, rituals, feelings, beliefs, institutional savvy, and so on are at issue because "student writers operate in very real, complicated rhetorical situations, ones that they know quitewell how to manipulate, situations where plans, goals, and performance have different values from those outlined in published research" (93).

A research report based in student writers' experiences, which respected students' views, gave my students support for exploring their own writing. They felt that their dirty linen could finally be aired and that the generally not-talked-about-but-important-aspects of writing, like procrastination or grades, could be raised. They were pleased to encounter a composition article which spoke to them and appeared to detail student writing experiences authentically.

After the response this essay received, I began looking for writing research studies that complicated my understanding of students' contexts and processes, and looked for discussions that emphasized students' voices, stories, reactions, corrections, and contributions to our field: student-present rather than student-vacant projects. While doing this, I found it essential to consider the development of composition research, asking why as researchers we had neglected to tap students' contributions, asking why they weren't more fully in our professional gaze?

Professionalizing Composition—Some Gains, Some Losses

By all accounts, from the turn of the century to the early 1960s, composition was the least valued strand of English studies. If we read the institutional histories of Gerald Graff, Terry Eagleton, James Berlin and Robert Connors, authors whose writings are informed by very different politics and beliefs, a great degree of consensus still exists. In the late 1800s, literary studies displaced an existing oratorical, classical college culture in America; members of developing English departments adopted the scientific educational model prevalent in German universities, annexing scientific prestige to their own work through a philological and linguistic emphasis, by "responding to the text as an historical artifact to be studied scientifically" (Berlin 191).

Graduate programs in English began in the late 1870s, and the new university offered education to anyone who could meet the entrance requirements, focussing attention on preparation for entrance exams. Entrance testing begin in 1874 at Harvard, as did the freshman composition sequence. During the next seventy years, in over-enrolled and often unrewarding undergraduate writing classrooms, the classical rhetorical aim of invention was overshadowed by a focus on arrangement and style and an unnatural emphasis on correctness. Writing was not subjective and student-oriented or student-directed. Writing was a scientific and objective skill that could be delivered through proper instructional strategies and copious instructor intervention; in essence, writing became what we now term current-traditional.

In the 1960s, revolutions took place both outside and inside the writing classroom. Increasingly, current-traditional instructional methods weren't preparing new open admissions students to write with much success (see Shaughnessey), and writing was being viewed anew as a medium for self-knowledge, and self-expression, as a way of thinking. The scientific objective view of knowledge-out-there was being replaced with a subjective view of knowledge in-here. Expressivist views on writing instruction were popularized by several writing-teachers-turned-expert-witnesses. Peter Elbow and Ken Macrorie and Donald Murray and others started telling stories of what was working and wasn't working in the classroom, what worked and didn't work for them *as writers*, and how well students responded to a different kind of teaching, essentially writing workshops.

Just at the time critical theorists were challenging and changing the larger edifice of English studies, dominated by the study of literature, the writing classroom was also infused with energy: despair over conditions and excitement over possibilities. There were more and more students involved, creating *more and more teaching positions*. And, finally—if our field was to follow traditional academic models—there was a need to professionalize. Stephen North explains, "The freshman course was something nearly all of the rapidly increasing number of college students would take and represented in many cases the largest chunk of an English Department's budget" (14). He dates the birth of composition with a capital C from Albert Kitzhaber's address to the Conference on College Composition and Communication and publication of Kitzhaber's book-length study of college writing. In addition, the National Council of Teachers of English formed an ad hoc Committee on the State of Knowledge about Composition which called for research, specifically scientific research—rigorous, controlled, repeatable. Writing research was generally conducted and answers offered within the social science tradition because writing teachers were being asked to "provide information about their activities and programs and about their students' performance and abilities to audiences . . . used to information being presented in the traditions of social science research" (Lauer and Asher vi),

Attempts to create composition as a profession, then, did not simply result in networking or calls for the development of new pedagogies. Professionalization requires and results from the credentialing of teachers and development of testing procedures, the organization of graduate programs and their curriculums, and the production of tenure-gaining publication through research: "composition instructors in increasing numbers are being trained in rhetoric and composition Ph.D. programs, and are generating the necessary publication that will enable them to reap the same benefits as their colleagues elsewhere in the university" (Berkenkotter "Paradigms" 155).

As did literary studies before it, composition annexed the scientific model of empirical research and publication. Still, thirty years after NCTE's call for improved and rigorous research, the scientific model is proving as problematic for composition studies as did the philological model for literary studies. At issue is the very definition of *human science* (Berkenkotter "Paradigm" 152–153). The legacy of positivism in the human sciences is the decontextualized cognitive research that gained great visibility in composition from the early 1970s and retained that visibility through the late 1980s. Cognitive research is currently under some scrutiny though, primarily for what is seen as its practitioners' ". . . reluctance to explore the ethical or political dimensions of writing in favor of the disinterested scientific stance [which] lends its conclusions about composing to indiscriminate application in the economic setting . . ." (Berlin 218).[1]

Few in composition deny the usefulness of early cognitive research, but many question the valorization of the scientific method and its dominance in composition studies.[2] For instance, the scientific research report which was so difficult for me to learn to write and my students to learn to read often feels as if it distances us from the very students and classrooms we need to understand. The research report presents a stable, controlled environment very unlike the messy, complicated and always changing writing classrooms most of us inhabit. The research report makes claims for objectivity, while masking a researcher's ideology and subjectivity through the use of author-vacant language, what William Firestone calls a cool style. Cool style can be used to project a rhetorically convincing, impartial and accurate "scientific" persona: "If one of the threats to the validity of a conclusion comes from the writer's own biases, as is considered to be the case in science, then any technique that projects a lack of emotion has considerable persuasive power" (17).

According to the researcher's training and community, the report he or she writes will be intensely rhetorical, adhering to the conventions of the community. This is so because research is not only a method for making knowledge it is a means of professionalization, for initiating the novice researcher into the research community he or she hopes to join. Stylized research reports, then, provide the research community with this researcher's "new" information, showcased in a sanctioned, and therefore, safe format: "Thus what is original (and potentially threatening) in the study is neutralized through its being contextualized into the community's existing knowledge." (Berkenkotter "The Legacy" 76)[3]

In choosing writing research methods, then, much more is at stake that simply choosing the best tool for answering the research question at hand. Research initiates the novice, and increases field membership; usually it maintains rather than challenges community consensus. All research follows this path, but not all researchers have been able to admit this self-serving and subjective view of knowledge-making. Particularly, a subjective view contradicts key tenants of the positivistic epistemology.

Lately, in composition, there has been some questioning of the prevailing research tradition—and our acceptance of the positivistic research paradigm—and that is not surprising for, currently, "science" is under review in many branches of academic study. As researchers in our own and in other fields have become alert to their own rhetoric (their ways of reporting their research and advancing their own and their community's claims) many, as I have, have increasingly questioned the choice of those in composition studies who borrow the scientific model as the most appropriate one for studying spoken and written discourse and for validating the results of research to others within the academy.

Self-analysis is not easy; it is not surprising that composition as a field has not looked at the ramifications of its belated but rapid professionalization process and its choice of research paradigms. It is surprising to me, however, that we have so often ignored our own strengths. We are humans studying humans as they write. In order to suit the parameters of any research model, such a field should not, as Lad Tobin claims we tend to do, deny the value of the subjects who are being studied, student writers:

> That most student conceptions of their own composing process have been overlooked is not surprising: there exists a deep-rooted distrust of all retrospective student accounts. See, for example, Barbara Tomlinson ("Talking"), Linda Flower and John R. Hayes ("Images"), and Louis Rubin. The basic argument in each case is that student writers lack the experience, perspective, metacognitive sophistication, and technical language to describe accurately and fully their own composing processes. However, although all of these authors warn against uncritical acceptance of student retrospective accounts,

they also admit that such accounts can be valuable in certain ways for student and teachers. ("Bridging" 456)[4]

However, by ignoring students' voices, we emphasize the need for our professional intervention and do this at the risk of obliterating any notion of student expertise.

Thomas Newkirk makes the argument that most educational research, including empirical research in composition, develops its claims by "establishing the inadequacy of the more traditional sources of knowledge . . . custom, ritual, 'common sense,' and personal experience" (122). Thus, researcher knowledge is more valuable than teacher's experience (see North). In a similar way, we are at risk of seeing researchers' and then teachers' knowledge as always more valuable than students' knowledge and experiences. In a *required* first-year writing class (where enrollment has been mandated by knowing "authorities"—whether institutional, local or state) students' views, opinions, and experiences are easily suppressed. The implied illogic seems to run something like this: if they had any say in the matter, we know most wouldn't be in these classes; if they are in these classes, therefore, they must not have anything valuable to say about the matter.

Let me share a literacy story, told to me by a friend. Before she entered first grade, my friend's daughter could already read entire beginner's books by herself. The first week of school she was given a reading-readiness test, which she failed. She was sent home with a note telling her parents she would only be allowed to work on some basic exercises for the first few months of the year until she was ready to undertake more demanding tasks, all aimed at preparing her for reading. At that point, her father went to see the teacher and said: "Would you just ask her if she can read?"

As researchers considering student writers, we need more often just to ask. That's what my students felt when they read empirical research reports followed by the research essay by Kate Ronald and Jon Volkmer. Essentially, they were telling me, "if researchers had just asked us, we could have told them that we procrastinate, that we avoid writing, that we care a great deal about grades."

Convention-Making and Convention-Breaking Research

Experimental research studies serve our professionalization process too well when they "verify" the obvious and the commonsensical or when they exclusively serve community interests, asking questions about writing or writing students in a manner that supports the research community's agendas. Additionally, such studies may exclude conflicting, complicated, or ambiguous research directions since empirical research seldom focuses on questions of gender, race, and class, nor does it challenge current structures of institutional power. Such moves may be part of a traditional academic strategy that discredits personal experience, especially the experiences of disenfranchised individuals; consider the large number of women who form the majority of composition teachers and the students they teach, students who actually "experience" the results of research through curriculum mandates and pedagogical experimentation (sentence-combining and CAI and WAC and process workshops and competency based education and minimum competency testing) (see Newkirk).

When subjectivity, context, and human roles are bounded-in, writing research changes. Then, what we might label experimental shades quickly to quasi-experimental, a positivistic qualitative study may be reconsidered as a phenomenological qualitative study and clinical case studies are sometimes better understood as teacher-reserchers' reports and stories. The few guides to research available to our field still group all "valid" qualitative studies under the umbrella of scientific, empirical study; but the fit is becoming uncomfortable as ethnographic writing researchers become more insistent that they are working in different ways and with different ideological intentions, that they are working within a different epistemology.

Analysts of research paradigms have always had trouble bracketing and confining qualitative research. Stephen North finds that ethnography doesn't fit well where he places it, under the general category of "researcher" which includes experimentalists, formalists, and clinicians (136–140). And Janice Lauer and William Ascher and Carol Berkenkotter ("Paradigm") separately define qualitative methodology as research grounded in the rigors of the scientific method, including controlled data collection, coding, analysis, triangulation, and reporting. However, those very invocations to rigor may be protecting the scientific status quo and keeping a diverging strand of thought and research safely contained under the umbrella of empirical academic research.

I know that the "fit" is problematic, for I completed an ethnographic dissertation that was grounded with positivistic warrants ("A Microenthography"), and then I began to understand that work from a more phenomenological perspective, as constructed narrative (*Something Old, Something New*). Linda Brodkey suggests that qualitative research can be critical, and I'm not the first to discuss the way storytelling works in research (Bishop "Reliable"; see also Murphy). My views derive from postmodernist discussions within anthropology (see Geertz and James Clifford); for some anthropologists storytelling is an adequate—perhaps the only possible—reporting strategy, a strategy that accentuates a researcher's situatedness and subjects' voices. This is necessary, since we all carry a certain amount of our professional baggage along with us at all times. Still, I believe qualitative, ethnographic, phenomenologically grounded research-in-context, offers composition researchers an exciting and productive way of knowing that can accommodate and validate students' stories about their own writing.

While qualitative research seems a useful way to afford such accommodation and validation, it is not the only way. In composition, more projects are slowly appearing which use a variety of methodologies, yet take into account students' perspectives and contexts. For instance, Susan Wyche-Smith has investigated students' writing rituals and compared students to each other (those whose habits aided their own composing and those whose habits hindered their own composing). By doing this, her study is unlike early cognitive or clinical reports that often compared student writers to expert writers, with students always in the implied "deficient" position. And, like Ronald and Volkmer, Wyche-Smith found student writing activities were embedded in demanding life scripts where teachers, classrooms, and writing itself vied for student attention and often lost: "College is hard. It's a big change for me. The very first week of this semester I was out of it, totally out of it. But now I'm trying to get back on the ball. But I messed up, I'll probably have to take some classes over" (4), says one of her students. Through questionnaires and interviews, Wyche-Smith found students spent less than ten hours per week on homework for fifteen unit loads and double that amount of hours at jobs (8). Why aren't students drafting better papers? In part, because they're working too much.

When I say research methods, questions, and contexts are changing, I don't mean to imply that there is no need for further change. In my opinion, far too few reports like Ronald and Volkmer's and Wyche-Smith's are published, and they receive far too little attention. Scientific research is still dominant and that type of research, by definition, narrows the focus of the researcher's lens to a point so small that—theoretically—no explanation can be missed because no variable is unaccounted for. However, context-intensive researchers, their work derived from a phenomenological epistemology, insist that by reducing the lens size to such a small point, explanatory power is actually lost. Humans cannot be understood out of context. With small lenses, we may become "blind to the logic of a students' interpretation and the ways that interpretation might be sensibly influenced by the students' history" (Hull and Rose 287). With small lenses, we may focus on parts of a process or piece together a grand model, but we do so at the risk of missing students' stories and side-stepping their realities.

Myopia, blindness, the bracketed view of scientific research have led many researchers to design less focussed-down, more context-based research projects, even within the positivistic tradition. For instance, Jennie Nelson looks at the ways students *and* teachers view assignments, whereas ten years ago such research might have investigated a much smaller aspect of assignment-making. Nelson asked students and their teachers about assignments and discovered they held entirely different perspectives on the same activity ("This assignment should be challenging"—claims a teacher, and "This was an easy assignment"—claims one of that teacher's students). Nelson finds that "the special nature of school settings, with their emphasis on rewards for products, may have an important impact on the way students define and approach writing tasks" (392). I find it heartening that she has taken care in her study to include student perspectives and voices and to consider context, something that early cognitive writing research did not manage to do and which practitioners are now considering or advocating (see Berkenkotter "Paradigm" and Flower).

In addition, there are both formal and informal research reports available that accept and acknowledge students as knowing contributors to research. Finding his own and his students' metaphors for composing at a variance, much like the teachers and students whose assumptions Jennie Nelson studied, Lad Tobin began informally to listen to, collect, and study those metaphors, discovering:

> . . . not only that Michael and I had very different models of composing, but also (and more importantly) that metaphor offers student and teachers a significant (but little used) means of communication . . . there is still a disturbing failure of communications about composing—between students and teachers and between students' conscious knowledge and vocabulary and unconscious attitudes and strategies. ("Bridging" 445)

Tobin's observations suggest that teaching students the most productive habits of expert writers may not be a useful classroom strategy if we fail when doing so to acknowledge the conditions under which student writers compose:

[M]uch of these student writers' dissatisfaction is with the process itself, the inevitable frustration of trying to translate thoughts into written language, but even more of it seems a result of the scene or situation in which they find themselves—of being forced to write on demand, to write in a way that makes them feel powerless, to write for a grade. (Tobin "Bridging" 450)

And, despite our good intentions, we in composition may have been ignoring students' contexts in our enthusiasm to share our research-informed expertise, wanting students to tell us what they have learned—about what we have learned—about the writing process. We may offer them "new" information but neglect to ask them what they already know.

To start research where students are, rather than to suit our own or our graduate program agendas, we need to acknowledge students as legitimate contributors and to study their emotions and feelings. Since the study of feeling and affect requires a wide lens and a wide gaze, these areas have not seemed very amenable to empirical study or popular among scientific researchers. Alice Brand reminds us that: "It should come as no surprise that any movement to examine the emotions of writers is without members and that emotions theory is without place in contemporary writing research" ("Hot Cognition" 7); in a more recent article, she notes several important moves in the direction of investigating writers' emotions:

> We know that affective traits and personality overlap conceptually and empirically (Plutchik and Kellerman). We are just now recognizing that personality may govern discursive style (Jensen and DiTiberio; Selzer), just as discursive style has an impact on personality (Brand, *Therapy*; Denman). In fact, how personality influences the way writers function is the direction I think composition research is ultimately headed. ("The Why" 441)

I agree with Brand, for I see this movement in the work of Robert Brooke and John Hendricks, whose ethnographic study was galvanized when students didn't respond as well as expected to Brooke's writing instruction. Students' unexpected responses led Brooke and Hendricks to investigate the role of personality in writing. And Brooke's most recent study of writing workshops focuses almost exclusively on the way identify-formation drives the responses and realities of writing students in those classes; along the way, he develops an impressive theory-after-the-fact for a model of writing instruction which has been used for many years.

Today, then, some researchers are entering landscapes that were formerly off limits because of our profession's intentionally limited experimental gaze. Ethnographers (who are often also teacher-researchers are studying student affect and emotions and considering writing motivation, and some of these individuals have gone one step further and set up research teams that include and rely on students. While studying academic writing, Susan Miller and five student-researchers found more than they were looking for. Miller claims she:

> . . . originally thought we would be discovering how many and what kind of writing assignments and evaluations students encounter, and perhaps connecting this information to teaching practices in other disciplines. But I increasingly became aware that as a particular kind of teacher, I was facing delicate questions about my own course content and disciplinary identity . . . Increasingly [research] made me self-conscious about my own version of academic literacy. (Anderson 27)

Like the work of Tobin and Ronald and Volkmer, this study of writing in institutional contexts did not focus-down on a limited picture. Instead, a team of students-as-researchers entered several academic classrooms to observe, question, discuss, and report; these researchers looked for patterns and told stories; they explored ways that the institution drove the students and the students agreed to be driven:

> I consequently also need to reconsider the students' repeatedly documented isolation, even from their classmates, and the distancing strategies, humor, and anger they found to naturalize it. It took no special training in psychology to realize that our frequent group discussions of how often each one fell asleep in class and while studying, Alycia's legalistic view of attendance, Worth's calculated visits to professors, and John's assessment of what he pays professors to do were all expressions of admittedly WASP students, stinging and stung by a system they fully expect to join. (Anderson 31)

These researchers asked difficult, complex questions about writing, writers, and writing in context. In their work, the dream of positivistic unity is abandoned. Their research asks questions about individuals-in-contexts more than it attempts to discover large-scale explanations for the big questions that might reside out there in the universe of composition studies—a universe that they experience in myriad and often conflicting ways.

This kind of research will change composition studies. When teachers become researchers and students' stories, interpretations, and contributions count, then knowlege-making and professionalization come into better balance. I have seen this happen over the last ten years as I have traced the trajectory through many of the positions I've described here—student writer, writing teacher, aspiring professional researcher, teacher-researcher. And, I am inclined by these experiences to fight the negative effects of my own professionalization by attempting always to bring my work back to the classroom, sharing it with writing students and new teachers of writers. In this, my suggestions for reform are something like the suggestions of the middle-class recycler that I am. Yes, I still buy too many canned, bottled, and packaged foods, but I also try to recycle and compost and do my part. Yes, my own research is situated and, yes, my own discussions of writing teachers and students work to advance my professional career, but they can also advance the success of the writing classes I teach to the extent that I focus my research there and to the extent that I help students and new teachers join in the previously closed conversations of my profession.

Because my gaze is determined, subjective, situated, I am inclined in the direction of context-based research although I know it is not the only way to solve the problems I have raised. A context-rich methodology, however, lets me make my subjective, situated, and ideological claims through interrogation of my subjectivity, situatedness and ideology; when I research, I am learning as much about myself—my group, my norms, my profession—as about the students I study. And I don't believe a research methodology is useful unless it allows for some degree of this type of self-critique, unless it encourages and achieves some degree of methodological meta-knowledge. Without such self-knowledge something gets lost.

Too often in the past what got lost was the student, the student writer who inspires a large portion of our work. (I'm aware of those who argue that not all research has to return us to the classroom; but a great deal of it already does.) Therefore, we must challenge prevailing paradigms. And our gaze must be wide since our methods address a writing classroom that is conflictual, interactive, dynamic. In her research analysis which borrows from Baktinian critical theory, Joy Ritchie says:

> The experiences of this teacher and these students suggest that we cannot describe the process of learning to write as a tidy, predictable process. . . . We must resist reductive descriptions of our students' development as writers.

Each student comes to our class with a unique history, with different assumptions about writing, and different needs. So we should expect that each writing workshop will compose a different "polyphony" of disparate elements which each student will appropriate and reshape in different configurations. The process does not end with the writing class, and it may not appear to have the same characteristics in any two students. (171)

Challenges to positivist research come from these polyphonic classrooms. Reliability is not at issue here; writers-as-humans are as complex as the communities they form and can never be studied the same way twice, exactly. Validity is not at issue here; we don't always study what we thought we were setting out to study, but we are still learning from reflective practice.

We need to realize that composition came out of eclipse and moved toward academic professionalization within a very short time-span, and while such changes have been taking place, the gaze of composition research, like the gaze of any community, has been variable—looking at what is profitable, convenient, safe and sure. But our profession, I'm proud to say, is quite a bit more ornery than that. I think the most promising studies are those that challenge the conventions even as we try to set them up. If qualitative studies are increasing, it is because they offer if not perfect vision then an engaging type of double-vision: a way to look at the researcher, who is often a teacher, as well as a way to look at those researched, often that researcher's own students. In my own projects, I try to listen to the stories of the students I work with, as well as to those of my colleagues, and I always find I learn by considering cases and stories, by attending to metaphors and sketching out analogies. (I also learn by reading scientific research.)

And, I try to avoid the hubris of feeling that my gaze is the best gaze or only gaze by taking any knowledge gained back with me to the writing classroom. When I share writing research about students, *with students*, they are sure to respond with the story of what it really is like for them; and my job is to listen. Mike Rose suggests:

We need an orientation to instruction that provides guidance on how to determine and honor the beliefs and stories, enthusiasms, and apprehensions that students reveal. How to build on them, and when they clash with our curriculum—as I saw so often in the Tutorial Center at UCLA—where they clash, how to encourage a discussion that will lead to reflection on what students bring and what they're currently confronting. (236).

Equally, we need approaches to research that honor "the beliefs and stories, enthusiasms, and apprehensions that students reveal" (Rose 236). Listening to students' stories helps me to remember that we occupy only a small portion of their lives while they loom large in ours. How students are included in composition research is for me a continuing issue.

Notes

1. For a published conversation-of-sorts on this topic, see also Berkenkotter, John Clifford, Flower, Foster, Reynolds, Schilb.
2. See Reynolds, however, for a counter-claim that experimental studies are not dominant.
3. This essay, for instance, demonstrates the problems of academic writing style; as I compose, my practitioner (teacher's) anecdotes vie for a place within my graduate program–trained literature-review and heavily cited discussion. And I develop an important (to me) "argument" without myself believing in or feeling comfortable with traditional argumentative essay conventions.
4. And this important claim is found in a footnote, not in the body of Tobin's essay.

14

Attitudes and Expectations
How Theory in the Graduate Student (Teacher) Complicates the English Curriculum

COLLEGE AND UNIVERSITY ENGLISH DEPARTMENTS ARE ATTEMPTING curricular change in response to institutional critiques and analyses like those by Robert Scholes and Gerald Graff. The work of both scholars helps us understand how English departments have developed. In *Textual Power*, Scholes outlines the pitfalls of current English department stratification, showing how most departments over-value the consumption of literary texts and under-value non-literary and pseudo-non-literary texts, particularly student compositions. In examining this hierarchy, he claims:

> For me the ultimate hell at the end of all our good New Critical intentions is textualized in the image of a brilliant instructor explicating a poem before a class of stupefied students . . . . Our job is not to intimidate students with our own superior textual production; it is to show them the codes upon which all textual production depends, and to encourage their own textual practice. (25)

According to Scholes, we need to begin sharing our complicated textual practices with all students, examining these practices together, making them more comprehensible and more democratic.

In *Professing Literature*, Gerald Graff traces the history of "English" from a course of undergraduate study in the nineteenth century, focused on classical texts, to the development at century's turn of graduate programs modeled on European universities with their philological and linguistic emphases (22–23, 57). Through periods of intense change,

English departments survived—in fact, they grew—because they remained flexible. Over time, however, this flexibility would prove problematic. In his more recent work, *Beyond the Culture Wars,* Graff again points out the self-serving benefits of English studies' "amiable rule of laissez-faire" and then focuses on the problems this rule has created. In essence, the still-dominant "field-coverage" model allows departments to create a new category for every challenge to existing categories, absorbing and defusing the interests of alien constituencies. By doing this, English departments have ". . . enabled the American curriculum to relieve the increasingly conflicting pressures placed on it by painlessly expanding its frontiers, adding new subjects, courses, and programs without asking those in control of the already established ones to change their ways" (7).

Field-coverage allows English to keep the lid on a simmering pot. Recently, though, the heat has been turned up in response to changes in American academic culture,and the pot has started to boil over. Feminists, compositionists, new historicists, post-structuralists are all claiming "voice" in English department matters and challenging the status quo that field-coverage supports. Graff urges us to avoid the pitfall of developing a false consensus *yet again.* He believes we should teach the conflicts of our positions through various forums that support a new vision of department integration, airing perspectives and discussing conflicts within all classrooms and through the development of department-held conferences and symposia.

Many English departments are paying serious attention to these institutional critiques even as our solutions fall short of accomplishing what is being suggested.[1] For instance, in my department we have debated the usefulness of an undergraduate course in critical theory. We have instituted theory and multi-cultural course requirements in our graduate curriculum, reviewed graduate degree requirements, and renamed some of our graduate courses. However, it is very easy for well-intentioned programs like ours to compromise their own larger vision in the elusive search for department unity. If teaching the conflicts is relegated to a few courses and requirements are changed but content is not, field-coverage has prevailed. It can only be hoped that departments currently able to institute multiple-course reconfigurations will eventually become departments, willing, at a future date, to consider more radical *and integrative* curricular reform, reform that takes place vertically—within graduate and undergraduate programs simultaneously—as well as horizontally—reconceptualizing fields and periods of study.

As a profession, we have changed the way we talk more than we have changed our daily practices. In these discussions, post-modern theory offers several lenses for our discipline and the language of critical theory may prove to be a lingua franca among sub-disciplines. However, while a rhetorician and a literature scholar can attempt to find common ground regarding curriculum reform, most of us have failed to consider how the "theory" in our graduate student (teacher)s complicates any changes we hope to introduce into the culture of English studies. New graduate students in English—including those who track into degree programs in literature, rhetoric *and* creative writing—are constituted by the theories of learning that they bring with them. In the rest of this essay, I'll illustrate the degree to which our students are sites of conflicting theories and suggest that we need to "read" them better if we truly aim to improve our programs. Overall, it is necessary to ask our graduate student (teacher)s to share their attitudes and expectations, to articulate their tacit theories, for tacit theories rapidly come into conflict with the explicitly new theories being introduced into many programs whether through coursework, or dialog, or both.

I come to this discussion from my position as a teacher educator. Each summer I introduce current research and pedagogy in composition and rhetoric to a diverse set of graduate teaching assistants, studying at the M.A. and Ph.D. levels. In the summer course, Teaching Writing in College, I reverse the usual English department hierarchy and privilege writing over reading, composition over literature, at least temporarily, in order to ask new teachers to consider seriously the learning needs of their prospective first-year writing students. Through ethnographic study and informal observation, I know such reversals cause resistance and conversion—temporary to enduring—and are part of this educational process; new teachers must try on personas as well as explore practices as they include *first-year writing instructor* as one of their graduate program identities (see Bishop, Brooke). However, "trying on" an identity is not the simple shrugging into a new coat that the metaphor predicts; teachers aren't always aware (nor are their teacher educators or graduate professors) of the firm theories they have and upon which they often base their attitudes toward classrooms, graduate school, and professors (see Welch). I use theory here in the largest sense—a reasoned prediction, often based on observation, about how things work—and often these tacit theories combine to form an individual's world view.

New teachers are obviously influenced by their chosen area of study. Those tracking into the literature program, for instance, predictably resist the de-emphasis of literature that can occur in a writing teacher education course, and those on the creative writing track may embrace the elements of writing process pedagogy that are most congruent with the creative writing workshop model of instruction. What is less clear is the degree to which field-coverage and traditions of compartmentalization in English studies—majors and minors, strands or tracks—has produced a compart-mentalization of GTA thought, and to what degree GTAs' theories of learning lead them into particular educational choices even as their professors attempt to mold these seemingly "blank slate" new students to the professors' professed fields of study or critical approaches.

I have experienced the impermeability of the boundaries between tracks. I am often surprised at the lack of transference between teacher education at one level (first-year classrooms) to GTA teachers' practices at other levels (second- and third-year classrooms). I attended a workshop at my university composed entirely of experienced first-year writing teachers. In designing the workshop, we intended together to brainstorm ways to use writing more often in 2000 and 3000 level introduction to short story and literature courses, courses often taught by senior GTAs. As the workshop leader asked each table to report back on strategies for using writing in the literature classroom, I heard a disappointing litany of exercises where writing was still used primarily to test knowledge: pop-quizzes, short essays, research papers. Drafting, response groups, student-led discussion from journals, question-making, and ungraded free writings—writing-to-learn activities—were all left in the dust of the first-year sequence.

Last summer, a GTA—one of a group of promising students who are deeply immersed in the study of critical theory—sent me a letter and a draft of a version of the common first-year curriculum that he hoped to teach. In this proposal, he derives his teaching theory from post-structural theory, choosing a ten-year-old, fifth edition of a well-known language reader, and selections from Orwell and other classic essayists. I read this student as well versed in critical theory but poorly versed in composition theory, research and practice. He planned for extensive discussions using technical theoretical language and provided less support for writers in the process of constructing texts. Since this teacher entered our program with credit for previous teaching exempting him from our summer teacher education courses, it was impossible to tell what composition texts he had read, but it felt like not very many. Clearly, theory was already in the student.

I can most clearly illustrate how filled by theory or theories our graduate students are by sharing excerpts from a year-long research study. These excerpts show how one Ph.D. student entering the literature track, without previous training but with strong attitudes and expectations about English studies and the value of literary texts, tested a new theory of learning against the strong one he already had. Again, while this student—whom I call Dennis—represents a literature student incorporating and resisting instruction in writing theory, he proved also to be resistant—because unacquainted with—the postmodern critical theories that are beginning to under gird our literature track.[2]

As we'll see in the case of this student, departments can mandate program requirements for theory, but they can't put theory into their faculty nor into their students. By "reading" Dennis, we can see that "theory" in the largest sense develops within the complicated territory of a GTA's experiential theories of learning and of school. For instance, Dennis relied on degrees-held: always pay more attention to a graduate student than an undergraduate, to the M.A. than the B.A., to the Ph.D. than the M.A., and so on. Equally, Dennis expected his students to learn from him based on a similar premise: they should pay attention and believe him because he was a graduate student and they were freshmen, because he was an experienced academic writer and they weren't yet experienced, and so on.

I want to annotate very small portions of a much more extensive set of taped interviews that I conducted with Dennis over a twelve-month-period when he was training to be a teacher and I was participant-observer in his teacher education class (the summer before I was to begin teaching that class myself). Dennis enrolled in two three-credit teacher education courses and mentions the teachers of those courses—Bonnie and Rick—in the transcripts below. After the summer 1990 courses, I continued to interview Dennis as he began doctoral work in English literature and taught his first two semesters of first-year writing. I need to emphasize the illustrative nature of my readings and excerpts. The quotes I've chosen to use are representative although, of necessity, they are extracted from the rich context of the ethnographic study (which includes data collection with twenty eight other new teachers and case studies of seven other teachers besides Dennis).

I also want to mention Dennis's successful negotiation of the English program. During the month I am composing this draft, Dennis is preparing his dissertation prospectus. In his third year of teaching for the first-year writing program, he is in good standing as a teacher and as a student. In the last three years, some of his strong theories of learning and classrooms have modified and others have proved resilient. Changes in the graduate curriculum—undertaken to emphasize multi-cultural perspectives and incorporate contemporary critical theory—have been instituted within this English department, as I mentioned above, mainly by adding more course requirements in those subjects. The movement toward theory and multi-culturalism is less clearly instituted across the English department curriculum by an equal transformation within the *teaching* of all department professors. Graduate students, naturally, gravitate toward faculty members who teach in familiar ways, say by offering the familiar rewards of *A* grades for New Critical literary analysis essays. Due to undergraduate literature course sizes of forty-five or more students, due to a large number of linked 4000/5000 literature courses of the same size or graduate courses of twenty or more, due to unfamiliarity with contemporary writing theory, and due to preference, most professors continue to teach by the lecture/exam or lecture/literary analysis and research essay method at both the undergraduate and graduate levels (see Sullivan).

My reading of Dennis illuminates the degree to which our graduate students are already fully-formed, tacit theorists about to mix and match the theories that they are presented with—by an English department which itself is driven by multiple and conflicting theories—into a functional graduate student outfit.

Professors as (Male) Authorities

Dennis found composition theory particularly difficult to accept because it conflicted with his theory about teachers, particularly college professors. Professors were authorities, usually right about issues by virtue of their degrees and long experience:

7/12/90
Wendy: There's something that prompted you to feel that you should consider this [composition theory] at least?
Dennis: Yeah, I mean, the basic fact is that Rick's a Ph.D. These guys [Rick and Bonnie] are Ph.D.s and I'm not. You've been doing this for a hell of a lot longer than I have.

7/17/90
Dennis: Doesn't a teacher have to trust his knowledge and instincts? And what else do I have to give the student if not the sum of my knowledge and understanding?

7/30/90

Dennis: I mean, on the one hand, these people are Ph.Ds and they've been teaching for thirty years so they have, I mean roughly thirty years, so they have a system of thought. Like I've never been uncomfortable with the fact that a classroom isn't a democracy. It really bugs some students, I've never really been bothered with it. Because, that's a professor, he has a certain point of view, learn it! . . . now if you want other points of view, take another class . . . You're guaranteed that you're going to get another point of view, because it's a different person teaching it.

Dennis did know that professors were contradictory creatures—not all professors agreed with each other—but, as a group, he vested them with wisdom because they had achieved a place in the English department hierarchy that Dennis himself wished to achieve. If they contradicted each other, so be it; the student's job then is to endure, engage (he often chooses battle metaphors) with each professor, and go on to the next until he gains the needed status from which to assert his own authority. The authoritative professor evoked by Dennis is a male; his female professor, Bonnie, is grouped into "you guys," for professors are always designated in his speech with the pronoun he. This is not surprising given that Dennis appeared to enroll in (or recall) courses from his M.A. program taught only by men, and his first fall courses at this Ph.D. program were also taught by men. Senior women professors in his academic life were as scarce as they are in the profession in general, and those he encountered in the summer of 1990 taught composition and women's studies.

In Bonnie's class Dennis was asked to write on freshman tasks, which he resented (I explore this attitude in more detail below). As important as the task, though, was the course context: Dennis was writing here for a female professor whose opinion he doubted since she praised him for texts he himself could not value:

Dennis: And she loved it [his last paper], I don't know why.

Wendy: You thought for sure this is writing with a small *w* and she's saying, hey, for me, this is writing with a large *W*. And go back to your argument of "She's been doing this a long time, she's in the system, she has a Ph.D." Does that shake things up a little?

Dennis: Hum, no, then I would probably be tempted to say that she's just being nice. I don't know.

Wendy: Because she's a woman?

Dennis: I didn't say that!

Wendy: I asked it. I'm a woman, I can ask that.
Dennis: I didn't say that. I refuse to get into an argument. I just read the articles on sexual discrimination.

Dennis is normally eager for an argument—relishing the academic war of words that I discuss below—but here he denies his female professor a normal academic's authority when her advocacy for informal, exploratory writing threatens to undermine his trained preference for literary essay writing. For Dennis, professors are authorities, but some professors have more authority than others, based on gender. In this, he reflects the values of English studies during the last hundred years, for only slow changes have occurred in the gender make-up of English departments over the last twenty years.

Teaching and Learning as Battle

Because knowledge, in Dennis's theory, is developed through personal authority, wresting such authority from a classroom turns learning into a battle. I am not the first to point out that the battle metaphor often signals an interest in hierarchy and a degree of comfort with confrontational argumentation. Although composition scholars, feminist scholars, and many other academics who identify themselves as part of marginalized sub-disciplines in English studies tend to challenge such seemingly masculinist tropes, the tropes are still prevalent. As a student of literature, still the dominant group within English studies, Dennis could be expected to partake of this contentious metaphoric tradition:

7/30/90 [regarding writing his papers for professors]
Dennis: It was always a "me versus you" type of mentality . . . I went and looked up their [professors] articles and book, I could tell, so I had these strategies. If you know where the enemy is, you know how to fire upon him.

[regarding a particular professor]
He ran the class basically like 1930s Germany. It was strictly lecture. He could come in, we did three books, *Scarlet Letter, Moby Dick, Huckleberry Finn,* and he basically would come in and would read the book to you. And every sentence, he would interpret every other sentence.

In this battle, the experienced, (male) degreed professor has the edge and students push the limits of his authority at their own risk.

7/30/90

Dennis: He didn't want anyone else's opinion . . . Out of class, I argued with him and I didn't agree . . . basically, I learned after the first exam, after *The Scarlet Letter*, the type of symbolism that he wanted . . . and the same with another professor. I wrote basically the same essay on an exam roughly four times, almost word for word, I think. Or at least, types of sentences were the same. "Man's a creature in possession of language . . . "All I had to say for this one professor is that "Keats celebrates language as an event through this particular device." Then the next time: "Virginia Woolf celebrates language in this way . . . I have yet to find a professor that doesn't want in some shape or pattern his own opinions. No matter how much [they] say "I want to see original thinking. . ." that's a lie.

Given Dennis's theory of learning as a battleground with the tables turned in the favor of the professor, it's no surprise that he has trouble with the collaborative, student-centered, feminist instructional model advocated in his teacher education classes. Even as he is being instructed to consider classrooms as something other than academic battlegrounds, Dennis's most prized day of the summer occurs when he takes over his GTA mentor's writing class:

7/12/90

Dennis: . . . what I thought was the best day . . . there were so many people talking and I was firing questions off. I really enjoyed that. That was good. That's the way I'd like to run the class, an hour and a half battle.

Dennis has recreated his own educational past: he's at the helm, captain of the ship, the officer calling the charge, firing off questions, in the heat of the battle and the center of the action. However, during his training, he is asked to give up his hard won superiority and advantage. And it is not that Dennis is unaware of other theories of learning; before he began his summer teacher education courses, he predicted this problem on a questionnaire. In answer to "What do you need to learn about teaching writing?" Dennis answers: "I know how to teach effectively. I know how not to hurt the feelings of others. I do not know how to do both." For Dennis, in the necessary classroom war, someone is bound to be wounded, and teachers do not dare become too sensitive on the battlefield of knowledge. Dennis feels he needs no other teacher preparation than his careful observations of his own previous classrooms from which he has abstracted this functional theory of learning. School is a bracing battle that unfortunately often hurts.

Conflicting Theories

Dennis's theory of learning, attitudes toward professors, and expectations for his classrooms based on his observations of literature courses he has enrolled in, immediately set him in opposition to both composition *and* reception theory:

7/16/90

Dennis: How can students, who by definition lack specific knowledge simply stumble upon knowledge? No, I am not underestimating their capabilities. But I am questioning the students' ability to teach themselves to write. It seems to me to be the blind leading the blind. I thought the provision of guidance was our function. I thought that's what a teacher did. Current thought reduces my role to absurd tour-guide, a man with a dim flashlight waving at tourists wandering aimlessly in the dark. It's not only wishful thinking but it's a disservice to the students themselves. When I enter a classroom, I expect to be offered something that I did not have before. But that offering comes from the instructor; what he knows becomes part of me.

Dennis's opposition is based, of course, on his experiences with the transmission and banking models of the teacher-centered instruction he has experienced. His role with former professors was to profess their way of reading. His role with his students, since he's senior to them, should be to show them the way, to offer them something. Student-centered learning represents the blind leading the blind, since knowledge—in Dennis's theory—is something transmitted from master to novice. Yet, in his education courses, he has been strongly introduced to an alien model of learning.

7/17/90

Dennis: Students find it difficult enough to communicate effectively without worrying about their membership in an interpretive community. And if we hold to the postmodern premise that reading and meaning are relative, then I can never read the student paper "correctly," can never give the "right" response. I'm defeated before I begin. I can't accept that. I have to go with what I think is right and hope the students *are* learning to write—even if they are only conforming to the standards of my own interpretive community.

Certainly Dennis is able to understand the premises of post-structural theory. But he is unable to inhabit those positions, for by accepting multiple readings and teachers as senior-learners he might risk losing the classroom war; he would do this by being untrue to his past school experiences and the theories he had abstracted from his M.A.–level literature studies.

Theories of Writing

Dennis knows how to write papers to please his professors. He's a successful graduate student. Here's how he goes about it:

7/30/90
Dennis: You have the due date looming over you . . . by the time I finish [reading the assigned] text, there'll usually be a few things that have stuck out that I'll have noticed, so I'll drop some notes, and we'll raise questions in class . . . then when we're approaching the paper, I usually have a general idea in mind. And then I start systematically, "Okay, this is the point I'm going to prove." I'll have a thesis . . . And then I'll go into the text and see if I'm right, before I start taking real notes, because I'll specifically quote. "This quote matches what I want to say, this quote doesn't." Once I get a body of quotes and notes, then I usually start making an outline. So I'll take every quote that I want to use out of the text, put it on a couple of sheets of paper and then dismiss the text . . . .
Wendy: Do you go much to outside critical work??
Dennis: I kind of rely more on my own critical theory. I don't see the purpose of rehashing what everyone else has written . . . usually what I'll do is I'll find a nice set of quotes from the research that I've done and then have that as a "set of quotes #2,"—there's a set of quotes from the text and a set from the [critical] literature. And then I'll stick them in where I want them, where I think they'll look good.

Dennis has developed an effective method for writing traditional academic literary essays. When he enrolls in a teacher education course intended to teach him current process theories of writing instruction, there is an immediate mismatch. He hates writing the class assignments which require him to do the same type of papers he'll be assigning in first-year writing: "Now those papers I turned in for Bonnie—the last one, I should have had my M.A. rescinded. It was that bad. And she loved it; I don't know why." Dennis has trouble appreciating the informal, exploratory, multi-draft essay; in his view, more elementary types of writing will take place in first-year writing. Equally, he feels he is wasting his time writing such prose, for his standards have been molded around literary analysis and research essays with their sets of references and techniques of close reading:

7/30/90

Wendy: So even within formal academic style, you don't like informal academic style?

Dennis: Even if I'm writing a letter it's always big *W* [writing]—I mean, it's always I'm just in this big *W* set. I've just been taught, I have to "do something" that's better than it was before. Sometimes it's just like I don't want to do it [write]. That's why I don't write as much as I used to, because it's like climbing the big *W*.

Wendy: You have really high standards but you also agree with those standards?

Dennis: Yeah. Hey, it just hit me. I think in the class [teacher education], maybe I want big *W* and Rick is willing to settle for the little *w*?

Dennis, like many new writing teachers, wrestles with issues of response and the difficulties of grading student texts. He has always preferred literary text to *all* other texts, including those by students and by theorists:

8/1/90

Dennis: Finally, after nearly six weeks of abstractions, of rhetoric and composition duckspeak, I finally was able to get to my first love: literature. Now I understand that the ENC1102 class is structured as Writing *Through* Literature. But nevertheless, I was quite pleased to hear the names Faulkner and Kafka rather than Elbow and Murray.

Dennis is fighting some new battles here as he enters an English department that gives at least minimal acknowledgment to the value of different types of text and new types of academic writing. Dennis is a graduate student proficient at the thesis-statement literary paper. Even when convinced he should use certain writing invention strategies in the first-year classroom, making the move to *believing* in those strategies or a new view of the writing process is very difficult. Dennis is pained at having to write writing with a lowercase *w* and chooses to teach invention strategies not on the basis of how effective they might be for student writers but instead on the basis of how they strike him personally:

9/12/90

Dennis: Well, it's a struggle because I don't use them [invention strategies]. I know how to do this stuff already. It's more internalized so it's hard for me to distance myself from it and not come off saying—and I found myself doing it at first—that may have been why I had so much trouble [teaching invention strategies] doing it at first—I may have come off saying "Well, this is stupid but we're doing it anyway." And I can see the problems resulting from that . . . and, in some respect, I do think these things are stupid, but that may just be because I don't need them anymore. Like, I, I absolutely refuse to do the house thing [draw a floor plan of a former home]. I thought it was utterly a waste of time, so I haven't done it.

What I find interesting when I read across this year of interviews with Dennis is not only his resistance but also his successful adaptation. Changes did occur in his attitudes toward teaching, in the shape of his classrooms, and even in his theory of learning (at least for first-year writing). However, Dennis overall remained much the same in his expectations about graduate school learning simply because the new theories offered to him did not prove more compelling than the old ones he held.

Dennis's original theories proved profitable; his first semester graduate literature professors rewarded him for his already developed literary analysis writing skills and did nothing to reinforce the writing and learning theories raised in his summer education courses. In one of his two American literature courses, Dennis received a grade of 95 for a paper on "Who is the Catcher in the Rye?" which begins: "One does not always have to read a novel to enjoy a finely crafted and highly symbolic work of fiction" and received a professor's comment of: "Excellent paper, intelligent, clearly argued, written with grace and precision. Parallel is exact—and your analysis leaves little doubt as to cogency of your argument. Hey, you write good!" Dennis had brought off another capital *W* production.

Another paper he shared with me was from the second American literature course. "The Split Reality of the Puritan Sensibility" as a title suggests a course lecture phrase, and the essay opens with the thesis statement: "Any consideration of the seventeenth and early eighteenth century American—specifically Puritan—sensibility must proceed from the assertion that Puritan culture was theocentric in its focus, revolving around a constant attention to the relationship between God and man." This paper received the response: "A+ Well-organized and clear exposition. Good explanation." More notable are the drafts from this paper: On five separate pages, Dennis hones the opening thesis paragraph, a sentence at a time, adding one more sentence each page. The last several draft pages represent the single hand-written draft of the full paper which proves his carefully wrought thesis. Both literature course essays capitalize on the skills and process Dennis was able to articulate the summer before he enrolled in those Ph.D. courses and bear scant resemblance to the forms or process of writing required in the first-year classes he was teaching.

The year long study of Dennis's teaching, of course, illuminates the complicated play of old and newly encroaching theories and suggests the resiliency of field divisions. To some degree, Dennis changed his attitudes toward process instruction and his first-year writing classes (changed them particularly from the more current-traditional model he *thought* he would institute before being trained that summer), but his life in the newly theorized English department curriculum remained compartmentalized for many reasons: he enrolled in the courses of professors who themselves were not engaged in theoretical and curricular debates, and when he was introduced to theory it was in the education or critical theory course, cordoned off from his daily practice.

Having spent one year with Dennis as a participant-observer and another two years as a department friend who continued to undertake good-natured verbal "battles" concerning the value of composition theory, the problem of subjectivity in grading, the shape and direction of English studies, and the value of literary and student texts, among many other topics, I believe Dennis is the perfect example of a student who would benefit from Gerald Graff's proposal that we teach the conflicts in the curriculum, for clearly they are being played out every day when his attitudes and expectations intersect with those of his professors and students in the halls and classrooms of the English building. However, his case also reminds us that the situation is far too complicated to be resolved by *structural* curricular change. Dennis needs to see his literature and his composition teachers in dialog—co-teaching, participating in department conferences and colloquia, negotiating in a lingua franca—making it harder for Dennis to claim total allegiance to one discourse and deny credibility for another. That means, of course, that the professors under whom Dennis studies would need to learn about and respect each other's work. It means that departments need regularly to promote meritorious women to the rank of full professor, eliminating the associate professor level "glass ceiling" that can develop as a larger number of women, many of whom are completing exemplary but often non-traditional work, enter departments. And that means departments will have to pay attention to the hierarchy of texts identified by Robert Scholes in order to examine their own valorization of certain academic genres during times of curricular revision and during annual and tenure reviews. If a department doesn't value composition textbook writing equally with the writing of critical essays and "creative" prose, drama and poetry, and allow those texts to count toward tenure, faculty will play out the department's value system in the classroom and in department interactions. And Dennis will be watching and learning.

The issues I've outlined here as being at play in a typical research university also play out in two- and four-year colleges. Graduate students like Dennis will mostly take up teaching positions within our two- and four-year colleges, replicating the habits they developed in their graduate teaching and imitating the practices of professors they studied under, including those in their undergraduate pasts. If their professors taught writing and reading quite differently or taught writing as if it were a course in reading, these graduate student/(teacher)/s will be influenced in the same direction. If graduate students at my institution teach first-year writing and junior- and senior-level literature based on different theories of learning, they are likely to continue to do the same as they teach undergraduates at other institutions.

Important questions remain to be answered: Is the move to theory only another battle and in what type of war? How do we shape change when professors, students, and curriculums are informed by tacit and explicit theories, many of which directly contradict the others? Even as Dennis wanted and needed to change his attitudes towards first-year writing instruction, he noted that such change was incredibly difficult.

12/5/90
Wendy: So, in a way, you thought they [first-year writers] would be fully formed writers with just bad habits . . . ?
Dennis: . . . Maybe I was thinking they should all be like me type of thing, you know, because I considered myself a decent writer when I got into college.
Wendy: You have an in-the-head criteria of great freshman writing?
Dennis: I don't know great. I don't like the word great.
Wendy: Your criteria of freshman writing . . . ?
Dennis: uh huh
Wendy: It's not your rankings of literary writing?
Dennis: No. No. No. That's one thing I have managed to separate.
Wendy: I've been advocating viewing students' writing as literature . . .
Dennis: Their grades would sink. Their grades would sink. Don't make me do that.
Wendy: No, I'd rather have you reconsider literature, but we'll talk about that another time.
Dennis: Okay (laughter). Seems like an argument there.

Wendy: Literature with a regular, healthy, small l.
Dennis: Oh no. We talked about that before with a *w.* (Laughter) I don't want to get into that again.
Wendy: Okay.

Reading Dennis, we find that learned theories of reading and writing are always foregrounded against a backdrop of tacit theories of learning, classrooms, and teaching roles that have been built up through a student's astute observation of professors and English studies as an institution. Such a complicated matrix of interactions suggests that we can't just talk theory talk and ask our students to do the same. Instead, we have to examine the roles graduate student/(teacher)/s are asked to assume in our classrooms, in their own classrooms, as writers and as readers, in every course in the English curriculum. Equally, we have to make our own tacit assumptions about these issues explicit as we discuss the future and directions of programs. At the least, we may have to give up some autonomy to develop curricular comprehensibility—some of us trying to do some of the same things, more or less, some of the time—for this will encourage dialog. I'm not suggesting that we all teach the same way—that's an impossible and unappealing solution—but I do believe we should agree to talk about how our theory exists in practice as we recalibrate curriculums. We need to learn from all our fields, that is—from each other. For even when we think we are conducting the decision-making process in the private forum of department faculty meetings, Dennis's case shows that our students are internalizing our conflicting theories and creating strategies for survival in every English course they take, and those strategies will affect an enormous number of students in undergraduate English classrooms in the future.

Notes

1. The textual stratification that Scholes points to marks such a great division between different strands of English studies that Graff himself, according to Christy Friend, problematically ignores one of the largest department level issues—the relationship of literature and composition.
2. Collection of Dennis's case study data was funded, in part, by a grant from the Research Foundation of the National Council of Teachers of English.

15

Having Been There
The Second Ethnography and On

*I had thought . . . that the process of becoming authoritative was much
quicker than this. But then again, I was forgetting the lessons of process
pedagogy. Just as I learned about the process of doing research and could
now design a better ethnographic project, I am also learning about the
process of writing it up. At least, [after completing my ethnographic
dissertation] I will be somewhat more prepared with the stamina and
determination required for a lengthy project next time.*

Donna Sewell (233–234)

ETHNOGRAPHY CHANGES THE ETHNOGRAPHER. CONDUCTING A FIRST
ethnography changes our relationship to the field, to research methods, to
our own authority, and, often, to our research subject(s). We're no longer
the complete novice, and, as Donna Sewell explains, we're somewhat sea-
soned and certainly sobered. A naturalistically-oriented writing researcher,
after her first study is completed, not unexpectedly feels that she could do
it better—next time. And there often seems to be a "next time" since
many of us are drawn to ethnography because it *is* a complicated and
compelling activity. As Paul Atkinson explains:

> The ethnography embeds and comments on the stories told by informants,
> investing them with a significance often beyond their mundane production. It
> includes the ethnographer's own accounts of incidents, "cases," and the like.
> They too are transformed and enhanced by their recontextualization in the
> ethnography itself. These narrative instances are collected and juxtaposed in
> the text so that their meaning (sociological or anthropological significance) is
> implied by the ethnographer and reconstructed by the reader. (Atkinson 13)

In 1990, when I completed and published *Something Old, Something
New: College Writing Teachers and Classroom Change*, a book-length study

on the learning processes of teachers, I had just negotiated, to some degree, the complex issues of becoming an ethnographic writing researcher. This new writing research methodology demanded that I learn both how to *be there* in the field—entering a community, observing, participating, collecting data—and how to *be here* on the page (see Geertz). After transcribing tapes, tabulating questionnaires, coding and analyzing journals, reviewing field notes, I had to create a believable authorial persona and prepare persuasive textualized accounts of my data and findings.

Ethnographic research methods were the most effective way of answering my research questions, the most theoretically sound way of studying the processes of writers, writing teachers and writing classrooms, and the most engaging use of skills I already possessed as a writer. For instance, the process of "textualizing" research data—that is, turning events into textual representations of those events—shared similarities with the methods of textualization taught in English literature departments and followed by creative writers who composed fictions and factions. Further, by completing an ethnography, I met several extrinsic goals, primarily, completing a Ph.D. in rhetoric and composition and being hired as an assistant professor of English.

When it came time to embark on "the second ethnography," another long-term study of college teachers, I felt well-prepared, having learned the most basic lesson of research under the guidance of my major professor, Donald McAndrew: have a good plan (prospectus, outline, grant application, etc.) and the rest will follow. He taught me, and taught me well, that you can never improve a poor plan at the last minute. With Don's help, I created a workable plan and after the project was done I was hooked on ethnographic research. I wanted to go on because I agreed with Sonda Perl that such research provides rich (and personally and professionally profitable) tasks:

> [W]e view both writing and teaching as personal and social acts created by individuals within particular contexts. When we take this kind of approach to such complex phenomena we don't end up with neat research designs, clear-cut boundaries and controlled variables. But we do find ourselves involved in an enormously rich task that often requires us to respond on a human level. (Perl 11)

Therefore, I began the second ethnography (Working Title: *Composing the New Teacher of College Writing*) following closely on the good plan of my first project. In my first study, I looked at experienced teachers as they returned to summer school to study theories of writing and teaching. In this study, I would be looking at new graduate teaching assistants beginning their graduate studies and training to be teachers for first time. Both groups were learning about writing theory and pedagogy but each group was at a different point in their professional careers and attending different schools under different time constraints. The difference in the two projects resided in the population and location of the school, then, but not in my data collection methods because I hadn't realized yet that new populations and locations might (probably do) require individualized data collection strategies.

Other problems arose. First, it was time for a project for this assistant professor on a tenure-line. Second, there were funding opportunities available. And third, that's what academics did, continued to research, as far as I could see. Luckily, I liked research and saw no problem with continuing. Although supported in-part by an NCTE research grant, and although all the data was collected according to plan, the second book-length ethnography, much to my regret, is still incomplete. Reams of collected data languish in blue plastic storage crates and I've published only one of many potential essays—"Attitudes and Expectations: How Theory in the Graduate Student (Teacher) Complicates the English Curriculum"—(with plans and personal commitment to a second) out of a wealth of data collected over fifteen months from the gathered materials of eight case study teachers' generously shared lives.

I realized—after data collection—that there were two major flaws in my second project. First, I had forgotten that the ethnographic moment is not replicable (evidence of this comes from my staying too close to my first project design, from not realizing that two groups of "teachers" could vary so much) since each investigation is created through the interactions of research design *and* researcher *and* community:

> This worldview [holistic, participative] sees human beings as cocreating their reality through participation: through their experience, their imagination and intuition, their thinking and their action (Heron, 1991). As Skolimowski (1992) puts it "We always partake of what we describe" (p. 20), so our "reality" is a product of the dance between our individual and collective mind and "what is there," the amorphous primordial givenness of the universe. This participative worldview is at the heart of inquiry methodologies that emphasize participation as a core strategies. (Reason 324)

Second, by modeling this second investigation so strongly on my first, I became less engaged, more a technician and less a participant-observer.

I had moved my lens too slightly, focused too firmly, and did not allowed my project to breathe. I was more interested in the teachers as individuals (partly because they taught in a writing program I was about to become director of) but less drawn into the project as a whole (partly because of my looming WPA apprenticeship). I knew (philosophically and method-ologically) but did not understand (practically) the degree to which: "The ethnography is bound in time and place. The ethnography is uniquely shaped by the sensibilities and style of its individual author. The ethnographer is, we know, the 'research instrument' par excellence. The fieldwork is the product of a personal and biographical experience" (Atkinson 29).

It was not until I had collected data and faced my writing-it-up respon-sibilities that I learned that I had overdetermined the outcome of my sec-ond major research experience. I did not see until then that I should have embarked on my second project for different reasons and in order to cover different territory by different means. I was exercising my skills but sel-dom reinventing and augmenting them. I had reversed the problem Mary Louise Pratt mentions when she complains about dull or poorly written research narratives. She asks: "For the lay person, such as myself, the main evidence of a problem is the simple fact that ethnographic writing tends to be surprisingly boring. How, one asks constantly, could such interesting people doing such interesting things produce such dull books?" (33). I had sabotaged my own work by making the "doing" itself dull. Data col-lection complete, my involvement in the project waned. At a growing dis-tance from the intrinsic interest of interviewing human informants—real live teachers whose lives and work I was always interested in—I became too easily distracted by other projects. I found that I was not writing this research according to plan; I found that research was no longer a prospec-tus to dissertation proposition. Suddenly, I entertained the distractions of my new job and lacked the pressures of the job hunt that would send me back day after day to the data.

Certainly, too, during the time of this second ethnography, I moved toward other interests—writing classroom textbooks and conducting teacher-research and pursuing personal essay writing about literacy and education—and these multiple interests (which I couldn't afford to enter-tain during the dissertation process) seduced me from the time-consum-ing, sometimes tedious, work of writing up my research. Writing *about* ethnography overtook and surpassed writing *up* my second project data. Particularly since writing *about* could take place in essay or chapter sized chunks of writing time and those chunks could add up to enough understanding to compose a handbook (for instance, see *Ethnographic*, "I-Witnessing" and "The Perils"). Also, writing *about* suddenly took on new importance as I began to teach research methods classes and direct dissertation projects. My line of writing followed my lines of immediate need.

Perhaps such developments might not have created such a guilt-filled year, when everything I wrote seemed to come at the "expense" of the "second project," if I had remembered some of my initial readings. For instance, in *Tales of the Field*, John Van Maanan mentions the tendency in anthropology for initial field work to produce the same effect. For many, the anthropological ethnographic experience may still require three to five years in residency, but the ethnographic life thereafter often focuses on writing about issues in ethnography rather than on continued fieldwork since the researcher has often left the community (the anthropologist leaves the country and the classroom researcher leaves the class at term's end). When I first read this observation I was disturbed by it; now, I have experienced a similar trajectory. I began to teach research methods courses in ethnography, I began to read post-modern ethnographic theorists, I began to push the boundaries of methods and writing style in smaller-scale research projects. In that sense, I was more fully living the ethnographic life than I had earlier. Such a life was no longer "out there"—a project to be done for credentialling—but it was also "in here," all mixed up, a part and parcel of my academic and writing life and I had to learn to accept and negotiate this new, seemingly boundary-less, existence. As Clandinin and Connelly put it, I was learning to live, tell, relive and retell *my story*. This chapter, of course, is part of that process. Clandinin and Connelly claim:

> We imagine, therefore, that in the construction of narratives of experience, there is a reflexive relationship between living a life story, telling a life story, retelling a life story, and reliving a life story. As researchers, we are always engaged in living, telling, reliving, and retelling our own stories. (418)

Returning to *Tales of the Field* I also find an argument that important research narratives had been left out of my training; rarely had I read about work that didn't work, for rarely do we share our tales of research misfortune: "The implied story line of many a confessional tale is that of a fieldworker and a culture finding each other and, despite some initial spats and misunderstandings, in the end, making a match" (Van Maanan 79). Clearly, researchers need to learn from their mistakes as much as any other learners do, as we encourage writers to do. And, equally clearly, they need to be telling problem stories as well as success stories; I consider my second ethnography a problem though not a failure—I failed to achieve full written closure though I certainly have learned much as I researched and as I contemplated the project. Still, it is rare for me to talk about my work as I am in this chapter, just as it is rare to read published reports of "projects where the research was presumably so personally disastrous to the fieldworker that the study was dropped or failed ever to find its way to publication" (Van Maanan 79).

In this chapter, I am clearly sharing a confessional tale, but I don't completely agree with John Van Maanan that more honest confessions would uncover scores of disastrous, failed, dropped, or unpublished work. It might uncover—and fruitfully—some of this. But also, confessional tales provide accounts of the process of learning ethnographic practices and adapting to the ethnographic life, detailing researchers' adjustments, compromises, and confusions that inevitably occur in a first anything (that will of necessity occur in some degree in subsequent anythings, too).

Given this pocket history of one life in research, in the space that remains I want to offer as preliminary advice a few observations intended to improve life after the first ethnography. If the second ethnography is a continuation or elaboration of our journey and therefore part of our professional meditations, where might it take us and what do we need to do to make sure we arrive somewhere? To pose tentative answers to such a question, I'll look at four areas: goal-setting, learning from the process, understanding one's own research authority and direction(s), and accepting—for some this means embracing—the ethnographic life.

Intrinsic and Extrinsic Research Goals

It's crucial for the researcher to make professional goals personal goals, to merge extrinsic and intrinsic motivation. Ethnographic research is highly amenable to this strategy since what we learn in our work often improves our teaching, deepens our understanding of writers, encourages us to "read" educational settings more critically and carefully. While a researcher may be required in her job to conduct research, that same individual will probably benefit personally as a teacher by studying those issues that seem crucial to her. And, quite simply, to offer a good reading of our data we must find that data compelling, because the ethnographic process requires that we return to it again and again. If, in returning, we are not engaged, or if, because of design predictability or impoverishment, the return is tedious, we will not fare well. Therefore, to even attempt the ethnographic practice of creating an on-going "thick-description" of a culture the researcher must be engaged at all levels of meaning-making.

Ethnography offers narrative representations of how a researcher evokes a particular culture at a particular time. The ethnographic report is always several steps removed from the culture, being, as Thomas Schwandt points out, "an inquirer's construction of the constructions of the actors one studies" (118). Therefore, I think we'll find the culture and the construction-making most compelling when we have both private and professional commitments to making meaning out of the events we're co-creating with our ethnographic attention. For humanist—rather than social scientific—researchers; for writing program administrators wanting to know more about programs; for teachers eager to understand classrooms; for writers determined to learn more about writing—the intrinsic case study will seem preferable:

> In what we may call intrinsic case study, study is undertaken because one wants better understanding of this particular case. It is not undertaken primarily because the case represents other cases or because it illustrates a particular trait or problem, but because, in all its particularity and ordinariness, this case itself is of interest. (Stake 237)

Finally, when undertaking the second ethnography, we are already more authoritative than we were in the first project. Now we may need to worry less about closeness to a culture (as when a graduate student studies a peer's classroom and has to determine/explore the degree prior friendship and assumptions about the teacher and classroom will influence the "scene of research") and more about guaranteeing our engagement and committing our time . This is probably best done by setting up intrinsic goals that are as strong or stronger than extrinsic goals. For instance, when applying for grant funding, as I did, making sure that a fundable research design doesn't overdetermine a project's direction (this is one explanation of what may have happened in my case).

To stay engaged with my data and my writing commitments, I've had to do as William Stafford suggests and "lower my standards" in order to begin at all. Instead of dreaming of a book that I'm not writing, I accept the value of producing an essay-length case study and working to understanding what I learn from the writing-up process. In doing this, I learn to accept the fact that I can't always produce products I facilely promise.

Learning from The Process

Just as we learn a great deal about writing by the act of writing, whether our work sees the light of public print or not, we learn important lessons from the ethnographic research process—even when we need to let the data go or even when our final reports take an unexpected turn. This is a lesson I have to re-learn with each project, large and small, and it's a lesson I see my students learning, and re-learning. For instance, my data collecting skills have improved through practice while my second more frustrating experience led me to "study" ethnographic theory and philosophies and to question my own relationship to the method. The quote from Donna Sewell, which opens this chapter, shows the degree to which every new researcher reinvents insight(s) into the process. In research classes, my students and I have seen that short-term, mini-ethnographies can teach us great deal: from what it's like to be stood up by informants to what it's like to enter a new culture, alone and insecurely.

Ethnographers learn from seeing, doing, being there and then being here on the page. Since they can't enter the stream of a particular culture in the same place twice, it stands to reason that they'll constantly learn (and want to learn) from the process. Process writings, whether they show up in a final product in a manner now being undertaken by some postmodern ethnographers or in the form of intermediary texts that are later edited out of the final product, still, all, allow us to learn. Devan Cook, who recently completed her first ethnography that explores the lives of student writers who work, found herself including poems on how to be an ethnographer and personal narratives of her own work/writing life in the course of her many dissertation drafts. Some remain, some became texts on their own, circulating in literary journals, still others are now filed away. Stephen North suggests we should expect to do this juggling of realities and genres given that ethnographers, as he sees it, are "Serving as a kind of alternate reality brokers, they [ethnographers] deliberately juxtapose one imaginative universe with another, struggling, in the effort, to make both more intelligible—to themselves, to us, to the inhabitants of those alternate universes" (North 279).

Research Authority Creates Research Direction(s)

The second entry to the field may represent the first time we truly feel professional. It becomes time to claim our membership in our research discourse community (particularly as we try to turn school-writing into journal or book-writing) and help (re)see the direction of our continuing research. For instance, in the five years since my first ethnography and now, my own movement toward more narrative reporting was confirmed by my wider readings in poststructural discussions that began in anthropology and are currently affecting the way we define ethnographic writing research. Learning about these discussions accelerated my move to cultivating an informal, narrative research writing style that allows me to investigate ethical, political, and writerly concerns more freely.

No one can give us a sense of authority. We must earn it *and* we must take it. The credentialling process of dissertation writing can only take us so far; reflection on our own position will take us another necessary part of the way. For instance, Donna Sewell ended her dissertation with this meditation on authority and researcher roles:

> While I fully realize the main function of dissertations is to credential scholars, at times I managed to forget my probationary status, just as I did when I completed studying for preliminary examinations. During those times I felt most like a researcher and less like a novice. After the first two disorienting weeks in the "field," I could see the project coming together even as I struggled frantically to keep interview appointments and collect documents. Especially during that first summer, I was a researcher.
>
> Within the academic year, though, my roles became multi-layerd again, as I was called upon to teach, mentor, serve on committees and do research; the next summer moved me back into a researcher role, but the role of researcher as writer, a new and scary one. And now, of course, in another academic year [as a new assistant professor], I am balancing mostly researcher and teacher [roles] again. (Sewell 233)

Living (and Enjoying) the Ethnographic Life

Finally, completing the first ethnography and then going on, as a learning, fallible, yet engaged researcher, helped me realize that living (and enjoying) the ethnographic life overall is what I've really been learning about; and, if the life fits, I'd say, wear it. As my initial research goals were achieved and then complicated by continuing research, I found my life in general has been enriched by thinking ethnographically. There are few things so pleasurable as participating in the imaginative and systematic thinking that an ethnographic stance requires. The drafting of texts also activates many writerly qualities and challenges that I value:

[T]his issue, negotiating the passage from what one has been through "out there" to what one says "back here," is not psychological in character. It is literary. It arises for anyone who adopts what one may call, in a serious pun, the I-witnessing approach to the construction of cultural descriptions. . . . To place the reach of your sensibility . . . at the center of your ethnography, is to pose for yourself a distinctive sort of textbuilding problem: rendering your account credible through rendering your person so. . . . To be a convincing "I-witness," one must, so it seems, first become a convincing "I." (Geertz 78–79)

There is something very satisfying about working to become a convincing "I," although that I changes regularly. The I of my first ethnography has given way to the I of the second project who in turn engendered the I of this account. Each witness needed to be constructed, each journey taught me, and each continues to encourage me to travel on. Having been there and back again, I hope you'll allow yourself to learn from both failure and success, to be both idealistic and pragmatic as you embark on your research travels once again.

Part V

Composing Ourselves as (Creative) Writers

Writing captured me and composition helped me understand that captivation. After unbraiding and uncomposing my selves within the academy in order to learn specialized skills and certain discourses, in order to participate in elect and select societies, I decided intentionally to rebraid and recompose my self through teaching creative and compositional strategies together. Just as I believe we return to the site of our family to understand ourselves as partners and parents and siblings and sons and daughters, I return to my life as a writer, particularly my life as an academic creative writer, to understand who I am in composition studies today. It is for this reason that I believe that the good and the bad (or indifferent or spotty or dramatic or quiet) teaching I experienced as a student still informs me. It must be critiqued, assimilated, accommodated, transcended, reprocessed.

To do this, I've helped found professional special interest groups, I've proposed and attended workshops and readings, I've depended on classroom and on extracurricular writing groups. And I've written. Still, I think it can never be adequately explained or explored, this (creative) writer's life. The journal on my desk filled with loves, travels, desires doesn't fully do it nor do conversations, explanations, and essays. Still, a mixture of writing about and writing within has developed some insight.

"Crossing the Lines: on Creative Composition and Composing Creative Writing" published in Writing on the Edge *in 1993 is based on earlier essays and has become an ur-text of my understandings. It was reprinted in a 1994 collection* Colors of a Different Horse: Rethinking Creative Writing, Theory and Pedagogy *(co-edited with my regular co-author Hans Ostrom, whose thinking in this area, along with that of Katharine Haake, has greatly influenced my own) and led directly to the more personally situated argue for the benefits of combining creative writing and composition studies, or at least*

aspects of and knowledges from both fields. In "Learning" I revisit scenes of creative writing that at first kept me from being a comfortable or effective teacher in that field. I work in these two essays, as I worked in earlier essays, to defuse and/or detonate counter-productive myths, attitudes, and beliefs about these worlds of writing and teaching writing. I say defuse and/or detonate because neither move alone seemed then, or seems now, enough to shake up and reconstitute the institutional, professional, fiscal, emotional, practical divides that have developed.

"Poetry as Process: Realigning Art and the Unconscious" comes at institutional problems from a different angle. Not only are writing programs divided, but institutions divide us from our own best relationships to the work we value—in this case, for me, the writing of poetry. In this 1995 essay I explore my current impulse to find the process of writing poetry equal to or often greater than the end-goal I once aspired to—that of becoming a well-published professional academic poet. In this essay, I look again at a writer-who-teaches relationship to institutional politics as well as the politics of taste.

One result of the successful breaking down of barriers between composition and creative writing (or the rebraiding of naturally congruent elements) is the access this gives us as writers and teachers to all genres of writing. In the case of "What We (Might) Write About When We Write (Autobiographical) Nonfiction" I take the confluence of fields as an encouragement to talk about a formerly undervalued creative genre (nonfiction) and to do so experimentally. This 1995 essay provides a meta-analysis of one class, is filled with student and professional voices, and pushes the boundaries of the genre under discussion and the genre of presentation (the how-to essay). The following essay, "The Shape of Fact," is also an enactment of principles and processes. In "The Shape of Fact" I use the freedoms of multivoice writing to explore creative nonfiction as genre, to include sections of literacy autobiography as I was practicing the form in classes I taught, and to end with classroom critique turned meta narrative as I wove in student responses to my nonfiction essay as a way of enlarging the scope of that essay. Drafted in 1992, "The Shape of Fact" led in part to the class developed and discussed in "What We (Might) Write About." I include these two pieces as practical proof that only by crossing the artificial institutional borders that I was trained in—first as a creative writer—next as a compositionist—was I able to write the more exploratory and thought-provoking pieces that end this section—was I able to better compose my writing life.

16

Crossing the Lines
On Creative Composition and Composing Creative Writing

WE NEED TO BE CROSSING THE LINE BETWEEN COMPOSITION AND CREATIVE writing far more often than we do. In fact, we may want to eliminate the line entirely. To support this claim, I hope to describe what it has felt like to enter the creative writing classroom as a composition specialist and the world of composition studies as a creative writer, before suggesting that we rethink undergraduate writing curriculums and revise graduate education for writing teachers.

To begin, consider this undergraduate's journal entry, discussing creative writing *and* composition:

> I'm really confused here. What's the difference between the two? Most of the time I use the two words interchangeably . . . . For all I know, it is a grave sin to use one for the other. If I think really hard, I can see a line of distinction begin to form between the two ideas. Is creative writing stuff that is done for fun, and composition stuff that the teacher makes you do? That's what it meant in elementary school, and later. Composition was writing about a specific topic, picked out by the teacher and had to be a certain length and certain form. Creative writing was anything you felt like putting down on paper. My creative writing was most often poetry, or a short story. Composition was an essay. So it's fun stuff vs. required stuff. Then I wrote a paper that was required, and it turned out to be fun. What??!? Yes, and it was an English (ugh! don't say it!) *term* paper. I chose my own topic, so I wouldn't get bored with it. Something *totally* off the wall, so fascinating that its appeal overwhelmed my intense hatred of term papers. It was on parapsychology.

This student, Fran, found composition a dreary, teacher-imposed task and creative writing something done to pass time, for fun. In her world view, students in creative writing classes seemed launched on a teacherless field-trip and students in composition classes entered a kind of academic prison. Fran was confused even as this line formed when she realized that the distinction between fun stuff and required stuff, creative writing and composition, broke down when she chose and wrote on her own topic, parapsychology. Equally important, from the view of the two writing professions, Fran doesn't make nearly as much of the genre distinction as her teachers make—that is, that creative writing results in poetry and stories, non-nonfiction, while composition results in essays, non-fiction (terms I use intentionally to highlight problematic distinctions). Finally, there's a hint of guilt in Fran's story; she had fun, became engaged, and even learned in a composition class only when she broke the rules.

My second story moves from unintentional to intentional confusion. A first-year college writer calls home to talk to her mother, a former director of composition and a friend of mine. Composing her first college paper, this writer, Lee, was resistant. She told her mother that she didn't like the first-year writing teacher, the assignment, or the grade she received—a C—and reported current first-year lore that claimed a first paper grade would be a student's end-of-semester class grade.

For the second paper, students were asked to go off campus and interview someone about their work and writing. Lee didn't have time, didn't want to—knew she was going to get a C. But, a week later, Lee reported that she had received a B-minus on the interview paper and strong teacher encouragement. Then, she explained to her mother that she had *invented* the interview and that during a revision conference for this paper the teacher asked Lee about a detail relating to her imagined "real" interviewee. "I'll go back and ask him," Lee assured her teacher. And, real interviews or not, Lee was encouraged by her improving class performance; she made a high B on her third paper and the same for her final class grade.

The semester after this story unfolded, I continued to reflect on Lee's experiences, for I believed that they would be replicated by students enrolled in my own writing program—again and again. First-year writing for Lee was no fun; she was disengaged, at least until she redefined her assignment by turning in a piece of "imaginative" writing for the required factual interview. Genres seem to have little to do with her new success with writing.

In a third and final story, this one from the creative writing side of the line, we see that confusion can result in self-doubt. Despite Fran's assumption that creative writing is the fun stuff, writing with which we're more readily engaged, students who enroll in creative writing classes for the first time may have to overcome an overwhelming sense of unworthiness. Since creative writing is usually an elective class, those who elect it may be English majors, more steeped than fellow students in the traditional canon.

If creative writing is the class in which literature is made, as an English studies–influenced student tends to think, she or he will wonder: Am I good enough to make literature with a capital L? Frank writes in his class journal:

> I think I was misleading myself for a very long time. I had so many grand ideas about writing that I had forgotten that you have to write to be a writer. . . . [Now,] instead of pondering over ideas and waiting for the perfect one, the one to make me famous, I take small ideas and make them good ones. I just recently finished a short story that I am very proud of. It was 8 pages long, the longest one I had ever written. It had scenes, summaries, dialogue. I love it. I didn't really ever think I had it in me. I was putting so much pressure on myself to write the masterpiece that all of my writing was overdramatic, didn't say anything and was shallow. I have learned to write in stride, write for myself & let my ideas flow. Although I really do picture my audience as I write, I now write with much less apprehension and try not to make them my cornerstone.
>
> I have realized that just by sitting down and writing many different ideas just pop into your head. It is as if you turn on a hose that has been lying out in the sun. You expect cold water to come out & then are amazed that you get scalded by the water that has been heating in its length.

For some of us a ready response to Frank's entry is to shake heads and think he's more than a little misguided. Famous? A masterpiece? For, depending on our feelings about who should be encouraged to pursue "creative" writing, we may find Frank's hose metaphor an indication of promise or a prediction of mediocrity.

As I moved as a teacher between these worlds of composition classes and creative writing classes, my pedagogy in each became more similar. However, because the culture I inhabited—English studies—didn't support such commonalties in instruction, I hadn't examined very well my growing beliefs that it was more productive to cross the line than to create a separate teaching persona on either side. If there was limited use in making so many distinctions between the areas, I needed to understand why I continued to make some of them and what was at stake.

***

I was formally trained to teach composition. I was not formally trained to teach poetry. However, I write poetry and not compositions, at least not the type of essays—in the modes—that I was first hired to teach to my students. Jim Corder is one of the few composition teachers I know of who regularly reports his attempts to write essays with his students, although theorists now often advocate such a practice. And Corder admits to the difficulty of the enterprise; sometimes he even cheats, recycling old papers and creating pastiche compositions so as always to be there with students as a fellow author (see "Asking for a Text"). Most writing teachers, however, don't write with their students, if they write much at all. When we do write, it seems safe to say, we don't produce the type of writing we ask students to produce. Lynn Bloom argues that "teachers of writing should write literary nonfiction, assuming that is what we teach, and we should publish what we write . . . writing regularly should be as much a part of the teacher's activity as meeting class, and as unremarkable" (87). Additionally, like me, many of the new teachers of writing I train never took first-year writing, having tested out of those classes and wandered back into the fold via literature and creative writing; therefore, we have underdeveloped personal schemas for those classrooms.

These attitudinal and experiential problems compound. While graduate students in creative writing programs inevitably see themselves as writers, M.A. and Ph.D. candidates in English literature traditionally have prepared themselves for lives as "scholars," defined by their abilities to read. Undergraduates' careers as students of great literature may ill-prepare them for naming themselves as writers as graduate students. "The problem for many of us," explains Harvey Kail, "is that authors became our heroes long before we began to think of ourselves as writers willing to compete with those heroes for a reader's attention" (89). And Patricia Sullivan's study of graduate-level literature instruction shows that writing abilities are usually assumed and not taught, deficits being attributed to problems in the student not to problems with English graduate education.

While it's easy to imagine readers who resist my claims with the simple counter-claims that they *do* write and teach, these individuals would be ignoring the toll taken on many of their colleagues by teaching loads, department assignments, institutional attitudes, and personal life—constraints that work to keep the majority of writing teachers from publishing or even from viewing themselves as authors. Mimi Schwartz found this to be true to a surprising degree. She opens *Writer's Craft/ Teacher's Art* in this way:

> This book began on Martha's Vineyard three years ago, with this question: "How many of you consider yourself writers?" I was teaching a two-week seminar on writing to twenty-five writing teachers from twenty states, mostly from English Departments. . . . Two hands went up. "What about the rest of you?" I asked, somewhat surprised. "We're not good enough . . . famous enough . . . creative enough. What we write—memos, letters, articles, reports, diaries, grants—that doesn't count," said the Noes. (ix)

These writers did not feel that their academic writing was valid or valuable. And clearly, academic writing may be as distinctly unpleasurable for some teachers as composition is for many of their students since academic writing is, to a degree, as compulsory within institutional life as is first-year writing for a first-year student. Compulsion has the same counterproductive results, both constituencies avoid writing; Maxine Hairston suggests "that at least two-thirds of college professors publish nothing after the dissertation" ("When Writing" 62).

These, then, are just a few of the problems that arise. Many teachers don't write; those who do write specialize. Creative writers compose primarily imaginative work and composition instructors excel at the academic essay or, more likely, the memo and class handout. Graduate level tracking into creative writing *or* academic writing has been strenuous and successful. And creative writing teachers with an unhealthy sense of author hero-worship may transmit those feelings to a student like Frank who for a long time saw writing primarily as the act of producing a masterpiece in order to gain fame. And composition teachers may tend to perpetuate the conservative writing class Fran mentioned—students writing only on teacher-specified topics of restrictive length and form. This will be particularly likely if these teachers have underdeveloped writers' identities, experience negative institutional pressures (either they *must* write and/or they're given *no* opportunity to write), and have never experienced first-year writing from the inside—as students or as teachers who write with their students.

***

It is important to emphasize that teachers participate in a complicated acculturation process within Departments of English. As graduate students, many progress through the various strands of English studies looking for a home. For instance, I started in creative writing, quickly added literature, discovered and moved into rhetoric, and all the while kept up my interests in all my earlier types of writing and reading. I wanted to connect my knowledge of writing and reading, discovered in the separate "strands," but was not encouraged to do so. I don't think, from conversations with colleagues, that mine is simply a naive academic *Bildungsroman* for there is rarely an easy initiation into English studies. But I have been able to begin sorting my confusions with the help of the institutional histories and professional critiques that are becoming more available.

One examination of the lines that divide us has been provided by Robert Scholes in *Textual Power*. Scholes describes how the institution of English studies has always valued the consumption of texts (interpretation and reading) over the production of texts (all writing) and that in the four-tiered textual hierarchy of the traditional English department, creative writing ranks as pseudo-literature (literature in the wings) and is valued over composition (pseudo-nonliterature). Both, in turn, are subservient to literature because literature calls for interpretation, the highest ranked form of consumption. In spite of these apparently stable, ranked positions, however, creative writing developed with composition.

The two writings were in unison at the turn of the century after which, according to David Meyers, composition became a routinized operation for teaching the large numbers of students to write (for composition history, see also, of course, Berlin). Robert Connors traces an equally efficient institution-serving movement, claiming "Narration and description seceded to become the nuclei of creative writing courses, and argumentation, finding itself more of an orphan in English departments, took refuge in speech departments and became largely an oral concern for many years" (30). From a creative writing historian's or composition historian's point of view, composition was left with the stripped down expository, non-fiction, essay form that we now recognize, while literary composition was viewed generally as unsuitable for "the masses" who weren't qualified to appreciate or practice literary art. "It was foundations of grammar and usage that students required" (Meyers 103). The lessons here are obviously political ones; fundamentals precede art and art writing is for the elite (endlessly, the white, literate, at least middle-class kind), and composition writing is for those who need nothing more than *basic* literacy (although what that is no group has yet been able to agree upon) (see Eagleton and Graff *Professing*).

There are conflicts here then of class and an issue of genres being asserted to represent class interests. But actual writers—student writers—

don't fall neatly into categories. I point to Fran, Lee, and Frank, to the ways they found that one genre is not more valuable than another for learning about writers and writing; specifically, Frank in a creative writing class is as engaged with his work as is Fran writing her self-chosen term paper on parapsychology in a composition class. Because they are engaged with their writing, choosing topics and using writing to learn more about themselves and their worlds, Fran and Frank are writers-more-than-students. However, when students remain students-more-than-writers, when instruction is top-down, for their own good, they quickly become disenfranchised.

Often students believe essay writing is a chore. They also believe in what I'll call the myth of "free creativity" in creative writing classes, as expressed here by Bill: "In creative writing, I feel that there is no set guidelines. It leaves room for experimentation and you can go into any angle or direction. In expository prose you have set guidelines of what you must write and how you should write it." This "free creativity" belief is as devastating for the creative writing class as it is for composition classes. When students arrive in creative writing classes with dichotomous attitudes—composition is no fun, creative writing therefore must be fun—creative writing classes can appear surprisingly restrictive since novice writers are often expected to learn conventions like the intricacies of formal verse or plotting and point of view rather than simply given free rein to "find some exotic, fun, brilliant way to say things" as Ashley had hoped.

No doubt, students are confused about the relationship between composition and creative writing because English studies as a profession is confused. Early in his history of the subject, Meyers defines creative writing:

> As it is loosely applied today, creative writing seems to denote a class of compositions once simply called fiction. . . . As such it is a makeshift, omnibus term for poems, novels, novellas, short stories, and (sometimes) plays; for the invented as opposed to the historical; for the imaginary in contradistinction to the actual; for the concrete and particular as distinguished from the thorny and abstract. In short, for non-nonfiction. . . . (2)

The textual creations that Meyers catalogs as fixed genres will be found by many current compositionists (and literary theorists) as convenient, contingent and situated. The historical must be discovered through the ideologically based author; the actual can only be apprehended through the representations of language and constructed texts; and the thorny and abstract may provide valid but (currently) not sanctioned ways of learning about the concrete and particular.

Essentially, our categorical systems work to maintain order within our communities. And our communities—to maintain and preserve order—insist that we adhere to our categories and their hierarchies. When genres blur, it is necessary to remind ourselves that categories are *constructed* and that genres are *defined*: "*Genre*," Scholes reminds us, "refers to things regularly done and *style* to a regular *way* of doing things" (2).

English studies is not the only academic field that is considering these problems. Particularly relevant is the situation of ethnographers who are entertaining critiques of one hundred fifty years of field research, purporting to detail the "real" life of other cultures. Anthropologist Clifford Geertz explains:

> [The idea] that the writing of ethnography involves telling stories, making pictures, concocting symbolisms, and deploying tropes is commonly resisted, often fiercely, because of a confusion, endemic in the West since Plato at least, of the imagined with the imaginary, the fictional with the false, making things out with making them up. The strange idea that reality has an idiom in which it prefers to be described . . . leads on to the even stranger idea that, if literalism is lost, so is fact. (140)

Discussing the construction of ethnographic narratives, certain anthropologists argue that ethnographic reporting involves "telling" the life of the researcher as much or more as the life of the studied culture. Influenced by current critical theory, these individuals acknowledge the subjective and ideological nature of their profession, based as it is on human experience. Human science, then, becomes more similar to than dissimilar from humanistic study; field notes are texts, and text *are interpreted* by highly trained, skilled, but situated authors. Those exploring these views challenge anthropology's original values, those of positivistic research, an empiricism grounded in "true" facts and "pure" data.

It would seem that the strands of English studies—literature, composition, and creative writing—are also laboring under, have actually even helped to establish and maintain, similar self-limiting ideas of the "true" relationship of fact and fiction: if literalism is lost, is fact? What of the imaginative reality of Fran's fabricated composition interview? Would we do better to consider the degree to which non-nonfiction writing always evolves out of its composer's fact-filled existence and the degree to which nonfiction is shaped by its composer's judgments, desires, and imagination?

Whether we sanction it or not, when fact and fiction do blend we need other ways of looking at and of teaching writing.

***

These considerations return me to the writing classroom. As a composition teacher, I was trained to have the unique ability to grade individual first-year texts. I learned to invoke the generic "college-level" rubric (essentially thesis, development, organization, mechanics) that my teacher preparation class and textbooks taught me. And I rarely doubted my abilities to rank what might seem a bewildering array of "essays." I could identify not only superior and inferior examples of writing but every range in-between.

From my earliest moment teaching poetry writing, however, in spite of my own experience with the genre—which included far more practice with the form and far more reading in it—I was sure that it is impossible to evaluate (grade) the single poem, and I have never done so. Although I know a few individuals who grade single pieces of "art" writing, most do not. And never would I grade my student's first poem, although early in my teaching I was regularly required to grade first freshman essays in freshman composition. And oddly, in creative writing classes, the *adequate* story or poem (call it average or C-level) was rarely discussed and never assumed to be a normal base for future growth.

Although I now grade all writing classes—composition and creative writing—by the portfolio method, as a writing program administrator and institutional representative, I must note that I still sanction more controlling attitudes and practices toward first-year writing and writers. Certainly, I *am* accountable to certain state, university, and program mandates and constraints. But also, I suspect that I agree to institutional pressures in part because I have never taken first-year writing and never had regularly to produce those pieces of "student writing." As I wrote this essay, I changed that situation, and the process of meeting the deadlines and writing demands of my own advanced composition class *as I taught it* proved sobering, informative, and tough. It also prompted me to improve my classroom design.

By writing and rewriting this essay, by writing with, for, and to my writing students, I'm exploring the degree to which I am a product of my own literary education, taught to value the "fictional" work (pseudo-literary text) over the essay (pseudo-non-literary text), and I still find myself in situations where I may talk about the average essay although it remains impossible (not-creative-writing-field-sanctioned) to hold serious discussions about the *average* poem or story. All this despite my willingness to tell you that I believe writing in each genre to be more similar to writing in other genres than it is different from them.

I am of course influenced by what Linda Brodkey calls the "scene of writing." In the modern scene of writing, the artist is locked into a garret, writing masterpieces alone. Brodkey warns of the danger of this image, ". . . those who teach as well as those who take composition [and all writing] courses are influenced by the scene of writing, namely, that all of us try to recreate a garret and all that it portends whether we are writing in a study, a library, a classroom, or at a kitchen table, simply because we learned this lesson in writing first" (397). One result of this lesson is an overvaluation of—a worship of—literature. Over and over, we come to non-nonfiction with "the attitude of the exegete before the sacred text" (Scholes 16).

Not surprisingly, the "scene of writing" and its image of "solitary genesis," as Valerie Miner calls it, affects our students' views of texts. They quickly learn that the most *valuable* texts are puzzles; they learn to solve puzzles in literature classes and they come to creative writing hoping to learn puzzle-construction, to escape to a garret and reappear hours later with a soon-to-be-acknowledged masterpiece. The role of author is seductive, as you've seen from Frank's journal entry and, no doubt, from the responses of your own creative writing students. And the roles as apportioned leave nothing to composition classes except the predictable drudgery of delivering unpuzzling texts to uncomplicated readers. No wonder neither students nor their teachers look forward to such a workplace.

***

It is possible to point out that institutions have rigid and self-maintaining categorical systems—field coverage, composition *or* creative writing, fact *or* fiction, and so on. It is less easy to discover how these systems work within research agendas—say the ones of the composition community. classic studies in composition research often compared and contrasted the basic and the expert (non-fiction) writer. Difficult areas—student engagement (or lack of), individual talent, cognition and creativity, writer's affect—were generally bounded out of research projects, influenced as they were by the positivistic research tradition. Even today, there are few studies of "creative writers" and there is little encouragement to conduct such studies (published exceptions include those by Armstrong, Brand, and Tomlinson). As compositionists model the writing process, what will be known when we claim to present this thing we call the *non-fiction writing process?*

Creative writing as a composition research area, then, is generally ignored in spite of cross-the-line pedagogical raiding; compositionists have borrowed effective teaching methods from the creative writing work-shop—particularly group response sessions and portfolio evaluation—improved on those borrowings and gone beyond them. Seldom discussed are the basic commonalties of writing a poem and writing an essay. That is, many teachers in both writing areas deny commonalties while a few teachers are exploring connections. Anthony Petrosky feels that, despite surface differences, the processes of poetry and essay writing are produc-tively similar (209). Marie Ponsot and Rosemary Deen believe all students of writing are creative, that they are always writing literature, and that writing processes have basic commonalties:

> [S]tudent writing is literature, that is, free and disinterested, a product of imagination and thought. In our experience and the experience of those we know, there is no essential difference between writing a poem and writing an essay, except, as we must often say, that writing a poem is easier, its conven-tions being so much clearer and more plentiful. (65)

Their claim that essays are more difficult to compose may seem hard to believe until we remember those teachers of composition who rarely themselves write first-year compositions. So, for many of us, perhaps, writing a poem would be easier than writing an essay since we are well schooled, if literature majors, in the conventions of poetic form. We are also schooled in that school never to view student writing as Literature (despite what that vision promises for the project of responding to stu-dents' drafts). Literature is what is past, what is old. Ponsot and Deen, however, redefine literature through language, claiming "What[ever in a text] we pay attention to is literature" (68) and then show how this defin-ition helps both teacher and student: "When we name and praise the liter-ature in a student's writing, she sees, sometimes for the first time, what she has done. Then she sees that what she has originated is not peculiar to her but is part of her culture" (68).

Ponsot and Deen's claim does not advocate chaos but it does alert us to complexity. Critical and discourse theories constantly complicate our defi-nitions of literary writing (as the primary imagination [Coleridge]; aes-thetic [Rosenblatt], poetic [Britton et al.], discursive [DeQuincy; Langer]; and so on). (Winterowd discusses these categories in *The Rhetoric*.) Reader-response theory persuades that meaning does not reside solely in the text, inserted once and for all by authorial agency. Meaning is constructed by authors in conjunction with a reading and a reader. And several theorists have provided readings of texts as non-literary–seeming as lists left on blackboards (Fish) to computer instructions and phone booth directions (Winterowd *The Rhetoric),* in order to show that literary texts are those *to which we pay attention in particular ways and by community sanctioned agreement.* In fact, our response to and interpretation of a first-year theme will change over time. In his essay "The Drama of the Text," W. Ross Winterowd reads a twenty-five-year-old student theme in three ways: "Between 1965 and the present, the paper changed radically . . .it has become sexist. . . . It has been, successively, (1) an inadequate structure, (2) an inadequate statement of selfhood, and (3) a perfectly normal exemplar of a pseudo-genre." (22–23)

That students can see the literature within their own writing in order to understand text-building is not a radical notion if we use current theories of texts to let us understand that Literature with a capital *L* is primarily a canonized set while writing literature with a small *l* may be thought of as writing in order to understand genre conventions, writers' choices, readers'-responses: the exhilarating act of experiencing textuality, as defined by Scholes and commented upon by others.

What is lost by these views? Certainly the idea that not everyone can be a writer, for everyone should be able to learn to see the texts within his or her texts. We also come closer to understanding student writing practices. Imagine, as I have been doing lately, the vast network of first-year writing instruction as we know it today. Consider that for years we may have been reading a wealth of "imaginative" and "creative" essays even when we assigned them and evaluated them as non-fiction work. It is also possible then to visualize the infinity of shaped "family stories" and "true experiences" that comprise the beginning compositions of generations of creative writing students (and comprise the published texts of many of their teachers, myself included). The old, limiting distinctions, I maintain, were given primacy because they helped keep our selves and our academic territories well and safely sorted.

These days, we might ask for research agendas that help us to take a closer look at genre expectations and their influence on composing. I think we must note, for instance, the way the essay is moving back into the three-genre literature anthology and ask what it means when two recent books from a "composition" press focus on *Literary Nonfiction* and *The Rhetoric of the "Other" Literature.* This movement, I believe, may represent either a bridge between literary studies and composition studies or a movement on one side (literature) to co-opt the power rhetoric has gained in English departments when: "[T]he "literature of fact" is being rehabilitated within the literary establishment, and rhetoric is being repatriated after nearly a century of exile from the literary establishment" (Winterowd ix).

Or, it may represent a movement on one side (composition) to assert a primacy for itself as strong as that asserted in literary studies: "[T]hat literary nonfiction, by its nature, reveals to us the complexity and power and rhetorical possibilities of language—and that the complexity and power and possibility of language ought to be the unifying concern of rhetoric and composition as a discipline" (Anderson xxiv). The latter may be a significant political move in composition, an area that has traditionally felt undervalued, members of which still debate the wisdom of a suggestion that first-year programs leave English departments and create academic programs of their own (Hairston "Breaking"). The moves on either side seem, however unfortunately, to be revisiting old categories and ways of viewing English studies and simply looking to reapportion power.

***

In several of the scenarios I've sketched above, claims are being raised formally that we can (and should) read non-fiction as non-nonfiction. To me, these claims suggest that some of the deepest categorical assumptions of our writing classrooms and writing research models may be simplistically exclusionary; we have assumed, due to our own English studies institutional hierarchy, that comparing non-fiction to non-nonfiction is like comparing apples to oranges. Maybe.

Maybe, though, we have we talked ourselves into using a single-lens, the wrong lens, one out of several possible category systems. What if non-fiction is apples and non-nonfiction is apples, too, and both must be looked at that way and/or categorized in other ways?

To start, I believe we should teach "creative" writing in the first-year program, as has been done at my school for many years with good effects—particularly on student and teacher attitudes—and no reported harm. Students are well prepared for future academic writing when they explore creativity, authorship, textuality, and so on, *together, all at once*. In fact, I suggest that they are more prepared to think about and perform the complicated act of writing when they study this way. Currently, many of our students pick up conflicting understandings about textuality from traditional courses, the ones that define writing or reading very narrowly, focus on skills rather than on active learning and process, or that offer only a naive theory of texts (if any). Understanding writing as a subject, I believe, aids the development of written products. And, certainly during the college years, if not earlier, a well-developed metacognitive and metalinguistic understanding of the demands of writing and reading enables a student to develop flexible responses to class-assigned or self-assigned writing tasks.

Next, in our classrooms, the results of writing research should be welcome beside the testimonial of expert (and/or famous) writers. Equally, we should read and study the best, most exciting, most creative texts in all genres (this includes scientific and technical texts), whether the authors of such texts have invested more heavily in fact or fiction. We should remember, also, that when conducting a writing class, we are convening a discussion among writers who happen to be students. We should consider the extent to which "literary interests" have defined the creativity quotient of other kinds of writing (usually as zero). When we see the individuals on our rosters as writers-more-than students, we distance ourselves from the demeaning, disempowering concept of "student writer" with its inevitable implications of eternal deficiency. Our students aren't writers the day they are finally hired as writers in the workplace or the day they publish in "professional" forums. They are writers whenever they write, and they will believe us when we say so only when we acknowledge their rights through our course designs and our attitudes toward their work.

Finally, throughout their graduate education, prospective teachers should be trained as writers, composing extensively and gaining an introduction to the many discourses of English studies (and when feasible to the discourses of fields outside English). While doing this they should receive help and encouragement. Teachers shouldn't need to apologize for having a writing strength or a weakness ("I'm never going to be a poet"; "I can't write a critical essay to save my life"; "I don't think of myself as a [creative] writer"; "I write, but I guess the type of writing I do isn't creative") as long as they are willing to explore writing in the same manner and along the same dimensions that I'm suggesting for first-year college writers: as a complex human endeavor, requiring practice and analysis, involving beliefs and emotions, resulting in failure and success. Teachers don't have to profess writing but they should experience it, and that experience, as any graduate of National Writing Project training will attest, is life-changing. It's possible, I guess, to teach writing without ever having felt like a writer, but shouldn't we insist that it be otherwise?

Anyone interested in writing and reading in academic settings will have realized by now that a wealth of issues and questions can be raised on both sides of the line that seems to divide composition from creative writing; I tend to believe that our categories don't suffice and that questions—now—are essential. And our questions need to move into both territories from this disturbing spot in no-person's land where we reside together with Fran and Lee and Frank. For instance, there is much to be asked, too, about the world of creative writing instruction. Why is the institutional history of creative writing the last to be written? In the creative writing class, why do we devalue critical theory and writing research? In what ways does it hurt us to find out that the muse can have regular habits and hours and that our writing processes can be illuminated, adapted, enhanced and changed? What do we gain when we lose complete authority over our texts? And finally: Who is served by the assumption that the academy taints "creative" writers and that composition taints "creative" writers even worse than the generic "academy?" It isn't a sin, as Fran worried, to ask these questions. Surely, it's time to find more answers and then to return, renewed, to our work.

17

On Learning to Like
Teaching Creative Writing

I've often felt an outsider to the world of creative writing "society" and insecure about my forays into that particular café. I need to testify to my own education, though, because it is the mis-educational parts of that experience that drive me to improve instruction. "How do you inscribe difference without bursting into a series of euphoric narcissistic accounts of yourself and your own kind?" Asks Trinh Minh-ha, author of *Woman Native Other*. "Without indulging in a marketable romanticism or in a naive whining about your condition? . . . Between the twin chasms of navel-gazing and navel-erasing, the ground is narrow and slippery. None of us can pride ourselves on being sure-footed there." (28)

I am not sure of being sure-footed, but I have talked to others about teaching creative writing who feel as I do. We were in creative writing classrooms a lot but didn't feel supported there. Some of us were simply muddling along, trying to right the wrongs we felt done to us by our own previous teachers. Some of us had internalized a destructive self-doubt that it wasn't just teaching that our poetry or fiction teachers disdained, maybe it really was us, the young aspiring writers in their classes, that they despaired of.

What, if anything, had been withheld from some of us? Has anything changed? Where are we going as teachers? It is time to look around and see what has been made, to find a language in which to express divergent perspectives, to avoid, if possible, narcissism, romanticism, and whining. With my Capricorn goat-feet, I hope to stay somewhat sure-footed as I investigate this difficult terrain, for, oddly, I feel that I had to *learn to like* teaching creative writing.

Learning to Learn

I had two clear credentials for writing poetry. I had family stories that needed telling and a way with words after I developed into a childish agoraphobic, determined to escape family fights not by moving out into the world but by moving into books, becoming a consumer of words, more words, more words until they finally had to be returned in kind, in elementary school poems that angled for teacher approbation. What fifth grade teacher could resist the seventeen rhyming quatrains of "The Grunion Run" and fail to honor me? Certainly I became addicted to the distinction of being the family "smart one" "reader" and finally "writer." Easily, I gave in to my addiction. As the sounding board for my high school girlfriends, I wrote "portraits" of each as gifts and, as I widened my audience, soon won high school writing competitions and published for the first time.

Now, part of me has been schooled to find something horrible in this confession, for later, in college, I was trained to see writing, poetry, art— as art, nothing more. To allow art to serve me, help me understand myself, make me feel good, was to tarnish somehow the profession with schoolgirlishness. At the time of my college education (and perhaps still) New Criticism held sway. The canon was strong and entering it was the (impossible) goal; art that *felt* or *helped* was wrong.

"Instead of moving the audience and bringing pressure to bear on the world," explains Jane Tompkins, "the work is thought to present another separate and more perfect world. . . . The imputation that a poem might break out of its self-containment and perform a service would disqualify it immediately from consideration as a work of art. *The first requirement of a work of art in the twentieth century is that it should do nothing*" (210, emphasis added). Of course, and I didn't know this then, the Do-Nothing School of Art was a strategic move to keep insiders safe and outsiders safely out. The still hotly debated issue of art as political action illuminates the insider/outsider struggle. And, the outsider struggle has been most evident for women and for those not raised in the canon. Canonical arguments are convenient diversions away from larger problems, like those pointed out by Mike Rose in his book *Lives on the Boundary*: "Although a ghetto child can rise on the lilt of a Homeric line—books *can* spark dreams—appeals to elevated texts can also divert attention from the conditions that keep a population from realizing its dreams" (237).

"And writers at the margins," says Toni Cade Bambara, "are more likely to link thought and body, writing to the body, the writer to the community, writing for dear life. A writer, like any other cultural worker, like any other member of the community, ought to try to put her/his skills in the service of the community" (qtd. in Minh-ha 9–10).

The problem for the sixties and seventies was class, remains class. Classes. How did so many, from so many places, of so many colors, with so many unrecognized strengths and too easily labeled deficiencies, enter the academic realm? Open admissions policies produced waves of irreconcilable Otherness.

As a senior in college in 1974, I asked my boyfriend to take a poetry workshop with me; he said "yes" but didn't show up on the first day of class. Here I am, then, in a college writing workshop for the first time. I'm assigned a riddle poem. I buy a book of Old English verse. I write. I recapture my early writing successes under the guidance of an involved woman teaching assistant who praises and encourages us. Somehow, she has already learned to like teaching creative writing, perhaps because she is *not* a creative writer, though we can tell that she dearly loves poetry (though later she leaves the university, Ph.D. complete, unable to get tenure-line work in the Bay Area). I double my art major to English, spend a fifth undergraduate year finishing my creative writing major, entering, as I envision it, classes full of word making and book reading, imagining I've come home.

Then, after being a good student in several undergraduate workshops, I am let into graduate school where the distinction of being the quiet brainy child who read books was negated in the matter of months. In a theory class I thought I was listening to a foreign language (and I was). In a poetics class, I already lacked several hundred years of preparation. I was surprised to find my undergraduate confidence and excitement draining away. I didn't know that I wasn't able to be a poet because I was a woman. The Master Poet I studied under claims: "Poets, like people in love, always behave badly, except on occasion" (Shapiro 55). If I were to behave badly, then I would not be let into the club of women who swelled the workshops, the conferences, the famous writers' lunches, professors' trysts. In the role of a bad girl—one wanting respect and attention for her writing—I would not be contributing *to*, I would be asking *of.* And that would not do. To begin with, there was not enough room in the world for great poets of the first rank. Competition was necessarily fierce for the few places in the pantheon for women who were writers (writers who were women?). It was understood: If you make it, you're a poet; if you fail, you're a woman poet. "Exceptionalism," Nadya Aisenberg and Mona Herrington point out in their book *Women of Academe* "condemns the voices of most women to silence." (143).

In my first-year graduate workshops, young men and women sit in a half-circle around a famous white-haired poet. He smokes a pipe, pages through our work, drops matches, and doesn't intervene during our remarks to each other. No comments beyond the significant twitch of an eyebrow or speedy movement to the next text.

I thumb the *Norton Anthology of Modern Poetry* to figure out what poets write about. I am embarrassed by the woman—Sylvia and her anger and Anne and her body. I mention loudly that I never want to be called a woman poet. I never mention that I have bought all of Anne Sexton's books and read them, yet rarely buy the assigned others: Wordsworth floated outside my experience—a young man's life, what was that to me? I say none of this in class, although I write a lot, like the women of academe in Aisenberg and Herrington's study who "prefer the written to the spoken voice, because in this form they can project authority and influence without engaging in confrontations that raise confusing issues of appropriate response" (74).

Although I didn't know I couldn't be a poet, I did know I felt terrible when it came to my voice. I stumbled if I read aloud. Attending poetry readings, I'd see *real* poets: How could I impress in the manner of William Everson, Robert Bly or Gary Snyder, low, vibrant voices seducing audiences with words?.

As a fellowship student at a summer writer's conference, I was momentarily mentored. The poet reviewing my manuscript suggested that I not use the name "Wendy" to publish under. I obeyed him, using W.S. Bishop for five years in my insecurity.

During that time, I wrote about my family. My young loves. A chapbook compiled for me by a willing small press editor seemed to be composed primarily of those of my poems that had the word *thigh* in them.

My second year of graduate workshops consisted of hours of meeting with a group of other aspiring poets not to be taught. Our egos grew to the degree that they were not sated. Cliques, competitiveness—some of us thrived, at a cost. Deborah Churchman interviewed Johns Hopkins creative writing faculty and students in the mid-1980s to find:

In most programs, weekly seminars tear through students' works line by line, giving criticism that may or may not be constructive. "You're generally naked here," said Professor Barth, "and if you've botched it, it's there for all to see."

"It was fiercely competitive," said Miss Robison of her year at Johns Hopkins, "though now those students are like family. But it took pounds off me.'"(43)

We spent our time waiting for our Master Poet to say: "This is good." We read his books and liked his work. He was a poet. He did not teach us, we assumed, because we were not ready, worthy, or worth it. He told us stories of his own battles. If we stayed, we built our own armor, were launched into the world from indifferent degree committees.

"What are you going to do now?"

"Submit my book to The Yale Series of Younger Poets."

Polite embarrassed silence.

I submitted my manuscripts for fifteen years in anger. And never won. I proved my masters right instead of learning from them. And it was bred in the bones that my growing joy in teaching as a graduate student was one more mark of non-achievement. Here is my Master Poet's verse on teaching:

CREATIVE WRITING

English was in its autumn when this weed
Sprang up on every quad.
The Humanities had long since gone to seed,
Grammar and prosody were as dead as Aztec.
Everyone was antsy except the Deans
Who smelled Innovation, Creativity!
Even athletes could take Creative Writing:
No books, no tests, best grades guaranteed,
A Built-in therapy for all and sundry,
Taking in each other's laundry.
No schedule, no syllabus, no curriculum
No more reading (knowledge has gone elsewhere).
Pry yourself open with a speculum
And put a tangle in your hair.
(*Shapiro* 27)

This teacher in the years I studied with him returned no annotated texts, gave no tests, shared no grading standards, kept to no schedule or syllabus, designed no curriculum. That's the way it was: master knows, disciples wait for enlightenment. Follow the rules, the Poet suggests:

> Rules live in masterpieces.
> Get them to read the masters, let them
> Learn some humility for art;
> Let them copy, let them imitate,
> Memorize models, learn languages,
> Above all master their own.
> *(Shapiro 56)*

But over the years, I would learn to distrust rules like these: learn the master plots, imitate the masters, aim for clarity, coherence and correctness. Trinh Minh-ha suggests, "Clarity is a means of subjection, a quality both of official, taught language and of correct writing, two old mates of power: together they flow, together they flower, vertically, to impose an order." (16)

Learning to Teach

Although teaching creative writing at the university where I first began to do so was an assignment of honor, I viewed my first classes with some terror. I could not demand emulation, even if I had believed emulation was the solution, which I didn't. "It's not a question of teaching without theory," Francois Camoin suggests, "—we can be goats and monkeys in the halls and at department parties, but in workshops the students want more from us than 'Be like me. Write,' which is not very useful advice, finally" (5).

At first I was barely able to keep a step ahead of my students, whether opening my first grammar handbook to "grade" my first set of essays or reading anthology poems for the first time in a blur the night before attempting to teach them. Finally, I stopped trying to stay ahead, I fell back, I was with my students, and I developed the exciting idea of learning together that I have never left. The classroom—that I needed to make over into a success story—became my haven. If being a poet meant teaching badly—I suppose so I could stay home and wait for my poems—then I couldn't do it.

In the first place, it was boring and unproductive to stay home and wait for poems. My poems, I knew, arrived because I willed them into being—due for a class, generated by a need to learn my life and share it, prompted by self-imposed exercises because working with words was so damn pleasurable in itself. And anyway, I wanted to write stories, novels, essays, too, any and everything. I hated writers' conference panels on: "The possibility of creative writers succeeding in *two* genres." I remember with some anger the colleague who told me he didn't think he *believed* in the prose poem.

After a few quarters, I had some teaching success, but I didn't yet know how well creative writing could be taught because teaching it well had built-in risks. For example, it was okay to teach but not to say that writing could be taught. When I said: "here's what I did, it worked," I seemed to become a conversational pariah. And, not unexpectedly, my Master Poet still didn't agree with me—in his published poems—or in my head:

> Creative Writing classes are the pits,
> Yet by some osmotic-symbiotic-
> Empathetic catalysis people learn,
> At least the two percent with talent learn.
> The others do their own spontaneous thing.
> Surrealism as a rule.
> The worst start all their poems with I
> And end with *me*. And nobody reads.
> How did they get this far? Who let them in?
> Are these rooms holding-pens?
> *(Shapiro 55)*

I started with different questions. Why hadn't we been let in before (women, minorities, lower-classes)? Why was I given and asked to give out so many rules? Why was I supposed to read books that signified nothing to me but a world that excluded me, folded me down, hid me away? Why were the benefits of workshops extolled or assumed and the dangers never examined? Lynn Domina says

Writing about what you know often implies writing about what other members of the workshop will not know, which is easily enough dealt with if what you know about is running a dairy farm or swimming competitively or communicating with an Australian via short-wave radio, less easily dealt with if what you know about is prostitution or incest or addiction, and much less easily handled if what you know about is anger at your exclusion from a culture by white people or by wealthy people or by men or by heterosexuals, who are all your classmates and/or your teacher. (33)

Why were only two percent of human beings talented? Were they? What was at stake? Katharine Haake says

> Even after I began to recognize these incursions into other peoples' texts/stories/lives as colonizations, I kept it up, not knowing what to replace it with. Over time, I began to realize that what students need to know is not how to "fix" any given story, but how to read, instead, the conventions of the discourse—in general, any discourse, and in particular, a fictional literary narrative text. Where a writer decides to locate herself and her work within the context of these conventions is a decision that should not involve the teacher. I am not saying not to "advise" students; I am saying to respect who they are, and also to trust their decisions. (draft of "Teaching")

Clearly, I could not teach the way I had been taught. At a teaching loss, I analyzed my own poems and made assignments for students from self-assignments that had worked for me. I also looked sideways, stealing from my composition classes—for I had received some training to teach composition—repaying my thefts, a little, with what was developing in my creative writing workshops. Nowadays that's less new. Rex West says: "As I see it, if someone walks past my classroom and can't tell whether I'm teaching expository or creative writing, that's a good sign" (Turkle et al. 50). But in 1981, cross-fertilization between composition and creative writing just wasn't done, though I did it. If my composition students were benefiting from sharing drafts—comparing an early draft with a later one—I borrowed that for my poetry workshops, sharing my own, realizing that I had *never* seen my own teachers' work in draft.

Robert Scholes puts the classroom and real-life divide that is indicated here in perspective when he reminds us:

> [A]ll who write, whether in an ivy-covered study or a crowded office, are involved in a process that moves from practice to earnest, beginning with dry runs, trial sessions, rough drafts, scratchings out, and crumpled sheets in the wastebasket. There is, then, something inescapably academic about all writing, whether in school or out of it, and many a text begun in school has finished in the world. The "real" and the "academic" deeply interpentetrate one another. (10).

In my own education, I was not offered the commonalities between ivy-covered study and crowded office that Scholes describes, but I started to explore commonalties in the classes I taught. If in poetry workshop poems were never graded poem by poem, then the method would suffice for essay writing, too. If I was already trained in essay conferencing, then I would need to have poetry students in my office doing the same. I asked creative writing students to read a draft aloud and talk about it. Soon I asked for portfolios that showed the process of writing poems and stories. I tried to learn where (creative) writers' ideas came from, what they didn't understand, what they did. I attempted praising development, change, and risk, and, better, I figured out how to reward these attributes by articulating my grades.

As I began to see creativity as more than a two percent issue, I found genre and writer's myths twin tyrants in the workshop, lingering on to trick me and my students into self-hatred long after my Master was a ghost in the corner of my classroom, sleeping mostly, if awake a trifle condescending or amused. Fighting myths and received ways of doing things meant asking difficult questions and assuming difficult (non-traditional) views, as Robert Scholes does when he claims:

> We must help them to see that every poem, play, and story is a text related to others, both verbal pre-texts and social sub-texts, and all manner of post-texts including their own responses, whether in speech, writing, or action. *The response to a text is itself always a text.* (20)

As Trinh Minh-ha does when she asks:

> Why view these aspects of an individual which we imply in the term 'writer' or 'author' as projections of an isolated self and not of our common way of handling texts? (Minh-ha 35)

As Katherine Haake points out, when she explains:

> We could be a long time debating, for example, such a question as whether we write the writing, or the writing writes us. (87)

And despite what could be seen as a series of triumphs—a first-generation college-student, army-brat from the suburbs, becomes a writer and teacher of poetry and composition, I still felt an outcast from creative writing. *I could claim* that I write many genres, speak theory and pedagogy and art; *it could be claimed* that I let my energies be sapped and diffused between teaching and parenting and writing. Worse, I am not a name poet and haven't published a book with a university press, yet I inhabit an academic system where that matters. Instead, I have published several books of writing about writing and find, ironically, that I'm still subdued by genre. We all know that in the Do-Nothing School of Art a book of elegant verse is worth more than many hard-working books of pedagogy or criticism. Trinh Min-ha captures my feelings:

> Accumulated unpublished writings do stink. They heap up before your eyes like despicable confessions that no one cares to hear; they sap your self-confidence by incessantly reminding you of your failure to incorporate. For publication means the breaking of a first seal, the end of a 'no-admitted' status, the end of a soliloquy confined to the private sphere, and the start of a possible sharing with the unknown other—the reader whose collaboration with the writer alone allows the work to come into full being. Without such a rite of passage, the woman-writer-to-be/woman-to-be-writer is condemned to wander about, begging for permission to join in and be a member. (8–9).

Are we policing *quality* or *society* with our stiff publication competitions, with our focus on measurable products and our neglect of intangible and multiple processes? The amount of unproductive competition and anti-pedagogical thinking in this field strikes me oddly since it often comes from those who also rail at anti-intellectual thinking. In my experience, creative writers continue to be exceptionally worried about the taint of the academy where a majority of them live. Francois Camoin recalls: "I remember watching William Least Heat Moon take off his boots at a convention in St. Louis, and talk about squelching his feet into the mud of life. Who would ever have thought that he had a Ph.D. in Renaissance Lit.? Who'd have thought that he would be so ashamed of it? (3–4)

And yet, and yet, it is by training in rhetoric in composition after my training in creative writing and by writing pedagogy that I've come to find myself as a writer, I've learned to like teaching creative writing, and, finally, in doing so, been freed to like my own.

Learning to Like Teaching Creative Writing

I'm hoping for nothing less than to change our profession, so that the parts of it which proved incredibly valuable for me and others like me are not lost to the kind of anger and difficulties you can hear in my story: "[T]he lure of teaching for many women," Aisenberg and Herrington found, "is the desire to reinvoke the transformational experience, their own experience of growth and change, for others. It is not, that is, simply an extension of the nonintellectual gifts of mothering transplanted to another, professional, scene, but something far more radical—women invoking change in others." (39)

To keep the affirmation in my daily life, I've had to rewrite the story of learning and teaching creative writing as I'm trying to do here. The story of my own workshop education was, in many ways, this one, narrated by Peter Elbow:

> We write something. We read it over and we say, "This is terrible. I *hate* it. I must work on it to improve it." And we do, and it gets better, and this happens again and again, and before long we have become a wonderful writer. But that's not really what happens. Yes, we put it in a drawer and vow to work on it—but we don't. And next time we have the impulse to write, we're just a *bit* less likely to pick up the pen. ("Ranking" 199)

That's the type of workshop education that derives from the critical, doubting, winnowing, elite form of the master-teacher workshop. But the workshops we need to develop—and I think there are many ways to orchestrate them—read like this story, again narrated by Elbow:

> What really happens when people get to write better is more like this: We write something. We read it over and we say, "This is terrible. . . . But I *like* it. Damn it, I'm going to make it good enough so that others will like it too." And this time we *don't* just put it in a drawer, we actually work hard on it. And we try it out on other people too—not just to get feedback and advice but, perhaps more important, to find someone else who will like it. ("Ranking" 199–200)

Peter Elbow's retellings of the story of the growth of writers echoes all the way back through my confessional history. Something in that terrible poem "The Grunion Run" made me like it. The sheer pleasure of having gotten from beginning to end in rhyme. Because I didn't keep it hidden in a drawer, I found a teacher who could like it too. And while my story is also one of sheer dogged insistence in the face of poor teaching, proving that it is possible to buck the odds and learn alone, my productive writing addiction was actually generated in that first undergraduate poetry workshop where my work was liked. I was not making a McPoem; I was making me.

Elbow argues that liking work allows us to be more demanding of the writer. He also suggests that good writing teachers feel able to like student writing. If they like students' work, they can be more demanding. If they're more demanding, the work improves. Liking creates a positive chain reaction.

If we enter the creative writing class expecting to limit the size of the playing field, keep closed the floodgates on "too much damn writing," we certainly will. Conversely, if we enter with expectation, appreciation, and excitement, we have the possibility of engendering intrinsic rewards in writers and demanding vast amounts of high quality work from them. What writer would work hard to fail, to be dubbed uncreative, to not publish or converse in a public forum? Whenever we set up doubtful and doubting classes, we encourage our students in their inwardness, their paranoia, their grievances, their narrow world view; we keep them in the limited therapeutic state of writing to fix the past instead of the perhaps equally therapeutic but more important state of writing to construct the future. "Shake syntax," exclaims Trinh Minh-ha, "smash the myth, and if you lose, slide on, *unearth* some new linguistic paths. Do you surprise? Do you shock? Do you have a choice?" (20)

The benefit of liking our students is manifold, for we talk to them and learn them and celebrate their progress rather than bar it. Truly, they are not going to displace us before our time. Rather than two percent with talent, there are probably only two percent of our students who will follow us into this profession. To the degree that we like their work and know we're orchestrating learning, to that same degree we can raise our class standards, asserting the truth: improvement in writing results from long-term, serious attention to writing, from drafting, response, reading, pushing, experimenting, and succeeding *even just a little bit.*

The benefit of liking our teaching is manifold. Primarily, we don't feel our class time is stolen from our writing time. If we write with our students in class, write about our classes, read theory and writers with an eye to developing the students in class and the student in ourselves, we develop an ecologically sound system for our writing lives. We find other teachers to share with rather than complain to. We find our students' own small successes cause as much celebration as our own small successes. We tend not to procrastinate in responding to student texts; we like their texts better because they are better texts and because ours is no longer the only valuable opinion or suggestion.

The benefit of liking our colleagues, our English departments, our professional organizations, is manifold. For a new generation of creative writer-teachers, it is becoming easier to teach with involvement and distinction. Unfortunately, many others of us—those who are one, two, and even three generations older than currently enrolled M.A., M.F.A., and Ph.D. students—matured in a climate that did not encourage pedagogical and theoretical thinking about creative writing, an upbringing I've woven together in this essay through my own personal testimony and the contrapuntal voices of writers I admire.

Change in this climate has only come lately though I hope it will continue rapidly. In the last five years the Associated Writing Programs have started hosting annual workshops and sessions focusing on pedagogy, and teachers who do not teach at the graduate level have started to discuss undergraduate creative writing instruction during the meetings of a special interest group at the Conference on College Composition and Communication and are developing a strong voice in that organization. In the same five-year period, the booklists of the Teachers and Writers Collaborative, Boynton/Cook-Heinemann Publishers and the National Council of Teachers of English have increased greatly, responding to a growing interest among readers in creative writing pedagogy and theory by publishing a number of collections of note. And finally, within the last five years, we have regularly heard discussions of new undergraduate and graduate course listings that explore and feature the intersection of creative writing, composition, theory and pedagogy.

I'd like to argue now that this pedagogical change needs to be undertaken more actively in all degree programs in creative writing. Learning to teach better is tough, exhilarating, and possible. I'm talking here about the need I see for a deep revision of what it means to teach and learn creative writing, a reprioritization of products and processes, a curriculum that investigates itself, that denounces old premises, topples myths, renames and reaffirms: "Substantial creative achievement," Trinh Minh-ha suggests, "demands not necessarily genius, but acumen, bent, persistence, time" (7). We can start fostering acumen and bent by instituting pedagogy seminars; we can give to teaching and learning the persistence and time they require. Here is the response of a graduate student to one creative writing pedagogy seminar.

> Quite, frankly, I think this should be a required course—part of the M.F.A. program requirements. Many of us would like to go out and get a job teaching—but without having thought a great deal about teaching creative courses, so we end up doing the same thing we did in our courses in school. Pretty sad. Some people may find out they don't want to think about their craft in this way, and that is useful, too. They'll steer away from teaching.

How well do we know our graduate students? How willing are we to let them carve out careers different from the dominant (and often unattainable) one of "star" writer. Our students will be teaching under conditions and in locations we can only speculate on. How do we prepare a teacher to teach creative writing in nursing homes, hospitals and prisons? Much support is needed for much is at stake. Diane Kendig found:

> One colleague, who has taught English in prison for years, had a student come to her to explain why he could not write a response journal for her literature class. He had made it a practice, he explained, to eat any personal writing in his possession. She was at first unfazed, assuming that "eat" was prison slang for "getting rid of," and then she was shocked to hear the inmate explain that he had actually chewed and swallowed every piece of paper he had written or received personal writing on during his incarceration. To maintain such a diet, one must not produce many meals, and he knew he literally could not swallow what she was asking him to produce. (159)

A writer as a cultural worker does put his/her skills in the service of difficult-to-support communities.

And a pedagogy seminar does not take valuable time *away* from the study of literature or the practice of craft, for it can address theory, research and practice; it can and should include writing and workshopping; it should address what we know and what we need to know—how to design courses, how to grade; it should take a student and a teacher beyond the boundaries of what they themselves have experienced, into investigations of alternatives, into deeper understandings of students, into broader examinations of cultures, politics and institutional systems.

Often, our graduate students are trained to teach composition and benefit from it. Now they need to be taught to teach writing both generally and specifically, to examine the "creative" in creative writing. Today, the separation between composition and creative writing programs is still so firm that the two fields rarely converse except in the overtaxed brain of the university teaching assistant. Too often, this TA learns that those professors she studies under believe little overlap does or should exist between these fields with a resulting puzzlement similar to the Irish individuals in this story:

> When a sufficient number of specialists are assembled on a college faculty, the subject of which each knows only a small part is said to be covered, and the academic department to which they all belong is regarded as fully manned. In

ancient Ireland, if legend is to be trusted, there was a tower so high that it took two persons to see to the top of it. One would begin at the bottom and look up as far as sight could reach, the other would begin where the first left off, and see the rest of the way. (Erskine, quoted in Graff 111)

I'd like to question the division of our writing programs so that some individuals are assigned views of the bottom half of the tower—exposition—and others are assigned the top half of the tower—imagination. Encouraged to talk about their field and to view themselves as teaching professionals in that field, allowed to evaluate models of teaching and question received wisdom, creative writers turned students of pedagogy grow into individuals who can see and appreciate the entire tower. I want to offer some testimonials, because I see myself as the mirror here:

A writing *for* the people, *by* the people, and *from* the people is, literally, a multipolar reflecting reflection that remains free from the conditions of subjectivity and objectivity and yet reveals them both. I write to show myself showing people who show me my own showing. (Minh-ha 22)

After a pedagogy seminar, these graduate students showed me my own showing. They felt:

That students can be trained to critique each other's work rather than left to "catch on" as is expected in a standard workshop.

That invention exercises are as important for creative writing students as they are for composition students.

That there is no comparing graduate (trained) and undergraduate (untrained) writers. I'm not sure I want to work with untrained writers.

That it's harder to neglect an intriguing bit of invention that's already on paper than it is an abstract idea in your head. Being forced to invent in a prescribed way is useful and enlightening in spite of my resistance to prescription. I can produce something worth showing to people in only one week. I can share early drafts.

That, as instructor, it is important to participate also. It's important to sit around a big table, to read aloud samples, to try various workshop formats and share students' reactions, to provide unguided holistic response to writing.

That there is sexism in the field.

That it is possible to deal with student writers' block.

That I'm sensitive about my own creative efforts and felt exposed sharing spontaneous work.

That what it all boils down to for me is that students get the respect they deserve in classrooms. I don't think it matters what we're teaching—literature, composition or creative writing—what we're helping students to achieve is the ability to empower themselves through language. When we understand this, the tools—literature, essays or poems or stories or criticism—take on an equal weight, one is no more primal than the other. What is most important is that students experience language, discover it and clarify their relationship to it.

These changes—to encounter writer/teachers like this—seem to me as rapid and surprising as second-wave feminism must have seemed to first-wave feminists. So I hope that as a profession we have finally moved from feeling the need to be horses of a different color—individuals steeped in a romantic creative writing culture that valorized the hard-drinking, sweet talking, solitary and usually male author. The romantic creative writing culture sanctions the star system with out the underlying capital to support that system (most authors we know, lifelong, will make very little money, directly, for their work) and a set of cultural stances that encouraged us to inhabit rigid positions that made us feel unrealistically exalted and more often not very valuable, as we've tried to explain.

These attitudes linger, hopefully, more truly in the minds of those who once suffered from the classroom and publishing climates created by such thinking; we have indications that the day-to-day learning life of younger creative writers is more tolerant and informed, or that it could be if we honored teaching and offered courses to prepare those writers who continue on in the academy. That they should continue is fine by us since there's a pretty good life to be had here. The stunningly notable increase in interest in creative writing, practice and instruction, indicates that we are ready to reconceptualize this field and all creative practitioners not as writer *or* teacher, not as famous *or* failed, not as infamous *or* boring, not as first *or* second rank, not as contributing to a glut of creative work and therefore *never* contributing to a conversation about art through art. In this, we also reconceive our metaphor—we aim toward different distinctions, not to be a product only, a horse of different color, but to become part of a process, a work and thought community that constructs the colors of a different horse, creative writing in new hues and configurations, a collaborative and energetic intellectual and creative project undertaken inside and outside universities, alone at home and together in the classroom.

18

Poetry As a Theraputic Process
Realigning Art and the Unconscious

HERE ARE SOME THINGS WE DON'T OFTEN SAY ABOUT WRITING POETRY, AT least not in poetry writing classes in our universities: poetry is active, alive, and pleasurable. It may be part of a therapeutic process, because poetry is conversational, meditative, and (self) historical. It is a practice that can heal us, as well as let us testify to personal and public issues. It allows us to explore and it can go along with us wherever we go. Obviously, these are not statements about aesthetic value—what makes writing good or bad, technical aspects of crafting a poem, schools or trends or political issues in contemporary poetry. These are statements about writers, humans, and their relationships to poetry.

> Did anything [about this class] surprise me? Well, I must say, I had no idea so many people had the desire to write poetry.(Poetic Technique student)

A friend, listening to me talk on e-mail about drafting this essay about why poetry is important to me, tells me why poetry—an act she's allowing herself again after five years working on a composition Ph.D.—is important to her:

> I guess, in part, I'm hoping that it [your essay] complicates the term "confessional"—a term I don't like too much, although I know that my poetry would fall into that category. But the term has taken on nuances that make me uncomfortable. And, I think, glosses over other reasons people have for writing poetry. I don't feel as much as if I'm confessing as I feel I'm realizing, then because I share it with others, I'm confessing. (Gay Lynn)

Have we all, I wonder, learned to define "confessional" negatively (as in confessional poets, as in self-revealing, as in writing about taboo topics, as in going too far into self and self-indulgence, as in one- or self-sided)? What was once a cultural/historical phenomena, labeled for convenience a "school" of poetry, is now an ingrained bias—"that's too . . . [confessional, personal, sentimental, easy, unearned]" a chorus will go up in a writing workshop and the poet will wish she had never shared her *realizing* with others.

Let me start this exploration of the "other" side of poetry another way. One of my students last summer thought I was a hippie teacher though I don't think I am. In classes, I demand a lot of writing, I demand attention and conversation, I ask for experiment and exploration, for in-class and out-of-class writing, for revisions and small and large group response, for reading and writing journal entries, for final portfolios of beautifully produced (temporary) products. But, I also ask for jazz, play, and innovation—I ask students to bring objects to class (this time seashells or rocks) and write about them, to discover unused senses (sharing favorite candies from our youths and writing about them; sharing smells in brown paper bags—I'm afraid this was the last "hippie" straw for this student), to be present in writing, to explore the universal through the personal particular, to dive into poems, to see the class as part of what I hope will be their longer, life-long writing journey, but always also to consider our writing as public writing, as we bring what we are realizing together.

I know I'm not a hippie teacher because I went to college in the seventies and experienced truly hands-off, off-beat and arbitrary teaching. It was a time of amateur and drug-induced enthusiasms for Jungian theory and Zen philosophy. It was a time when contemporary confessional poets like Robert Lowell, Sylvia Plath, and Anne Sexton produced stunning poems. Attention to new philosophies and new poetries got tangled up in a time of free and public expression, to the point that anything invoking self and self-discovery was labeled, by default, easy, indiscreet, excessive, unacademic, playful, juvenile, or just unserious:

Poetry plunged out of the classics, out of the modern masters, out of all standards, and plopped into the playpen. (Karl Shaprio, *The Poetry Wreck*, quoted in Packard *The Art* 27)

Since words like *craft*, *initiation*, and *art* dominate the talk of contemporary poets, it is no surprise that words like *best* and *worst* do also. They are concerned with the products they make and the public circulation of those products, what some term "the poetry biz." Poetry is not, in this manifestation, a democracy. For instance, the tiny republics of professional poets (modernists, surrealists, symbolists, traditionalists, imagists, post-modernists, Beats, confessionalists) with their royal families of famous poets were in danger of being overrun in the seventies in open-admissions institutions and their poetics were in danger of being diluted by unorthodox approaches. In fact, these republics were at war with each other; say Beats with modernists, and poets didn't have much interest to spend on the student-as-poet (a novel concept) or the too many unsorted students who threatened to overrun the palaces by enrolling in popular elective classes. These students, to the poets teaching newly formed creative writing courses, seemed discouragingly untutored in the genre.

Giving "just anyones" free access to *art* was untenable, for what happens to craft, initiation, good and bad, if one takes a Zen approach to poetry? As Gary Snyder put it, we might work toward the "practice of an intuitive capacity to open mind and not cling to too rigid a sense of the conscious self" (quoted in Packard *The Poet's* 274). He also argued for a holistic approach to poetry: "poetry as a healing act . . . it means healing psychological distress, integrating people in the Jungian sense, their inner discontinuities harmonized . . . to be healed is to be sane, and to be sane is to be very energetic, rather than tranquilized" (274–275). Passed off as beat at the time (off-beat?) and submerged in the more pragmatic poetic thinking of the eighties and early nineties, poets hare rarely, if ever, returned to ideas like this, for they seemed dangerously non-academic, difficult to impossible to teach, and alarmingly egalitarian. Producing an energized poetry populace was simply not important to the poet/teacher struggling as he/she was/is in the academy and the poetry biz.

Along the way, though, popular interest in poetry led to the development of many—a still growing number of—college elective courses in the subject. Today, there are a lot of us, poets and would-be poets, poetry programs and poetry students. And we're living in an age that has divided art and the unconscious with some devastating repercussions. As poetry continues its high art course, the general public has remained suspicious of poetry, resentful of poetry, wary of poetry. And this—as a person who finds poetry an integral part of my life—bothers, disturbs, and alarms me.

To recap, here is how I was trained and trained to train others, by identifiable precepts: write in isolation, when ready (after long dedication) submit your poems for publication, if the poems are worthwhile, they'll attract attention and book publication, you'll get a job teaching other creative writers and attend writers' conferences, give readings, improve and refine your craft.

Certainly, being a good student, I tried. It was hard to write in isolation once I had children. It takes time and money and dull office labor to submit poems for publication (200+ published, so far, but what then?). The market for book publication is flooded (for a new poetry book series, Sarabande Books' 1995 contest rejection letter mentions "Approximately 1500 poetry manuscripts and 700 fiction manuscripts were received. Needless to say, competition was especially keen; a great many of these works were of the highest quality"—mine was one of 1500 and I guess I hope of the highest quality; I tried, anyway to make it so).

I teach—and feel conflicted over the institutional subtext that urges me to create in each student writer a desire to write the 1501st poetry manuscript that will be submitted to Sarabande Books' contest next year. I attend a few writers' conferences where the topics are often the glut of bad poetry and the lack of readers/appreciators of (the participants') poetry. No, this isn't what I meant at all. This is entirely about the products of poetry and I've come to know and value poetry as a life process, certainly a process involved in the making and contemplating of artistic texts, but an art that is also, and as importantly, a journey back to the unconscious, a relearning and realigning of selves.

There are ways I live poetry now and would teach it to others.

I go on a vacation, the first in several years. Before I return, members of my poetry writing group, one that has met once a week to share new poems for two years now, are getting more restless than ever; no one can stand the break between summer and fall term and Devan and Jennifer are scheming a way to start meeting earlier, even if we all can't attend. This once-weekly group meeting has proved a site of teaching, healing, and meditation. We borrow writing strategies (one bringing in poems with impossibly hidden structural patterns and self-challenges), we see each other mine and re-mine themes of love, loss, separation (ex-husbands and children), we see each other create worlds and personas (one writing about a imaginary couple traveling in imaginary foreign countries).

I send three friends every new poem on e-mail, each for a separate reason: with one it's a diary of my life, as poems sometimes are for me; with one it's a signal of trust; with one I can preen and be proud as I'm not supposed to be in public. Communication, sharing, pure pleasure.

My eleven-year-old, sixth grade daughter reads my weekly poems. "Neat" she says, each time.

For the eighteenth birthday of each of my children (a son, too, who is eight), I plan to make each a book of "their" poems. I think about this pleasantly, lazily, since there's plenty of time.

When a poem about my children is published, I show them and they wander away from it; for them, too, there's plenty of time.

Within the following poem, not yet published, I store a particular memory (I can remember composing it, sitting in my back work room, feeling like I could hear my daughter growing older in the evening darkened house for I could, literally, hear her breathing); the poem was also written to have a text to share the next day with my poetry group, and to explore a form—quatrains—I would be teaching that week to my poetry students, and includes thematically recurrent motifs for me. I was reading the *I-Ching* checked out from the library; I had been doing a lot of writing about writing and remembering old travels. Before children I traveled a lot and now I saw I was traveling through them. Vaulted into my own future by my daughter's aging, actual life felt dream-like, causing me to remember one of my own recurrent (and I knew common enough) dreams, that of floating over a city. All these flashforwards and flashbacks combined into one interwoven meditation; what I call the process of writing a poem.

NIGHT SONGS

My daughter sings herself older in her bedroom
before sleeping. This is the sound of her self-flute:
tones float through a darkened house, loose
lean counterpoint to my evening's journey.

Sleep-awake myself, I leaf through anthologies,
throw I-Chings of poetry. Craft can frame
old messages a new way, blow longings secretly
into bottles: they drift along the inland waterways

of personal history. Enough densely scored songs,
enough possibility, and she falls to dreams. I have
that one we all have: float high above the city—not waving
not worried—assume I've finally pinched myself awake.

On the first day of writing classes, though, if I'm not careful, I *won't* talk about the way the poetry group helps each member re-finding and re-defining through words; how friends like Gay Lynn use poems for "realizing" selves, how I use poems about daughters to talk to my daughter (as well as to the daughter I was to my mother and to other writers who mother poems), how writing is meditation and rehearsal for my friend Devan as she walks around Lake Ella and then later shares that insight with me on e-mail, part of our poetry conversation.

> I keep thinking about the Renaissance commonplace books of poetry that circulated, and how like they are people e-mailing each other poems and setting up Web pages with their Web pages with their stuff. Nobody was thinking, "Great! I'm the Earl of Sidney, and I'm going to write the first sonnets in English and people are going to be kissing my butt for eons." (I like Sidney, actually). No, he was thinking about being in love. This is my new thing: writing is contextual, localized, situated, and transitory. Actually, it's not my new thing—it's Derrida's old thing, but you know, it makes me feel better and helps me just enjoy writing this whatever-it-is right now, the person I am this minute . . . I think about Natalie Goldberg's idea of "mental writing" (the poem I write in my mind while walking around Lake Ella) being a different poem—specific for that time, place, and circumstance—than the one I write when I get home—even though I'm attempting (and constantly, constantly failing) to finish or take off from that earlier mental poem. (Devan)

If I'm not careful, the-profession-and-the-teacher-over-my-shoulder will whisper that I should not talk about how Devan's meditations on writing help my own writing, that I should only emphasize craft, solitude and aesthetic distance. And there's a reason for this impulse; it was how I was taught: being told to read more and more, to write, to refine an aesthetic taste, to live that art-oriented Poet's Life—

> In the spring of 1970, I was finishing my first year of graduate school as a teaching fellow it the Ph.D. program in English at SUNY/Buffalo. Living alone in a two-room, $85.00-a-month apartment, I had plenty of time (too much) to reflect upon my existential fate as a nascent poet, a mere 23 years old, loving the genre for no inherently practical reason. (Baldwin, 32)

That is one Poet's Life, described by Neil Baldwin in a recent *Poets and Writers Magazine* column, and it could stand for an exemplary, if modest, version of the vision that is handed from initiate to initiate. The Poet's life includes an eschewing of popular culture and a cultivation of a particular taste for the art poem:

> We're talking here about reading really worthwhile books—not reading a lot of cheapo schlock paperback romances that are only one step ahead of the sick

TV sitcoms that do nothing but rot the human imagination and take away one's desire to write. (Packard *The Art* 191)

Because of the necessity of resistance, the best contemporary poetry will remain the American art least contaminated by other media and, as a result, the least popular art in America. (Holden 12)

It has taken me only minutes with the books and magazines on my shelves to re-prove to myself that currently the "professional" view of poetry that my affiliations, memberships, academic training suggest I need to align myself and my students with is aesthetic, public, hierarchical (consider the words "best," "least contaminated," and the valorization of "least popular" as somehow more valuable than readily popular, in the quote above). But this is not the poetry of every class member being interested, of my poetry group impatient to re-meet and share, of less than solitude when it comes to writing (consider the fruitful cacophony of family life and e-mail discussions of drafting and the meaning of poetry), of poetry as a life's journey, of poetry as the moment we dive deeply into the private to reemerge, healed perhaps, energetic if lucky, more whole and able to function in the public sphere. But I want, of course, to argue for such a (re)joining of interior to exterior and to argue that in so seeing poetry, we realign, heal, and energize the practice of poetry.

A few more instances of the problem, as I see it. Because poets, departments, the professional world of letters is dominated by aesthetic beliefs, I should, I fear, urge this writing student to resist, erase, remove the following entry from his writers' journal:

I am writing me. On this paper is essentially the bones of who I am. Everything and every time I write, it is all from me. There is nothing in my writing that does not scream ME when I read it. I tell the truth here in printed word because this is where I feel safest. (Rhain)

Instead, I have set up a classroom that encourages personal statement and personal exploration. And later on the same page, this writer moves from self only to seeing the self in context:

In the end, who can designate a specific place of ending for a writer. As we write, we take small journeys into the various levels of our mind. Who can say where we will go or where we will hit a rock or a fresh spring of topic. (Rhain)

These journal entries helped me understand the thought processes of a gay student who talked about his life freely in small group discussion but who, initially, hid behind his writing topics in the safety of cliché and archaic language like this:

LOVE'S LIGHTHOUSE

crashing waves against a rocky shore
we are all lonely ships in the darkness
darkness in our hearts
screams signaling from the bow of each ship
from each heart

(continuing for six more stanzas)

Rhain hid because he had great difficulty believing I was urging him to write about the specifics in his life, not because he was protecting those specifics. I argued that it was there he would find his universals, his understanding of love, loneliness, darkness and issues of the heart. For him, this suggestion seemed, well, too easy, too simple, too un-poetic. He had expected to don the Poet's Life, to talk about himself as a lonely ship in a dark sea (to live like a lonely ship in a dark sea). Instead, I asked him to do something more difficult, to find his life in poetry. And this turned out to take many drafts, and most of the term, the turning point arriving in the shareable honesty he achieved in his poems of the last two weeks of class. This is one that I admired:

NOT IN MY ROOM

I've never slept with anyone in my room
It's a private place, just for me
A place I'm not willing to share with any man

I won't pretend, I won't play charades in my room

I've slept with men in nice cars and on worn, green velour couches
In mildewed showers and on dark quiet beaches
In black closets in rooms other than my own

I won't play power games in my room

Outside my room, I am a superman with no emotions, no regrets
No inhibitions and no secrets
But in my bed, in my room, I am only me, I have no masks
Unloved, except for the love of the cat who knows who I am.

(Rhain)

In this poem, Rhain realizes and renders and taps into the deep images of his life—here, too, love is dark but found in the vivid darkness of closets and couches, and here he explores masks he wears, super-human and real human, the hero? seen only by his cat.

This is not confession, it's rendering, and no doubt Rhain will re-render his experiences differently across his writing life. But he allowed me as reader to accompany him on this level of the journey, the journey that many of us turn to poetry to take:

As a writer of poetry, I think I have a lot to learn, but I also think I have come a long way. This does not discourage me, however, because to be a "good" writer is a lifelong journey. Every time you put your pen to the page, you train your mind, your inner voice, your vision to express itself so that everyone may hear the intensity of your thoughts. (Chantelle Couba)

I no longer see the poem as an ending point, perhaps more the end of a journey, an often long journey that can begin years earlier, say with the blur of the memory of the sun on someone's cheek, a certain smell, an ache, and will culminate years later in a poem, sifted through a point, a lake in my heart through which language must come . . . (Joy Harjo, Quoted in Coltelli 68)

Once a line is written she can step out onto it. The line is like a train and she a passenger curious to learn its destination. Each line is an idea that carries her to the next idea. Yes, she is taking the poem somewhere, but the poem is also taking her. (Rita Dove, discussed in Herrington 15)

Again, it did not take me long to find quotes from three writers (one who was a student, two whom my readers will recognize) that illuminate this sense I have of writing poetry as being part, a necessary part, of a life's journey. This is not an indulgent journey in any sense or "mere confession"—these writers describe the journey as one that requires training, receptivity, attention, willingness, and curiosity, all attributes I'd have any writer cultivate. I would have my student poets see this by carrying their writing journals with them everywhere, by writing poster poems and performance tapes to be played in class and circulated on campus, by taking home our class books of workshop poems to their families at Christmas—their poetry workshop writing interleaved with other magazines, advertisements, and books on the household coffeetable. When my students travel to Europe, I want them to whisper what they remember of Gerard Manley Hopkins's poem "Summer and Fall" to the first fall leaves in Norway and to compose their own poem about the horrible bus stop in Puno, Peru, or describe what it's like to work at IHOP every hot day of the long summer. When they go through the campus bookstore, I want them to find themselves in the eddy of the poetry section as often as they lean over the discount CD table. Not always, not every time, but fluidly, I want positive memories of poetry and poetry as an aid to memory to filter through their lives.

In published writers' journals we see poets exploring deep unconscious connections between image and symbol and the events of their lives. Poems that result from journal exploration are in many ways equivalent to Jungian dreamwork: poets retell fairy tales, plumb family stories for archetypes, find the symbolic in daily processes, undertake heroic journeys of self and social healing. Poetry students can too. They grow by being encouraged to take the rigorous dive or journey back to earlier selves. And I work on this by assigning just those activities—retelling fairy tales, exploring and re-telling family stories, looking for the recurrent patterns in everyday life, exploring the meaning of a life as journey, for this is exactly how we all reach the universal that the aesthetic school would champion:

> But this realm, as we know from psychoanalysis, is precisely the infantile unconscious. It is the realm that we enter I sleep. We carry it within ourselves forever. All the ogres and secret helpers of our nursery are there, all the magic of childhood. And more important, all the life-potentialities that we never managed to bring to adult realization, those other portions of ourselves, are there; for such golden seeds do not die. If only a portion of that lost totality could be dredged up into the light of day, we should experience a marvelous expansion of our powers, a vivid renewal of life. . . . In a word: the first work of the hero is to retreat from the world scene of secondary effects to those causal zones of the psyche where the difficulties really reside, and there to clarify the difficulties, eradicate them in his own case (i.e., give battle to the nursery demons of his local culture) and break through to the undistorted, direct experience and assimilation of what C.G. Jung has called "the archetypal images. (Campbell 17–18)

Combining art and the unconscious, the products and practices of poetry, means writing courses start from a new premise. We do not have to don the Poet's Life like a coat, grow up, mature, have life experiences before we write, but rather, we have actually to dive back down to who we were to see who we are, find the golden seeds, clarify and bring to realization. This is a systematic as well as an intuitive process because we are re-reading ourselves.

At this point, I'm arguing that poetry is the stuff of the self, and that reading poetry leads us to produce better readings of the self. Contemporary theories of reader-response show us that we can't step in the same spot of the river of the self twice. That is, every time we read the "seed" moment, evoke a text, we evoke a different text because we ourselves have changed, however imperceptibly. So re-reading our writing, that is drafting our poems, is to take a journey through the self, not of indulgence or of solution, but of educational attention. Poetry as life journey yields the respectable benefits of attention: the ability to see connections, to make predictions, to interpret the past, present and future. Poetry is not equal to therapy, it is only—but usefully—a therapeutic *process,* a mode of thinking. We don't "solve" ourselves, but we do see and re-see; we say what we didn't know needed to be said and then make some (never complete) sense of such sayings. This is part of the practice of seeing, writing, thinking and we do it as a practice, a hazard, a working-through:

> Any poem is therapy. The art of writing is therapy. You don't solve problems in writing. They're still there. I've heard psychiatrists say, "See, you've forgiven your father. There it is in your poem." But I haven't forgiven my father. I just wrote that I did. (Anne Sexton qtd. in Packard, 110)

I want to take the circular path and return to my opening list, to affirm once more why I want new ways to talk about writing poetry, life in poetry, poetry in life. I work as hard as I can for you, reader, and you, contemporary poetry community, to shape my daughter poem "Night Songs" into a lasting art object. I'm proud of the four line stanzas, the half-rhyme, the allusions, the risks (will you let me get away with "I-Chings of poetry" or is it too arty); the way (if you read my unpublished book of poetry) you'd see this poem builds on earlier poems in terms of theme, image, symbol, sophistication; the way it represents, for that moment eighteen months ago, my dedication to the Poet's Life. I was/am still writing and participating in the public life of poems, revising my book manuscript for Sarabande book's next contest, sending my individual poems out like beloved children to call on the world of literary journal editors, writing a textbook on using form for invention. As important, I am going to my poetry writing group next Monday night, with stories of this essay: How I tried to, wanted to capture what poetry can mean. Poetry is part of a therapeutic process, poetry is conversation, poetry is meditation with the potential to heal, to lead us into a more energized relationship with lives, both private and public.

So, look for this daughter poem someday in a literary journal; it will be out on the rounds, seeking public sanction and an academic home, and in so doing it measures my life and hopefully means something to yours. But also look around you the next time you're in a local restaurant. Those people laughing and teasing each other, reading drafts aloud, making a time and place to meet again, sharing selves, rendering lives, they're probably making poetry, also. And they're lucky enough to know they need to.

19

What We (Might) Write About When We
Write (Autobiographical) Nonfiction

IN WHAT READERS DESCRIBED AS THE "POSTMODERN, FRAGMENTARY, collage-like, 'bricolage-like'" text that you are about to read, you will find my own last assignment, written for and shared with a graduate level seminar in the theory and practice of literary nonfiction that I designed and taught, spring 1995. The exact assignment—Class Writing 6—is described in the "What We Wrote" bibliography at the end of the text. In the last two weeks of the class, we all shared drafts that were either meta-analyses of the course or potential "teaching chapters" of a book on literary nonfiction that I proposed we might (if all things went well) start collecting together. Although we never got far enough along to assemble a complete book, class members wrote "chapters" that I will share with future classes—for instance, one on letter writing (written in letter form), one on travel writing, and so on—and others wrote insightful meta-analyses of their own work and the class. I combined both options and shaped a text that is simultaneously a teaching chapter and a meta-analysis. In it, I weave together sections of class members' writing, and in doing this I need to thank the following individuals: Rebecca Lee Bailey Archer, Devan Cook, Amy Cashulette-Flagg, Faith Eidse, Ronald DePeter, Heidi King, Kathleen Laub, Melanie Rawls, Jennifer Wheelock for their many contributions to our mutual scholarship. They are quoted with permission.

Since the genre of nonfiction has received renewed attention lately, there was a great deal of material to choose from for a text like this. The writing, by scholars and by class members, was often questioning, speculative, circular, and/or open-ended, and that's how our course of study progressed: we read, we wrote, we considered, we made lists, and we came to temporary conclusions, shared here. My purpose in sharing is fairly simple . I try to recreate the feel of the class, by taking you, today's reader, through our term's work. Consider this a "how-to" essay in another key. I think "how-to" or "how-we-did-what-we-did" essays are unfortunately undervalued these days, perhaps because they are often written in a conventional, predictable style. By changing the assumed shape of a how-to essay, I aim to recuperate and open up this genre for your consideration even while sharing what I hope are provocative glimpses of one classroom as it existed at one time.

***

For fifteen weeks we have been (un)defining and (re)exploring nonfiction.[1]

We learn that there is no agreement, for by defining, we keep expanding what we might write, what we might consider.

We've developed a class vocabulary—"What about the reader contract? Does this text tell us how it is to be read?" "Faction"—not less than fiction nor more. But different. We've reframed the questions. "Similar in what ways?" has come to seem more productive. How to have a place and a voice from which to author in an authorless age?

Some of us in our secret hearts may still prefer the formal essay ("Death of a Moth," "Once More to the Lake") and the nature and travel and science essayists with literary voice (*Living by Fiction, The Lives of a Cell, Coming Into the Country*). Others of us are toppling accepted constraints and guideposts, then find ourselves a little too adrift (Can I say this, and this? Do you read that and that?)

Still, we sought to discover the issues in narrative, the tectonics of fact and fiction (does one plate overlay another? Is there a Marianna's trench where the magma of fiction dissolves into the core of fact?) and the possibilities of voicing across genres while riding the teeter-totter of revelation (what informs this voice?).

As a graduate-level seminar in theory and practice of literary nonfiction, we tried to write freely into unfree territory, our autobiographies and literacies, families and fascinations.

Try this:
Write about your voice(s), when you had it, didn't have it, how many you have, who you borrow from, what you sound like, inside, outside, alone, with others, when you had none, what you'd like to say but haven't yet:

I've never experienced anything. Someone called Devan has experienced a lot, but she's not me, exactly: I've made up her life. (Devan)

This is a story I have had published, and for some reason I find the "voice" of the piece to be truer to my personality than many nonfiction essays I write, truer than the nonfiction here. (Ron)

Write about language:

Ugly is a funny word, the way my mom uses it—to describe behavior usually, or language. *Pregnant* is ugly. She prefers *expecting*. . . . when Ellie's only daughter, Lisa, conceived a child out of wedlock at the age of 15 in our tiny little Tennessee town, she was *expecting* because she had *been tacky*. (Jennifer)

And for me he brings Julius Caesar to life, removes the mist from "Chackes-piri," as *abuela* would say it. And for those in the room not as fascinated by Julius Caesar or Prince Hamlet or poor Willy Loman as I am, those who are—in teacher talk—disruptive, Mr. D. forgoes the pink slip to the principal, meets the disrupter downstairs in the gym, twelve-ounce gloves, the matter settled. He has a broad definition of art. He knows the world—and he understands the block, *el bloque*, what kids today call "the hood." (Victor Villanueva *Bootstraps*, 2)

Write about names, nicknames, given names, imagined names, personas, naming others, naming yourself, place names:

My name—Devan—floated in my mind over a map of North Alabama, looking for a person to land on who could tell me what really happened. Someone told me that it is a name more often used for boys than for girls, which I can believe, and that it is an old name occasionally used by a group of families—a clan of sorts—around Birmingham. (Devan)

I named a gerbil "Nibbles." He was cute. He ran up my brother's back and got into his long hair. Nibbles ate Cheerios from my palm. He chewed up toilet paper rolls and died in one too. (Ron)

Some mornings I wake up and I'm Faith Eidse, other mornings I'm Faith Kuhns. I never officially changed my name. Other people did that for me. And I let them. (Faith)

Melanie, which means "black" in Greek (oh, felicitous naming!) is black damask. My middle name, Annette, is French, means "grace" (very nice, yes?), and is angular and the color of magnolia seeds. Black grace. We run to strange nicknames in my family. My family name is Ginny (pronounced with a hard "g"). My dear Aunt Essie used to call me "Goo." My father used to call me "Mudzin." Nicknames bestowed in my family include Boochie, Donnie, Raytee, Michee, Fats-pedly-edly, Boo-hoo-ca-howrie, Pouch, Bugs, Thumper, Tootie, Scooterpoos, Scoot, Bal-Ball, Ari-belle, Kelli-bear, Pud, Pudman, Tammi-lamb, Nato-potato, Beady, Brown Sugar, and Boo (twice). (Melanie)

Write about weather, climate, landscape:

But first some facts: I have taught for seven years and am a tenured professor at Cal State Northridge, the exact epicenter of California's latest earthquake. Today is day four. We are beginning to dig ourselves out. Even on the Westside of Los Angeles, where I live with my husband and two sons, it has been rocky. (Haake "This is Geology to Us," 3)

Florida has never felt like home, despite its best efforts at grounding me in sand and pastel. North Florida seems an adequate escape—compromise, for the time being. At least primary color exists here in change of season, and in the soil. The further inland you get from water, the deeper you find yourself in red clay. (Becky)

Write about architectures, houses you've loved or hated, places you've built, cities, human-made forms and figures, space within and without, materials, meanings:

Think, for example, of your houses: the one you live in now, if you have one, and the ones you have inhabited before. I am writing a book about your houses. You never lived in a yellow house on the coast of Maine? No matter. You have had such a house, perhaps a long time ago, not perhaps your chief house, the one you spent the most time in, but the one that you return to now most frequently in dreams, whether you remember them or not, a locus for you, inexplicably, of mystery and desire. I will write about the yellow house. You will read about your house. If I do my job, the book I write vanishes before your eyes. I invite you into the house of my past, and the threshold you cross leads you into your own. (Nancy Mairs *Remembering the Bone House: An Erotics of Place and Space,* 11)

Back door, rusty hinges, the kind of door that stays so wide open even when it's shut that frogs can hop through the crack. Holes torn into the screens, or bitten through by insects. Bare light bulb. Cinder block bookshelves along the baseboards; an occasional roach. Blue tortilla chips, pretzel rings on the wood table next to the antique typewriter. Everyone asks if Michael writes his poetry on it; "it makes me feel poetic," he says. "That's when it *comes* to me." (Ron)

Write about scars:

I wonder sometimes if all women hate their noses. I hated mine till I spent a few years living in Los Angeles. When I saw what some people go through to alter their noses, I embarked on a difficult journey—to the land of loving my nose. (Jennifer)

Somewhere on my head, grown into my scalp-line, is a curved scar from a window casing in St. Joe, Missouri, that I ran into on October 25, 1952, the day after I turned 5. Bright cool day, leafy bushes surrounding a damp poured concrete walk, house-like, high-ceilinged motel with long corridors. (Devan)

I remember my mother's body in death. Open, naked. I could not look for very long at it, anymore than I can look at my own in the light, except in pieces. Never from the waist down, except in the shower when I have to shave, and always avoiding glimpsing my abdomen. I put my face on with a towel around my waist. Mother learned shame from her mother, from her generation and culture—and from my father. I, too, learned in much the same way. (Becky)

Write about your inner worlds—illness, death, healing, dreams, wishes, lies, religions, values:

Marty is changed. She doesn't leave the hostel anymore unless she has to. She won't eat, says her breasts are too big, she's on a diet. After school and before bedtime, she walks endless laps around the living room and ping pong table, her eyes dull. Her bubbly laugh is gone, her cheeks hollow, elbows pointed. She sheds twenty pounds, forty. She catches hepatitis and is sent home, skeletal and yellow. (Faith)

In the years following my uncle's death I always imagined him sitting in a green, winged chair in an empty room. My aunt stood behind him, looking down with concern. I'm not sure where this vision came from, I suspect from stories I overheard at home. There was no funeral, and fewer and fewer visits from my aunt and cousin. My Uncle John is still the only person I've lost.

The "truth" of the story is that he didn't need to die. Apparently he felt the heart attack coming on and didn't go to the hospital. He took a shower and sat down while my aunt called the ambulance. He died before they got there. (Amy)

Write about time:

It focuses on a memory I have from my childhood, centering specifically on the nature of description as it affects us psychologically—my room, my mother's eyes, what were always powerful instruments of persuasion . . . even now that she is gone. (Becky)

Sundays and holidays are the worst, no mail will arrive, to, perhaps, give me some insight into my future. On these days I feel closed off from the world, my link to the schools is broken. I go to a bookstore to, at least, find more information on the schools, to find out how each one ranks and differs from the other, but all of the books are sold out. Then, I go on-line to see if anybody in the computer world can commiserate with my situation. There is a lot of talk about Law Schools but no one mentions feeling the seemingly eternal wait. (Kathleen)

Write about ancestors—real, imaginary, black sheep, genealogies, present realities, absences, presences:

It's a beautiful Sunday afternoon on that quiet campus in the heart of Atlanta. Glover and Dan, sitting on a wall, are lazing in the sun in the company of some young women. Three more young women walk by, headed in the direction of Spelman's gate.

Says Glover Rawls, "Oooh, man, look at those eyes!"

Dan Rawls looks. And looks and looks.

The young woman with the big eyes sticks out her tongue.

"She had the biggest eyes," Dan Rawls tells his daughters in later years. "Skinny, though. You couldn't see her if she turned sideways! But she had the biggest eyes."

According to Dan, he saw her later standing on the balcony of some building, probably a dorm. He stares some more and she sticks out her tongue before turning to go inside.

When she tells the story, she doesn't mention any sticking out of tongues. (Melanie)

Write about decisions, windows, chances, turns:

My parents prided themselves on an always unnamed amount of assistance of theirs that allowed Ruthie [who had worked as their maid in Japan in 1953] to come to the United States. . . . When I was in sixth grade, a visit was arranged and this woman who had not seen me since age three months came to Ventura. At some point as I was leaving the living room reminiscences to take a shower before bed, and she asked if she could help me bathe. I went very still. Showers were there for my furtive attention to my own new body, for fingering and feeling and escaping in hot clouds of steam. Not for backward memory but its adolescent equivalent—forward memory, prediction, and dreaming. This time my mother didn't force me. I said yes myself. And Ruthie, gray hair in her black hair, scooped water and laved me with a cloth, saying quiet, singing things, murmuring. (Wendy)

Write about habits, hobbies, obsessions and fetishes—the Comb Museum in Homer, Alaska, the way you gather rocks, the need you have to check—to recheck—the stove burners:

One thing that lies behind this writing that is absolutely true—I really do come from a family that ate mint and garlic sandwiches, and my grandmother really did win prizes at the Garden Club. (Devan)

Each spring Strat-O-Matic issued new recreations of the previous baseball season. I thumb through the fresh cards, checking statistics on the Boston Red Sox players. Strat-O-Matic was a game I grew up playing with my brothers. . . .
    I remember my brother could not stand to lose when we played Strat-O-Matic. He would scribble fiercely on his score sheets, break pencils, swear. . . .
    As I install the new computer Strat-O-Matic software, I think about the old player cards we owned, how fingered, dirty, and soft those cards became. The rubber bands would melt from the teams being stored in a shoe box in the closet, so over time I cut up little white strips of white paper to fold in between the rubber band and the team cards.
    I remember the tactile pleasure of Strat-O-Matic playing cards, and the quick flip I would do during games to check that player's home run total, his strikeouts or walks, his batting average. Was this guy living up to his real numbers? Exceeding them? (Ron)

David and I met on a blind date. Actually, we met over the phone, through a mutual acquaintance, a girl he had dated and that I now worked with. I was hooked from the moment I heard his voice, the voice that now causes my internal cavity to constrict against itself . . . (Becky)

Write about gender:

The harder I tried to keep out of it, the more pronounced "I" became . . . . Paradoxically, I somehow assumed the attitude that the "I" despised, that the personal pronoun "I" was sentimental, sloppy, undisciplined, self-indulgent—all the things that I had been taught not to be both at home and in school, grade one on up. I had been indoctrinated, as many women in this country continue to be, to deny my own existence as a meaningful, contributing, thinking as well as *feeling*, holistic being. (Becky)

The only time my father shared a highly personal moment with me he was driving with me one night. He spoke into the windshield. He told me he was proud of me for something. (Maybe I had just graduated from Eckerd College.) He wanted me to know that. He told me that he was never able to tell his father "I love you." He had wanted to so badly, but even when Papa was in the hospital, and my father knew he was dying, he still could not say the words. (Ron)

Write about travel—local and distant, returning and remaining, insiders and outsiders, landscapes and peoples, how you see a culture and how you're seen:

Had I included my personal experiences of growing up in this part of the country, the reader might learn about traveling snake shows with specimens that extended from one end of the school gym to the other, summer afternoons melted away by sucking on orange sherbet push-ups, and small town nights in a dry county that boasted a bootlegger with a drive-through window on the side of his mobile home. (Heidi)

So I traveled from steamy North Florida to the cold, rocky northeast coast of Ireland to start over. I wandered along fuchsia and blackberrry hedges, past stone fences and cropping herds of Belted Galloways (dairy cows); I listened to Medbh McGuckian and Thom McCarthy and Joan Newmann as they read poems and talked about them; I know because I wrote these things in my journal. Yet nowhere does the journal tell the real story of the journey . . . (Devan)

Write about taboos:

My first bleeding was copious and happened at school in my plaid dress. I didn't notice it until I got to my room at the hostel and stuck to my chair. I was alarmed. I'd never seen so much blood caked into a dress. I had thought menstruation would be discrete, a small leakage now and then. My dress was ruined, and I didn't have any to spare.

Aunt Nettie showed me how to soak it in cold water and gave me a sanitary belt and pad. Sitting under the twist-barred window in the bathroom, threading my first pad, I wondered at having a body that could produce babies. (Faith)

The day I came out to my mother, at the age of 29 (I'm a late bloomer, or a late confessor), the first thing she asked me, the *very first* thing, was, "Does anyone else know?" Knowing that she meant *anyone else in my hometown*, I told her no, and was surprised to discover that this was immeasurably more comforting to her than the news that two of her nieces—the daughters of her younger sister and her brother—are also lesbians. (Jennifer)

At home the things we did were predictable and orderly, so orderly that by four I had already established my lifelong persona as a rebel by refusing to eat—food came around with a grinding annoying regularity, peas and carrots and the unrelieved bland repetitiveness of milk. The only thing I liked to eat was candy orange sections or the lemon drops, peppermints, and gingerbread that my grandfather carried in the pockets of his sweater, and to escape meals I would wander out into the yard without my shoes, which I wasn't supposed to do, either, talk to the neighbors, talk to myself, play in the sandbox with Sharon who lived next door, and eat green apples until I was sick. (Devan)

Write about circles and sets—seasons, elements, four corners of the world, wonders of the world, dream catchers, webs, fates, muses, mysteries and initiates:

I know my education has made me a better writer and a better thinker in many ways. I fear sometimes, though, that it will make me too self-conscious to be honest. So I write about things I dream about as often as I can. Dreams, my dreams at least, are always honest. I dream my demons. I dream about abandonment and humiliation and failure and food and crying while someone laughs at me. In my dreams, the people I care about the most always turn on me. Whenever I can, I write the dreams down and turn them into poems—talismans or therapy. (Jennifer)

I look for signs, symbols that reflect and resound, move with a rhythm that is most like the peace that I have glimpsed in the night, lying prone on my back, feeling the pulse of wind through the pines dancing around me. It is there, waiting, hiding in the open. (Becky)

Write about family:

Wasn't sure what to write about. In a foul, overworked stressed-out, hyperactive mood; chose this story because it was amusing and silly and because it is one of my mother's favorite stories, so she means it to tell something about our family. (Devan)

I would sit with my Mama, who closed her eyes when she sang. Her eyelids would twitch. My Papa never sat beside her; he was always on the front pew because he was an elder. We always had to be on our best behavior when we sat with her; she'd reach over and pinch a plug out of our arm if we wiggled too much. . . . (Heidi)

Write about you writing:

My structure throughout has been to tell the story of growing up a Mennonite woman in post-colonial Zaire and Canada, and to do so in a way that evokes the colonizing of the body by religion. (Faith)

I keep thinking of writing process, that I'm sitting in my new chair from Office Depot, that I'm drinking room temperature Diet Pepsi, and that I put off doing these writings for as long as I could. (Amy)
    I taped photos of my mother and aunt all around my computer. This helped a great deal—helped me get at certain emotions. Finally, I find myself inevitably doing some fictionalizing, however little, in the nonfiction piece. (Jennifer)

What was problematic: How could we write about relatives? Did we have the right to speak for them? Whose stories are our stories? Could we tell their stories even if we tried? What's the difference between truthtelling and self-indulgence? Is it easier (better) to speak only of those who are no longer alive? Or, is it simply better not to send them the texts.

I don't think we have a responsibility to tell everyone's story. I can only tell my memories, my perceptions, and my truths. What I write is what I remember, and my memories are significant for reasons that other family members might not share. . .I don't believe we can speak for others, that we can imagine or suppose what they might have thought or felt. It is too complicated imagining what we think and feel to presume to do it for another person. But if we do write about our imaginings of their thoughts and feelings, we need to do so carefully, always admitting that they are no more true than the "characters" we create. (Amy)

I suggested that this term I would send my three sisters my writing. My parents, being dead, freed me to write of them. My sisters, were another issue. "Don't do it," said Faith, "Or at least be prepared for anything to happen."
    Of the three, the one portrayed most painfully, has yet to respond. The one who is oldest, most distant, called. I've yet to call back. The one portrayed most lovingly, wrote back—"The piece is so personal, so clear. The phone conversation between Gina (you, me, Nancy or Judy) and mom was IT. We've all experienced it, and you've captured it. My guess is there are others in the world who

may have shared a similar experience, but for me it was a snapshot. . . . Thanks again for sharing your writing with me. It is a gift I appreciate more than any other."

Gratifying, but I realize it is the silent sister I most want and fear to reach, at this moment of my writing life. (Wendy)

"I wouldn't share this with my brother" say Ron.
"I don't think I would either—share mine," says Melanie.
"Oh. Oh. You've got to. You've got to publish this," says Faith.
"My mother's been gone for nearly two years now," says Becky, "and I still worry about her reading my work."

Equally vexing—truthfulness versus artfulness. Does all fiction grow out of a matrix of nonfiction or do the two co-exist and the writer tips the see-saw—-changing the percentages of fact to facts-as-they-might-or-should-be?

Unless you don't mind being a "stealer of souls" or don't care if your family and friends never speak to you or trust you again, as a writer of personal essays, you will ask yourself over and over, "How much of a shared experience should I, as only one of the sharing parties, make public?" (Melanie)

A friend of mine has no sight. I don't know how he lost his sight, because he is reticent, reserved; and I don't ask about what he doesn't volunteer. The one time I made an oblique query about the lack of light in his life, he evaded me so definitively and with such deftness that I, as quickly, dropped the subject. (Melanie)

And I remember and still feel "new" feelings for the characters I created: even though based on real people, they became new then, somehow more tangible and accessible than the real ones. Sometimes it's easier to relate to and love fictional characters than it is real persons. (Ron)

What was fascinating: Setting definitions aside, we jumped in, got our words wet—we wrapped them to dry on the racks of memory, we turned fact to fiction or fiction to fact, intentionally, and compared the results. It worked this way:

Great-great-grandma Margareth Isaak   (fiction)
    I don't often sit for photos, so I feel a little stiff today, every button buttoned, every lace tied, every hair tucked in place. Photos are quite literally

graven images and some Mennonites don't believe in them. But my husband Abraham is a thinking man, and he's decided that a photo will mean more than a tombstone to our grandchildren. Besides I don't intend to worship this image when it's developed. We won't put it in a fancy frame like the ones the photographer showed us.

Great-great-grandma Margareth Isaak   (fact)

In the photograph my great-great-grandma sits with her hands cupped in her lap. There is a book balanced in her hands, but she is not holding it. It's probably just a prop, placed there by the photographer who has ideas about making his subjects look learned and wise.

So much for bright ideas. My great-great-grandma probably can't read English and she's no faker. But she could probably beat the photographer at the Railroad Studio Car in a Bible drill any day. Especially if she had her own well-thumbed Martin Luther translation. (Faith)

How They Met   (fact)

My mother and father met for the first time in the Fall of 1945. She was a first semester freshman at Spelman College in Atlanta, Georgia. He was a second semester freshman at Morehouse College.

He was also fresh from the army—he'd served in Africa and Europe during World War II, and was taking advantage of the GI Bill. He was twenty-eight years old, slim, brown, very very handsome, a cosmopolitan older man. She was just turned seventeen, slim, brown, big-eyed and very very pretty—and as confidant as any pretty young woman can be who was the somewhat spoiled baby of her family and had been away to Hampton Institute. No shyness here.

How They Met: 2   (fiction)

"Oooh, man, look at those eyes!"

You're a first semester freshman in a woman's college adjacent to a men's college positively notorious for its eligible young men. Good-looking men all over the place. Good-looking men only too happy to pay vocally appreciative attention to young women happy to have this attention paid to them, though since they're *ladies,* the cream of the nation's young Negro women, its best and brightest and prettiest and very much LADIES, the young women take pains not to acknowledge the attention too eagerly. (Melanie)

And we learned.

It was much easier to proceed from that [fictional essay] to non-fiction, especially since I could return to my own voice and write from personal experience (is there any other kind?). (Faith)

It never occurred to me to do any kind of wild, fictional exaggeration or extrapolation. For example, it never occurred to me to imagine, much less develop, a piece of fiction in which one of my parents was an extraterrestrial. It never occurred to me to create backgrounds or personalities wholly unlike what I have been told of the former and of what I have experienced of the latter. Do I have, now, a piece of fiction? Or is what I have a piece of slightly fictionalized biography? (Melanie)

As fiction can project us into alternate lives, nonfiction may return us to ourselves:

Another irony: you may remember that I started this class with the notion that I wanted to write personal/political essays because I was finding poetry and politics irreconcilable in my life. Partly due to the value I now see in the personal revelations of my peers in this class, and partly due to the article [I read], "What are Poets For?" in the most recent AWP Chronicle, I have done a 180. My poetry has become a place for politics—images I hope will invoke specific ideologies and events from the public sphere—while my essays are becoming more and more personal. In part I am challenging myself to do this. But it has also happened as something of a response to this class. (Jennifer)

Writing autobiography is not an indulgence of the self if it is done together, seeing what can and can't be said for individuals, pushing the risks of writerly selves against and with the faith of the community.

Questions that remain: Is it more fun (engaging) to write experimental autobiographical nonfiction than to read it? Is it foolishly therapeutic or functionally and healthfully honest? Which interests does it serve? And to borrow a famous question: How does it circulate?

I was a little surprised—taken aback by the confessional nature of the class. It made me feel defensive, unwilling to contribute in that way. Clearly, some members of the class have huge issues they are reconciling and I understand that. It tends to make talking to them outside this context a bit awkward, like I know more than I should, or want . . . (Ron)

The greatest "reward"—bad word, because I don't think it's an "earned" thing—gift of the class (holistic) has given me is a (relatively) safe place to be. Isn't that what we all need? . . . .[My professor] Bonnie Braendlin has remarked that my writing is much more focused now than it was 13 years ago. I certainly hope so. I was pretty fragmented then. Now I prefer to think of myself as (a) "narrative collage" (Dillard's *Living by Fiction*). Seemingly dis/unconnected, but fully cohesively rendered. Toned. (Despite some mid-life cellulite). (Becky)

In the postmodern world, a nonfiction workshop can give the self a place to stand and contemplate what can be known and not known, told truthfully and not at all, turned inside out and outside in. Individual lives make sense together.

Notes

1.   This course was a 6000 level seminar titled Theory and Practice of Literary Nonfiction. From the course information sheet: Together, in this class, we will examine definitions of the academic genre literary nonfiction, theories of writing that inform such definitions, and pedagogies that result from both. In addition, we will complete several writing exercises of a definitional nature, one to two pieces of original literary nonfiction shared in workshop and revised, and we will each write several short essays and bibliographic entries for a textbook on the same topic, intended to be used by undergraduate and graduate writers in the genre. Not unexpectedly, there will be lots of reading, writing, and sharing in this seminar.

2.   In the course, we read many contemporary essays on nonfiction—found in the What We Read list, below, as well as our own writings. In addition, we began the class, reading Nancy Mairs and ended reading Victor Villanueva as samples of academic autobiography. I've quoted them here because their voices were part of our discussions.

3.   Equally, I'm indebted to Katharine Haake for the loan of her exercises in narrative technique that I adapted to this course (particularly Class Writing 1 described in the What We Read list, below). It was only fitting, then, to include her nonfictional fictional voice also. For a discussion of her exercises, see her essay "Teaching Creative Writing If the Shoe Fits" *in Colors of a Different Horse: Rethinking Creative Writing, Theory and Pedagogy.* Eds. Wendy Bishop and Hans Ostrom. NCTE 1994. 77–99.

What We Read

Anderson, Charles. "Coming into the Country . . . and Living There: Literary Nonfiction and Discourse Communities." In Katherine Adams and John L. Adams, eds. *Teaching Advanced Composition.* Portsmouth, NH: Boynton Cook, 1991. 223–247.

Anderson, Chris. "Introduction: Literary Nonfiction and Composition." In Chris Anderson, ed. *Literary Nonfiction: Theory, Criticism, Pedagogy.* Carbondale, IL: Southern Illinois UP, 1989. ix–xxvi.

Atkins, G. Douglas. "Envisioning the Stranger's Heart." *College English* 56.6 (October 1994): 629–641.

Bloom, Lynn Z. "Creative Nonfiction, Is There Any Other Kind? In Katherine Adams and John L. Adams, eds. *Teaching Advanced Composition*. Portsmouth, NH: Boynton Cook, 1991. 249–265.

Bloom, Lynn Z. "Why Don't We Write What We Teach? And Publish It?" *Journal of Advanced Composition* 10.1 (1990): 87–100.

Brent, Doug. "Chapter 2: Reading as Construction; Reading as Communication" and "Chapter 3: From Interpretation to Belief." *Reading as Rhetorical Invention: Knowledge, Persuasion, and the Teaching of Research-Based Writing.* Urbana, IL: NCTE, 1992. 18–74.

Britton, James et al. "Chapter 5: An Approach to the Function Categories" and "Chapter 6: Defining the Function Categories." In *The Development of Writing Abilities (11–18)*. Urbana, IL: NCTE 1992 (First published in 1975). 74–105.

Corder, Jim W. "Hoping for Essays." In Chris Anderson, ed. *Literary Nonfiction: Theory, Criticism, Pedagogy*. Carbondale, IL: Southern Illinois UP, 1989. 301–314.

Creative Nonfiction, 1.1 (1993).

Dillon, George. "Fiction in Persuasion: Personal Experience as Evidence and as Art." In Chris Anderson, ed. *Literary Nonfiction: Theory, Criticism, Pedagogy*. Carbondale, IL: Southern Illinois UP, 1989. 197–210.

Elbow, Peter. "Introduction: About Voice and Writing." In Peter Elbow, ed. *Landmark Essays on Voice and Writing*. Davis, CA: Hermagoras, 1994. xi-xlvii.

Elbow, Peter. "The Pleasures of Voice in the Literary Essay: Explorations in the Prose of Gretel Ehrlich and Richard Selzer." In Chris Anderson, ed. *Literary Nonfiction: Theory, Criticism, Pedagogy*. Carbondale, IL: Southern Illinois UP, 1989. 211–234.

Foucault, Michel. "What Is an Author?" In Lodge, David, ed. *Modern Criticism and Theory: A Reader*. NY: Longman, 1988. 196–210.

Freisinger, Randall R. "Voicing the Self: Toward a Pedagogy of Resistance in a Postmodern Age." In Peter Elbow, ed. *Landmark Essays on Voice and Writing*. Davis, CA: Hermagoras, 1994. 187–219.

Goffman, Erving. "Character Contests." In Robert Scholes, Nancy R. Comley, and Gregory L. Ulmer, eds. *Textbook: An Introduction to Literary Language*. NY: St. Martins, 1988. 27–33.

Harvey, Gordon. "Presence in the Essay." *College English* 56.6 (October 1994): 642–654.

Hesse, Doug. "The Recent Rise of Literary Nonfiction: A Cautionary Assay." *Journal of Advanced Composition* 11.2 (Fall 1991): 322–333.

Hesse, Doug. "Stories in Essays, Essays as Stories." In Chris Anderson, ed. *Literary Nonfiction: Theory, Criticism, Pedagogy*. Carbondale, IL: Southern Illinois UP, 1989. 176–196.

hooks, bell. "'When I Was a Young Soldier for the Revolution': Coming to Voice." In Peter Elbow, ed. *Landmark Essays on Voice and Writing.* Davis, CA: Hermagoras, 1994. 51–58

Klaus, Carl H. "Essayists on the Essay." In Chris Anderson, ed. *Literary Nonfiction: Theory, Criticism, Pedagogy.* Carbondale, IL: Southern Illinois UP, 1989. 155–175.

Mairs, Nancy. *Remembering the Bone House: An Erotics of Place and Space.* NY: Harper and Row, 1989.

Pratt, Mary Louise. "Natural Narrative." In Robert Scholes, Nancy R. Comley, and Gregory L. Ulmer, eds. *Textbook: An Introduction to Literary Language.* NY: St. Martins, 1988. 2–12.

Villanueva, Victor. *Bootstraps: From an American Academic of Color.* Urbana, IL: National Council of Teachers of English, 1994.

Winterowd, W. Ross. *The Rhetoric of the "Other" Literature.* Carbondale, IL: Southern Illinois UP, 1990.

What We Wrote

Class Writing 1: In twenty minutes, write your complete autobiography, include information from the following list: childhood, coming of age, traveling, war, home, male/female awareness, spirituality, your body, dreams. Adapted from an exercise by Kate Haake. Read aloud and draw on this, if you'd like, for a piece to be workshopped with the class in a few weeks.

Class Writing 2: Bring an old family photograph. In class, looking at the photograph, follow these writing prompts: describe the photograph, literally; describe what is happening just outside the frame of the photograph; talk for one of the individuals in the photograph; describe how the photograph feels; who would like to be in the photograph but isn't? Look deeply into the eyes of one of the individuals and then speak for them; who is missing from the photograph and why? Read aloud and draw on this freewrite, if you'd like, for a piece to be workshopped with the class in a few weeks.

Class Writing 3: Write a short piece of fiction. Then write the same story as factual. Or, start with the non-fiction and move to fiction. Write a meta-commentary that discusses what you learned from the process. Copy all three parts to share and discuss in class.

Class Writing 4: Write about names, use any of the following prompts: tell how you were named—if you don't know, make up a story; share secret names you've had; share names you've chosen or would choose; talk about nicknames; talk about personas you've created or fictional character names you've chosen; describe names for your real or imagined children; talk about how you name;

discuss times you've remained unnamed. Copy one page of the exercise and share in class.

Class Writing 5: Share one piece of nonfiction writing of your choice for an in class workshop.

Class Writing 6: Write a teaching essay on writing nonfiction and/or a meta-discussion of your own writing and what you've learned in this class.

20

The Shape of Fact

THIS PROSE IS A FORAY, A TRY, AN ATTEMPT. I WANTED TO TALK ABOUT mothers and daughters and women more than men and childhood and adulthood; I wanted to talk about my mother and myself and my daughter. My only authority was that of having experienced and having written, enough, so far, to want to push further now. But the writing brought up other issues for me and for readers: what sanctions our sharing and what drives our need for protective coloration, concealment, privacy even when going public? And why go public with this life more than any other? For me or for readers?

Intentionally, I take pick-ax to acres of family midden, for, as one reader said of the first section, "It seemed as if I were witnessing with the author a discovery, an archeological dig back into the bones of this mother's depression." Since I know that all families trade in support and repression and most writers manufacture their fictions and factions from the intimate dross of their past, I was aware of wanting to cross the line from hidden writing to exposed writing, with due respect for all the dangers. Part I is the foray then, artful and naive. Part II is another try from another angle, say it is meta-faction, also artful and naive.

PART I

One

In my family of four daughters, I was youngest and lived longest with my mother when she was most ill. My life was shaped by her illness, more so, I've assumed, than the lives of my sisters who left early, each blowing away like seed from the dried head of a dandelion. But I could be wrong. My oldest sister, old enough to be a mother herself at fifteen when I was born, still has a never-look-backness that comes from making decisions, for herself, early in life. My next sister escaped to food, and endured my mother's enforcement of hare-brained diets. Those early powdered diet drinks tasted like ground up steer skulls. I remember this sister's bedroom as a bear's den of formless clothes and candy wrappers woven over and under bed slats, everything heavy with the dust of her privacy. The final sister before me *seemed* like my mother because she seemed *perfectly normal.* Of course I fell in love with her boyfriend and when that didn't work, from afar with his twin brother, and I tried to go with them everywhere, as I see it now, as their child.

Two

If you're the child of a manic depressive, you want several things. Certainly, you want for your mother not to be ill. Still, if she's going to be ill, you want her to be really ill—at pneumonia or severe cold level at least (some snot and Kleenexes would help, a surgical scar would be convincing, why not something really impressive like a cast or an invisible-man styled bandage?). Dearly, dearly you want tangible evidence, something to point at, the body announcing "here—look at this—this is what hurts and why." (Later, you want her to remain ill due to a new kind of fear. You get used to absence, that painful freedom when you feel with your tongue for a missing tooth and strike a seductively tender gum. Should the adult tooth come back, through an impossible rejuvenation process, it would feel unlike you, too dominant, new, hugely filling all the space, and so, intolerable.)

Also, you want to be a child. Your mother is always ill, so you have to be well.

Her need to concentrate on her own problems—what seemed like a mental hypochrondria—erased the daily ills of those around her. No words (I believe truly) can indicate the anguish of such a woman, lost within the boundaries of mind, trekking illegible trails each day and night, coming slam up short against blocked passages out of box canyons.

At the same time, the strain of understanding not-real-but-real illness, can make a child ill, imagined ill, sympathetic ill, actual ill.

Stomach aches were what I had, and I was prescribed bottles of green and red medicine. In the nurse's office, I would wait for my father to pick me up, wearing his uniform (he was a former WWII and Korea veteran and army recruiter). Resting on my back on a metal cot, I'd count the holes in the school's acoustic ceiling tiles and stare until the black and whites wavered many times before he arrived, tall, safe-seeming. The illness I had,

I think today, was wanting to be a child; the medicines tasted of despair, rankly red and green like bile. And I couldn't understand, then, why my stomach knotted like a fist. My sister's stomach, apparently, opened wide to the world, even as mine responded by turning away.

Often, you want to end her illness but can't imagine an end. In truth, it doesn't end.

Alarm over my mother continued years after I left home and didn't ease until she took her own life. Even at such an ending, I've found, questions and worry don't end. Her life appears to me as a giant joke of patterns, tangled in their force, hard to salvage, vivid. One pattern of her later years, advanced agoraphobia. Near the time of my parents' divorce, my mother stopped getting out of bed, regularly. After school, I'd find the sliding glass door from her bedroom to the patio still curtained. Her mind was a microcosm of that room, tightly shut. She'd number her failures, her griefs, her angers—real and legitimate angers, but angers for which she had no resource. Hospitals never helped. Drugs lofted her too far out of herself. Shock treatments, nothing to gain but the loss of parts of her memory. If I try, I see her Past and her Marriage perched like vultures on the bed in the dark. The few Durer prints and Goya etchings I've seen up close make me think less of the condition of humankind and more of the condition of my mother's mind. Her talk had the taut-lined frenzy of those prints. Of course, the more she was lost in and to herself, the less those of us around her could see her, could see in. We could do no more than project our imaginings upon her.

My parents were loud in their fights, yelling interspersed with threats about leaving. More impressive was their match. They were well-balanced enough to stay together in disharmony for twenty-one years. Of course, they aged and were no support to each other's age. In a series of pictures, my mother gains, turns heavy in the ruffled Ester Williams bathing suit that contours her childbearing and melted-hourglass figure. My father is tall but heavy, full-bodied, meat and potatoes, T-shirts stretch some and then a little more. Such stasis, neither could leave, at first; neither could stop blaming the other, to the last. And their daughters couldn't stop being daughters.

Three

Of course, I tried stopping, tried not being a daughter. Yet I inherited her. Certainly the writer in me inherited such a mother as theme, for always, she pushes, generates, lurks behind a story or a poem. In this one, I'm trying (after my father's earlier death) to sort out what I felt:

FAMILY HISTORY

My jack-sprat parents, full of spite and bile,
Would measure out their words in stunning ways
And amplify each other's torn-tongue style
In hard-barred, door-locked rooms of disarray.
They would defend each maneuver and slowly stockpile
An arsenal of faithless things to say.
As their days grew black (when their hopes grew thin),
They danced a vicious dance, alluring, grim.

My fairy-tale sisters (white slips for hair)
Would dress-up to kill and watch at the door.
They seemed to understand what would happen in there.
If I knew a little, they always knew more.
They would dress me in silk or knot-up my hair,
Convince me horses would move in next door
And never divulge just what they divined,
But I was content to spy on their spying.

The master is dead (and the mistress breaks).
The children are married but few are festive.
If we dream of those days it's with distaste
For the hours were hard and our hearts were restive
And we felt each night that familiar ache
As the spirit of our household was wasted
And love-lost faces fed on spite and guile.
We continue their life, fearing their style.

To deal with Family, I escaped from it. Like many, I went to college,
put my head down, and, when I had to, turned the shape of the fact of my
family into my versions, stories that appalled or pleased or elicited the
response I hoped for: solidarity, or comfort, or understanding. In doing
so, for a while, I gave up everything, years blanked out, facts were facts
only as I made them. By claiming a clean careful modified Yeatsian stanza
form, I turned myself into a clean careful (in control) story. When my
control loosened and the stories grew bolder, more insistent, more necessary, I tried to recapture my mother through her voice. In this story, I am
Gina, and my mother's roommate is given her name, Lillian, while she
herself remains generic, a mother:

The next day, she called her mother at the hospital.

A soft female voice answered. She asked for her mother. *That* voice, when it came, was too familiar—it was faint with a shrill warble of terror in it that horrified Gina. The edge of terror had always been there. It had never left her mother's voice. Gina held the receiver slightly away from her ear.

"How are you?" Gina asked.

"Well, I'm doing what I can."

"I just called to see how you are doing."

"Well, Gina, it has been a bad period, but I think I'm coming round now and the doctors hope so too. I was telling Lillian, my new roommate, that you were sure to call any day. It is good to hear you. I thought I'd hear from you last Sunday, but I know you have a busy life and it is good to hear you now. Excuse me dear, 'Lillian, Lillian, this is long-distance. My daughter Gina is calling me. I'm afraid you'll have to use another phone now.' Excuse me, Gina, it was just Lillian. How are you dear?"

Before Gina could answer, the voice began: "The doctors say that mine is a very interesting case. And, Gina, I got that new doctor I told you about. He's brilliant, just brilliant. Such a change. Why in ten minutes he and I had more rapport going for us than that other doctor and I could come up with in ten hours. It is so important with a depression like mine to force yourself to reach out and get the help you need. Would you believe it, no one here can ever believe I have problems. They all think I'm so strong. But inside I hurt, Gina, and I have to demand my share of reinforcement. Gina, you're so quiet. But now, I want to hear about you. You talk."

"I'm glad you're getting help. The new doctor sounds . . . sounds nice."

"Oh, it won't be a simple matter though. It will take time. I have to keep telling myself that, Gina. These things take so much time. But I want to know about you. How is Rod?"

"Rob."

"Her mother started coughing violently. "Just a little cough, Gina. It's the excitement of hearing from you at last. It will go away. *You talk.*"

"Rob moved away. There is something new though, but are you all right?"

"Just my cough. You know how I am. You remember, Gina. Oh, oh, a minute, dear, just a tiny minute while I get a drink."

'Long Distance,' she could hear her mother cry out, 'Please, Lillian, some water.' Gina could hear steps, the toilet flushing, and her mother saying grandly, 'Gina, my daughter, is on the phone.'

Her mother picked up the receiver again and said, "Good-bye," loudly. "Nice woman," she said, "But she's terribly sick and I don't have the time to talk to her right now. Now, before you have to hang up, are you taking vitamins? Good health is the key to everything. If you work too hard, you'll end up here like me."

Gina sighed. "I'm fine. I bought vitamins today."

There was no boyfriend named Rob. But these voices ring true to me. I've captured my mother. I've erased myself. At a safe distance, on the phone, I have no weight and no body.

Four

Something had to happen before I could inhabit that body. First, my mother died. Before she died, I was unwilling to consider having children. I worried about my ability to understand children, since I had been the long-time companion of a mother turned child. But there were children everywhere in my writing. Women with transparently ticking biological clocks. There were metaphors, there were voices, and of course there were perplexed *mes*: Gina or Jennie or Jean, asking why not?

Aging had to happen to reclaim that body. Living, myself, through my mother's ages, I had to see her body in my body, my visage moving back into her visage. In our thirties we had the same operation—intimate, female, and particular—the right ovarian cyst—removed thirty years apart. When I catch a glimpse of the back of my arms, I see my mother's arms. I most easily notice in myself those things about her I liked least. Naturally, then, I live through my mother's ages with some reluctance (those arms, that cellulite, the lines around the mouth—true I'm thinner, but I might, I might, I might. . . .) and with some sympathy (those terrible cramps we have and premenstrual tension). Did anyone then, I wonder, worry enough about the female body she was living through before slapping on cold gel at the temples? She was always too trusting of technology, so reliant on the safe, concerned, unlike-her-husband (she-thought) doctors.

Even as I live through my mother's ages, I live through my daughter's. To hazard a metaphor, I envision her with me as, hand in hand, we walk together out of a darkened room. Of course, my daughter and my son will have to shape the facts themselves, and their views will never follow the same angle or strike the same timbre as mine. Yet, at eight years, my daughter offers, like flickering candlelight on the cave wall, the possibility of seeing into the heart of things, a caught-out-of-the-corner glimpse of understanding.

I tried to catch this elusive hope in two stanzas from a longish poem called "Touching Liliana." The narrator is intentionally me, the author, and the five-year-old is intentionally my daughter, as she was three years ago. "Liliana" is not shorthand for my mother's name, "Lillian," since the story of the poem came from a TV documentary about a young Argentinian woman named Liliana who "disappeared" and with her was lost her child, her generation. Still the poem has resonance for me because the name of the lost woman was like my mother's own. Coincidences may simply be moments when we listen:

> I hold
> my five year old,
> A sandpiper of spring-rain fed
> Flesh and hollow hollow bone.
> She darts in a tide of my patience,
> Pecks, preens, cowers,
> And comes back, licked by waves,
> Licked by waves—"getaway."
> She plays in the shadow of
> My days—her forward
> Is my past. Her tease
> Is my torture—
> Life is centered in such delicate
> Passing breath.
>
> (later in the poem)
>
> Raising children, you see,
> Is the kind of archeology
> Most of us do best—
> Trace family skeletons
> And our biology:
> "Has your morning energy,
> My teeth in your jaw."
> Concatenation of genes,
> Such glories we meant
> To invoke.

I inherited my mother. I inherited this need to think her through (to think through her). And I inherited her actual, tangible effects. Her papers and my memories are married together in file cabinet and bookcase, inscribed deeply on computer disk and brain cells. I trace her body in my body, make stray sightings of us both in my daughter, and see her as a warning—and a need to witness. Facts, I'm learning, take their shape this way: I etch a new outline and slowly, slowly, find the encouragement to fill it in.

Part II: Shaping "The Shape of Fact"

P: I only wanted to know more—about the mother, about the four sisters, about your daughter, about you. I want to know more keenly the mother's problems, the manifestations of her depression in some scenes with the narrator, with the sisters, the husband.

W: That is a central issue—how many vignettes should I share? Which holds the key? The fact that my mother, raised in a Minnesota-Norwegian farm family of many brothers and sisters, might have been abused as a child but died before we talked about it. The fact that my parents were separated for four years during the wars that formed my older sister's earliest years, with my mother left to raise that first child alone. The fact that my army family moved eighteen times in the fifteen years before I was born. The fact that my mother couldn't face her family responsibilities, went to mental hospitals, became well—damn near ran the wards—returned home, and couldn't face us once again. The fact that my mother never had a career and always wanted one just as she never broke the bounds of 1950s conventions and always needed to. The fact that my father was not faithful in an age when this represented wellness in men and illness in women. The fact that four daughters later, my parents still made jokes about the never-engendered male heir.

Did I share only already fictionalized "scenes" like the one between Gina and Gina's mother because they are safe, fully filtered through my memory's censor? Is the problem that I can't share the sharp photos of family life that flash through my mind when asked about "more" or that I'm afraid that more, specific, information will de-sensationalize "my" story, make it just another family plot?

And there is the problem of authority. Did these things happen, and if they happened, did they happen as I remember them? Certainly I feel unable to "tell" stories for my sisters. We rarely disagree because we rarely meet. It is significant to me that my sisters and I each hold down a separate corner of the US map—California, Washington, New Jersey, Florida, isolated push-pins in the corners of safely distant pastel states.

Also, I worry that to tell too much,, too clearly is to sensationalize, to admit failings, to wallow, to sentimentalize, to feel sorry. "Why don't these people just straighten up and fly right" as my army father might put it.

P: Did it ever feel as if she were taking your life? Did you ever want her just to go ahead and die?

W: Sure. Yes. She took my life (and how I changed hers!).

I know I'm taking my daughter's. We struggled just last night over how to study for 2nd grade spelling tests. She was tired. I was controlling. She cried in frustration. We started over. And after some negotiation, we made it to the last word. She spelled always as *alwas*. I suggested writing it again. She couldn't allow me to say this—it was a simple mistake, she knew the word, why was I making her do it again? Crying, in her bedroom, she wrote *alowas* and showed it to me, with a "so there." I laughed. Forgive me, but the angry small letters jumped off the paper, proclaiming her personhood. I laughed at how hard it is to grow up with a mother. She felt I laughed at her. So last night, I took part of her life. She told me she'll never forgive me for that loud spontaneous belly-laugh, and I believe her.

S: Are you ever afraid that you may have inherited your mother's illness? Or that you might have "carried" it to your own children?
W: Of course. That is the essence of the essay, asking have I? Asking it of every family shading, asking it during down days, stressful times, after divorce and remarriage and growing older.

Why was I reluctant to have children until my mother died? Maybe knowledge hidden in my biology that I could inherit her depression and my daughter, then, mine. More simply, at that time, I didn't want her to come visit, and grandparents have the need to see their grandchildren. A child would have provided her with entry back into my house and heart. For we were estranged by the distance I had put between us, moving from California to Africa and then back to Arizona.

I once saw my mother sweep up my infant niece (against my sister's wishes), hold her too tightly to her bosom graced by a large piece of sharp costume jewelry and claim she had a right to see her granddaughter, didn't she? Well, it seemed clear, at first, no granddaughter—no claims.

S: Who is your audience? I am confused here. Even your title is "dense." You seem to think densely. However, the final paragraph gives the reader hope that you will continue to grow.
W: Questions about audience touch the writer's drive to make writing "art." Art has a never explicit but always accessible audience. If the language is good enough (never mind that we can't define good), then anyone would be glad to read it. Everyone is my audience, I'd suggest, and be wrong.

Not my remaining family. My sisters might be offended or offer up a different faction, destroying my contained and artful-fix on this problem. Maybe my daughter, by way of an explanation. But mostly other women and mothers and daughters and fathers and sons who make a study of mothers and daughters. It's an attempt at saying: testifying is okay. Talking about women is okay. Not okay—essential. Voice for silence, safety-valve for rage? Less melodramatic—a challenge to say what I haven't been able to say; this will free me to say other things at other times.

L: Your style is secretive in a way.
*W:*Secretive in a way. I actually like that phrase because I can reverse it: not secretive in a way, too.

D: The line that reads: "Alarm over my mother continued years after I left home and didn't ease until she took her own life." It was especially powerful because it took me off guard. I didn't know how to react—most people don't. I suppose it's human nature but I wondered—how?
W: I knew I was slipping this fact in. And I didn't want to dwell on this because I still haven't figured out how to announce suicide. My mother took too much of her medication on purpose and went swimming in her trailer park estate's clubhouse pool. She drowned. It's both riveting and plain.

I've written poems about her being found by someone I only imagine—a pool cleaner, a home owner's representative. And I've had trouble writing this fact down on medical forms. I'm not cowed by religious embarrassment, just social embarrassment. I've been schooled at her school: visits to the hospital were reported in town (by decree) as visits to her relatives (who never wanted her to visit, just to straighten up and fly right). It's like the illusion achieved through facing mirrors, the way reflections move back and back, into eternity: do I embarrass myself by saying she killed herself or do listeners find it so embarrassing that I reflect their discomfort?

I've had trouble explaining this to my daughter—how did her grand-mother die? By drugs, by drowning, by decision, by self, due to loss, due to depression. My daughter comes home from school, often, singing jingles learned at "Just Say No" (to drugs) assemblies. She worries about people dying from cancer. Lately, she's been asking what the holes in the ozone layer look like. I'm a bit at a loss myself about how to be more specific in a positive way about my mother's final decision. I have nothing against human nature.

L: I wondered if it might not be a more effective beginning if you just started your essay off with "If you're the child of a manic-depressive." I didn't think the sisters were developed enough to warrant beginning with them.
W: Somehow, though, I can't reach my mother without moving through and by my sisters. They were at first buffers, since they were my mothers to a large extent. Then, as they left home, and because I was the youngest, they were also the locus of my feelings of abandonment. Sure my mother went away, that story was familiar, she had most always been "away" in her own world. But as each sister left, so I was left. In this essay, I find my entry to some honesty by slipping quietly past my older sisters.

W: Maybe you could explain more about manic depression. Although we've all heard the term, many of us are unsure of the actual happenings, and some of the cures that are tried.

W: There are labels like the now current bi-polar disorder, and I could describe her six month down (depressed) and three month up (manic) cycles. Easier, I could refer to William Styron's discussion of depression—less common and less acknowledged among men—or evoke the movie *Play Misty For Me* and explain how the crazed female lead in that drama caught my mother's "bad" phases in tone and feeling, how I sat in the movie theater crying as I watched Clint Eastwood save me from my fears.

I'm less expert at self-diagnosis than my mother was; through her I learned a superficial history, from the use of electroshock, to the exploration of chemical imbalances in the human brain, to the development of effective anti-depressant drugs (all with side effects) to the emergence of new forms of psychotherapy, including family systems counseling, to the necessary surge in language that brings dysfunction and co-dependancy into the light of everyday discussion and inspection. In my essay, I aimed only to capture the confusion (and in her story, the failure) of treatments.

T: I think writings like yours are no doubt therapeutic for the writer. But— possibly run the risk of being dull to readers in general? I mean, why are you really writing this? Almost everyone has 'problems' with their parents to some extent, and maybe being reminded of them by reading someone else's isn't the funnest thing to do. . . .

W: No, it's generally not very fun. Most of us probably read confessional, personal history, especially female faction out of need—a need to hear another voice, to tap a similar experience. I read women's magazines and rather despise them, but I also keep reading them. Why do women? Why don't men?

F: On the last two pages of the essay, I wondered about what you were trying to say. I think I got the gist of it, but I felt that there was something that you were holding back, that you weren't coming out and saying.

W: In the last two pages I believe I'm carefully hopeful. As a parent, I'm tapping into the basic hope that people, especially as embodied in my own children, can be better. I suppose the qualification of "careful" comes from knowing that this is a very romantic hope in general but a fierce one. I'm hoping to change what might be my family's fate through attention to the particulars of my unfolding life with my own daughter.

E: This piece tilts in favor of a female audience, so I'm not into it as much as many of the other readers are.

W: This is both good and bad. Good, because I wanted to tap issues that I don't often feel sanctioned to tap. Bad, of course, in that I want you to read on, to care. Why don't you care the cares of a female audience? Why are they female?

M: I'm thinking of how I would like to write about my mother (especially now after reading about your own awareness of body changes that we share with our mothers). But I don't think I could write as honestly and clearly as I would like until after her death.

W: This essay isn't in the mail to my sisters any more than it would be to my mother if she were alive. Perhaps your writing is for my family and mine is for yours?

C: Watch out for your writer voice messing up your storyteller voice. Making your mother a literary device makes the reader [who is] intimately involved at this point, recoil a little—then you needlessly have to win me back. You do of course, but why mess with it.

W: Making my mother a literary device has been a long-time problem. Making myself a literary device is too. Or is it? The utility of faction for me resides in it's acknowledgment of shaping—this is my shape of these facts, me digging back through the past, me saying these facts fall this way into these patterns, for me, for now: want to see? want to talk about it?

S: [You're] hovering still, especially at the first of the piece . . . what's keeping you from landing? Fear? I doubt it. Guilt? Anger? I don't think so. Lack of curiosity? No. So what is the diagnosis? Can't be pin-pointed? Have all the tests been run? Every indication is that all results are normal, but still you find yourself hovering? Are you hovering alone? No? Then who do you keep company with? Why do you make that choice?

W: Exactly, Dear Reader, exactly. We have shared this much, until now. What do you think?

   If we have come this far, I think we're hovering together.

Note

"Family History" appeared in *Western Humanities Review* 34.3 (1980): 222 and "Touching Liliana" in *American Poetry Review* 20.1 (1991): 31–32.) The term faction is borrowed from Clifford Geertz who uses it in *Works and Lives: The Anthropologist as Author*. Stanford, CA: Stanford UP, 1988.

Part VI

Composing Ourselves
Through Teaching

Ten years ago I shared my teaching thoughts slumped in the spare chair in other teachers' offices or with friends beside coffee urns at conference book exhibits. Now I'm more likely to begin my sharing with others across the Internet. We ask "Has this happened to you?" "What did you do and why?" "Can you upload that exercise?" "Here's what I changed—here's what (didn't) work for me."

This morning alone I could respond to messages about creative writing programs in Germany, experiments in literary nonfiction, or ethics in ethnographic writing research (a continuation of a conference question and answer session). Friends have responded to a new poem I sent them, share news of relationships and tales of institutional folly. An invitation to participate in an MLA session pops up in the incoming mail as does a quote on the derivation of my name, forwarded by someone who knows I'm interested in writing about naming (it appears, as I've long suspected, that I was made up for the book Peter Pan). A former graduate student and research-subject resurfaces with news of her career in another field (she moved from English to social work) and a newer acquaintance, an MFA graduate student shares her decision making process toward choosing a Ph.D. program in rhetoric and composition. Friends of long standing share continuing life stories, writing progress, and job search news. An editor answers questions, shares his writing, teases. All of these individuals are teachers: they have taught, are teaching, will teach again. All are composing their (teaching) lives—and my teaching life.

Teaching—as you can see—remains central in my social and in my professional discussions. "If Winston Weathers Would Just Write to Me on E-Mail: A Response to David Bartholomae and Peter Elbow" is the original version of an essay that appeared by invitation in College Composition and Communication. I drafted the response in the summer of 1994 and it was cut by about fifty per cent when editor Joe Harris picked it up again to fit into a February 1995 issue. While the published version may be tauter and more to the point, the longer version shared here more fully represents my evolving writing style. I use twenty-two snapshots—grammar B "crots"—as introduced to our field and named by Winston Weathers in his book An Alternate Style: Options in Composition—in order to show how deeply writing and thinking about writing allow me to feel both social and individual—not either/or but both/and.

In December 1994, Hans Ostrom and I prepared the script for "Letting the Boundaries Draw Themselves" for a panel at the San Diego meeting of the Modern Language Association. We had been working for two years as editors of a collection on genre and writing and we wanted to illustrate the way coming to see genre as a social process had impacted our relationship(s) to language, style and scholarship. In the final essay of this collection "Teaching Lives: Thoughts on Reweaving Our Spirits"—drafted in 1995/96—I speak of the affective nature of our profession with need and affection. If teaching is a type of moving meditation, it is also (can be? should be?) a spirit-filled enterprise. Unrepentantly converted to composition studies, I want to name what has happened (still is happening) to me because I believe such investigations encourage others to undertake their own. When a teacher is lucky—as I have been lucky—a teaching life becomes indistinct from a lived life. And this development should be commented upon to the same degree that teaching crises and professional positions have been and will continue to be discussed.

Teaching, for me, has never been about sudden certainty. Instead, it has been about wandering determinedly, composing myself here and there—"I need to write about this, now this, now this." And suddenly, I would find myself—as I expect you find yourself—trying to figure out "how-to" something—that is, everything—else.

21

If Winston Weathers Would
Just Write to Me on E-Mail
A Response to David Bartholomae
and Peter Elbow

*In formulating your response, I hope that you will resist a simple taking
of sides or positions, and instead work to deal in issues rather than
personalities—to try to offer, that is, your own take on some of the
questions of criticism, credulity, voice, power, and classroom practices
that Dave and Peter raise.*

Joe Harris (letter, 28 March 1994)

1. I WAS OUTSIDE THE PARLOR THE DAY THE FIRST SET OF BARTHOLOMAE
and Elbow papers were presented, the large conference room was over-
flowing, I stood on my tired tip-toes in the hallway and looked in to see a
far platform—David and Peter—microphones, crowd at the back shuf-
fling, I walked away, down the corridor and toward the escalators. I had
missed the moment, reported to me again and again during the rest of the
conference, presaged in graduate classes I took in the past and played out
in those I would teach in the future: are we socially constructed or individually empowered?

2. The Bartholomae/Elbow dialog was/is. A moment. A turning point.
An important academic interlude. Here's another one, a student's:

Writing this last draft, which I've just finished has left me exhausted. I've
worked almost four hours tonight. I have a fever of over 101. I have more to
do. I'm whining too much. Somehow, from somewhere, it all came out again.
I must've changed 60 or 70 percent of the bloody thing. I found myself upset,
sore, crying. I was bitchy. But I think I made it work, and I discovered things I

didn't know. I like what I did. It came with some sacrifice and reward. I didn't take Dylan on a bike ride. I didn't give him his bath. But he came to visit, to ask about my writing, to sit on my lap and give me a hug. Erica, whom I live with, made me ginger tea, sat on my lap and gave me a hug. I'm glad I don't go through this every day. But I'm glad I went through it tonight.

3. A graduate student's essay from last term, his beginning exploration into A-student plagiarism has haunted me—what does the academic critique or the expressivist agenda matter if students aren't writing, for themselves (for their own sakes')? What does it mean if they aren't writing in collaboration with others in writers' (not plagiarists') ways? How should we feel when we learn that regularly some computers in some dorms are dedicated to extended social "borrowing" and "recycling." Isn't the idea of the classroom as the site of critical explorations into academic discourse as simple (I didn't say simplistic) in its hopefulness as is the writing classroom as "free" territory?

4. "The desire for an open space, free from the past, is a powerful desire . . . (DB). Why is open space, by definition, by appositive, free from the past? Rocks have their geological history, most meadows I've hiked to show scars of settlement, the west has its mythic and traceable histories, the dream of "freedom" is inevitably rooted in an individual, group, and cultural consciousness. Why is free or open or empowered assumed to be solely and of necessity, romantic, transcendent? My western "open" places are cluttered by connections and earthy: hobo jungles, with their runes of burnt tincans, railroad tracks, creosote and sagebrush, Anasazi ruins under phantom jet trails, dead and stinking possum or armadillo carcasses, mine tailings of instrumental savagery.

5. Is this an expressivist author-centered essay or am I constructing myself coyly within my discipline, trying to enter the parlor by speaking with textual freedoms? Why didn't I worry more four weeks ago about this response, or why didn't my worry, real and academic, push me to begin, to finish?

6. "We shouldn't think of ourselves as frontier guides but as managers, people who manage substations in the cultural network, small shops in the general production of readers and writers" (DB). I've got some explaining to do here as my heart is beating "no" and my head is nodding

"sure." As a writing program administrator I was a manager, and I did try to produce readers and writers. And I tried to define my own responsibility. And that wasn't always "in service of" the institution. I tried to be "in service of" the writers—like me, like students are. Anyway, I assumed that "fiction of service" as easily as any other. Of course I quit, stopped being WPA. I suspect Peter, Dave, and I each administer, teach, write out of our lives, romantic idea or not. Dave will have to tell me if I'm right or wrong. Peter has made this evident as he examines his life history in most of his writings. And me, I do have something to add to this conversation because I'm a woman and a creative writer and part of a different generation of compositionists, perhaps because I may experience fewer disharmonies and dichotomies than Peter does since I don't find my academic and writing lives so disparate, although they are often desperate.

7. Am I working with "the past," with "key texts," "other's terms," "struggling with the problems of quotation, citation and paraphrase" (DB)? I think so. How can writers who do so not reproduce our master narratives? The biggest master narrative I encountered as a woman in schools was that of academic discourse: certainty, logic, war, linearity, Grammar A, unitary, authoritative, author-evacuated. Untutored in that magic element of critical thinking (that I still fail mulishly to understand: what is critical thinking? Am I doing it? I think so, as I'm writing, I'm thinking, seriously, as deeply as I can, writing teaches me just as teaching helps me write). A student's literacy autobiography that I was reading today in the hot late spring Florida sun triggered my first draft of this, my late draft (sorry Joe). She says:

> Monday morning, draft 4. . . . I like the way writing this makes me feel, freer. Like I am admitting something, coming out of the closet and standing up for myself about my weird writing. Maybe it will make it more acceptable, interesting, if it's written about. You know that old thing about if it's real it's in print (Actually, that's backwards isn't it?). But if I write about my style, it will actually *be* a style.

8. From another process cover sheet, a suggestion of the writing that can be composed in the arbitrarily and temporarily though not necessarily "free" space of the classroom:

> As I stated in the opening paragraphs of the autobiography, this assignment really did turn into a monster. It was the map of the house, I think, that really

triggered the events. Without thinking about it, I found myself sketching out a diagram of my Grandmother's house in Canada. That particular house is the first place that I have any solid memory of, it is a place in which I lived some forty-two or forty-three years ago. I was amazed at what I was remembering; a flood of images and sounds that were kaleidoscopic but without any apparent theme. The sounds of the hall clock and the whistle of the train were very strong and were sounds, sensations, that I identified with when I went to bed each night. Those remembrances led to the memory of my father reading me stories before I went to sleep and then, finally, to the actual event of his reading *The Hollow Tree Stories*.

This writer is not without history or a sense of how life constructs us as we live it. And why can't we now talk together about master narratives of family life, how he/we/you/I shape triggered memories at the point of utterance?

9. Writing composed outside the classroom is often less free but not necessarily more academically constructed:

On Tuesday, I went to my boyfriend's house to start fresh. Sam's place is air-conditioned and quiet, whereas my apartment complex, which I call Rap Central b/c residents play bass music from their car stereos in the parking lot, is often not conducive to the thinking I need to start a writing project. Sunday, I set up on my laptop on the kitchen table and alternated between talking with Sam's sister-in-law, working on my 1102 class planning, and writing the literacy autobiography. I accomplished more in that setting than I would alone, when I wander off to other projects. Talking to Edith actually helped me to focus better, although our conversation had nothing to do with literacy. We discussed family issues, leading me to remember my grandmother's stories, which I added to the draft.

Writers think and write sort-of alone. Writers write with and through others.

10. "I find it a corrupt, if extraordinarily tempting genre. I don't want my students to celebrate what would then become the natural and inevitable details of their lives. I think the composition course should be part of the general critique of traditional humanism" (DB).

Two *tempting* critiques. One class writer says

I continued to keep a diary every year after fourth grade. My entries became longer and longer. Sometimes I would write pages at a time. The writing I did in my diary was a thousand times more real than any writing I did at school. It was not like the "Why the Sacrament of Confirmation Is Important" essay assigned by Sister Mary Peter. This was real life—my life. I was struggling with my life and creating order in my world by writing words on paper. I wrote all kinds of "essays" in my diary. The persuasive essay—"Why My Parents Should Let Me Date Juan." The informational essay—"My brother Mike Is a Disgusting Pig." The comparison-contrast essay—"Margarita Is a Better Friend Than Lourdes." I even wrote poems in my diary. They weren't haikus or sonnets, but they usually rhymed and they came straight from my heart. I was very proud of them.

Another—

As I began my outline for my paper, I could see the billboard in Mr. Biggers' classroom, "Better writers make better thinkers." I used to think he was wrong. Better thinkers make better writers. Through the years, I tested the two theories in many different ways. I was right; the better I wrote the better I thought. But Mr. Biggers had been right too. I could never really get down on paper what I was thinking as clearly as it was in my head. That meant the more I wrote and the better I got, the clearer I thought. I started saying to myself, "Gosh, I really am becoming a writer."

11. Corrupt and extraordinarily tempting, the personal essay. As WPA I remember run-ins with athletic programs, a time when I learned that entrance test scores on an in-house writing exam (grammar) were set at the pass level that would efficiently adjust the number of students that could be accommodated fiscally. I found that that I was viewed as troublesome and not very polite, that my field of study was not valued. I found it extraordinarily tempting to flee academic arenas full-tilt (in some ways I did) and return to the classroom and teach writing as best I could (I am)—as a writing teacher who writes with her students, who knows that the administration doesn't care what I do as long as it thinks it knows what I'm doing and nothing "goes wrong." My students don't care whether I got into the Bartholomae/Elbow presentations at 4Cs. And sometimes I don't think, actually, that the "debate" matters much to my teaching and their learning, except it does matter; it has kept me analyzing my desire to defend teaching writing as writing for the last seven weeks. Time to say here that I don't much like romanticism, humanism, traditional English

departments, critical thinking, academic discourse (as defined so far to me as I understand those definitions), or the myth of the unitary (mostly male) author. I don't want to feel that I've been a foolish and misguided teacher not to make politics or the academy or power relations the center of my classroom; and I don't have to because writers like this one do so for themselves:

> I often tried to write for professors and, in revamping my aesthetic judgment to make the grade, threw women and children overboard first. In my first college blue book final, I sold out Sylvia Plath to show that I'd outgrown sentimental girl poetry. Such clarity and emotion as Plath's would not measure up. I did a good job in savaging someone whose work I'd loved so much, if the professor's comments were any indication.

12. "It is writers who celebrate presence and readers absence" (PE). But I don't want to swing aboard the dichotomy train. Writers who are students may refuse too:

> By stopping at any of these stages, I would have developed a flat aesthetic of what is or is not good literature: it must be engaging; it must have a profound, shared message; it must challenge me as a reader rather than allowing me to wallow in its familiarity. These are all legitimate criteria and not mutually exclusive; I cannot work with or against them individually. In a similar fashion, my writing follows a progressive spiral where I re-visit old realizations about what's good on a regular basis and incorporate them anew.

13. Peter claims he likes an arrogant writer—I don't as much. In my classes, I have to battle him in a way that wastes time—show him I am, if I want to be, the authoritative teacher, but I don't choose to demonstrate my authority in ways he expects and reacts well to. Then again, I don't think Peter means arrogant that way, but as invested, interested, devoted, bewitched, lost in (academic) investigations of language. Is this naive unexamined romanticism or lived life?

> My third grader first learned to spell using inventive spelling. He snatched a sense of dominion over his own words. In our family when someone says bobwire, for barbed wire, we quickly claim it. It becomes a new word we adopt, expanding our vocabulary from their innate glimmers. Chuck E. Cheese has become tacky cheese, and somehow it fits so much better than what was served up to us. Some words I can't remember the 'right way' anymore because our new words become such second nature.

14. As the constructed author of the text you're currently reading, I need to point out that I'm thinking of the several friends with whom I share these same type of language stories and "new" words on e-mail. I'm thinking of the members of my poetry group who will be saddled with this draft tomorrow. We'll see if they understand how I wanted this response to BE a poem, really. I tell them how my own son turned "armpit" into "kneepit" and "exclamation points" into "excitement marks" and has just asked if after the year 1999 we go back to zero—an odometer vision of history.

15. Why did classroom literacy autobiographies prime me, prompt me, "free" me to write this response when Dave and Peter's good writing alone didn't? Why do I resist reading class writing and then when I do, marvel at all I learn? That students have the clues to their own construction:

> I am driven by everything I have ever read, from fiction to poetry, to children's books. Sometimes television still inspires me—Kodak commercials, the evening news.

16. Why do I have to learn again and again that students don't do all their growing as writers in their first year *or* in their fourth year writing class:

> Since freshman year, I have learned a lot. I've learned to shop for a week on twenty dollars. I've learned to pack up and move efficiently. I've learned that writing is an art applied to communication and that I have a tendency to stray from the communication aspect. I've learned to be honest with myself first, then people are honest with me. I've learned that I only need to water my plants once a week. I've learned to write papers like molding clay. Write like crazy, stop and turn it to the light, examine it. And never, never put it in the kiln until it can speak without you.

17. "Writing is a struggle and a risk. Why go to the bother unless what we say feels important?" (PE)

There are many ways to get to important. As I said, I expect that Peter and Dave and I are teachers of our own histories—Peter the importance of free and non-evaluative spaces (at first); Dave of writing that questions and complicates; me of writing as a mixture of mess and self-discipline, self-history to cultural history the only route I've been able to follow since

I started swinging way in and way out on the orbits of the academy (starting programs, finishing some, failing at others, teaching in my culture and out of my culture, writing academic essays and more and more blurring my genres publicly as they are blurred internally, experientially).

18. "Imagine, then, how different our classrooms would be if all academics and teachers felt themselves to be writers as much as readers" (PE).

19. I'd not treat the divorce paper writer critically *or* supportively, solely. Lately, I've been writing my own socially-constructed-yet-authored papers that leave me struggling with master narratives. And sharing these with my classes. I find that I can neither critique myself as writer from a distance or accept my own romantic evasions when I attempt to speak of what means something deeply to me. I'm betting that when Dave teaches "sentences and paragraphs" and "work on cultural politics" that that work, similar work, has been enormously valuable to him as a learner, writer, academic, critic. I can get there, too, differently, I believe, in the short space of a first-year class, without Adrienne Rich's text being closely examined (but, by the way, Rich is already there, I've "consumed her" and so she already influences this class I design, pushes me as a woman to share my personal experiences. Her text reacts in my writer's body chemistry, and maybe someday—one of my students who is an adult negotiating life in the academy—will bring Rich to class to share. I'm not the only one who consumes texts, by any means). I feel that my students 18–20 or reentry 30, 40, 50-year-olds need and require as much respect and attention as I've given my own academic and personal life these last long six months (mini-mid-life crisis) when I find myself only wanting to write what I want to write. Simple. Hard. Impossible. But I still can't help desire this. Desire—mine, theirs—won't be legislated by theory.

20. A class writer explains:

The way I approached things Freshman year was so extreme. I did everything to excess; thinking, smoking, drinking. I remember walking around the campus all night sometimes. Walking around smoking, so confused and overwhelmed about some things that I couldn't even talk about them. And when I did want to talk, nothing made sense or was so full of holes it wasn't worth arguing about. I was in a constant state of dilemma with myself, but I could always get alcohol. I was lost inside myself. It's kind of funny. I approached the "Love" paper with the same intense chaoticness that led my life at that point. I wrote papers/poems with the idea that 'this is how I write and if you don't get it then sorry.' I was writing things for myself to read and feel good about. Sitting on my bedroom floor [and reading this paper two years later] I laughed. I laughed again. I laughed for all of those who didn't when I told them the definition of love. I laughed for all the people who knew what I was going through, and still took me seriously.

21. Much of my (academic) world is constructed on the internet these days.

I
send poems,
flirt,
create,
critique,
arrange childcare,
transmit data,
respond to students,
schedule,
converse,
obscure,
share too freely,
get stuffy and irritated,
flattened out,
affectless,
elated
don't answer,
lose text,
find text I didn't expect,
invent a new world,
a friendly English Department
a universe.

Many of my students have been floating through this textual ether longer and farther than I have. It's their world. This is not utopia and free space. It is not ahistorical or uncritical. It is simply different and intensely interesting. For me, the writing classroom has such unique space potential. How we fill it, each and every one of us who teachwrites and writeteaches, is always worth examining as are David and Peter's dialogs that prompted my response. My goal is not only that students keep writing after my course (PE) but also that I become more aware and respectful of how much and how well they compose themselves before, in what varied media, with what full lives, acknowledging that they are part of the "weight" of the community as much as I am—I have power, but when I write with them I tap into their powers:

> I learned to write through a fog of voices, some clear and distinct, others muffled and encoded. By the time I entered kindergarten, I had lived in colonial French Africa and babbled in Chokwe, a Bantu language of Zaire. I had landed at my German Grandma's doorstep in Manitoba, Canada, a displaced pre-schooler.

22. And I've only read five of the twenty literacy autobiographies I had planned on for today (I'll share this draft in class tomorrow as my excuse and elaboration). The sun is sinking low—this "essay" is chaotic, first breath, in a momentary "free-space" of writers' faith, and I know I know it has to be shaped, lassoed in, made more acceptable. As I continue to read students' writings, I know mostly that I'll find bits and pieces that I'd like to share with you. But my students bore you. That's okay. As long as your classroom, your students fascinate you.

P.S. Dave—I hope at the next 4Cs we'll talk about our written wanderings. We'll meet face to face, rather than just word to word. Peter—I've just begun to untangle the complicated genealogy of your word-work and how it affects my academic life. I look forward to understanding more about the differences now that I've lived so long with the similarities. This is a way, I think, of finding out more about my own voice(s). Joe—like my students, I'm not sure if this is what you wanted. Readers—you're so so so hard to invent, really.

P.P.S. This text is "intentionally" composed in what Winston Weathers calls Grammar B style. It's a bitch to edit (sorry Joe). Weathers's insights are undercited, underappreciated and undertaught. If I had his e-mail address, I'd let him know that I think so.

22

Letting the Boundaries Draw Themselves
What Theory and Practice Have Been Trying to Tell Us—An Exchange

Wendy Bishop and Hans Ostrom

Hans

GENRES IN DOUBT, IN PLAY, IN FLUX—THE SIGNS SEEM TO BE EVERYWHERE these days.

A colleague who teaches literature seminars tells me one of his students wrote a long poem instead of an essay to fulfill a term paper assignment. "For an instant," the colleague says to me, "I thought of all the knee-jerk reasons for not accepting the poem, but I thought, this student probably put more work, analysis, and original thinking into the poem than she has in any of her traditional papers, so I accepted it, evaluated it, ended up giving it a high grade."

Andrea Lundsford visits our university, and in a colloquium several of us get on the subject of departments—departmentalism, if you will. We end up agreeing that department boundaries were not just out of date but often in the way: blocking many collaborations that seem so useful now. One example: I find myself collaborating more and more with colleagues from the political science department because we're all interested in representations of race and in relations between rhetoric and power. This work has made departmental boundaries seem arbitrary, at best.

The same can be said—and said for parallel reasons—about genres, genre boundaries. The boundaries are (were) convenient in their moment. However, to put this in Derridean terms (!), we reader-writer-teachers respond to genres by wanting to *supplement* them with something *different*—or dee-fer-aunt. And I think it's clear that ONE reason many of us now regard departmentalism as an affliction is that departments are, to a degree, based on textual genres, which are illusory, contingent, enforced but unenforceable.

The business of our colleagues in sciences is to describe the behavior of physical energy. The sites of their inquiry are cells, particles, organisms, light, matter, and lightmatter (Matter Lite). But it's energy description, all of it, as far as I can tell. And by the way, these colleagues are just as allergic to departmentalism as we are. A colleague in chemistry is delighted to tell me that he really "does physics," and biologists, of course, "do chemistry."

Over in social sciences our colleagues stratify, datify, measure data treasure, and demarcate contours of bodies politic. Energy of human masses; that's what they describe.

Our business is energy, too, and that's why genres are so maddening, so full of implications for what we do every day in our writing, reading, interpreting, teaching embodiments. Maddening in the sense that language moves, is moved, and moves boundaries that try to contain it; it can be said to form (transitive and intransitive), flow, accelerate, thicken, disperse, escape, solidify. It means and signifies, whatever that means, and it resists meaning and significance. It's particle, it's wave, it's light and matter and neither.

That old-time genre study was not and is not equipped to deal with such oceanic energy. Genre study didn't even used to be genre theory. It used to be more like surveying. Northrop Frye's *Anatomy of Criticism*, for example, combined myth and literary formalism to create a sparkling, tidy, well-surveyed city of genres. No wonder we are sometimes nostalgic for the time we spent there.

Now genres, genre-study, and genre-theory are explosively bothersome. For we are back to the original questions. How does verbal energy get formed? We have our Heisenbergian problems, too, in other words. More mundanely, but no less fundamentally, what genres should we, do we, teach—and why, and why not? If genre is "social action" couldn't it also be social inaction? Often (a speculation) the genre-training of college students is a way of quieting them, universalizing them, con-forming them, domesticating them, making them presentable to the corporate world— that is to say, the world. And when we are disappointed in our students' writing, perhaps we don't realize the degree to which genre-training has produced the disappointing writing.

Newt Gingrich knows "The Contract With America" is a performance poem and not a contract. Dan Quayle knows that a speech about family values is not a speech but a textual wink and nod evoking in his constituents' minds a precise image of certain kinds and colors of people. In some instinctual, Orwellian way, such politicians know more about genres that we do.

And the supposed shift from product to process in the composition curriculum has been illusory, at least in the sense that the writing processes we encourage still lead—across the curriculum and in English—to predictable pseudo-academic genres: things called papers. In 1994 as in 1974 and 1954, students have a bunch of papers due, which they don't like to write and we don't like to read.

College teachers enjoy reading about five per cent of the papers they get from students, and I'm being generous. Our goal in tossing out old products, introducing new ones, and letting the boundaries draw themselves should be to raise the pleasure percentage at least 50 per cent. This is what practice has been trying to tell us.

What theory has been trying to tell us is that genre boundaries and hierarchies are means of creating social capital. They mark status and buttress privilege and pretension. At least this is, in part, what Pierre Bordieu has argued. In academia—on campuses—this means that genres are a kind of play money. Their inherent value should be doubted. But the idea of their being *play* should be taken more seriously. Our field of English studies, its dizzying number of subfields, our classrooms—are all sites in which genres are in play, in doubt, in flux. Every discipline should embrace the fact that it is playing riffs on its own genre "melodies": its conventions and demarcations. The jazzing around should be out in the open. This is what theory has been trying to tell us.

Wendy

To prepare myself for the '94 MLA, a week in academic discussion, I iron five white shirts and reflect on my last three day's oasis of reading—*Women Writing the Academy, Seeing Yourself as a Teacher* and *The Peaceable Classroom*. I have to read, play with poems and iron, and send e-mail to Hans, to write a talk, and in doing that, I've broken down the boundaries between private and public, personal and academic, then, THEN I'm ready to go. I dance to Brazilian music, chomp on a carrot, hang up a blouse, write these lines, and go back to another blouse before the iron runs out of water, falls on the ironing board, burns the rug, the back room the whole house, everything I care about, and leaves me empty. I do *want* the cacophonous clutter of the world, though that world is a dangerous place, and I keep it in place with words—boundaries help, some, but so often they hinder.

Hans claims: "Language moves, is moved; it can be said to form (transitive and intransitive), flow, accelerate, thicken, disperse, escape, solidify. It means and signifies whatever that means, and it resists such behavior; it supplements and differs." Mary Rose O'Reilley adds "The inner world is what literature is all about. Why have we forgotten that?"

I've refurnished the rooms of every classroom I've ever entered. Literally, I haul podiums to corners, pick up trash, move flimsy armed desks nose to nose, erase old chalk marks, make new ones, dust handprints onto my jacket or jeans pockets, always try to adjust the melancholy thermostat. Equally, I've had to unteach a lot—I've had to teach A-earning high school students that experimental writing, taking risks, is not baby work and silly play. I've had to teach English majors who, like me, exempted from first-year writing, that they really did have a writing process and a need to understand it. More, that they had reading processes, internalized, hidden, dark, myopic and conventional or deficient-feeling and hang-dog. I've had to shove the couch of creative writing into the overcrowded parlor of composition and allow for the complexity of a literacy life (ironing, eating carrots, dancing to music, not writing, in order to read and write) to students whom some of my colleagues define as empty vessels, adrift in a sea of popular culture. Because we disrespect our students, we keep shoving them into smaller and smaller rooms, from the living room of English literature to the laundry room of writing or the back porch of intro-to-literature-for-non-majors.

Does it matter that one blouse isn't white? It has a pattern on it that almost loses the small stain I find while ironing. I wonder how I actually got that stain and I make up the story I might say about it if someone noticed it on my blouse when I wear it. Does it matter that I lied about having only white blouses? They were *predominately* white. I must have looked in the ironing closet and said to myself, all white, then everything I wear will match, but I realize, now, I can never resist the one last motion, to add a dash of something else.

I'm tired of penurious, parsimonious curriculums that never let my students choose something else, something *and*. I'm tired of genres that fit. Hans asks "Is genre a social inaction."

Mary Rose O'Reilley believes "Students do not really listen well to the answers to questions they have not learned to ask" (34).

Do you believe me about the four white and one patterned shirts? Does it matter that each shirt (white or multi-colored) is a text for its owner, ironer? The patterned shirt has it's story printed on it in the words *1987 Official Esprit Sport, FlexArama, Sun Club.* Should I be allowed to speak at the MLA wearing such a story?

In the Atlanta airport, a woman turned to me and said: "you must be going to MLA." I agreed. We exchanged university names like members of a secret society. Then she asked what I taught: "Rhetoric and Composition and Creative Writing," I said.

"Oh," she said—an 18th century literature scholar—"Why are you going to MLA?"

"They let some of us in now," I said.

Should I be allowed to speak at the MLA wearing such a story? I'd like you to feel the tenderness I feel for that patterned shirt, bought one summer in graduate school in rhetoric and reminding me still of steamy humid Pennsylvania days studying words and words, reminding me also of another shirt, lost in the airfreight back to what was then home, Fairbanks, Alaska. I have been arguing, lately, that we need to teach convention making and convention breaking together, in concord, in strife, in dialog. Mary Rose O'Reilley says "I believe it is possible to examine our subject matter, whatever it may be, through a glass of tenderness as well as through the glass of reason" (82).

What is our subject? Theory, practice, boundaries. No, students. No, ourselves. Mary Rose O'Reilley says: "because teaching is some kind of spiritual inquiry, what we learn is more important than what they learn. It is more important, at least, to our passage; they are going someplace else; they are in a different myth . . ." (72).

I once admired Georgia O'Keeffe when I read that she only wore white shirts and black pants. But look at the paintings. In our teaching, if we wear the institutional clothes, what are we painting in the classroom? Are we remembering the explosion of colors that is the kaleidoscope of thought?

Is the problem of boundaries one of gender, insiders and outsiders? Why the sudden interest in boundary rhetoric? What if we spill colors on our white shirts? Will we continue to wear them? Is there a reason on earth to or not to? I like the phrase *No Reason on Earth*—it's the title of a good friend, Katherine Haake's, collection of short stories. I like it because it reminds us, boundaries, contact zone, inner or outer circles or not, we are constructing the reasons and we can reason with the constructs. Aren't we unethical to agree to genre as social inaction? Listen to this writer in another discipline:

> Historians typically distinguish between "narrative" on the one side, which is this cute little storytelling mode, and "analysis" on the other, which is somehow something else that historians do ever so much better. The difficulty has been dichotomization. There's no reason on earth why you can't write an analytical narrative. But they ignore all the ways in which a narrative, by definition, is analytical: narrative involves intelligence; it makes assumptions and judgments; [it] shapes itself; [it] has an engine; it explains its progress. All of those things are part of narrative, and I don't quite know why the dichotomy as to be there. The institution ought to reconsider the categories. I'm not the only one who is disgusted. There are many, many historians who can't quite understand why we are still locked into these irrational categories. (Kirsch 120–121)

Boundaries can create intellectual inaction—theory and practice together produce stereoscopic vision, writing and reading are partners, all writing is creative if we allow it context and all students are writers if we allow them an existence in the context, the complicated matrix of their lives. In a recent promotion review letter, a composition scholar (or is he a writer, or theorist or practitioner?) whom I respect, shared observations on my professional attempts to break boundaries and gave me a key to what I've been getting at: ". . . rather than simply being pluralistically "eclectic" or "well rounded" and as it were, simply moving comfortably from one well-furnished room to another," he said, "She keeps insisting on redecorating the rooms with furniture from the others—and knocking down walls and partitions."

Changing the furniture in the classroom doesn't mean throwing the classroom out with the bathwater—it's still a classroom. But things happen when we sit different places, view different angles, accused neither of dilettantism or dilution. If you try to view my remarks through the lens of compassion, you'll see that I'm insisting that we make teaching and learning real life, the institution a real house, inhabited by real people.

Four of the shirts are white, one is patterned. I've had four offices in five years at my present school; I've taught at six schools in seventeen years. I eat a carrot and read a friend's good book on teaching and listen to Portuguese and African influenced music and think of talking to Hans about all this and iron, in order to arrive. When I return, I'll write three syllabi that borrow from each other—creative writing activities to inhabit literature, theory to explore the textual claims of the literary nonfiction texts we'll write and workshop, and poetic form to teach invention rather than convention.

Collaborating together in several genres, Hans and I have learned that our students, in a similar way, need to write themselves. They need to write about writing, about themselves as newcomers and lovers and scared tender souls thrown into the flux of university life to brazen it out. They have lives and those lives continuously burst through the boundaries and dams of English department control. Hydroelectricity might be helpful here—to draw on, use, create with, generate with—we've already lost the wild lakes and rivers in the damned up boundary wars of K–12 schooling. In *Howard's End*, E.M. Forester said, "Life demands that we connect the prose and the poetry" (qtd in O'Reilley 53). For us, letting the boundaries draw themselves means being drawn into what we teach and residing there more ethically, letting students iron shirts and eat carrots, too, in order to write, to redecorate when the classroom furniture gets mildewed and musty, to unlock irrational categories, to connect the prose and the poetry.

Because . . .

Hans

Because . . .

I am in the Seattle-Tacoma airport, waiting to fly to San Diego. Often when I go to conferences I buy a new white shirt, get it out of its plastic wrapping, unpin it, and put it on without ironing it. Doing so reminds me of black-and-white Hollywood movies, starring Alan Ladd or John Garfield, in which the hero is on the run. The hero unpacks his suitcase in a seedy hotel and takes out new shirts and throws them in a drawer before getting out a bottle of whiskey. I don't do the whiskey thing, but I still like the shirt thing. There's something adolescent and irresponsible (John Garfield, Robert Mitchum) about putting on a new shirt without ironing it, especially when you're headed for an unbearably responsible conference.

In order for my story to parallel Wendy's I would have to run into a woman at the Sea-Tac airport who would stare at my chocolate brown leather jacket, my shirt with the geometric fold lines on it, and my moussed-up (messed up) hair, and the woman would have to say, "Are you going to the O.J. trial," and I would have to say, "No, I'm going to MLA," and she would have to say, "What's that?" and I would have to say, "I can't tell you, but I can tell you that I think O.J. is guilty."

23

Teaching Lives
Thoughts on Reweaving Our Spirits

SPIRITUALITY IS A TROUBLING WORD TO ME. I TEND TO SHY AWAY FROM spirit even as I'm drawn to it. I tend to focus instead on humanist, on what it means to me to be humane, involved, and human—to be a person with a vocation that fills spiritual as well as material needs. I would have, as a for-years-but-no-longer-(and-never-very-convinced)-Methodist, equated spirituality with religion, or have found disturbing the idea that writing and the work of teaching could be a powerful form of meditation (too reminiscent of my cynical 1960s and '70s growing up in California).

For a long time, other words, like *emotion* and *intuition,* would seem equally problematic, proved by years in the academy where I felt too much (it seemed). Even when I was learning to suppress emotion and intuition, the idea of *knowing* still interested me ("Why did I go with that lesson plan? Well my guess was that this class would . . . "). Knowing in the self-sustaining, getting-connected-with-a-world-bigger-than-me sense, in the, well, I guess, spiritual sense. I gravitate to this word now because it clarifies certain aspects of my life and points to experiences bigger than *affect* and bigger than *mind:* that is, mind combined with affect creates an exciting experiential tapestry. For me, that tapestry represents the university campus and the university presents one form of *real* life, where writing is meditation and teaching is a spiritual journey, benefiting both teacher and student.

How long it's taken me to say so.

***

I was delighted with the term "felt sense" when I encountered it in research into composing processes and quickly applied the term to my experiences as a creative writer, as in felt sense, that moment of equipoise when the hair on the back of my neck rises, when I read a poem and it moves me, moves molecules; the same when my own teachers would read in a dull classroom and, despite the dullness, in the emotion of that reading, allow the poet's words to touch my spirit in an inexplicable way. In the same way, trying to understand my teaching life includes a tentative tour, *a feeling through* of these difficult to define words, *a feeling through* years of embracing and avoiding, *through* questioning, *through* half-remembered poems, those that were "taught" to me and those that I write as I teach. In *The Peaceable Classroom*, Mary Rose O'Reilley captures this journey-sense for me when she explains:

> But I stay in teaching because all the models we have for spiritual process—religious, mythic, what have you—tell us that it doesn't matter whether we are right or wrong or successful but merely that we remain faithful to a vision. And that when it's easy, it isn't worth much. Let me repeat and rephrase: because teaching is some kind of spiritual inquiry, what *we* learn is more important that what *they* learn. It is more important, at least, to *our* passage; they are going someplace else; they are in a different myth . . . . we cannot control their reactions, we can only determine our own inner weather. (72)

My own inner weather, after seventeen years of teaching, tells me that teaching is visionary and spiritual for me—it is what matters—and I return faithfully to the classroom year after year, needing that growing space, no doubt, as much or more than the classroom inhabitants need me.

***

Several years ago, I began to argue in teaching essays that writing is necessarily therapeutic, usefully so, unashamedly so, for whether sanctioned or not, students will write their lives in our writing classes (if we let them), and so we, as teachers, must write ours with them. I've learned that my intuitive understanding of the power of personal writing and my intellectual understanding of the force of discourse and culture need to commune—that heart and brain have to unite in teaching. When they do, I learn that teaching teaches me, heals me, helps me, centers me in my professional and personal life in a way I've seldom seen talked about.

I've learned that students will always write within the complicated matrix of their daily lives. Last term, students' writing process narratives again highlighted their lives' complexities: from a young man whose parents were divorcing at Thanksgiving; to a young woman pregnant and estranged from her abusive husband; to an older woman, a state worker, who was in two catastrophic car accidents; to another young man who just didn't feel like he wanted to do schoolwork anymore. Students' lives

impinge on their writing processes in serious ways that are seldom studied. The cognitive problem-solving model cannot, of course, provide an
equation for how these students might best be helped to write better.
Only a well-trained, invested, interested teacher has a hope of navigating
the inter-related cognitive and affective territory of the classroom.
Perhaps, only a teacher who comes to experience the confusions (collu-
sion?) of avocation and vocation, teaching as a way to confirm and recon-
firm, to weave and reweave, a life's vision, an act of faithfulness.

***

The affective map has been neglected, on several levels. There appears to
be a field-wide refusal to deal with the content of student writing and the
contexts of students' lives. I am not suggesting here that I become my students' professional counselor, knowing fully how untrained and unequal I
am for that task. But I'm perplexed by the degree of professional horror I
raise when I suggest that I am present as a person in the classroom, that
one part of the negotiation all writers partake in is that of their own lives;
I welcome a book like Robert Brooke's *Writing and Sense of Self* that looks
at the individual within the structure of the workshop and Lad Tobin's
recent *Writing Relationships* for the assertions it makes that what we do as
teachers is embedded in relational processes. If relationships in the classroom represent sticky, dangerous territories—the La Brea tarpits of the
mind—they are also the glue of writing as I know it, and must be
addressed. Mary Rose O'Reilley says:

> I would like to meet the concern about turning the classroom into "some kind
> of therapy group," then, by observing that good teaching *is*, in the classical
> sense, therapy: good teaching involves reweaving the spirit. (Bad teaching, by
> contrast, is soul murder.) . . . In general, I find it more productive to look at
> how things (like teaching writing and doing therapy) are similar, rather than at
> how they are, and thus should remain, different. (O'Reilley 47)

Soul murder? Strong language. Too strong or barely strong enough?

The student who mentioned that his parents were divorcing. He
lingers in my mind as a still-needing-to-be-understood teaching moment.
On a fairly dull Tuesday before last Thanksgiving, I asked my students to
complete a sure-fire invention exercise—writing fifteen metaphoric
responses about a person about whom they had strong feelings—to be
turned, later, into a portrait poem. I started the exercise near the end of
class, and, after most students had packed up and swept out, I waited
impatiently for this young man to finish—I was ready for Thanksgiving

break too. I was surprised he was still writing away since he usually was fairly perfunctory about the class. He looked up, said, "This is a neat exercise. I think I found a poem."

My teacher-self preened, and I almost replied before he said, "I don't really want to go home, my parents are getting a divorce and it's going to be strange."

My teacher-words died in my throat.

I myself had had a difficult fall term, personally, and I felt unable to respond, unable to offer either the dismissive brisk or the emphatic supportive reply. It bothers me now to think of that pedagogical pause, as I froze for a moment, saying nothing. I hadn't been writing along with my classes, as I often do and feel I always should, and I was distant from the teaching moment, deciding, finally, on a non-committed:—"Oh, well, good. Great, I'm glad you found something."

For me, that moment represents the opportunity, the danger, the lure and the confusion that teaching writing has always had for me, and because of my own busy life context, I willed it out of being: did not talk about the purposes or results of the activity, did not talk about how writing leads into and out of living, talked about nothing. The longer I teach, the more clearly I realize, my own and my students' lives are really at the center of what I do, however well or poorly I do it. By attending to my teaching, tracing and understanding my teaching life, I understand my life, period.

***

I've been thinking back over moments that brought me to this argument—that teachers should be telling about their emotional and spiritual lives as teachers. In 1992, for instance, I was at several sessions at the New Hampshire Conference on the writing process movement and I was struck by the number of times that conference speakers recited poems— by others or their own—about what they do. As a teacher of composition and poetry, I've learned that most of my students harbor a hidden "high school" poet inside themselves, and I know, from working with new teachers of writing, that many in English studies came to be where they are through their aspirations to write like author X, Y, or Z , to make, to create texts.

I continue writing in this manner, though, because I realized my poems, and more recently my literacy autobiographies, self-assigned in teacher-education classes I teach, offer me valuable new modes of understanding myself and my professional life. Thinking about teaching by writing, informally, in mixed genres, helps me solve or at least think differently, productively, creatively about teaching problems. It enriches my life. Literally, it reweaves my experiences into a usable whole. Not a permanent whole, for I often find the need to tear out the stitching, reconsider the pattern, and construct my understandings anew.

To do this, I use poetry in James Britton's sense of exploratory writing: my informal thoughts shaped into verse because verse shaping comes by now fairly naturally to me as a mode of thinking. Picking up a book of poetry on the public library shelves, I read "Poetry was part of the everyday social life of an educated man in China, and it was customary for friends and acquaintances to exchange poems on various occasions or to get together and compose poems on a particular theme" (Watson 9) and this tenth century poet, Su Tung-p'o has titles like "At Twilight, Fine Rain Was Still Falling" and "Feet Stuck Out, Singing Wildly" and "Letting the Writing Brush Go." Why, I wonder, is occasional verse anathema in the modern writing classroom. How lucky I was in New Hampshire, I think, to be around on a day when poetic testimony broke through professional decorum.

***

Jo'al was taking my poetry class while enrolled in the first-year writing class of a teacher I had educated to teach writing. Jo'al was "hearing" different writing rules in each class and became confused by the apparent contradictions.

JO'AL

tells me her other teacher
asks for "no metaphors, please,"
in the personal narrative,
tells me her poetry teacher,
me, asks for "images and no clichés
and the five senses, use them concretely"
but weirdly
make lungs ring like brass bells
make skin feel hot and foolish like caramel,
make eyes track lucid questions in sky blue—
guides to coax the day into formal
shapes she's hesitant to use.
Jo'al asks me, can she put metaphors
in poetry? Can she use her own words

like chitterlings and cornbread?
Pushed back from a heavy desk,
I see blocks of days,
some for creating, some for composing.
Then I say "yes." Yes.
Southern fried and hamhocks steaming,
naps, and plaits twisting patient hands.
I share my mother's lost Norwegian
farmlands and lilting syllables
flattened, all rules followed.
Jo'al listens between
the messages. Thanks me.
Her next poem, "When I Was
Black," her best.

After reading Su Tung-p'o's life in poems, I might retitle mine "The Day Jo'al Pointed Out Contradictions in Teaching and Learning" or "Letting the Writing Student Go."

***

I also see teaching and writing about teaching not simply as pedagogical or personal inquiry but also as civic action, a component in my personal and broadest definition of spiritual. Perhaps the analogy here is of piecing a quilt together, or raising a barn, if the needle is not comfortable to hand. I need only to think of my own dissertation director, Don McAndrew. When we get together to share a beer and teaching stories, we don't swap academic citations, we talk about our teaching, share what does and doesn't work. We talk about our writing, explore why we do it, what it means to have done it. We participate in a verbal reweaving. We consider our profession—ask tough questions about our places in it. It's love and passion for a profession that can make us consider leaving the classroom sometimes when we feel we may not make a difference.

It's love and passion and concern that sent this professor into his children's local school district to offer fifty free in-service days in whole-language workshops over a two-year period. He knew there were better ways to teach, and because he did, he had to share them. It is this type of committed teacher who grounds the teacher-research, expert-practitioner movement for me: I'm not suggesting that teachers all need to go out and volunteer more time. We're overworked as it is, most of us. But I do argue that it is this type of teacher, along with Nancy Sommers and Lynn Bloom and Mike Rose, who should be writing their teaching autobiographies, and exploring their teaching histories in print. When they won't, don't, or can't, I believe all of us who are hearing these stories should take note and pass the stories on: a pedagogical potlatch that moves beyond *mere* lore in order to highlight, value, respect, draw our attention to other ways of knowing, and saying, and being in the professional world. "But my pitch," says James Moffet, "is not so much that the university should provide spiritual sites of composing for the sake of therapy and spirituality . . . as that the university needs spiritual sites of composing for its own sake" (261).

***

Postmodern anthropology and feminist theory suggests alternative ways of reporting both practice and research—honoring story, testimony, observational anecdote, informal analysis, regularized lore and so on—and these movements may connect some of us back to our humanistic roots as writers and readers of fictional and factional texts. To the *spirit* of what drew us to our field(s). These are certainly new ways teachers may choose to share their teaching lives and such sharing leads to profound questioning of traditional ways of making knowledge, as we ask what is valuable as research and publication and what is learned in doctoral exams and what voice(s) should be allowed in dissertations. Many of us realize that the structures of the academy are *slowing* rather than accelerating learning; if we believe this is so, we have to redefine our terms and change our processes. It may take poems and journal notes, like these, to understand what we mean, for ourselves, as we work with others: "Failure, what makes a teaching failure? More a sense of disappointment—didn't workness—as if enthusiasm gets bottled up, backfires, and has nowhere to go—overwhelms me, the conduit or circuit not open, voltage doesn't flow. So success is—connection, flow, open circuits, transfer, electrons moving" (my personal journal from the 1994 New Hampshire conference).

***

Reweaving the spirit doesn't demand new, whole cloth. Reweaving requires attention as we darn, patch, embroider, look for connections:

Thought A: Many of us in composition/English departments are people who care deeply about reading and writing, and we need to testify and practice more visibly. We need to really question the ways we make students (first-year and graduate) produce texts we don't value and the way we agree to do this ourselves for academic promotion. We'll gain power if we refuse trends or theoretical movements that don't fit; yet, we'll only

know that they don't fit, of course, if we try them on, test them in the cru-
cible of the classroom.

Thought B: Some models and practices are enduring because they allow
for the personal and public to co-exist, to communicate. I'm thinking of
the way my expressivist heart negotiates daily with my social-constructionist brain, and how, as a writer and teacher of writers I wouldn't have it
any other way. I've been struggling for years now to take the "creative" out
of certain genres of writing and to (re)consider the active, creative well-
springs of all passionately engaged writers and writing.

Thought C: If we accept the job description of writing teacher, then
theory and practice, the public and personal, must form a web, a network,
a circle, an interconnected chain, a dialog, a mutual refrain in our teaching, a tapestry, quilt or momentarily well-constructed whole.

Thought D: We need to be more playful and tell more praise stories.
For instance, there are many reasons I love being a teacher and even this
essay is too empty of them. I value the way teaching lets me talk about
and practice my favorite subject, writing; the ways students change and
allow me to participate in that change; and the way my work puts me in
touch with like-minded, intelligent, committed colleagues around the
country.

***

Teachers can listen to students to understand their own worlds, can write
with and about the classroom to construct the spirit-full story of teaching.
A writer who in discussing a paper also discloses childhood abuse is not
simply "burdening" us with more than we're trained to handle—rather,
this student has connected to us, made our day more whole, more human,
more important. We can worry over him *and* marvel at him, at his
strength and survivor's skills, at his excitement right now, at the way he
has rewoven his spirit through writing.

It's almost that simple.

I believe in teaching.

Because I relearn my life as my students explore theirs.

Works Cited

Abercrombie, Minnie Louie Johnson. *Aims and Techniques of Group Teaching*, 3rd ed. London: Society for Research into Higher Education Ltd. 1974.

Aiken, Susan Hardy, et al. "Trying Transformations: Curriculum Integration and the Problem of Resistance." *Signs: Journal of Women in Culture and Society* 12 (1987): 255–275.

Aisenberg, Nadya and Mona Herrington. *Women of Academe*. Amherst: U of Massachusetts P. 1988.

Anderson, Chris. *Literary Nonfiction: Theory, Criticism, Pedagogy.* Carbondale, IL: Southern Illinois UP. 1989.

Anderson, Worth, Cynthia Best, Alycia Black, John Hurst, Brandt Miller, and Susan Miller. "Cross-Curricular Underlife: A Collaborative Report on Ways with Academic Words." *CCC* 41.1 (1990): 11–36.

Anson, Chris, Joan Graham, David Jolliffe, Nancy Shapiro, and Carolyn Smith. *Scenarios for Teaching Writing*. Urbana, IL: NCTE. 1993.

Applebee, Arthur N. "Problems in Process Approaches." *The Teaching of Writing*. Eighty-fifth Yearbook of the National Society for the Study of Education. Anthony Petrosky and David Bartholomae, eds. Chicago, IL: U of Chicago P. 1986.

———. *Tradition and Reform in the Teaching of English: A History*. Urbana: NCTE. 1974.

Armstrong, Cheryl. "A Process Perspective on Poetic Discourse." Paper presented at the Annual Meeting of the CCCC. ED 243108. 1984.

Atkinson, Paul. *The Ethnographic Imagination: Textual Constructions of Reality*. London: Routledge. 1990.

Baldwin, Neal. "Meditations on the Number 25 by a Few of Our Friends." *Poets and Writers Magazine* 23.5 (September/October 1995): 32.

Bartholomae, David. "Writing With Teachers: A Conversation with Peter Elbow." *CCC* 46.1 (1995): 62–71.

Battle, Mary Vroman. "Suicide: Students at Risk." *Teaching English in the Two-Year College* (1990): 253–259.

Baumbach, Jonathan. *Writers as Teacher/Teachers as Writers*. New York: Holt 1970.

Beach, Richard. *A Teacher's Introduction to Reader-Response Theories*. Urbana, IL: NCTE. 1993.

Beaven, Mary H. "Individualized Goal Setting, Self-Evaluation, and Peer Evaluation." *Evaluating Writing: Describing, Measuring, Judging.* Charles R. Cooper and Lee Odell, eds. Urbana, IL: NCTE. 1977. 135–56.

Belanoff, Pat and Marcia Dickson, eds. *Portfolios: Process and Product.* Portsmouth, NH: Boynton/Cook-Heinemann. 1991.

Belenky, Mary Field, Blyth McVicker Clinchy, Nancy Rule Goldberger, and Jill Mattuck Tarule. *Women's Ways of Knowing: The Development of Self, Voice, and Mind.* New York: Basic. 1986.

Berkenkotter, Carol, Thomas Huckin and John Ackerman. (1988). "Conventions, Conversations, and the Writer: Case Study of a Student in a Rhetoric Ph.D. Program." *Research in the Teaching of English,* 22 (1988): 9–44.

Berkenkotter, Carol. "The Legacy of Positivism in Empirical Composition Research." *Journal of Advanced Composition* 9 (1989): 69–82.

———. "Paradigm Debates, Turf Wars, and the Conduct of Socio-cognitive Inquiry in Composition." *CCC* 42.2 (1991): 151–169.

Berlin, James. "Rhetoric, Poetic, and Culture: Contested Boundaries in English Studies." *The Politics of Writing Instruction: Postsecondary.* Richard Bullock, John Trimbur and Charles Schuster, eds. Portsmouth, NH: Boynton/Cook-Heinemann. 1991. 23–38.

———. *Rhetoric and Reality: Writing Instruction in American Colleges, 1900–1985.* Urbana, IL: Southern Illinois UP. 1987.

———. *Writing Instruction in Nineteenth-Century American Colleges.* Urbana, IL: Southern Illinois UP. 1984.

———. "Writing Instruction in School and College English, 1890–1985." *A Short History of Writing Instruction: From Ancient Greece to Twentieth Century America.* Davis, CA: Hermagoras P. 1990.

Bishop, Wendy. *Ethnographic Writing Research: Writing It Down, Writing It Up, and Reading It.* Portsmouth, NH: Boynton/Cook-Heinemann, forthcoming.

———. "Genre as Field Coverage—Divisions in Writing Instruction Erase Our Common Ground." *Dialogue* 1.1 (Fall 1993): 28–43.

———. "I-Witnessing in Composition: Turning Ethnographic Data into Narratives." *Rhetoric Review* 11.1 (fall 1992): 147–158.

———. Jo'al. *Teaching English in the Two-Year College* 18.1 (1991): 4.

———. *A Microethnography with Case Studies of Teacher Development Through a Graduate Training Course in Teaching Writing.* Dissertation Abstracts International, 49, 11A: 1989.

———. "The Perils, Pleasures, and Process of Ethnographic Writing Research." *Taking Stock: Reassessing the Writing Process Movement in the 90s.* Thomas Newkirk and Lad Tobin, eds. Portsmouth, NH: Boynton/Cook, Heinemann. 1994. 261–279.

———. "Qualitative Evaluation and the Conversational Writing Classroom." *Journal of Teaching Writing* (Special Issue 1990): 267–284.

————. *Released into Language: Options for Teaching Creative Writing.* Urbana, IL: 1990.

————. "Research, Theory, and Pedagogy of Writing Peer Groups: An Annotated Bibliography." ED 276 035. 1987.

————. "Revising the Technical Writing Class: Peer Critiques, Self-Evaluation, and Portfolio Grading." *The Technical Writing Teacher* 16 (1989): 13–25.

————. "Risk-Taking and Radical Revision—Exploring Writing Identities Through Advanced Composition and Poetry Portfolios." Manuscript in circulation.

————. *Something Old, Something New: College Writing Teachers and Classroom Change.* Studies in Writing and Rhetoric. Carbondale, IL: Southern Illinois UP. 1990.

————. "Texts and Contexts: A Social-Rhetorical Model for Teaching Writing-With-Literature Courses." *The Writing Instructor* 5 (1986): 191–202.

————."Teaching Undergraduate Creative Writing: Myths, Mentors, and Metaphors." *Journal of Teaching Writing, 7.1,* (1988): 83–102.

————. *Working Words: The Process of Creative Writing.* Mountain View, CA: Mayfield. 1992.

————, ed. *The Subject Is Writing: Essays By Teachers and Students.* Portsmouth, NH: Boynton/Cook. 1993.

Bishop, Wendy and Hans Ostrom, eds. *Colors of a Different Horse: Rethinking Creative Writing, Theory and Pedagogy.* Urbana, IL: NCTE. 1994.

Bizzell, Patricia. *Academic Discourse and Critical Consciousness.* Pittsburgh: U of Pittsburgh P. 1992.

————. "Cognition, Convention and Certainty." *PRE/TEXT 3* (1982): 213–243.

————. "Composing Processes: An Overview." *The Teaching of Writing.* Eighty-fifth Yearbook of the National Society for the Study of Education. Anthony Petrosky and David Bartholomae, eds. Chicago, IL: U of Chicago P. 1986. 49–70.

————. "On the Possibility of a Unified Theory of Composition and Literature." *Rhetoric Review 5* (1986): 174–179.

————. "What Happens When Basic Writers Come to College?" *CCC* 37.3 (Oct. 1986): 294–301.

Bizzell, Patricia and Bruce Herzberg. *The Rhetorical Tradition: Readings From Classical Times to the Present.* Boston: Bedford. 1990.

Bleich, David. *Readings and Feelings: An Introduction to Subjective Criticism.* Urbana, IL: NCTE. 1975.

Bloom, Lynn Z. "Finding a Family, Finding a Voice: A Writing Teacher Teaches Writing Teachers." *Writer's Craft, Teacher's Art: Teaching What We Know.* Mimi Schwartz, ed. Portsmouth, NH: Boynton/Cook Publishers. 1991. 55–68.

————. "Why Don't We Write What We Teach?" *Journal of Advanced Composition* 10.1 (1990): 87–100.

Bolker, Joan. "Teaching Griselda to Write." *College English* (1979): 906–908.

Brand, Alice G. "Hot Cognition: Emotions and Writing Behavior." *Journal of Advanced Composition* 6 (1985): 5–15.

———. *The Psychology of Writing: The Affective Experience.* Westport, CT: Greenwood. 1989.

———. Therapy in Writing: A Psycho-Educational Enterprise. Lexington, MA: Heath. 1980.

———. "The Why of Cognition: Emotion and the Writing Process." *CCC* 38 (1987): 436–443.

Bridwell, Lillian S. "Revising Strategies in Twelfth Grade Students' Transactional Writing." *Research in the Teaching of English* 14 (October 1980): 197–222.

Bridwell-Bowles, Lillian. "Discourse and Diversity: Experimental Writing within the Academy." *CCC* 43.3 (Oct. 1992): 349–368.

Britton, James, Tony Burgess, Alexander McLeod, Nancy Martin, and Harold Rosen. *The Development of Writing Abilities (11–18).* London: Macmillan. 1975.

Britton, James. *Prospect* and *Retrospect: Selected Essays of James Britton.* Ed.Gordon M Pradl. Montclair, NJ: Boynton/Cook. 1982.

Brodkey, Linda. "Modernism and the Scene(s) of Writing." *CCC,* 49 (1987): 396–418.

———. "Writing Critical Ethnographic Narratives." *Anthropology & Educational Quarterly* 18 (1987): 67–76.

Brooke, Robert. "Lacan, Transference, and Writing Instruction." *College English* 49 (Oct. 1987): 679–91.

———. "Modeling a Writer's Identity: Reading and Imitation in the Writing Classroom." *CCC* 39 (1988): 23 41.

———. *Writing and Sense of Self: Identity Negotiation in Writing Workshops.* Urbana, IL: NCTE. 1991.

Brooke, Robert, Ruth Mirtz, and Rick Evans. *Small Groups in Writing Workshops: Invitations to a Writer's Life.* Urbana, IL: NCTE. 1994.

Bruffee, Kenneth A. "The Brooklyn Plan. Attaining Intellectual Growth Through Peer Group Tutoring." *Liberal Education,* 64 (1978): 447–469.

———. "Collaborative Learning and the Conversation of Mankind." *College English* 46 (1984): 635 52.

———. "Writing and Reading as Collaborative or Social Acts." *The Writer's Mind: Writing as a Mode of Thinking.* Janet L. Hays, et al., eds. Urbana, IL: NCTE. 1983.

Burnham, Christopher C. "Portfolio Evaluation: Room to Breathe and Grow." *Training the New Teacher of College Composition.* Charles Bridges, ed. Urbana, IL: NCTE. 1986. 125 138.

Camoin, Francois. "The Workshop and Its Discontents." Bishop and Ostrom, eds. 3–8.

Campbell, Joseph. *The Hero with a Thousand Faces*, 2nd ed. NJ: Princeton UP. 1968.

Carino, Peter. "Early Writing Centers: Toward a History." *The Writing Center Journal* 15.2 (spring 1995): 103–115.

Caywood, Cynthia L. and Gillian Overing, eds. *Teaching Writing: Pedagogy, Gender, and Equity*. Albany: State U of New York P. 1987.

CCCC Committee on Professional Standards. "A Progress Report from the CCCC Committee on Professional Standards." *CCC* 42.3 (Oct. 1991): 330–344.

"CCCC: Voices in the Parlor." *Rhetoric Review* 7 (1988): 194–213.

Chase, Geoffrey. "Accommodation, Resistance and the Politics of Student Writing." *CCC.* (1988): 13–22.

Churchman, Deborah. "Fertile Time for Creative Writing: More College Courses Every Year." *New York Times* 8 Jan. 1984: 42–43.

Clandinin, Jean D. and F. Michael Conelly. "Personal Experience Methods." *Handbook of Qualitative Research*. Norman K. Denzin and Yvonna S. Lincoln, eds. Thousand Oaks, CA: Sage. 1994. 413–427.

Clark, Beverly Lyon and Sonja Wiedenhaupt. "On Blocking and Unblocking Sonja: A Case Study in Two Voices." *CCC* 43 (1992): 55–74.

Clifford, James and George E. Marcus, eds. *Writing Culture: The Poetics and Politics of Ethnography*. Berkeley, CA: U of California Press. 1986.

Clifford, James. "On Ethnographic Authority." *The Predicament of Culture*. New Haven, CT: Harvard UP. 21–54.

———. "On Ethnographic Self-Fashioning." *The Predicament of Culture*. New Haven, CT: Harvard UP. 92–113.

Clifford, John. "Ideology into Discourse." *Journal of Advanced Composition* 7.1/7.2 (1987): 21–29.

———. "The Reader and the Text: Ideologies in Dialogue." *Practicing Theory in Introductory College Literature Courses*. James M. Cahalan and David B. Downing, eds. Urbana, IL: NCTE. 1991. 101–111.

Collins, James and Michael Williamson. "Spoken Language and Semantic Abbreviation in Writing." *Research in the Teaching of English* 15.1 (1981): 23–35.

Coltelli, Laura, ed. *Winged Words: American Indian Writers Speak*. Lincoln: U of Nebraska P. 1990.

Connors, Robert J. and Andrea A. Lunsford. "Teachers' Rhetorical Comments on Student Papers." *CCC* 44.2 (1993): 200–223.

Connors, Robert J. "Rhetoric in the Modern University: The Creation of an Underclass." *The Politics of Writing Instruction: Postsecondary*. Richard Bullock, John Trimbur and Charles Schuster, eds. Portsmouth, NH: Boynton/Cook-Heinemann. 1991. 55–84.

———. "The Rise and Fall of the Modes of Discourse." *CCC* 32 (December 1981): 444–55.

Cooper, Charles. "Measuring Growth in Writing." *English Journal.* (1975): 111–120.

Cooper, Marilyn. "The Ecology of Writing." *College English* 31 (1986): 134–142.

Corbett, Edward P.J. *Classical Rhetoric for the Modern Student.* 3rd ed. New York: Oxford UP. 1990.

———. "Literature and Composition: Allies or Rivals in the Classroom?" *Composition and Literature: Bridging the Gap.* Winifred B. Horner, ed. Chicago: U of Chicago Press. 1983. 168–184.

Corder, Jim W. "Asking for a Text and Trying to Learn It." *Encountering Student Texts: Interpretive Issues in Reading Student Writing.* Bruce Lawson, Susan Sterr Ryan, and W. Ross Winterowd, eds. Urbana, IL: NCTE. 1989. 89–98.

Crowley, Sharon. "A Personal Essay on Freshman English." *Pre/Text* 12.3–4 (1991): 156–176.

Daniell, Beth and Art Young. "Resisting Writing/Resisting Writing Teachers." Bishop, ed. *The Subject Is Writing.* 223–234.

Daniels, Harvey, and Steven Zemelman. *A Writing Project: Training Teachers of Composition from Kindergarten to College.* Portsmouth, NH: Heinemann. 1985.

Danis, Francine. "Weaving the Web of Meaning: Interactions Patterns in Peer-response Groups." Paper presented at the annual meeting of CCCC. ED 214 202. 1982.

Danis, Mary Francine. "Peer-response Groups in a College Writing Workshop: Students' Suggestions for Revising Compositions." *DAI* 41: 5008A-5009A. 1980.

Daumer, Elisabeth and Sandra Runzo. "Transforming the Composition Classroom." Caywood and Overing, eds. 45–64.

Davis, Kevin. Letter. 2 May 1989.

———. "What I Learned in Basic Writing: Negotiating Commitment." *Research in Teaching Developmental Education* 5 (1988): 35–42.

Dean, Terry. "Multicultural Classrooms, Monocultural Teachers." *CCC* 40 (1989): 23–37.

Democrat Staff and News Services. "Test States the Obvious: Kids Don't Read." *Tallahassee Democrat,* Friday, April 28. 1995: A1, A6.

Domina, Lynn. "The Body of My Work Is Not Just a Metaphor." Bishop and Ostrom, eds. 27–34.

Eagleton, Terry. *Literary Theory: An Introduction.* Minneapolis: U of Minnesota P. 1983.

Ede, Lisa and Andrea Lunsford. *Singular Texts/Plural Authors: Perspectives on Collaborative Writing.* Carbondale IL: Southern Illinois UP. 1990.

Elbow, Peter. "Being a Writer vs. Being an Academic: A Conflict in Goals." *CCC* 46.1 (1995): 72–83.

———. "Reflections on Academic Discourse: How It Relates to Freshmen and Colleagues." *College English* 53.2 (1991): 135–155.

———. "Methodological Doubting and Believing: Contraries in Inquiry." *Embracing Contraries*. New York: Oxford UP. 1986. 253–300.

———. "Ranking, Evaluating, and Liking: Sorting Out Three Forms of Judgment." *College English* 55 (1993): 187–206.

———. "Trustworthiness in Evaluation." *Embracing Contraries: Explorations in Learning and Teaching*. New York: Oxford UP. 1986. 217–232.

———. "The War Between Reading and Writing—And How to End It." *Rhetoric Review* 12.1 (1993): 5–24.

———. *Writing with Power*. New York: Oxford UP. 1981.

———. *What Is English?* New York: MLA. 1990.

———. *Writing without Teachers*. New York: Oxford UP. 1977.

Elbow, Peter and Pat Belanoff. "Portfolios as a Substitute for Proficiency Examinations." *CCC* 37 (1986): 336–339.

———. *Sharing and Responding*. NY: Random. 1989.

Emig, Janet. *The Composing Processes of Twelfth Graders*. Urbana:, IL: NCTE. 1971.

———. "Literacy and Freedom." *The Web of Meaning*. 171–178.

———. "Non-Magical Thinking: Presenting Writing Developmentally in School." *The Web of Meaning*. 132–144.

———. *The Web of Meaning: Essays on Writing, Teaching, Learning, and Thinking*. Dixie Goswami and Maureen Butler, eds. Upper Montclair, NJ: Boynton/Cook. 1983.

———. "Writing as a Mode of Learning." *CCC* 28.2 (1977): 122–128.

Faigley, Lester. "Competing Theories of Process." *College English* 48 (1986): 527–542.

Firestone, William A. "Meaning in Method: The Rhetoric of Quantitative and Qualitative Research *Educational Researcher* 16.7 (1987): 16–21.

Fish, Stanley. "Literature in the Reader: Affective Stylistics." Tompkins, ed. 70–100.

Flower, Linda. "Cognition, Context, and Theory Building." *CCC* 40 (1989): 282–311.

———. *The Construction of Negotiated Meaning: A Social Cognitive Theory of Writing*. Carbondale: Southern Illinois UP. 1994.

———. "Writer-based Prose: A Cognitive Basis for Problems in Writing." *College English* 41 (1979): 19–37.

Flower, Linda and John R. Hayes. "A Cognitive Process Theory of Writing." *CCC*, 32 (1981): 365–387.

Flower, Linda, David L. Wallace, Linda Norris, and Rebecca E. Burnett, eds. *Making Thinking Visible: Writing, Collaborative Planning, and Classroom Inquiry*. Urbana, IL: NCTE. 1994.

Flynn, Elizabeth. "Composing 'Composing as a Woman.'" *CCC* 41 (1990): 83–88.

————. "Composing as a Woman." *CCC* (1988): 423–435.

————. "Freedom, Restraint and Peer Group Interaction." Paper presented at the annual meeting of CCCC. ED 216 365. 1982.

Flynn, Elizabeth A., and others. "Effects of Peer Critiquing and Model Analysis on the Quality of Biology Student Laboratory Reports." Paper presented at the Annual Meeting of the NCTE. ED 234 403. 1982.

Foerster, Norman, et al. *Literary Scholarship: Its Aims and Methods.* Chapel Hill, U of North Carolina P. 1941.

Fontaine, Sheryl and Susan Hunter. "Rendering the 'Text' of Composition." *Journal of Advanced Composition* 12.2 (1992): 395–406.

Foster, David. "Hurling Epithets at the Devils You Know: A Response to Carol Berkenkotter." *Journal of Advanced Composition* 10.1 (1990): 149–152.

————. *A Primer for Writing Teachers: Theories, Theorists, Issues, Problems.* Upper Montclair, NJ: Boynton/Cook. 1983.

————. "What Are We Talking About When We Talk About Composition?" *Journal of Advanced Composition* 8 (1989): 30–40.

Frank, Francine Wattman and Paula A. Treichler. *Language, Gender, and Professional Writing.* New York: MLA. 1989.

Frey, Olivia. "Beyond Literary Darwinism: Women's Voices and Critical Discourse." *College English* 52.5 (1990): 507–526.

Friend, Christy. "The Excluded Conflict: The Marginalization of Composition and Rhetoric Studies in Graff's *Professing Literature.*" *College English* 54.3 (1992): 276–286.

Fulwiler, Toby. "Provocative Revision." *The Writing Center Journal* 12.2 (1992): 190–204.

————. "Writing to Reform the English Major." Paper presented at the Annual Meeting of the CCCC. 1992.

Garne, Michael. "Fictionalizing the Disciplines: Literature and the Boundaries of Knowledge." *College English* 57.3 (1995): 281–286.

Garrett, George. "The Future of Creative Writing Programs." Moxley, ed. 47–63.

Geertz, Clifford. *Works and Lives: The Anthropologist as Author.* Stanford, CA: Stanford UP. 1988.

George, Diana. "Writing with Peer Groups in Composition." *CCC* 35 (1984): 320–36.

Gere, Anne Ruggles. *Writing Groups: History, Theory, and Implications.* Carbondale, IL: Southern Illinois UP. 1987.

Gere, Anne Ruggles, and Robert D. Abbott. "Talking About Writing: The Language of Writing Groups." *Research in the Teaching of English* 19 (1985): 362–381.

Gere, Anne Ruggles. "Students' Oral Response to Written Composition." Seattle, WA: University of WA. ED 229 781. 1982.

Ghiselin, Brewster, ed. *The Creative Process.* Berkeley: U of California P. 1985, c1952.

Gilbert, Sandra. *Wrongful Death*. NY: Norton. 1995.

Gilligan, Carol. *In a Different Voice: Psychological Theory and Women's Development*. Cambridge, MA: Harvard UP. 1982.

Giroux, Henry A. *Ideology, Culture, and the Process of Schooling*. Philadelphia: Temple UP. 1981.

Gould, Eric. *Making Meaning: Reading and Writing Texts*. Belmont CA: Wordsworth. 1989.

Gradin, Sherrie L. *Romancing Rhetorics: Social Expressivist Perspectives on the Teaching of Writing*. Portsmouth, NH: Boynton/Cook, Heinemann. 1995.

Graff, Gerald. *Beyond the Culture Wars: How Teaching the Conflicts can Revitalize American Education*. NY: Norton. 1992.

———. *Professing Literature: An Institutional History*. Chicago: U of Chicago P. 1987.

Grealy, Lucy. *Autobiography of a Face*. Boston: Houghton Mifflin. 1994.

Haake, Katharine. "Teaching Creative Writing If the Shoe Fits." Bishop and Ostrom, eds. 77–99.

Haake, Katharine, Sandra Alcosser, and Wendy Bishop. "Teaching Creative Writing: A Feminist Critique." *AWP Chronicle*, 22.2 (1989): 1–6.

Hairston, Maxine. "Breaking our Bonds and Reaffirming Our Connections." *CCC* 36 (1985): 272–282.

———. "Using Nonfiction Literature in the Composition Classroom." *Convergences: Transactions in Reading and Writing*. Bruce T. Peterson, ed. Urbana, IL: NCTE. 1986. 179–188.

———. "When Writing Teachers Don't Write: Speculations about Probable Causes and Possible Cures." *Rhetoric Review* 5 (1986): 62–70.

Hall, Roberta and Bernice B. Sandler. "Academic Mentoring for Women Students and Faculty: A New Look at an Old Way to Get Ahead." Washington D.C.: Association of American Colleges. Project on the Status and Education of Women. ED 240 891. 1983.

Hansen, Ron and Jim Shepard. *You've Got to Read This*. NY: Harper Collins. 1994.

Harjo, Joy. *She Had Some Horses*. NY: Thunders Mouth Press. 1983.

Harrington, Walt. "The Shape of Her Dreaming: Rita Dove Writes a Poem." *The Washington Post Magazine*, May 7, 1995: 11–29.

Harste, Jerome C., Virginia A. Woodward and Carolyn L. Burke. *Language Stories and Literacy Lessons*. Portsmouth, NH: Heinemann. 1984.

Hartwell, Patrick. "Creating A Literate Environment in Freshman English: How and Why." *Rhetoric Review*, 6 (1987):4–21.

———. "The Writing Center and the Paradoxes of Written-Down Speech." *Writing Centers: Theory and Administration*. Gary Olson, ed. Urbana, IL: NCTE. 48–61.

———. "Writers as Readers." Paper presented at the Conference on CCC, March 1981.

Haswell, Janis and Richard H. Haswell. "Gendership and the Miswriting of Students." *CCC* 46.2 (1995): 223–254.

Hawkins, Thom. *Group Inquiry Techniques in Teaching Writing.* Urbana IL: NCTE. 1976.

Haynes-Burton, Cynthia. "'Hanging Your Alias on Their Scene': Writing Centers, Graffiti, and Style." *The Writing Center Journal* 14.2: 112–124.

Heath, Shirley Brice. *Ways with Words: Language, Life, and Work in Communities and Classrooms.* Cambridge, MA: Cambridge UP. 1983.

Hemingway, Ernest. "A Clean, Well-Lighted Place." In *Responding to Literature*, 2nd ed. Judith A. Stanford, ed. Mountain View, CA: Mayfield. 1996. 1162–1165.

Holden, Jonathan. "Poetry and Media." *AWP Chronicle* 28.1 (1995): 12–14.

Hull, Glenda and Mike Rose. "This Wooden Shack Place: The Logic of an Unconventional Reading." *CCC* 41 (1990): 287–298.

Johnson, David W., and Roger T. Johnson. "Cooperative Small-group Learning." Curriculum Report 14: 1–6. ED 249 625. 1984.

———. *Learning Together and Alone: Cooperation, Competition, and Individualization.* Englewood Cliffs, NJ: Prentice. 1975.

Kail, Harvey. "A Writing Teacher Writes About Writing Teachers Writing (About Writing)". *English Journal* 75 (1986): 88–91.

Kaplan, Ann E. "Popular Culture, Politics, and the Canon: Cultural Literacy in the Postmodern Age." *Cultural Power/Cultural Literacy.* Bonnie Braendlin, ed. Tallahassee, FL: Florida State UP 1991.

Kendig, Diane. "It Is Ourselves that We Remake: Teaching Creative Writing in Prison." Bishop and Ostrom, eds. 158–166.

Kennedy, Eugene and Sara C. Charles. *On Becoming a Counselor: A Basic Guide for Nonprofessional Counselors.* New Expanded Edition. New York: Continuum. 1990.

Kennedy, X.J. *Literature: An Introduction to Fiction, Poetry, and Drama.* 3rd ed. Boston: Little. 1983.

Kirsch, Gesa E. *Women Writing the Academy: Audience, Authority, and Transformation.* Studies in Writing and Rhetoric. Carbondale, IL: Southern Illinois UP. 1993.

Knoblauch, C.H. and Lil Brannon. *Rhetorical Traditions and the Teaching of Writing.* Upper Montclair, NJ: Boynton/Cook. 1984.

Kumin, Maxine. "The World's Best Kept Secret." *AWP Chronicle* May 1989: 15.

Lagana, Jean Remaley. *The Development, Implementation, and Evaluation of a Model for Teaching Composition Which Utilizes Individualized Learning and Peer Grouping.* Dissertation. U of Pittsburgh. ED 079 726. 1972.

Lauer, Janice M. and J. William Asher. *Composition Research: Empirical Designs.* NY: Oxford UP. 1988.

LeFevre, Karen Burke. *Invention as a Social Act.* Carbondale, IL: Southern Illinois UP. 1987.

Lindemann, Erika. "Freshman Composition: No Place for Literature." *College English* 55.3 (1993): 311–316.

———. "Three Views of English 101." *College English* 57.3 (1995): 287–302.

Lindley, Daniel A. Jr. "The Source of Good Teaching." *English Education.* 19 (1987): 159–170.

Lunsford, Andrea, Helene Moglen and James F. Slevin, eds. *The Future of Doctoral Studies in English.* New York: MLA. 1989.

MacKenzie, Nancy. "Subjective Criticism in Literature Courses: Learning through Writing." *Teaching English in the Two-Year College* 48 (1985): 364–375.

Marks, Elaine and Isabelle de Courtivron, eds. *New French Feminisms.* Brighton: Harvester. 1980.

Mayher, John S., Nancy B. Lester and Gordon M. Pradl. *Learning to Write/Writing to Learn.* Upper Montclair, NJ: Boynton/Cook. 1983.

Martin, Wanda. "Tenure, Status, and the Teaching of Writing." *Farther Along: Transforming Dichotomies in Rhetoric and Composition.* Kate Ronald and Hephzibah Roskelly, eds. Portsmouth: NH: Boynton/Cook-Heinemann. 1990. 122–136.

McCall, William. "Writing Centers and the Idea of Consultancy." *The Writing Center Journal* 14.2 (Spring 1994): 163–171.

McCormick, Kathleen. "Theory in the Reader: Bleich, Holland, and Beyond." *College English* 47 (1985): 836–850.

McDonald, James C. "Rethinking the Research Paper in the Writing Center." *The Writing Center Journal* 14.2 (Spring): 125–135.

McGee, Patrick. "Truth and Resistance: Teaching as a Form of Analysis." *College English* 49 (Oct. 1987): 667–678.

McInerney, Jay. *Bright Lights, Big City.* New York: Random. 1984.

McLeod, Susan. "Some Thoughts about Feelings: The Affective Domain and the Writing Process." *CCC* 38 (1987): 426–435.

McMillian, Terry. *Waiting to Exhale.* NY: Viking. 1992.

McQuade, Donald. "Living In—and On—the Margins." *CCC* 43 (1992): 11–22.

Mehan, H. "The Structure of Classroom Events and Their Consequences for Student Performance." *Children In and Out of School: Ethnography and Education.* Perry Gilmore and Alan Glatthorn, eds. Washington, D.C.: Center for Applied Linguistics. 1982. 59–87.

Meyers, David Gershom. *Educating Writers: The Beginnings of "Creative Writing" in the American University.* Northwestern University. 1989. DAI Order Number 9009673.

Miller, J. Hillis. "Composition and Decomposition: Deconstruction and the Teaching of Writing." *Composition and Literature: Bridging the Gap.* Winifred B. Horner, ed. Chicago: U of Chicago P. 1983. 38–56.

Miller, Richard. "Composing English Studies: Towards a Social History of the Discipline." *CCC* 45.2 (1994): 164–179.

Miller, Susan. *Textual Carnivals: The Politics of Composition.* Carbondale, IL: SIUP. 1991.

Miner, Valerie. "The Book in the World." Moxley, ed. 227–236.

Minh-ha, Trinh T. *Woman, Native, Other.* Bloomington, IN: Indiana UP. 1988.

Moffett, James. "Responses to Interchanges: Spiritual Sites of Composing." *CCC* 45.2 (1992): 258–263.

Moi, Toril. *Sexual/Textual Politics: Feminist Literary Theory.* London: Routledge. 1985.

Moore, Lorrie. *Self-Help.* NY, Penguin. 1985.

Morrow, Diane Stelzer. "Tutoring Writing: Healing or What?" *CCC* 42 (1991): 218–229.

Moursund, Janet. *The Process of Counseling and Therapy.* Englewood Cliffs, NJ: Prentice-Hall. 1985.

Moxley, Joseph. "Tearing Down the Walls: Engaging the Imagination." Moxley, ed. 25–46.

———, ed. *Creative Writing in America: Theory and Pedagogy.* Urbana, IL: NCTE. 1989.

Mueller, Martin. "Yellow Stripes and Dead Armadillos: Some Thoughts on the Current Sate of English Studies." *ADE Bulletin* 92 (1989): 5–12. Reprinted in *Profession 89.* New York: MLA. 1989. 23–31.

Munby, Hugh. "Metaphor and Teachers' Knowledge." *Research in the Teaching of English* 21 (1987): 377–397.

Murphy, Ann. "Transference and Resistance in the Basic Writing Classroom: Problematics and Praxis." *CCC* 40 (1989): 175–87.

Murphy, Richard. "Anorexia: The Cheating Disorder." *College English* 52 (1990): 898–903.

———. "On Stories and Scholarship." *CCC* 40 (1989): 466–471.

Murray, Donald. "All Writing Is Autobiography." *CCC* 42 (1991): 66–74.

———. *Shoptalk: Learning to Write with Writers.* Portsmouth, NH: Boynton/Cook-Heinemann. 1990.

———. "Writing as Process: How Writing Finds Its Own Meaning." *Eight Approaches to Teaching Composition.* Timothy Donovan and Ben W. McClelland, eds. Urbana, IL: NCTE. 1980.

Nelson, Jennie. "This Was an Easy Assignment: Examining How Students Interpret Academic Writing Tasks." *Research in the Teaching of English* 24.4 (1990): 362–396.

Newkirk, Thomas. "The Politics of Composition Research: The Conspiracy Against Experience." Richard Bullock, John Trimbur and Charles Schuster, eds. *The Politics of Writing Instruction: Post Secondary.* Portsmouth, NH: Boynton Cook. 1991. 119–135.

Noguchi, Rei R. *Grammar and the Teaching of Writing: Limits and Possibilities.* Urbana, IL: NCTE. 1991.

North, Stephen M. "The English Department and the Nexus of Discourse." Wendy Bishop and Hans Ostrom, eds. *Genre and Writing: Issues, Arguments, and Alternatives.* Portsmouth, NH: Boynton/Cook. 1997.

———. "The Idea of a Writing Center." *College English* 46.5 (1984): 433–46.

———. *The Making of Knowledge in Composition: Portrait of an Emerging Field.* Upper Montclair, NJ: Boynton/Cook. 1987.

———. "Revisiting 'The Idea of a Writing Center.'" *The Writing Center Journal* 15.1 (Fall 1994): 7–19.

O'Reilley, Mary Rose. *The Peaceable Classroom.* Portsmouth, NH: Boynton/Cook-Heinemann. 1993.

Ohmann, Richard. *English in America: A Radical View of the Profession.* New York: Oxford UP. 1976.

———. "The Function of English at the Present Time." *Politics of Letters.* Middletown, CT: Wesleyan UP. 1987. 3–17.

———. *Politics of Letters.* Middletown, CT: Wesleyan UP. 1987.

———. "Writing and Reading, Work and Leisure." *Politics of Letters.* Middletown, CT: Wesleyan UP. 1987. 26–41.

Olson, Gary, and Joseph Moxley. "Directing Freshman Composition: The Limits of Authority." *CCC* 40 (1989): 41–50.

Ostrom, Hans. "Undergraduate Creative Writing: The Unexamined Subject." *Writing on the Edge,* 1.1 (1989): 55–65.

Packard, William. *The Art of Poetry Writing: A Guide for Poets, Students, and Readers.* NY: St. Martin's. 1992.

———, ed. *The Poet's Craft.* NY: Paragon House. 1987.

Pennebaker, James W. "Self-Expressive Writing: Implications for Health, Education, and Welfare." *Nothing Begins with N: New Investigations of Freewriting.* Pat Belanoff, Peter Elbow, and Sheryl I. Fontaine, eds. Carbondale, IL: Southern Illinois UP. 1991. 157–170.

Perl, Sondra and Nancy Wilson. *Through Teachers' Eyes: Portraits of Writing Teachers at Work.* Portsmouth, NH: Heinemann. 1986.

Perl, Sondra. "The Composing Processes of Unskilled College Writers." *Research in the Teaching of English* 13 (1979): 217–238.

———. "Reflections on Ethnography and Writing." *The English Record* (1983): 10–11.

———, ed. *Landmark Essays on Writing Process.* Davis, CA: Hermagoras P. 1994.

Petrosky, Anthony. "Imagining the Past and teaching Essay and Poetry Writing." *Encountering Student Texts: Interpretive Issues in Reading Student Writing.* Bruce Lawson, Susan Sterr Ryan, and W. Ross Winterowd, eds. Urbana, IL: NCTE. 1989. 199–220.

Pianko, Sharon. "A Description of the Composing Processes of College Freshman Writers." *Research in the Teaching of English* 13 (1979): 5–22.

Ponsot, Marie and Rosemary Deen. *Beat Not the Poor Desk.* Upper Montclair, NJ: Boynton/Cook. 1982.

Pratt, Mary Louise. "Fieldwork in Common Places." *Writing Culture: The Poetics and Politics of Ethnography.* James Clifford and George E. Marcus, eds. Berkeley, CA: U of California Press. 1986. 27–50.

Preminger, Alex, ed. *The Princeton Encyclopedia of Poetry and Poetics.* Revised edition. New Jersey: Princeton. 1965.

Qualley, Donna. "Using Reading in the Writing Classroom." *Nuts and Bolts: A Practical Guide to Teaching College Composition.* Thomas Newkirk, ed. Portsmouth: Boynton/Cook- Heinemann. 1993. 101–127.

Rankin, Libby. *Seeing Yourself as a Teacher: Conversations with Five New Teachers in a University Writing Program.* Urbana, IL: NCTE. 1994.

Raymond, James C. "*College English*: Whence and Whither." *College English* 49 (1987): 553–557.

Reason, Peter. "Three Approaches to Participative Inquiry." *Handbook of Qualitative Research.* Norman K. Denzin and Yvonna S. Lincoln, eds. Thousand Oaks, CA: Sage. 1994. 324–339.

Reid, Catherine and Katherine Lord. Personal communication. May 1992.

Reigstad, Thomas J. and Donald A. McAndrew. *Training Tutors for Writing Conferences.* Urbana, IL: NCTE. 1984.

Reynolds, John Frederick. "Motives, Metaphors, and Messages in Critical Receptions of Experimental Research: A Comment with Postscript." *Journal of Advanced Composition* 10.1 (1990): 110–116.

Rich, Adrienne. "Taking Women Students Seriously." *On Lies, Secrets, and Silence: Selected Prose 1966–1978.* New York: Norton. 1979. 237–246.

———. *On Lies, Secrets, and Silence: Selected Prose 1966–1978.* New York: Norton. 1979.

Ritchie, Joy S. "Beginning Writers: Diverse Voices and Individual Identity." *CCC* 40 (1989) 152–174.

Rogers, Carl R. *On Becoming a Person.* Boston: Houghton. 1961.

Rohman, D. Gordon and Albert O. Wlecke. *Pre-writing: the Construction and Application of Models for Concept Formation in Writing.* East Lansing, MI: Michigan State UP. 1964.

Ronald, Kate and Jon Volkmer. "Another Competing Theory of Process: The Student's." *Journal of Advanced Composition* 9 (1989): 81–96.

Rose, Mike. *Lives on the Boundary.* NY: Penguin. 1980.

———. "Rigid Rules, Inflexible Plans, and the stifling of Language: A Cognitive Analysis of Writer's Block." *CCC,* 31 (1980): 389–399.

Rosenblatt, Louise M. *Literature as Exploration.* 4th ed. New York: MLA. 1983.

———. *The Reader, the Text, the Poem: The Transactional Theory of the Literary Work.* Carbondale: Southern Illinois UP. 1978.

Roskelly, Hephzibah. "A Marriage of Convenience: Reading and Writing in School." *Farther Along: Transforming Dichotomies in Rhetoric and Composition.* Kate Ronald and Hephzibah Roskelly, eds. Portsmouth: NH: Boynton/Cook-Heinemann. 1990. 137–148.

Sachocis, Bob. *Easy in the Islands.* NY: Penguin. 1985.

Salvatori, Mariolina. "Reading and Writing a Text: Correlations between Reading and Writing." *College English* 45.7 (1983): 657–666.

Savage, Mary C. "Writing as a Neighborly Act: An Antidote for Academentia." *ADE Bulletin* 92 (1989): 13–19.

Schatzberg-Smith, Kathleen. "Passing the Torch: Mentoring and Developmental Education." *Research in Teaching Developmental Education* 5 (1988): 47–51.

Schilb, John. "Ideology and Composition Scholarship." *Journal of Advanced Composition,* 8 (1988): 22–29.

———. "The Ideology of 'Epistemological Ecumenicalism': A Response to Carol Berkenkotter." *Journal of Advanced Composition* 10.1 (1990): 153–156.

Scholes, Robert. *Textual Power: Literary Theory and the Teaching of English.* New Haven, CT: Yale UP. 1985.

Scholes, Robert, Nancy R. Comley, and Gregory L. Ulmer. *Textbook: An Introduction to Literary Language.* New York: St. Martins. 1988.

Schultz, Lucille M. and Chester H. Laine, and Mary C. Savage. "Interaction Among School and College Writing Teachers: Toward Recognizing and Remaking Old Patterns." *CCC* 39.2 (1988): 139–153.

Schwandt, Thomas A. "Constructivist, Interpretivist Approaches to Human Inquiry." *Handbook of Qualitative Research.* Norman K. Denzin and Yvonna S. Lincoln, eds. Thousand Oaks, CA: Sage. 1994. 118–137.

Schwartz, Mimi. "Wearing the Shoe on the Other Foot: Teacher as Student Writer." *CCC* 40.2 (1989): 203–209. Also in Moxley, ed. 227–236.

———, ed. *Writer's Craft, Teacher's Art: Teaching What We Know.* Portsmouth, NH: Boynton/Cook Publishers. 1991.

Schweickart, Patrocinio. "Reading Ourselves: Toward a Feminist Theory of Reading." *Gender and Reading.* Elizabeth Flynn and Patrocinio Schweickart, eds. Baltimore: Johns Hopkins UP. 1986. 31–62.

Sewell, Donna. *Encountering Writing: The Literacies and Lives of First-Year Students.* Dissertation, Florida State University, Summer 1995.

Shamoon, Linda K. and Deborah H. Burns. " A Critique of Pure Tutoring." *The Writing Center Journal* 15.2 (Spring 1995): 134–151.

Shapiro, Karl. *The Old Horsefly.* Orono, MA: Northern Lights. 1992.

Shaughnessy, Mina P. *Errors and Expectations: A Guide for the Teacher of Basic Writing.* New York: Oxford UP. 1977.

Showalter, Elaine, ed. *The New Feminist Criticism.* New York: Pantheon. 1985.

Slevin, James F. "Depoliticizing and Politicizing Composition Studies." *Politics of Writing Instruction: Postsecondary.* Richard Bullock, John Trimbur and Charles Schuster, eds. Portsmouth, NH: Boynton/Cook-Heinemann. 1991. 1–21.

Smith, Frank. *Understanding Reading: A Psycholinguistic Analysis of Reading and Learning to Read.* 5th ed. Hillsdale, NJ: Lawrence Erlbaum. 1994.

Sommers, Nancy. "Between the Drafts." *CCC* 43 (1992): 23–31.

———. "Revision Strategies of Student Writers and Experienced Adult Writers." *CCC* 31 (1980): 379–88.

Spender, Dale. "The Gatekeepers: A Feminist Critique of Academic Publishing." *Doing Feminist Research.* Helen Roberts, ed. London: Routledge and Kegan Paul. 1981. 186–202.

———. *Man Made Language.* London: Routledge. 1980.

Sperling, Melanie, and Sarah Warshauer Freedman. "A Good Girl Writers Like a Good Girl: Written Response to Student Writing." *Written Communication,* 9 (1987): 343–369.

Stafford, William. "Traveling Through the Dark." *Traveling Through the Dark.* NY: Harper. 1962.

Stake, Robert. "Case Studies." *Handbook of Qualitative Research.* Norman K. Denzin and Yvonna S. Lincoln, eds. Thousand Oaks, CA: Sage. 1994. 236–247.

Steinberg, Erwin R. "Imaginative Literature in Composition Classrooms?" *College English* 57.3 (1995): 266–280.

Stewart, Donald C. "Two Model Teachers and the Harvardization of English Departments." *The Rhetorical Tradition and the Teaching of Writing.* James J. Murphy, ed. New York: MLA. 1982. 118–129

———. "What Is an English Major, and What Should It Be?" *CCC* 40 (1989): 188–202.

Strenski, Ellen. "Disciplines and Communities, 'Armies' and 'Monasteries,' and the Teaching of Composition." *Rhetoric Review* 8 (1989): 137–145.

Strickland, Ronald. "Confrontational Pedagogy and Traditional Literary Studies." *College English* 52 (1990): 291–300.

Student Counseling Center. *Handbook for Counseling Referral.* FSU Division of Student Affairs, April. 1991.

Sullivan, Patricia A. "Writing in the Graduate Curriculum: Literary Criticism as Composition." *Journal of Advanced Composition* 11.2 (Fall 1991): 283–299.

Summerfield, Geoffrey and Judith Summerfield. *Reading(s).* NY: Random. 1989.

Tate, Gary. "Notes on the Dying of A Conversation." *College English* 57.3 (1995): 303–309.

―――. "A Place for Literature in Freshman English." *College English* 55.3 (1993): 317–321.

Thomas, Trudelle. "The Graduate Student as Apprentice WPA: Experiencing the Future." *Journal of Writing Program Administrators* 14.3 (1991): 41–52.

Tobin, Lad. "Bridging Gaps: Analyzing Our Students' Metaphors for Composing." *CCC* 40.4 (1989): 444–458.

―――. "Reading Students, Reading Ourselves: Revising the Teacher's Role in the Writing Class." *College English* 53 (1991): 333–348.

―――. *Writing Relationships: What Really Happens in the Composition Class.* Portsmouth, NH: Boynton/Cook-Heinemann. 1993.

Tobin, Lad, and Thomas Newkirk, eds. *Taking Stock: the Writing Process Movement in the 90s.* Portsmouth, NH: Boynton/Cook-Heinemann. 1994.

Tomlinson, Barbara. "Cooking, Mining, Gardening, Hunting: Metaphorical Stories Writers Tell About Their Composing Processes." *Metaphor and Symbolic Activity* 1 (1986): 57–79.

―――. "Tuning, Tying, and Training Texts: Metaphors for Revision." *Written Communication* 5.1 (1988): 58–81.

Tompkins, Jane. *Reader-Response Criticism: Form Formalism to Post-Structuralism.* Baltimore: Johns Hopkins UP. 1980.

―――."The Reader in History: The Changing Shape of Literary Responses." Tompkins, ed. 201–232.

Torgersen, Eric. "Loving (Hating) the Messenger: Transference and Teaching." *AWP Newsletter* (1988): 1, 12, 14–15.

Turkle, Ann, Julene Bair, Ruth Anderson Barnett, Todd Pierce, and Rex West. "Life in the Trenches: Perspectives from Five Writing Programs." In Bishop and Ostrom eds. 35–53.

Ulmer, Gregory L. "Textshop for Psychoanalysis: On De-Programming Freshman Platonists." *College English* 49 (1987): 756–769.

Van Maanen, John. *Tales of the Field: On Writing Ethnography.* Chicago, IL: U of Chicago P. 1988.

Waldrep, Tom. *Writers on Writing.* NY: Random House. 1985.

Waller, Gary, Kathleen McCormick, and Louis Josephs Fowler. *The Lexington Introduction to Literature.* Lexington, MA: DC Heath. 1987.

Watson, Burton, trans. *Selected Poems of Su Tung-p'o.* Port Townsend, WA: Copper Canyon Press. 1994.

Weathers, Winston. *An Alternate Style: Options in Composition.* Rochelle Park, NJ: Hayden. 1980.

Weaver, Constance. *Grammar for Teachers: Perspectives and Definitions.* Urbana, IL: NCTE. 1979.

Weiner, Harvey S. 1986. "Collaborative Learning in the Classroom: A Guide to Evaluation." *College English* 48 (1986): 52–61.

Welch, Nancy. "Resisting the Faith: Conversion, Resistance, and the Training of Teachers." *College English* 55.4 (1993): 387–401.

Wilbers, Stephen. *The Iowa Writers' Workshop: Origins, Emergence, and Growth.* Iowa City: U of Iowa Press. 1981.

Winterowd, W. Ross. "The Drama of the Text." *Encountering Student Texts: Interpretive Issues in Reading Student Writing.* Bruce Lawson, Susan Sterr Ryan, and W. Ross Winterowd, eds. Urbana, IL: NCTE. 1989. 21–34.

———. *The Rhetoric of the "Other" Literature.* Carbondale, IL: Southern Illinois UP. 1990.

Wyche-Smith, Susan. "Writing Rituals or Time, Tools, and Talismans." Bishop, ed. *The Subject Is Writing.* 111–123.

———. "Teaching Invention to Basic Writers." *A Sourcebook for Basic Writing Teachers.* Theresa Enos, ed. New York: Random House. 1987. 470–479.

Yancey, Kathleen Blake, ed. *Portfolios in the Writing Classroom.* Urbana, IL: NCTE. 1992.

Yancey, Kathleen Blake and Irwin Weiser, eds. *Situating Portfolios: Four Perspectives.* Logan, UT: Utah State UP. 1997.

Young, Art and Toby Fulwiler, eds. *When Writing Teachers Teach Literature.* Portsmouth, NH: Boynton/Cook-Heinemann. 1996.

Zawacki, Terry Myers. "Recomposing as a Woman—An Essay in Different Voices." *CCC* 43.1 (1992): 32–38.

Ziv, Nina D. "Peer Groups in the Composition Classroom: A Case Study." Paper presented at the annual meeting of the CCCC. ED 229 799. 1983.

Index

"Attitudes and Expectations: How Theory in the Graduate Student (Teacher) Complicates the English Curriculum." *Critical Theory: Curriculum, Pedagogy, Politics*. Eds. James Slevin and Art Young. Urbana, Il: National Council of Teachers of English, 1996. 207–222.

"Co-authoring Changes the (Creative) Writing Classroom: Students Authorizing the Self, Authoring Together." *Composition Studies/Freshman English News* 23.1 (Spring 1995): 54–62.

"Crossing the Lines: On Creative Composition and Composing Creative Writing." *Writing on the Edge* 4.2 (Spring 1993): 117–133.

"Designing a Writing Portfolio Evaluation System." *The English Record* 40.2 (1990): 21–25.

"Helping Peer Writing Groups Succeed." *Teaching English in the Two Year College*, *15.2* (1988): 120–125.

"If Winston Weathers Would Just Write to Me On E–Mail: A Response to David Bartholomae and Peter Elbow." *College Composition and Communication*, 46.1 (February 1995): 97–103. [IN A SLIGHTLY DIFFERENT VERSION.]

"Learning Our Own Ways to Situate Feminist and Composition Studies in the English Department." *Journal of Advanced Composition* Special Issue: Feminism, Culture and Ideology.10.2 (1990): 339–355.

"Let Me Tell You About the Rocks" *The Phoenix* 7.1 (1986/1987): 49–55.

"Letting the Boundaries Draw Themselves: What Theory and Practice Have Been Trying to Tell Us—An Exchange." (co-authored with Hans Ostrom). *Cream City Review*, 19.2 (1996): 150–157.

"The Literary Text and the Writing Classroom." *Journal of Advanced Composition*, 15.3 (fall 1995):435–454.

"On Learning to Like Teaching Creative Writing." Appeared in a slightly different form as "Afterword—Colors of A Different Horse: On Learning to Like Teaching Creative Writing." *Colors of a Different Horse*. Eds. Wendy Bishop and Hans Ostrom. NCTE, 1994. 280–295.

"The Shape of Fact." *Writing on the Edge*, 5.1 (Fall 1993): 55–66.

"Students' Stories and the Variable Gaze of Composition Research." *Writing Ourselves into the Story: Unheard Voices from Composition Studies*. Eds. Susan Hunter and Sheryl Fontaine. Carbondale, IL: Southern Illinois University Press, 1993. 197–214.

"Teaching 'Grammar for Writers' Means Teaching Writing as Writers." *The Place of Grammar in Writing Instruction: Past, Present, Future*. Eds. Susan Hunter and Ray Wallace. Portsmouth, NH: Boynton/Cook Heinemann, 1995. 176–187

"Teaching Lives: Thoughts on Reweaving Our Spirits." *The Spiritual Side of Writing*. Eds. Regina Foehr and Susan Schiller. Portsmouth, NH: Boynton/Cook Heinemann, 1997. 129–135.

"Teaching Writing Teachers to Teach Reading for Writers." *Reader: Essays in Reader-Oriented Theory and Pedagogy*. Special Issue on the Teaching of Teaching. Ed. Mariolina Salvatori. 33/34 Spring/Fall (1995): 38–67.

"'Traveling Through the Dark': Teachers and Students Reading and Writing Together." *Reader: Essays in Reader-Oriented Theory, Criticism, and Pedagogy* 24 (1990): 1–20.

"What We (Might) Talk About When We Talk About Writing Literary Non-Fiction." *Dialogue* 3.1 (spring 1997): 5–22.

"You Can Take the Girl Out of the Writing Center." Was published under the title "Some Reflections on the Sites We Call Centers." *Focuses: A Journal Linking Composition Programs and Writing Center Practice* 8.2 (Winter 1995): 89–100.

"Writing Is/And Therapy?: Raising Questions about Writing Classrooms and Writing Program Administration." *Journal of Advanced Composition, 13.2* (1993): 503–516.

"Writing Teachers and Writing Process: Combining Theory and Practice." Arizona English Bulletin, 29.3 (1987): 34–41.